Rembrandt
and the Bible

Stories from the Old and New Testament,
illustrated by Rembrandt in paintings,
etchings and drawings.

Composition and explanatory notes by
Hidde Hoekstra.

MAGNA BOOKS

Self-portrait with Cap Pulled Forward
Etching, 5 × 4.2 cm. Fifth state of six.
Ca. 1631.
Amsterdam, Rijksprentenkabinet.

A survey of Rembrandt's life is given at the end
of this book.

Published by Magna Books
© 1990 by Uitgeverij Het Spectrum, Utrecht, Netherlands
© 1990 English translation by Royal Smeets Offset bv, Weert,
Netherlands
All rights reserved.
No part of this book may be reproduced in any form by print,
photoprint, microfilm or any other means without prior
written permission of the copyright holder.
Translated by Tony Langham and Plym Peters
Produced by Royal Smeets Offset bv, Weert
Bound by Reliure Industrielle de Barchon, Belgium
ISBN 1 85422 146 9

SOME PRELIMINARY REMARKS

Translation of the Bible

As regards the translation of the Biblical quotations, it
is not certain which Dutch translation Rembrandt
would have used. Probably the 'old Bible' mentioned
in his inventory of 1656 was a 16th-century Reformation
translation, but it is possible that in referring to it as
'old', he meant a pre-Reformation Bible. It is doubtful
whether Rembrandt ever had a Staten translation of
the Bible, as this was only published in 1637. Like all
new versions, it initially encountered a great deal of
opposition, and it was not until the end of the 17th
century that it replaced the other Dutch Bible
translations.

Literature

In the literature listed for each illustration, the
author's name is used to refer to the catalogues and
anthologies of Rembrandt's paintings, etchings and
drawings mentioned in the bibliography. Similarly, the
literature mentioned after an oblique stroke (/) refers
to publications which are exclusively concerned with
Rembrandt's Biblical work.

States of etchings

When changes are made to the plate of an etching
after prints have been made, a print of the altered
plate produces a second 'state'. There are several states
for most of Rembrandt's etchings, sometimes involving
significant changes.

Contents

THE OLD TESTAMENT

Genesis 3, 4, 6, 7, 12, 16, 17, 18,   8
        19, 21, 22, 24, 25, 27, 28,
        29, 32, 33, 37, 39, 40, 41,
        42, 43, 44, 45, 47, 48

Exodus 1, 2, 3, 32   82
Numbers 22   88
Judges 4, 13, 14, 15, 16   92
1 Samuel 17, 18, 19, 20, 28   106
2 Samuel 1, 11, 12   120
Ruth 1, 2, 3, 4   130
1 Kings 11, 16, 17, 18, 19   136
2 Kings 4, 6   146
2 Chronicles 36   150
Esther 2, 4, 5, 6, 7, 8   152
Tobit 2, 3, 4, 5, 6, 7, 8, 9, 10, 11, 12   164
Daniel 2, 5, 6, 7, 8, 13   196
Judith 12, 13   216

THE NEW TESTAMENT

Luke 1, 2   222
Matthew 2   244
Luke 2, 3   266
Matthew 4   298
John 4   300
Matthew 4   306
Luke 5   308
Mark 1, 4, 5   310
Matthew 14, 15   316
Luke 10, 12, 15   324
Matthew 19, 20   340
Luke 17   344
John 9, 11, 2   346
Matthew 22, 24, 25   356
John 8, 13   362
Matthew 26   368
Luke 22   376
Matthew 26, 27   378
John 19   388
Luke 23   390
Matthew 27   396
Mark 15   402
Matthew 28   414
Mark 16   416
John 20   418
Luke 24   422
John 20   430
Luke 24   434

SUMMARY OF REMBRANDT'S LIFE   436

EPILOGUE   438

BIBLIOGRAPHY   446

The Old Testament

She took of the fruit thereof, and did eat

Genesis 3

NOW the serpent was more subtil than any beast of the field which the LORD God had made. And he said unto the woman, Yea, hath God said, Ye shall not eat of every tree of the garden?

2 And the woman said unto the serpent, We may eat of the fruit of the trees of the garden:

3 But of the fruit of the tree which *is* in the midst of the garden, God hath said, Ye shall not eat of it, neither shall ye touch it, lest ye die.

4 And the serpent said unto the woman, Ye shall not surely die:

5 For God doth know that in the day ye eat thereof, then your eyes shall be opened, and ye shall be as gods, knowing good and evil.

6 And when the woman saw that the tree *was* good for food, and that it *was* pleasant to the eyes, and a tree to be desired to make *one* wise, she took of the fruit thereof, and did eat, and gave also unto her husband with her; and he did eat.

7 And the eyes of them both were opened, and the knew that they *were* naked; and the sewed fig leaves together, and made themselves aprons.

8 And they heard the voice of the LORD God walking in the garden in the cool of the day: and Adam and his wife hid themselves from the presence of the LORD God amongst the trees of the garden.

9 And the LORD God called unto Adam, and said unto him, Where *art* thou?

10 And he said, I heard thy voice in the garden, and I was afraid, because I *was* naked; and I hid myself.

11 And he said, Who told thee that thou *wast* naked? Hast thou eaten of the tree, whereof I commanded thee that thou shouldest not eat?

12 And the man said, The woman whom thou gavest *to be* with me, she gave me of the tree, and I did eat.

13 And the LORD God said unto the woman, What *is* this *that* thou hast done? And the woman said, The serpent beguiled me, and I did eat.

14 And the LORD God said unto the serpent, Because thou hast done this, thou *art* cursed above the cattle, and above every beast of the field; upon thy belly shalt thou go, and dust shalt thou eat all the days of thy life:

15 And I will put enmity between thee and the woman, and between thy seed and her seed; it shall bruise thy head, and thou shalt bruise his heel.

16 Unto the woman he said, I will greatly multiply thy sorrow and thy conception; in sorrow thou shalt bring forth children; and thy desire *shall be* to thy husband, and he shall rule over thee.

17 And unto Adam he said, Because thou hast hearkened unto the voice of thy wife, and hast eaten of the tree, of which I commanded thee, saying, Thou shalt not eat of it: cursed *is* the ground for thy sake; in sorrow shalt thou eat *of* it all the days of thy life;

18 Thorns also and thistles shall it bring forth to thee; and thou shalt eat the herb of the field;

19 In sweat of thy face shalt thou eat bread, till thou return unto the ground; for out of it wast thou taken: for dust thou *art,* and unto dust shalt thou return.

20 And Adam called his wife's name Eve; because she was the mother of all living.

21 Unto Adam also and to his wife did the LORD God make coats of skins, and clothed them.

22 And the LORD God said, Behold, the man is become as one of us, to know good and evil: and now, lest he put forth his hand, and take also of the tree of life, and eat, and live for ever:

23 Therefore the LORD God sent him forth from the garden of Eden, to till the ground from whence he was taken.

24 So he drove out the man; and he placed at the east of the garden of Eden Cherubims, and a flaming sword which turned every way, to keep the way of the tree of life.

And when the woman saw that the tree was good for food, and that it was pleasant to the eyes, and a tree to be desired to make one wise, she took of the fruit thereof, and did eat, and gave also unto her husband with her; and he did eat. (Genesis 3:6)

The fall of Adam and Eve, the moment at which, according to the Bible, suffering and death became an aspect of human existence, was one of the most important themes in Christian art from its very beginnings. This event was depicted even on the walls of the catacombs in Rome.

Since the Renaissance it had been customary to represent the figures of Adam and Eve as examples of perfect human beauty: idealized, perfectly proportioned nude figures which expressed the harmony of the earthly paradise. In this etching dating from 1638, Rembrandt deliberately refrained from using this traditional image. With uncompromising realism he showed the first human couple as two impermanent creatures in whom the traces of decay were visible at the moment of their fall from grace. Adam raises his finger at Eve in warning, but at the same time greedily reaches for the forbidden fruit with

which she is tempting him. Rembrandt shows the serpent in this story (Satan) in the form of a dragon, probably basing this on Dürer's engraving *The Descent of Christ into Hell*, in which Adam and Eve are the first to be liberated from the power of Satan, after the Saviour has conquered death. By representing the tempter as a monster with legs, Rembrandt in a sense adhered more closely to the text of the Bible than many of his predecessors had done, for it was only after the Fall that the serpent was condemned to crawl on its belly (see Genesis 3:14).

Apart from this etching and two drawings related to the print (Benesch I, nos. 163 and 164), this theme does not recur in Rembrandt's work.

Etching; 16.2 × 11.6 cm. Second state of two.
Signed and dated: *Rembrandt f. 1638.*
Amsterdam, Rijksprentenkabinet.

Literature: Bartsch, no. 28; Hind, no. 159; Münz, no. 177; Boon, no. 140; Filedt Kok, no. B 28/Hofstede de Groot, *Rembrandt Bijbel*, V.T.e.1; Rotermund 1963, no. 1; 'Bijbelse Inspiratie', no. 21; Tümpel 1970, no. 1.

Where *is* Abel thy brother?

Genesis 4 AND Adam knew Eve his wife; and she conceived, and bare Cain, and said, I have gotten a man from the LORD.

2 And she again bare his brother Abel. And Abel was a keeper of sheep, but Cain was a tiller of the ground.

3 And in process of time it came to pass, that Cain brought of the fruit of the ground an offering unto the LORD.

4 And Abel, he also brought of the firstlings of his flock and of the fat thereof. And the LORD has respect unto Abel and to his offering:

5 But unto Cain and to his offering he had not respect. And Cain was very wroth, and his countenance fell.

6 And the LORD said unto Cain, Why art thou wroth? and why is thy countenance fallen?

7 If thou doest well, shalt thou not be accepted? and if thou doest not well, sin lieth at the door. And unto thee *shall be* his desire, and thou shalt rule over him.

8 And Cain talked with Abel his brother: and it came to pass, when they were in the field, that Cain rose up against Abel his brother, and slew him.

9 And the LORD said unto Cain, Where *is* Abel thy brother? And he said, I know not: *Am* I my brother's keeper?

10 And he said, What hast thou done? the voice of thy brother's blood crieth unto me from the ground.

11 And now *art* thou cursed from the earth, which hath opened her mouth to receive thy brother's blood from thy hand;

12 When thou tillest the ground, it shall not henceforth yield unto thee her strength; a fugitive and a vagabond shalt thou be in the earth.

13 And Cain said unto the LORD, My punishment *is* greater than I can bear.

14 Behold, thou hast driven me out this day from the face of the earth; and from thy face shall I be hid; and I shall be a fugitive and a vagabond in the earth; and it shall come to pass, *that* every one that findeth me shall slay me.

15 And the LORD said unto him, Therefore whosoever slayeth Cain, vengeance shall be taken on him sevenfold. And the LORD set a mark upon Cain, lest any finding him should kill him.

16 And Cain went out of the presence of the LORD, and dwelt in the land of Nod, on the east of Eden.

Cain Slays Abel *... and it came to pass, when they were in the field, that Cain rose up against Abel his brother, and slew him.* (Genesis 4:8)

Immediately after the story of the Fall, death makes an entry to claim its first innocent victim, Abel, the shepherd, who is killed by his own brother. In his only representation of this traditional theme, a drawing dated *ca.* 1650, Rembrandt depicts the fratricide in a way that is characteristic of his method of working. In order to locate the events within the context of the story, he refers to the sacrifices Cain and Abel had made earlier by showing the two altar stones in the background. The creature collapsed on its forelegs on the lower rock is the sacrifice of Abel, who chose one of the firstborn of his best sheep. Crops of the field can be seen on the high altar of Cain, the farmer.

The diagonal line of the composition ends with the dramatic scene in the foreground. Cain violently throws himself on his younger brother, who has dropped his shepherd's staff and tries to protect himself against the blow with his hands. As in traditional versions, Abel is killed with a donkey's jawbone, although the actual text in the Bible does not mention a weapon. God looks sadly down from heaven at the first murder on earth. He will soon exact a punishment from Cain. By relating the main subject in a meaningful way to the narrative elements which refer to earlier and imminent events, Rembrandt successfully evokes the whole story.

Abel, the shepherd, murdered by his own brother, was traditionally viewed as a forerunner of Christ, 'the good shepherd' (John 10:11-16), who was killed by the authorities of his own people.

Drawing in pen; 16.9 × 24.7 cm.
Ca. 1650.
Copenhagen, Kobberstiksamling.

Literature: Benesch V, no. 860 (*ca.* 1650)/Rotermund
1963, no. 5.

Thou shalt come into the ark

Genesis 6 5 And God saw that the wickedness of man was great in the earth, and *that* every imagination of the thoughts of his heart *was* only evil continually.

6 and it repented the LORD that he made man on the earth, and it grieved him at his heart.

7 And the LORD said, I will destroy man whom I have created from the face of the earth; both man, beast, and creeping thing, and the fowls of the air; for it repenteth me that I have made them.

8 But Noah found grace in the eyes of the Lord. [...]

13 And God said unto Noah, The end of all flesh is come before me; for the earth is filled with violence through them; and, behold, I will destroy with the earth.

14 Make thee an ark of gopher wood; rooms shalt thou make in the ark, and shalt pitch it within and without with pitch.

15 And this *is the fashion* which thou shalt make it *of*: The lenght of the ark *shall be* three hundred cubits, the breath of it fifty cubits, and the height of it thirty cubits.

16 A window shalt thou make to the ark, and in a cubit shalt thou finish it above; and the door of the ark shalt thou set in the side thereof; *with* lower, second, and third *stories* shalt thou make it.

17 And, behold, I, even I, do bring a flood of waters upon the earth, to destroy all flesh, wherein *is* the breath of life, from under heaven; *and* every thing that *is* in the earth shall die.

18 But with thee will I establish my covenant; and thou shalt come into the ark, thou, and thy sons, and thy wife, and thy sons' wives with thee.

19 And of every living thing of all flesh, two of every *sort* shalt thou bring into the ark, to keep *them* alive with thee; they shall be male and female.

20 Of fowls after their kind, and of cattle after their kind, of every creeping thing of the earth after his kind, two of every *sort* shall come unto thee, to keep *them* alive.

21 And take thou unto thee of all food that is eaten, and thou shalt gather *it* to thee; and it shall be for food for thee, and for them.

22 Thus did Noah; according to all that God commanded him, so did he.

Genesis 7 6 And Noah *was* six hundred years old when the flood of waters was upon the earth.

7 And Noah went in, and his sons, and his wife, and his son's wives with him, into the ark, because of the waters of the flood.

8 Of clean beasts, and of beasts that *are* not clean, and fowls, and of every thing that creepeth upon the earth,

9 There went in two and two unto Noah into the ark, the male and the female, as God had commanded Noah.

10 And it came to pass after seven days, that the waters of the flood were upon the earth. [...]

17 And the flood was forty days upon the earth; and the waters increased, and bare up the ark, and it was lift up above the earth.

18 And the waters prevailed, and were increased greatly upon the earth; and the ark went upon the face of the waters.

19 And the waters prevailed exceedingly upon the earth; and all the high hill's, that *were* under the whole heaven, were covered.

20 Fifteen cubits upward did the waters prevail; and the mountains were covered.

21 And all flesh died that moved upon the earth, both of fowl, and of cattle, and of beast, and of every creeping thing that creepeth upon the earth, and every man:

22 All in whose nostrils *was* the breath of life, of all that *was* in the dry *land,* died.

23 And every living substance was destroyed which was upon the face of the ground, both man, and cattle, and the creeping things, and the fowl of the heaven; and they were destroyed from the earth: and Noah only remained *alive,* and they that *were* with him in the ark.

24 And the waters prevailed upon the earth an hundred and fifty days.

And Noah was six hundred years old when the flood of waters was upon the earth. And Noah went in, and his sons, and his wife, and his sons' wives with him, into the ark, because of the waters of the flood.
(Genesis 7:6-7)

This composition in broad penstrokes is a characteristic example of the monumental way in which Rembrandt gave expression to his imagination in about 1660, at the start of the last stage of his life: there are no details, but the people and things are shown in a single impressive image in a very suggestive way rather than in clear outlines.

In contrast with the prevailing fashion, Rembrandt restricted his representation of the loading of the ark to the human aspect and does not use the subject as a pretext for drawing a colourful procession of wild and domesticated animals following Noah and his family into the ark, two by two. The upper half of the vessel, built according to God's instructions, looks like a large storage barn, and the dark bulk runs across the drawing. In the middle the railing is open for a wide

gangplank, and a group of people - a heavily laden man and several women with a child - are laboriously making their way up, looking like émigrés who are leaving their homeland with pain in their hearts. The small, bent figure awaiting them at the top is probably the 'patriarch' Noah, who is six hundred years old. In the foreground on the left, Rembrandt shows two of the people who will be drowned by God in the Flood because of their sins. Ignorant of their imminent judgment, they are observing from a distance; they have their own opinions about old Noah and his ark.

Pen and brush drawing; 19.9 × 24.3 cm.
Ca. 1660.
Chicago, the Art Institute of Chicago.

Literature: Benesch V, no. 1045 (*ca.* 1659-60)/Rotermund 1963, no. 6.

Noah's Ark

I will make of thee a great nation

Genesis 12 NOW the LORD had said unto Abram, Get thee out of thy country, and from thy kindred, and from thy father's house, unto a land that I will shew thee:

2 And I will make of thee a great nation, and I will bless thee, and make thy name great; and thou shalt be a blessing:

3 And I will bless them that bless thee, and curse him that curseth thee: and in thee shall all families of the earth be blessed.

4 So Abram departed, as the LORD had spoken unto him; and Lot went with him: and Abram *was* seventy and five years old when he departed out of Haran.

5 And Abram took Sarai his wife, and Lot his brother's son, and all their substance that they had gathered, and the souls that they had gotten in Haran; and they went forth to go into the land of Canaan; and into the land of Canaan they came.

6 And Abram passed through the land unto the place of Sichem, unto the plain of Moreh. And the Canaanite *was* then in the land.

Genesis 16 NOW Sarai Abram's wife bare him no children: and she had an handmaid, an Egyptian, whose name *was* Hagar.

2 And Sarai said unto Abram, Behold now, the LORD hath restrained me from bearing: I pray thee, go in unto my maid; it may be that I may obtain children by her. And Abram hearkened to the voice of Sarai.

3 And Sarai Abram's wife took Hagar her maid the Egyptian, after Abram had dwelt ten years in the land of Canaan, and gave her to her husband Abram to be his wife.

4 And he went in unto Hagar, and she conceived: and when she saw that she had conceived, her mistress was despised in her eyes.

5 And Sarai said unto Abram, My wrong *be* upon thee: I have given my maid into the bosom; and when she saw that she had conceived, I was despised in her eyes: the LORD judge between me and thee.

6 But Abram said unto Sarai, Behold, thy maid *is* in thy hand; do to her as it pleaseth thee. And when Sarai dealt hardly with her, she fled from her face.

7 And the angel of the LORD found her by a fountain of water in the wilderness, by the fountain in the way to Shur.

8 And he said, Hagar, Sarai's maid, whence camest thou? and whither wilt thou go? And she said, I flee from the face of my mistress Sarai.

9 And the angel of the LORD said unto her, Return to thy mistress, and submit thyself under her hands.

10 And the angel of the LORD said unto her, I will multiply thy seed exceedingly, that it shall not be numbered for multitude.

11 And the angel of the LORD said unto her, Behold, thou *art* with child, and shalt bear a son, and shalt call his name Ishmael; because the LORD hat heard thy affliction.

12 And he will be a wild man; his hand *will be* against every man, and every man's hand against him; and he shall dwell in the presence of all his brethren.

13 And she called the name of the LORD that spake unto her, Thou God seest me: for she said, Have I also here looked after him that seeth me?

14 Wherefore the well was called Beerlahairoi; behold, *it is* between Kadesh and Bered.

15 And Hagar bare Abram a son: and Abram called his son's name, which Hagar bare, Ishmael.

16 And Abram was fourscore and six years old, when Hagar bare Ishmael to Abram.

And Sarai said unto Abram, My wrong be upon thee: I have given my maid into thy bosom; and when she saw that she had conceived, I was despised in her eyes: the Lord judge between me and thee. But Abram said unto Sarai, Behold, thy maid is in thy hand; do to her as it pleaseth thee. (Genesis 16:5-6)

The history of the patriarchs, and thus of the people of Israel, begins with the promise to Abram (later known as Abraham), the paragon of faith who continued to trust in God's word, no matter what befell him.

Like his direct predecessors who painted Biblical scenes, Rembrandt was fascinated by the fortunes of the patriarchs. No one really knew what the world had looked like for these semi-nomadic tribes living in tents; there had been virtually no Biblical archaeology at that time. In the customary manner of the period, Rembrandt indicated the Biblical character of a scene by dressing the figures appearing in it in Eastern clothes or old-fashioned dress, and by showing the background in outdoor scenes as a clearly southern, rocky landscape of the type used by his teacher, Pieter Lastman, in his paintings. He concentrated on showing the emotions felt by the characters in the scene as clearly as possible.

The subject of this drawing from the first half of the 1640s is the conflict which has arisen between Abram's wife Sarai and her slave Hagar. In order to give her husband a child, Sarai, who was infertile herself, had given her Egyptian slave Hagar to Abram. According to the law of the time, she could claim the child conceived by Hagar as her own. However, when Hagar realizes she is pregnant by Abram, she thinks she can adopt a condescending attitude towards her mistress, and Sarai does not tolerate this. She angrily goes to Abram and loudly demands that he restore the correct balance in the relationship between them. In his representation of this moment, which is rarely depicted, Rembrandt makes a sharp contrast between the withered Sarai, bent with old age and leaning on her stick, and her young, self-assured rival, proud as the peacock which stands behind her at the entrance to the house. Abram's conciliatory gesture to Sarai is equally clear: henceforth Hagar will once again be wholly under her authority.

Pen and ink drawing; 18.9 × 30.3 cm.
Below right, signature added later: *Rembrandt.*
Ca. 1640-45.
Bayonne, Musée Bonnat.

Literature: Benesch III, no. 549 (*ca.* 1643-44); Slive II, no. 356 (*ca.* 1640-43)/Rotermund 1963, no. 10.

*Sarai Complains
to Abram About Hagar*

Then Abraham fell upon his face, and laughed

Genesis 17 AND when Abram was ninety years old and nine, the LORD appeared to Abram, and said unto him, I *am* the Almighty God; walk before me, and be thou perfect.

2 And I will make my covenant between me and thee, and will multiply thee exceedingly.

3 And Abram fell on his face: and God talked with him, saying,

4 As for me, behold, my covenant *is* with thee, and thou shalt be a father of many nations.

5 Neither shall thy name any more be called Abram, but thy name shall be Abraham; for a father of many nations have I made thee.

6 And I will make thee exceeding fruitful, and I will make nations of thee, and kings shall come out of thee.

7 And I will establish my covenant between me and thee and thy seed after thee in their generations for an everlasting covenant, to be a God unto thee, and to thy seed after thee.

8 And I will give unto thee, and to thy seed after thee, the land wherein thou art a stranger, all the land of Canaan, for an everlasting possession; and I will be their God.

9 And God said unto Abraham, Thou shalt keep my covenant therefore, thou, and thy seed after thee in their generations.

10 This *is* my covenant, which ye shall keep, between me and you and thy seed after thee; Every man child among you shall be circumcised.

11 And ye shall circumcise the flesh of your foreskin; and it shall be a token of the covenant betwixt me and you.

12 And he that is eight days old shall be circumcised among you, every man child in your generations, he that is born in the house, or bought with money of any stranger, which *is* not of thy seed.

13 He that is born in thy house, and he that is bought with thy money, must needs be circumcised: and my covenant shall be in your flesh for an everlasting covenant.

14 And the circumcised man child whose flesh of his foreskin is not circumcised, that soul shall be cut off from his people; he hath broken my covenant.

15 And God said unto Abraham, As for Sarai thy wife, thou shalt not call Sarai, but Sarah *shall* her name *be*.

16 And I will bless her, and give thee a son also of her: yea, I will bless her, and she shall be *a mother* of nations; kings of people shall be of her.

17 Then Abraham fell upon his face, and laughed, and said in his heart, Shall *a child* be born unto him that is an hundred years old? and shall Sarah, that is ninety years old, bear?

18 And Abraham said unto God, O that Ishmael might live before thee!

19 And God said, Sarah the wife shall bear thee a son indeed; and thou shalt call his name Isaac: and I will establish my covenant with him for an everlasting convenant, *and* with his seed after him.

20 And as for Ishmael, I have heard thee: Behold, I have blessed him and will make him fruitful, and will multiply him exceedingly; twelve princes shall he beget, and I will make him a great nation.

21 But my covenant will I establish with Isaac, which Sarah shall bear unto thee at this set time in the next year.

22 And he left off talking with him, and God went up from Abraham.

*I am the Almighty God; walk before me and be thou perfect.
And I will make my covenant between me and thee, and will
multiply thee exceedingly. And Abraham fell on his face:
and God talked with him, saying, As for me, behold, my
covenant is with thee, and thou shalt be a father of many
nations.*
(Genesis 17:1-4)

While the Almighty, floating on the edge of a cloud
and accompanied by two angels, holds forth, Abraham
lies prostrate on the ground, covering his face with
both hands in awe. Referring to God's final promising
words, Rembrandt also shows Sarai in the background:
henceforth she will be called 'Sarah'. For, however
incredible it may seem to Abraham, it is not his son
conceived by Hagar, Ishmael, the child of the
agreement, who is to be the heir to the 'eternal
covenant', but a son of Sarah, Isaac, the child that is

promised. The way to the future will not be held open
by agreement, but by trust in God's word.

It is probable that for this drawing, dated *ca.* 1655,
Rembrandt drew inspiration from an engraving of
Raphael's composition 'God Appears to Noah', on the
ceiling of the *Stanza dell' Eliodoro*, one of the richly
painted rooms in the Vatican buildings.

Pen and ink drawing; 19.7 × 26.6 cm.
Ca. 1655.
Dresden, Staatliche Kunstsammlungen,
Kupferstichkabinett.

Literature: Benesch V, no. 1003 (*ca.* 1656); Slive I, no. 142
(*ca.* 1657)/Rotermund 1963, no. 8; Colin Campbell,
'Raphael door Rembrandts pen herschapen' in *De
kroniek van het Rembrandthuis*, 27 (1975), pp. 20-32.

*God Reveals his
Covenant to Abraham*

Wherefore did Sarah laugh?

Genesis 18 AND the LORD appeared unto him in the plains of Mamre: and he sat in the tent door in the heat of the day;

2 And he lift up his eyes and looked, and, lo, three man stood by him: and when he saw *them,* he ran to meet them from the tent door, and bowed himself toward the ground.

3 And said, My Lord, if now I have found favour in thy sight, pass not away, I pray thee, from thy servant:

4 Let a little water, I pray you, be fetched, and wash your feet, and rest yourselves under the tree:

5 And I will fetch a morsel of bread, and comfort ye your hearts; after that ye shall pass on: for therefore are ye come to your servant. And they said, So do, as thou hast said.

6 And Abraham hastened into the tent unto Sarah, and said, Make ready quickly three measures of fine meal, knead it, and make cakes upon the hearth.

7 And Abraham ran unto the herd, and fetcht a calf tender and good, and gave *it* unto a young man; and he hasted to dress it.

8 And he took butter, and milk, and the calf which he had dressed, and set *it* before them; and he stood by them under the tree, and they did eat.

9 And they said unto him, Where *is* Sarah thy wife? And he said, Behold, in the tent.

10 And he said, I will centainly return unto thee according to the time of life; and, lo, Sarah thy wife shall have a son. And Sarah heard *it* in the tent door, which *was* behind him.

11 Now Abraham and Sarah were old and well stricken in age; *and* it ceased to be with Sarah after the manner of women.

12 Therefore Sarah laughed within herself, saying, After I am waxed old shall I have pleasure, my Lord being old also?

13 And the LORD said unto Abraham, Wherefore did Sarah laugh, saying, Shall I of a surety bear a child, which am old?

14 Is any thing too hard for the LORD? At the time appointed I will return unto thee, according to the time of life, and Sarah shall have a son.

15 Then Sarah denied, saying, I laughed not; for she was afraid. And he said, Nay; but thou didst laugh.

Abraham Entertains the Three Angels

And he took butter, and milk, and the calf which he had dressed, and set it before them; and he stood by them under the tree, and they did eat.
(Genesis 18:8)

In his 1646 panel, Rembrandt painted Abraham's three visitors as angels, as they had frequently been portrayed in the past. As described in the Bible story, he shows the patriarch as the perfect host, making sure that his honoured guests, seated in front of his house by the oak of Mamre, have all they need. The main figure is the shining white one in which the Invisible shows itself to man, the 'angel of the Lord', who tells Abraham that his wife Sarah (listening in a doorway in the background) will bear a child in a year's time.

It is not surprising that in medieval art this visit of God to Abraham served repeatedly to anticipate the message of the Angel Gabriel to Mary (Luke I:26-28). In 17th-century Dutch art, which often had a strongly moralizing content, the scene was popular as an image of the virtue of hospitality (see Hebrews 13:2).

Panel; 16 × 21 cm.
Signed and dated: *Rembrandt f.* 1646.
Private collection.

Literature: Bredius, no. 515; Bauch, no. 27; Gerson, no. 214; Bredius-Gerson, no. 515/Tümpel 1970, under no. 4.

And he took butter, and milk, and the calf which he had dressed, and set it before them; and he stood by them under the tree, and they did eat.
(Genesis 18:8)

In the etching which was made ten years after the painting, the same theme was depicted in a totally novel way. To give the scene an exotic emphasis, Rembrandt sought inspiration from one of his earlier drawings, based on Indian miniatures, a picture of four wise men seated under a tree (Benesch V, no. 1187).

This time the Lord appears in the guise of an aged man in Eastern dress, who, seated on a carpet, together with his two winged assistants, enjoys the meal served by Abraham. Again we see Sarah listening attentively, half-concealed behind the door. The boy playing with a bow and arrow is Ishmael. After the birth of the son promised to Sarah, Ishmael and his mother Hagar are rejected and the boy becomes a proficient archer in the desert (Genesis 21:20).

Etching; 16 × 13.1 cm. Only state.
Signed and dated: *Rembrandt f.* 1656.
Amsterdam, Rijksprentenkabinet.

Literature: Bartsch, no. 29; Hind, no. 286; Münz, no. 185; Boon, no. 276; Filedt Kok, no. B 29/Hofstede de Groot, *Rembrandt Bijbel*, V.T.e.2; Rotermund 1963, no. 14; 'Bijbelse Inspiratie', no. 22; Tümpel 1970, no. 5.

Escape to the mountain, lest thou be consumed

Genesis 19 AND there came two angels to Sodom at even; and Lot sat in the gate of Sodom: and Lot seeing *them* rose up to meet them; and he bowed himself with his face toward the ground;

2 And he said, Behold now, my lords, turn in, I pray you, into your servant's house, and tarry all night, and wash your feet, and ye shall rise up early, and go on your ways. And they said, Nay; but we will abide in the street all night.

3 And he pressed upon them greatly; and they turned in unto him, and entered into his house; and he made them a feast, and did bake unleavened bread, and they did eat.

4 But before they lay down, the men of the city, *even* the men of Sodom, compassed the house round, both old and young, all the people from every quarter:

5 And they called unto Lot, and said unto him, Where *are* the men which came in to thee this night? bring them out unto us, that we may know them.

6 And Lot went out at the door unto them, and shut the door after him,

7 And said, I pray you, brethren, do not so wickedly.

8 Behold now, I have two daughters which have not known man; let me, I pray you, bring them out unto you, and do ye to them as *is* good in your eyes: only unto these men do nothing; for therefore came they under the shadow of my roof.

9 And they said, Stand back. And they said *again*, This one *fellow* came in to sojourn, and he will needs be a judge: now will we deal worse with thee, than with them. And the pressed sore upon the man, *even* Lot, and came near to break the door.

10 But the men put forth their hand, and pulled Lot into the house to them, and shut to the door.

11 And they smote the men that *were* at the door of the house with blindness, both small and great: so that they wearied themselves to find the door.

12 And the men said unto Lot, Hast thou here any besides? son in law, and thy sons, and thy daughters, and whatsoever thou hast in the city, bring *them* out of this place:

13 For we will destroy this place, because the cry of them is waxen great before the face of the LORD; and the LORD hath sent us to destroy it.

14 And Lot went out, and spake unto his sons in law, which married his daughters, and said, Up, get you out of this place; for the LORD will destroy this city. But he seemed as one that mocked unto his sons in law.

15 And when the morning arose, then the angels hastened Lot, saying, Arise, take thy wife, and thy two daughters, which are here; lest thou be consumed in the iniquity of the city.

16 And while he lingered, the men laid hold upon the hand of his two daughters; the LORD being merciful unto him: and the brought him forth, and set him without the city.

17 And it came to pass, when they had brought them forth abroad, that he said, Escape for thy life; look not behind thee, neither stay thou in all the plain; escape to the mountain, lest thou be consumed.

18 And Lot said unto them, Oh, not so, my Lord:

19 Behold now, thy servant hath found grace in thy sight, and thou hast magnified thy mercy, which thou hast shewed unto me in saving my life; and I cannot escape to the mountain, lest some evil take me, and I die:

20 Behold now, this city *is* near to flee unto, and it *is* a little one: Oh, let me escape thither, (*is* it not a little one?) and my soul shall live.

21 And he said unto him, See, I have accepted thee concerning this thing also, that I will not overthrow this city, for the which thou hast spoken.

22 Haste thee, escape thither; for I cannot do any thing till thou be come thither. Therefore the name of the city was called Zoar.

23 The sun was risen upon the earth when Lot entered into Zoar.

24 Then the LORD rained upon Sodom and upon Gomorrah brimstone and fire from the LORD out of heaven;

25 And he overthrew those cities, and all at the plain, and all the inhabitants of the cities, and that which grew upon the ground.

26 But his wife looked back from behind him, and she became a pillar of salt.

And when the morning arose, then the angels hastened to Lot, saying, Arise, take thy wife, and thy two daughters, which are here; lest thou be consumed in the iniquity of the city. And while he lingered, the men laid hold upon his hand, and upon the hand of his wife, and upon the hand of his two daughters; the Lord being merciful unto him: and they brought him forth, and set him without the city. (Genesis 19:15-16)

This drawing again clearly shows how Rembrandt's primary concern in portraying a theme was to convey the human emotions as clearly as possible. Concentrating on the main figure, he portrays Lot as a deeply shocked man who is desperate when he realizes that he must unexpectedly leave his home for ever.

Frightened and hesitating, he moves in the direction he has been shown, though the angel is urging him to hasten.

This drawing is one of Rembrandt's most beautiful sketches dating from the mid-1630s, and is an excellent example of the virtuoso style which he adopted in his pen and ink drawings during this period (also see p. 23).

Pen and ink drawing; 22.1 × 23 cm.
Ca. 1635.
Vienna, Albertina.

Literature: Benesch I, no. 129 (*ca.* 1636).

Lot's Departure from Sodom

Come, let us make our father drink wine

Genesis 19 30 And Lot went up out of Zoar, and dwelt in the mountain, and his two daughters with him; for he feared to dwell in Zoar: and he dwelt in a cave, he and his two daughters.
31 And the firstborn said unto the younger, Our father *is* old, and *there* is not a man in the earth to come in unto us after the manner of all the earth:
32 Come, let us make our father drink wine, and we will lie with him, that we may preserve seed of our father.
33 And they made their father drink wine that night: and the firstborn wen in, and lay with her father; and he perceived not when she lay down, nor when she arose.

34 And it came to pass on the morrow, that the firstborn siad unto the younger, Behold, I lay yesternight with my father: let us make him drink wine this night also; and go thou in, *and* lie with him, that we may preserve seed of our father.
35 And they made their father drink wine that night also: and the younger arose, and lay with him; and he perceived not when she lay down, nor when she arose.
36 Thus were both the daughters of Lot with child by their father.
37 And the firstborn bare a son, and called his name Moab: the same *is* the father of the Moabites unto this day.
38 And the younger, she also bare a son, and called his name Benammi: the same *is* the father of the children of Ammon unto this day.

Lot and his Daughters *And the firstborn said unto the younger, Our father is old, and there is not a man in the earth to come in unto us after the manner of all the earth: Come, let us make our father drink wine, and we will lie with him, that we may preserve seed of our father. And they made their father drink wine that night ...*
(Genesis 19:31-33)

Many versions of this story were depicted, and in the late Middle Ages it was sometimes seen as one of the historical examples of 'the power of the woman over the man' - events from the Bible, or in ancient legends, in which a man is deceived, betrayed or led into disaster by a woman's sophisticated intrigues and temptations. Another example of such feminine intrigue, which is much more often portrayed, was the story of Samson and Delilah (Judges 16:4-21; pp. 102-05). In the treatment of this subject, Renaissance and baroque artists emphasized the sensuality of the female body, and consequently their representations of Lot and his daughters not infrequently had an erotic quality. This does not apply to Rembrandt's drawing shown here, which is focused on the psychological contrast between Lot's naïvety and his two daughters' guile.

The flair and speed with which this diagonally composed composition was executed on paper suggests that the drawing was done at the same time as the one reproduced on the previous page, *ca.* 1635.

In the bottom right-hand corner there is a fragment of Goethe's collector's mark. Johann Wolfgang von Goethe (1749-1832) had an extensive collection of drawings and graphic art, and during the last years of his life he marked his favourite sheets with his own collector's mark.

Pen and ink drawing; 15.2 × 19.1 cm.
Ca. 1635.
Weimar, Goethe Nationalmuseum.

Literature: Benesch I, no. 128 (*ca.* 1636); Slive I, no. 209
(*ca.* 1635)/Rotermund 1963, no. 19.

Cast out this bondwoman and her son

Genesis 21 AND the LORD visited Sarah as he had said, and the LORD did unto Sarah as he had spoken.

2 For Sarah conceived, and bare Abraham a son in his old age, at the set time of which God had spoken to him.

3 And Abraham called the name of his son that was born unto him, whom Sarah bare to him, Isaac.

4 And Abraham circumcised his son Isaac being eight days old, as God had commanded him.

5 And Abraham was an hundred years old, when his son Isaac was born unto him.

6 And Sarah said, God hath made me to laugh, *so that* all that hear will laugh with me.

7 And she said, Who would have said unto Abraham, that Sarah should have given children suck? for I have born *him* a son in his old age.

8 And the child grew, and was weaned: and Abraham made a great feast the *same* day that Isaac was weaned.

9 And Sarah saw the son of Hagar the Egyptian, which she had born unto Abraham, mocking.

10 Wherefore she said unto Abraham, Cast out this bondwoman and her son: for the son of this bondwoman shall not be heir with my son, *even* with Isaac.

11 And the thing was very grievous in Abraham's sight because of his son.

12 And God said unto Abraham, Let it not be grievous in thy sight because of the lad, and because of thy bondwoman; in all that Sarah hath said unto thee, hearken unto her voice; for in Isaac shall thy seed be called.

13 And also of the son of the bondwoman will I make a nation, because he *is* thy seed.

14 And Abraham rose up early in the morning, and took bread, and a bottle of water, and gave *it* unto Hagar, putting *it* on her shoulder, and the child, and sent her away: and she departed, and wandered in the wilderness of Beersheba.

15 And the water was spent in the bottle, and she cast the child under one of the shrubs.

16 And she went, and sat her down over against *him* a good way off, as it were a bowshot: for she said, Let me not see the death of the child. And she sat over against *him,* and lift up her voice, and wept.

17 And God heard the voice of the lad; and the angel of God called to Hagar out of heaven, and said unto her, What aileth thee, Hagar? fear not; for God hath heard the voice of the lad where he *is.*

18 Arise, lift up the lad, and hold him in thine hand; for I will make him a great nation.

19 And God opened her eyes, and she saw a well of water; and she went, and filled the bottle with water, and gave the lad drink.

20 And God was with the lad; and he grew, and dwelt in the wilderness, and became an archer.

21 And he dwelt in the wilderness of Paran: and his mother took him a wife out of the land of Egypt.

And Abraham rose up early in the morning, and took bread, and a bottle of water, and gave it unto Hagar, putting it on her shoulder, and the child, and sent her away.
(Genesis 21:14)

The Bible story indicates that Sarah, who had once been rejected, realized better than Abraham himself how to ensure the future of his lineage as the 'promised people'. To prevent her son Isaac having to share his father's inheritance with Hagar's son Ishmael, she demanded that Abraham drive out this servant girl and her son. God told Abraham that it would be sensible for him to listen to Sarah. He would have to suppress his natural love for Ishmael, no matter how difficult this was, for it was only through Isaac, 'the promised son', that the blessings he had been promised would pass to his descendants.

In view of the profound human emotions which conflict so violently here, it is not surprising that the story of Hagar - and particularly the drama of her rejection by Abraham - was one of the most popular Old Testament themes amongst Dutch 17th-century historical painters, particularly Rembrandt and his

pupils. In virtually all their works, the powerless pity which Abraham feels for Hagar when he has to follow Sarah's wish against his will is depicted every bit as strongly as Hagar's desperate sorrow.

In Rembrandt's 1637 etching the figure of Abraham is central. Hagar and Ishmael have already departed. While Hagar weeps and sets out for unknown parts with Ishmael, the patriarch's only remaining link with her is a gesture of blessing, while his right foot is already stepping back into his house. The young Isaac, on whose account these things are happening, stands diffidently at a distance in the doorway next to his mother, who is pleased to see Hagar and Ishmael depart.

Etching; 12.6 × 9.7 cm. Only state.
Signed and dated: *Rembrandt f. 1637.*
Amsterdam, Rijksprentenkabinet.

Literature: Bartsch, no. 30; Hind, no. 149; Münz, no. 174; Boon, no. 133; Filedt Kok, no. B 30/Hofstede de Groot, *Rembrandt Bijbel*, V.T.e.3; Rotermund 1963, no. 22; 'Bijbelse Inspiratie', no. 23; Tümpel 1970, no. 6.

Abraham Sends Hagar and Ishmael Away

**Abraham Sends Hagar
and Ishmael Away**

*And Abraham rose up early in the morning, and took bread,
and a bottle of water, and gave it unto Hagar, putting it on
her shoulder, and the child, and sent her away.*
(Genesis 21:14)

In a lengthy essay, the German art historian Richard
Hamann showed that the majority of the
representations which Rembrandt and his pupils
devoted to this subject, mostly drawings, were strongly
influenced by a painting by Rembrandt's teacher,
Pieter Lastman, dating from 1612. In his composition
the three central figures, which Rembrandt copied in a
chalk drawing in about 1635 (Benesch II, no. 447), are
closely interrelated: Abraham looks at Hagar and
places his hand on her arm, while his other hand rests
on the head of Ishmael, who stands between them.
Thus in Lastman's work the emphasis is no longer on
her rejection, but on the last moment of tenderness
between Abraham, Hagar and their child Ishmael, just
before their final parting.

From about 1640, Rembrandt also emphasized this in
his drawings, as in this one, in which Abraham lays his
right hand on Ishmael's head for a last time to bless

him before the unhappy couple depart. Meanwhile, he
tries to alleviate Hagar's sorrow with a placatory
gesture and soothing words. In the background Sarah
keeps a careful eye on matters with her head round
the door.

The figure of Abraham was incorporated in the
drawing on a different piece of paper to replace the
first version, which was cut away. Rembrandt used this
method of correcting his work several times.

Pen and brush drawing; 18.5 × 23.6 cm.
Ca. 1640-43.
London, British Museum.

Literature: Benesch III, no. 524 (*ca*. 1642-43); Slive I, no.
102 (*ca*. 1640-43); Haak, no. 41 (*ca*. 1642-43)/R. Hamann,
'Hagars Abschied bei Rembrandt und im
Rembrand-Kreise' in *Marburger Jahrbuch für
Kunstwissenschaft* 8-9 (1936), p. 471VV; Rotermund 1963,
no. 21.

And Abraham rose up early in the morning, and took bread, and a bottle of water, and gave it unto Hagar, putting it on her shoulder, and the child, and sent her away.
(Genesis 21:14)

In this sombre drawing from the early 1650s, Rembrandt produced the most beautiful version of the moving moment at which Abraham was finally forced to bid farewell to Hagar and Ishmael. The composition of the three figures is virtually identical to that in the previous drawing, but they form a closer unit and Hagar's expression particularly, broken with sorrow, is much more effective. In the distance Sarah looks on, unmoved, standing in front of a tall house with little Isaac under her wing. Referring to Genesis 21:20, which describes how Ishmael developed in the desert to become a competent archer when he was an adult, Rembrandt usually depicts the boy in this scene with a bow in his hand and a quiver of arrows on his back. On page 18 it was pointed out that he represented Ishmael playing with a bow and arrow for the same reason in his etching *Abraham Entertains the Three Angels*, dating from 1656.

In the catalogue of the exhibition 'Biblical Inspiration', it was remarked with regard to this drawing by Rembrandt that Abraham's farewell, which had played such an important part in northern Dutch representations of this subject, may well have had its origin in the fact that in a number of pre-Reformation translations of the Bible, Genesis 21:14 reads, 'And he let them go', instead of, 'And he sent her away', as in the Staten translation of 1637.

Pen and ink drawing; 17.2 × 22.4 cm.
Ca. 1650-53.
Amsterdam, Rijksprentenkabinet.

Literature: Benesch V, no. 916 (*ca.* 1652-53); Slive II, no. 547 (*ca.* 1650-52)/Rotermund 1963, no. 24; 'Bijbelse Inspiratie', no. 54.

Abraham Sends Hagar and Ishmael Away

27

God will provide himself a lamb for a burnt offering

Genesis 22 AND it came to pass after these things, that God did tempt Abraham, and said unto him, Abraham: and he said, Behold, *here* I *am*.

2 And he said, Take now thy son, thine only *son* Isaac, whom thou lovest, and get thee into the land of Moriah; and offer him there for a burnt offering upon one of the mountains which I will tell thee of.

3 And Abraham rose up early in the morning, and saddled his ass, and took two of his young men with him, and Isaac his son, and clave the wood for the burnt offering, and rose up, and went to the place of which God had told him.

4 Then on the third day Abraham lifted up his eyes, and saw the place afar off.

5 And Abrahm said unto his young men, Abide ye here with the ass; and I and the lad will go yonder and worship, and come again to you.

6 And Abraham took the wood of the burnt offering, and laid *it* upon Isaac his son; and he took the fire in his hand, and a knife; and they went both of them together.

7 And Isaac spake unto Abraham his father, and said, My father: and he said, Here *am* I, my son. And he said, Behold the fire and the wood: but where *is* the lamb for a burnt offering?

8 And Abraham said, My son, God will provide himself a lamb for a burnt offering: so they went both of them together.

9 And they came to the place which God had told him of; and Abraham built an altar there, and laid the wood in order, and bound Isaac his son, and laid him on the altar upon the wood.

10 And Abraham stretched forth his hand, and took the knife to slay his son.

11 And the angel of the LORD called unto him out of heaven, and said, Abraham, Abraham: and he said, Here *am* I.

12 And he said, Lay not thine hand upon the lad, neither do thou any thing unto him: for now I know that thou fearest God, seeing thou hast not withheld thy son, thine only *son* from me.

13 And Abraham lifted up his eyes, and looked, and behold behind *him* a ram caught in a thicket by his horns: and Abraham went and took the ram, and offered him up for a burnt offering in the stead of his son.

14 And Abraham called the name of that place Jehovahjireh: as it is said *to* this day, In the mount of the LORD it shall be seen.

15 And the angel of the LORD called unto Abraham out of heaven the second time,

16 And said, By myself have I sworn, saith the LORD, for because thou hast done this thing, and hast not withheld the son, thine only *son*:

17 That in blessing I will bless thee, and in multiplying I will multiply thy seed as the stars of the heaven, and as the sand which *is* upon the sea shore; and thy seed shall possess the gate of his enemies;

18 And in thy seed shall all the nations of the earth blessed; because thou hast obeyed my voice.

19 So Abraham returned unto his young men, and they rose up and went together to Beersheba; and Abraham dwelt at Beersheba.

The Angel Prevents the Sacrifice of Isaac

And Abraham stretched forth his hand, and took the knife to slay his son. And the angel of the Lord called unto him out of heaven and said, Abraham, Abraham: and he said, Here am I. And he said, Lay not thine hand upon the lad, neither do thou anything unto him.
(Genesis 22:10-12)

Isaac lies on the woodpile with his hands bound behind his back. As Abraham pushes the boy's head back to cut his throat, the angel suddenly intervenes and in shock the old man drops the sacrificial knife.

The dramatic turning point in the story is depicted as dynamically and realistically as possible in this large canvas, dating from 1635, when Rembrandt's style was closest to the European baroque style. In a second version, signed 'Rembrandt', changed and painted over, 1636 (Munich, Alte Pinakothek), the ram which Abraham sacrificed on the fire instead of Isaac is shown in the bush in the background.

Canvas; 193 × 133 cm.
Signed and dated: *Rembrandt f. 1635.*
Leningrad, Hermitage.

Literature: Bredius, no. 498; Bauch, no. 13; Gerson, no. 74; Bredius-Gerson, no. 498/Hofstede de Groot, *Rembrandt Bijbel*, V.T.p.3.

Abraham and Isaac

And Isaac spake unto Abraham his father, and said, My father: and he said, Behold the fire and the wood; but where is the lamb for a burnt offering? And Abraham said, My son, God will provide himself a lamb for a burnt offering. (Genesis 22:7-8)

When Abraham was commanded to sacrifice his own son Isaac to God on a fire, the tension of Abraham's story reached its zenith. Had the promise of many descendants been an empty promise after all? Abraham's trust seemed unshaken. There was no sign of any inner conflict. Surrendering completely ('Here am I'), he carried out what he was commanded to do by God, the Lord of life and death. In this way it was shown all the more clearly at the end that Israel, the promised nation, owed its existence only to God's mercy.

In contrast with the climax of the story, Isaac's sacrifice being prevented at the very last minute, the conversation between the father and son which preceded this was rarely depicted. Deviating from the text of the Bible in this etching dating from 1645, Rembrandt showed this as taking place not on the way

to the place of sacrifice, but actually at the place itself. The unsuspecting boy had already taken the wood collected for the sacrifice from his shoulder. On the left we see the fire, an iron pot with glowing coals, and the large sacrificial knife lies at Abraham's side. The father points upwards: 'God will provide himself a lamb for a burnt offering, my son.' The trusting answer sounds vague and evasive, but will turn out to be prophetic. Although the composition is simple and almost static, Rembrandt has succeeded in expressing a great inner tension in this work.

Etching; 15.7 × 13 cm. Only state.
Signed and dated: *Rembrandt f. 1645.*
Amsterdam, Rijksprentenkabinet.

Literature: Bartsch, no. 34; Hind, no. 214; Münz, no. 180; Boon, no. 196; Filedt Kok, no. B 34/Hofstede de Groot, *Rembrandt Bijbel*, V.T.e.4; Rotermund 1963, no. 28; 'Bijbelse Inspiratie', no. 24; Tümpel 1970, no. 8.

Lay not thine hand upon the lad, neither do thou anything unto him.
(Genesis 22:12)

Twenty years after the painting of 1635, Rembrandt concentrated particularly on Abraham's emotions in this etching of the same subject. The father mercifully holds his hand in front of the boy's eyes as Isaac bends forward as meek as a lamb, waiting only for the knife. Then the heavens open and Abraham realizes that he must go no further. Following artistic tradition, Rembrandt again showed the angel of the Lord intervening physically, although the text in the Bible says only that he calls to Abraham from heaven. A torrent of light descends over the tortured man and his child. Soon they will return together to the two servants waiting at the foot of the mountain with the donkey.

Etching; 15.6 × 13.1 cm. Only state.
Signed and dated: *Rembrandt f. 1655.*
Amsterdam, Rijksprentenkabinet.

Literature: Bartsch, no. 35; Hind, no. 283; Münz, no. 184; Boon, no. 263; Filedt Kok, no. B 35/Hofstede de Groot, *Rembrandt Bijbel*, V.T.e.5; Rotermund 1963, no. 30; 'Bijbelse Inspiratie', no. 25; Tümpel 1970, no. 9.

The Angel Prevents the Sacrifice of Isaac

33

Behold, Rebekah came out

AND Abraham was old, *and* well stricken in age: and the LORD had blessed Abraham in all things.

2 And Abraham said unto his eldest servant of his house, that ruled over all that he had, Put, I pray thee, thy hand under my thigh:

3 And I will make thee swear by the LORD, the God of heaven, and the God of the earth, that thou shalt not take a wife unto my son of the daughters of the Canaanites, among whom I dwell:

4 But thou shalt go unto my country, and to my kindred, and take a wife unto my son Isaac.

5 And the servant said unto him, Peradventure the woman will not be willing to follow me unto this land: must I needs bring thy son again unto the land from whence thou camest?

6 And Abraham said unto him, Beware thou that thou bring not my son thither again.

7 The LORD God of heaven, which took me from my father's house, and from the land of my kindred, and which spake unto me, and that sware unto me, saying, Unto thy seed will I give this land; he shall send his angel before thee, and thou shalt take a wife unto my son from thence.

8 And if the woman will not be willing to follow thee, then thou shalt be clear from this my oath: only bring not my son thither again.

9 And the servant put his hand under the thigh of Abraham his master, and sware him concerning that matter.

10 And the servant took ten camels of the camels of his master, and departed; for all the goods of his master *were* in his hand: and he arose, and went to Mesopotamia, unto the city of Nahor.

11 And he made his camels to kneel down without the city by a well of water at the time of the evening, *even* the time that women go out to draw *water.*

12 And he said, O LORD God of my master Abraham, I pray thee, send me good speed this day, and shew kindness unto my master Abraham

13 Behold, I stand *here* by the well of water; and the daughters of the men of the city come out to draw water:

14 And let it come to pass, that the damsel to whom I shall say, Let down thy pitcher, I pray thee, that I may drink; and she shall say, Drink, and I will give thy camels drink also: *let the same be* she *that* thou hast appointed for thy servant Isaac; and thereby shall I know that thou hast shewed kindness unto my master.

15 And it came to pass, before he had done speaking, that, behold, Rebekah came out, who was born to Bethuel, son of Milcah, the wife of Nahor, Abraham's brother, with her pitcher upon her shoulder.

16 And the damsel *was* very fair to look upon, a virgin, neither had any man known her: and she went down to the well, and filled her pitcher, and came up.

17 And the servant ran to meet her, and said, Let me, I pray thee, drink a little water of thy pitcher.

18 And she said, Drink, my lord: and she hasted, and let down her pitcher upon her hand, and gave him drink.

19 And when she had done giving him drink, she said, I will draw *water* for thy camels also, until they have done drinking.

20 And she hasted, and emptied her pitcher into the trough, and ran again unto the well to draw *water,* and drew for all his camels.

21 And the man wondering at her held his peace, to wit whether the LORD had made his journey prosperous or not.

22 And it came to pass, as the camels had done drinking, that the man took a golden earring of half a shekel weight, and two bracelets for her hands of ten *shekels* weight of gold;

23 And said, Whose daughter *art* thou? tell me, I pray thee: is there room *in* thy father's house for us to lodge in?

24 And she said unto him, I *am* the daughter of Bethuel the son of Milcah, which she bare unto Nahor.

25 She said moreover unto him, We have both straw and provender enough, and room to lodge in.

26 And the man bowed down his head, and worshipped the LORD.

27 And he said, Blessed *be* the LORD God of my master Abraham, who hath not left destitute my master of his mercy and his truth: I *being* in the way, the LORD led me to the house of my master's brethren.

Elieser et Rebeca gen. 24. v.14.

And the servant ran to meet her, and said, Let me, I pray thee, drink a little water of thy pitcher. And she said, Drink, my lord: and she hasted, and let down her pitcher upon her hand, and gave him drink. And when she had done giving him drink, she said, I will draw water for thy camels also ... (Genesis 24:17-19)

The meeting between Abraham's oldest servant (called Eliezer in Genesis 15:2) with the beautiful Rebecca by a well in the evening was, for a long time, one of the most popular Old Testament subjects in Western European art. In his robust pen and brush drawing of this scene, Rembrandt depicted the gesture with which Rebecca gives the man a drink from her water jug with as much love and the same precision as it is described in the Bible. The thirsty camel, a tall, humped figure behind Eliezer and Rebecca by the trough, serves as an indication that the girl will soon spontaneously offer to give the camels water as well. In this way the sign Eliezer asked for is given, and he knows with certainty

that this is the girl that God intended for his master's son (see Genesis 24:14).

The camel, which Rembrandt drew from memory, reveals that he was familiar with this exotic animal, which he had already drawn from life - as shown in two sketches dating from about 1633 (Benesch II, nos. 453 and 454).

Pen and brush drawing; 21 × 33 cm.
Bottom left in later handwriting:
Elieser et Rebeca gen. 24.v.14.
Ca. 1640-45.
Washington, National Gallery of Art,
Widener Collection.

Literature: Benesch III, no. 503 (*ca.* 1640-42)/Rotermund 1963, no. 32.

Eliezer and Rebecca at the Spring

Sell me this day thy birthright

Genesis 25 20 And Isaac was forty years old when he took Rebekah to wife, the daughter of Bethuel the Syrian of Padanaram, the sister of Laban the Syrian.

21 And Isaaac intreated the LORD for his wife, because she *was* barren: and the LORD was intreated of him, and Rebekah his wife conceived.

22 And the children struggled together within her; and she said, If *it be* so, why *am* I thus? And she went to enquire of the LORD.

23 And the LORD said unto her, Two nations *are* in thy womb, and two manner of people shall be separated from thy bowels, and *the one* people shall be stronger than *the other* people; and the elder shall serve the younger.

24 And when her days to be delivered were fulfilled, behold, *there were* twins in her womb.

25 And the first came out red, all over like an hairy garment; and they called his name Esau.

26 And after that came his brother out, and his hand took hold on Esau's heel; and his name was called Jacob: and Isaac *was* threescore years old when she bare them.

27 And the boys grew: and Esau was a cunning hunter, a man of the field; and Jacob *was* a plain man, dwelling in tents.

28 And Isaac loved Esau, because he did eat of *his* venison: but Rebekah loved Jacob.

29 And Jacob sod pottage: and Esau came from the field, and he *was* faint:

30 And Esau said to Jacob, Feed me, I pray thee, with that same red *pottage;* for I *am* faint: therefore was his name called Edom.

31 And Jacob said, Sell me this day thy birthright.

32 And Esau said, Behold, I *am* at the point to die: and what profit shall this birthright do to me?

33 And Jacob said, Swear to me this day; and he sware unto him: and he sold his birthright unto Jacob.

34 Then Jacob gave Esau bread and pottage of lentiles; and he did eat and drink, and rose up, and went his way: thus Esau despised *his* birthright.

Esau asks Jacob for the Red Pottage

And Esau said to Jacob, Feed me, I pray thee, with that same red pottage; for I am faint: therefore was his name called Edom. And Jacob said, Sell me this day thy birthright. (Genesis 25:30-31)

The story of Jacob begins with the birth of the twins, Esau and Jacob. After his grandfather Abraham and his father Isaac, he was the third patriarch, the man who finally gave the whole nation its new name, Israel. Israel's twelve tribes stem from his twelve sons.

The prenatal clash between Esau and Jacob was a portent: a power struggle would arise between the twin brothers, and Esau, the firstborn and therefore the natural heir to God's blessings, was to taste defeat. God chose with sovereign freedom, and through his choice, Jacob (the nation of Israel) became the firstborn, destined to be the bearer of the promise. Esau, who was considered as the ancestor of the Edomites, Israel's hostile neighbouring nation, was rejected, just like Ishmael.

The prophecy of their birth (verse 23) was first fulfilled in the well-known incident of the mess of pottage. Unlike in two earlier drawings of this story, which depicted the moment at which Esau confirmed his agreement with Jacob with a handshake, as was usual for this subject (see pages 38-39), Rembrandt portrayed the events leading up to the rash exchange. Tired out and hungry after a day's hunting, Esau can think of only one thing, the mess of pottage in his brother's hands. He motions to Jacob who stands still but pretends he is about to walk away.

Jacob's clothes suggest that Rembrandt was familiar with 17th-century Indian miniatures; he based a series of drawings on these in about 1655 (Benesch V, nos. 1187-1206).

Pen and brush drawing; 15.9 × 20.3 cm.
Ca. 1650.
Berlin, Kupferstichkabinett der Staatlichen Museen.

Literature: Benesch III, no. 647 (*ca.* 1649-50)/Rotermund
1963, no. 33; Tümpel 1970, no. 11.

Esau Sells his Birthright to Jacob

And Jacob said, Swear to me this day; and he sware unto him: and he sold his birthright unto Jacob. Then Jacob gave Esau bread and pottage of lentiles ...
(Genesis 25:33-34)

Esau and Jacob shake hands across the table to seal their agreement. The observer looks straight into the weathered face of Esau, who is dressed as a hunter, and sees a growing suspicion in his eyes about his brother's intentions.

'Rarely has the inner contrast between two people, who are unified by a handshake, been characterized so sharply as in Esau and Jacob in this drawing by Rembrandt, dating from the early 1640s' ('Bijbelse Inspiratie', no. 56).

Drawing in pen and ink; 16.6 × 15.7 cm.
Ca. 1640-45.
Amsterdam, Amsterdams Historisch Museum.

Literature: Benesch III, no. 564; Slive II, no. 424 (*ca.* 1645); Haak, no. 43 (*ca.* 1644-45)/'Bijbelse Inspiratie', no. 56.

And Jacob said, Swear to me this day; and he sware unto him: and he sold his birthright unto Jacob. Then Jacob gave Esau bread and pottage of lentiles ...
(Genesis 25:33-34)

In his second drawing of the same subject, Rembrandt showed the hunter Esau standing next to the table, so that the handshake sealing the agreement between the brothers can be seen more clearly than in the previous version. At the same time, he expressed more strongly the rashness with which Esau squandered his inheritance. It seems as though Esau has just returned from his trip, and hungry as he is, he agrees with the exchange even before taking off his hunting clothes. '... And he did eat and drink and rose up and went his way; thus Esau despised his birthright.' Again there is a beautiful contrast between the rough, restless outdoor character of Esau, and the quieter and more contemplative Jacob, who is more attached to the home.

Pen and brush drawing; 20 × 17.3 cm.
Ca. 1648-50.
London, British Museum.

Literature: Benesch III, no. 606 (*ca.* 1648-49)/Rotermund 1963, no. 35.

Esau Sells his Birthright to Jacob

Who *art* thou, my son?

AND it came to pass, that when Isaac was old, and his eyes were dim, so that he could not see, he called Esau his eldest son, and said unto him, My son: and he said unto him, Behold, *here am* I.

2 And he said, Behold now, I am old, I know not the day of my death:

3 Now therefore take, I pray thee, thy weapons, thy quiver and thy bow, and go out to the field, and take me *some* venison;

4 And make me savoury meat, such as I love, and bring *it* to me, that I may eat; that my soul may bless thee before I die.

5 And Rebekah heard when Isaac spake to Esau his son. And Esau went to the field to hunt *for* venison, *and* to bring *it.*

6 And Rebekah spake unto Jacob her son, saying, Behold, I heard thy father speak unto Esau thy brother, saying,

7 Bring me venison, and make me savoury meat, that I may eat, and bless thee before the LORD before my death.

8 Now therefore, my son, obey my voice according to that which I command thee.

9 Go now to the flock, and fetch me from thence two good kids of the goats; and I will make them savoury meat for thy father, such as he loveth:

10 And thou shalt bring *it* to thy father, that he may eat, and that he may bless thee before his death.

11 And Jacob said to Rebekah his mother, Behold, Esau my brother *is* a hairy man, and I *am* a smooth man:

12 My father peradventure will feel me, and I shall seem to him as a deceiver; and I shall bring a curse upon me, and not a blessing.

13 And his mother said unto him, Upon me *be* thy curse, my son: only obey my voice, and go fetch me *them.*

14 And he went, and fetched, and brought *them* to his mother: and his mother made savoury meat, such as his father loved.

15 And Rebekah took goodly raiment of her eldest son Esau, which *were* with her in the house, and put them upon Jacob her younger son:

16 And she put the skins of the kids of the goats upon his hands, and upon the smooth of his neck:

17 And she gave the savoury meat and the bread, which she had prepared, into the hand of her son Jacob.

18 And he came unto his father, and said, My father: and he said, Here *am* I; who *art* thou, my son?

19 And Jacob said unto his father, I *am* Esau thy firstborn; I have done according as thou badest me: arise, I pray thee, sit and eat of my venison, that thy soul may bless me.

20 And Isaac said unto his son, How *is it* that thou hast found *it* so quickly, my son? And he said, Because the LORD thy God brought *it* to me.

21 And Isaac said unto Jacob, Come near, I pray thee, that I may feel thee, may son, whether thou *be* my very son Esau or not.

22 And Jacob went near unto Isaac his father; and he felt him, and said, The voice *is* Jacob's voice, but the hands *are* the hands of Esau.

23 And he discerned him not, because his hands were hairy, as his brother Esau's hands: so he blessed him.

24 And he said, *Art* thou my very son Esau? And he said, I *am.*

25 And he said, Bring *it* near to me, and I will eat of my son's venison, that my soul may bless thee. And he brought *it* near to him, and he did eat: and he brought him wine, and he drank.

26 And his father Isaac said unto him, Come near now, and kiss me, my son.

27 And he came near, and kissed him: and he smelled the smell of his raiment, and blessed him, and said, See, the smell of my son *is* as the smell of the field which the LORD hath blessed:

28 Therefore God give thee of the dew of heaven, and the fatness of the earth, and plenty of corn and wine:

29 Let people serve thee, and nations bow down to thee: be lord over thy brethren, and let thy mother's sons bow down to thee: cursed *be* every one that curseth thee, and blessed *be* he that blesseth thee.

30 And it came to pass, as soon as Isaac had made an end of blessing Jacob, and Jacob was yet scarce gone out from the presence of Isaac his father, that Esau his brother came in from his hunting.

And he came unto his father, and said, My father: and he said, Here am I; who art thou, my son? And Jacob said unto his father: I am Esau thy firstborn; I have done as thou badest me: arise, I pray thee, sit and eat of my venison, that thy soul may bless me.
(Genesis 27:18-19)

After Jacob had cheated his brother Esau out of his birthright, he also obtained the blessing of his father, which he so desired, by means of lies and trickery. With this second story about the mystery of Jacob's preference over Esau, the Biblical story confirmed the comment in Genesis 25:28: 'And Isaac loved Esau, because he did eat of his venison: but Rebecca loved Jacob.' The scene in which Jacob, urged on by his mother, succeeded in craftily obtaining the blessing of Isaac which was intended for his brother was particularly popular in Rembrandt's circle. There are many examples of paintings of it by Rembrandt's pupils, but only a few drawings by Rembrandt himself are known. This drawing, dating from the middle of

the 1650s, depicts the first stage of the deception. Pretending to be Esau, Jacob has just gone to his blind, bedridden father and asked him to sit up and gather his strength to give him his blessing. On the low table next to the bed there is a dish of goat's meat, served as venison. Rebecca's role is now at an end, and in the Bible story she is not present in this scene. However, Rembrandt has followed artistic tradition and shows her to remind us of the part she played in the deception. In the drawing on page 43, she stands at the foot of the old patriarch's bed, as she is commonly depicted; here Rembrandt shows her in the background, characteristically eavesdropping as she had done before (see verse 5).

Drawing in pen and ink; 16.2 × 22.6 cm.
Ca. 1655.
London, British Museum.

Literature: Benesch V, no. 984 (*ca.* 1655-56).

Jacob Asks his Father Isaac for his Blessing

41

31 And he also had made savoury meat, and brought it unto his father, and said unto his father, Let my father arise, and eat of his son's venison, that thy soul may bless me.

32 And Isaac his father said unto him, Who *art* thou? And he said, I *am* thy son, thy firstborn Esau.

33 And Isaac trembled very exceedingly, and said, Who? where *is* he that hath taken venison, and brought *it* me, and I have eaten of all before thou camest, and have blessing him? yea, *and* he shall be blessed.

34 And when Esau heard the words of his father, he cried with a great and exceeding bitter cry, and said unto his father, Bless me, *even* me also, O my father.

35 And he said, Thy brother came with subtilty, and hath taken away thy blessing.

36 And he said, Is not he rightly named Jacob? for he hath supplanted me these two times: he took away my birthright; and, behold, now he hath taken away my blessing. And he said, Hast thou not reserved a blessing for me?

37 And Isaac answered and said unto Esau, Behold, I have made him thy lord, and all his brethren have I given to him for servants; and with corn and wine have I sustained him; and what shall I do now unto thee, my son?

38 And Esau said unto his father, Hast thou but one blessing, my father? bless me, *even* me also, O my father. And Esau lifted up his voice, and wept.

39 And Isaac his father answered and said unto him, Behold, thy dwelling shall be the fatness of the earth, and of the dew of heaven from above;

40 And by thy sword shalt thou live, and shalt serve thy brother; and is shall come to pass when thou shalt have the dominion, that thou shalt break his yoke from off thy neck.

41 And Esau hated Jacob because of the blessing wherewith his father blessed him: and Esau said in his heart, The days of mourning for my father are at hand; then will I slay my brother Jacob.

42 And these words of Esau her elder son were told to Rebekah: and she sent and called Jacob her younger son, and said unto him, Behold, thy brother Esau, as touching thee, doth comfort himself, *purposing* to kill thee.

43 Now therefore, my son, obey my voice; and arise, flee thou to Laban my brother to Haran;

44 And tarry with him a few days, until thy brother's fury turn away;

45 Until thy brother's anger turn away from thee, and he forget *that* which thou hast done to him: then I will send, and fetch thee from thence: why should I be deprived also of you both in one day?

And Jacob went near unto Isaac his father; and he felt him, and said, The voice is Jacob's voice, but the hands are the hands of Esau. And he discerned him not, because his hands were hairy, as his brother Esau's hands: so he blessed him. (Genesis 27:22-23)

In this drawing and in several others dating from the 1640s (Benesch III, nos. 509 and 510), Rembrandt concentrated on the moment at which the tension in this story reaches its peak. Confused by Jacob's voice, Isaac, who is dependent on his other senses because of his blindness, wishes to feel his son to find out whether it is Esau before him or not. Jacob seems to be absolutely terrified as his father feels his hands. On the other side of the bed Rebecca watches tensely to see whether the boy will succeed in tricking the old man.

Rembrandt showed Isaac's actual blessing of Jacob in a drawing dating from *ca.* 1652 (Benesch V, no. 892).

Pen and brush drawing; 12.5 × 17.4 cm.
Ca. 1640-42.
Groningen, Groninger Museum.

Literature: Benesch III, no. 508 (*ca.* 1640-42)/Rotermund 1963, no. 36.

*Isaac Feels
Jacob's Hands*

I *am* with thee

Genesis 28 10 And Jacob went out from Beersheba, and went toward Haran.

11 And he lighted upon a certain place, and tarried there all night, because the sun was set; and he took of the stones of that place, and put *them for* his pillows, and lay down in that place to sleep.

12 And he dreamed, and behold a ladder set up on the earth, and the top of it reached to heaven: and behold the angels of God ascending and descending on it.

13 And, behold, the LORD stood above it, and said, I *am* the LORD God of Abraham thy father, and the God of Isaac: the land whereon thou liest, to thee will I give it, and to thy seed;

14 And thy seed shall be as the dust of the earth, and thou shalt spread abroad to the west, and to the east, and to the north, and to the south: and in thee and in thy seed shall all the families of the earth be blessed.

15 And, behold, I *am* with thee, and will keep thee in all *places* whither thou goest, and will bring thee again into this land; for I will not leave thee, until I have done *that* which I have spoken to thee of.

16 And Jacob awaked out of his sleep, and he said, Surely the LORD is in this place; and I knew *it* not.

17 And he was afraid, and said, How dreadful *is* this place! this *is* none other but he house of God, and this *is* the gate of heaven.

18 And Jacob rose up early in the morning, and took the stone that he had put *for* his pillows, and set it up *for* a pillar, and poured oil upon the top of it.

19 And he called the name of that place Bethel: but the name of that city *was called* Luz at the first.

20 And Jacob vowed a vow, saying, If God will be with me, and will keep me in this way that I go, and will give me bread to eat, and raiment to put on,

21 So that I come again to my father's house in peace, then shall the LORD be my God:

22 And this stone, which I have set *for* a pillar, shall be God's house: and of all that thou shalt give me I will surely give the tenth unto thee.

Jacob's Dream *And behold, the Lord stood above it, and said, I am the Lord God of Abraham thy father, and the God of Isaac: the land whereon thou liest, to thee will I give it, and to thy seed. (Genesis 28:13)*

The main content of Jacob's dream is a verbal revelation which is introduced by the famous vision of a ladder between heaven and earth. Apart from in the etching he was commissioned to do in 1655 (see p. 47), Rembrandt always left out the so-called 'Jacob's ladder' in his versions of this subject that are known to us, and he has laid the emphasis on the encouraging message which the boy received in his dream. One day the land where he is lying, and which he must flee because he is threatened by Esau's vengeance, will be restored to him and his descendants. One day he will return cleansed to the land promised to Abraham and Isaac, and bring a blessing to all people as the heir to the promise. The only reference in this drawing to the image of the ladder with angels climbing up and down in Jacob's dream is formed by the cherubim floating above him and descending from heaven.

The number 44 written in Rembrandt's handwriting at the bottom right probably refers to the year (1644) in which he did the drawing. What Rembrandt might have meant by the word 'doopt' (baptizes) underneath is not clear.

Drawing in pen; 17.8 × 19.6 cm.
Dated (bottom right): *44* (1644).
Paris, Ecole Nationale Supérieure des Beaux-Arts.

Literature: Benesch III, no. 555/Rotermund 1963, no. 43.

And, behold, I am with thee, and will keep thee in all places whither thou goest, and will bring thee again into this land; for I will not leave thee, until I have done that which I have spoken to thee of.
(Genesis 28:15)

Bending forwards slightly, the angel of the Lord protectively spreads his hands above the sleeping boy, who possesses only a crook, a flask and a shepherd's bag, apart from the clothes he is wearing. However, he need not fear the future, for God is behind him. The God of Abraham and the God of Isaac will also be the God of Jacob. The promises made to Abraham will be fulfilled in him and his descendants. How surprising it is that Jacob, the deceiver, is not reproached in any way. The impenetrable nature of the reason why he is chosen is illustrated once again.

A less impressive version of this drawing can be found in the Boymans van Beuningen Museum in Rotterdam (Benesch III, no. 558). The surviving part of a drawing (Benesch I, no. 125) dating from *ca.* 1635, showing only the sleeping figure of Jacob, and a drawing dating from *ca.* 1655 (Benesch V, no. 996), together with the drawings shown here from the first half of the 1640s, clearly show that Rembrandt was interested in this subject throughout his career.

Pen and brush drawing; 25 × 20.8 cm.
Ca. 1640-45.
Paris, The Louvre.

Literature: Benesch III, no. 557 (*ca.* 1644); Slive I, no. 163 (*ca.* 1640)/Hofstede de Groot, *Rembrandt Bijbel*, V.T.d.8; Rotermund 1963, no. 42; 'Bijbelse Inspiratie', under no. 58.

And he took of the stones of that place, and put them for his pillows, and lay down in that place to sleep. And he dreamed, and behold a ladder set up on the earth, and the top of it reached to heaven; and behold the angels of God ascending and descending on it.
(Genesis 28:11-12)

Jacob's Dream

This etching is one of the four illustrations done by Rembrandt for the Spanish book by the Jewish scholar, Menasseh ben Israel, entitled *Piedra Gloriosa o de la estatua de Nebuchadnezzar* (The Glorious Stone, or About the Statue of Nebuchadnezzar). The book, which was published in 1655, was a Messianic explanation of Nebuchadnezzar's dream described in Daniel 2:31-35. He sees a large statue which is smashed before his eyes by a stone which has worked itself loose without any help from man. According to Menasseh, this stone was the one on which Jacob was sleeping when he dreamed about a ladder which connected heaven and earth; and it was the stone with which David slew Goliath. For this 'glorious stone' is the Messiah, and when he comes the kingdom of Israel will be established.

In the first copy of this print, Rembrandt finished the ladder at Jacob. In the second and third copies he continued it to the bottom edge because for Menasseh the middle of the ladder represented Jerusalem, and according to his interpretation, that is where Jacob slept.

Etching; 10.6 × 7 cm. Third state of three.
Signed and dated: *Rembrandt f. 1655.*
Amsterdam, Rijksprentenkabinet.

Literature: Bartsch, no. 36; Hind, no. 284; Münz, no. 183; Boon, no. 264; Filedt Kok, no. B 36 and B 36B/Hofstede de Groot, *Rembrandt Bijbel*, V.T.e.6; Tümpel 1970, no. 39.

Know ye Laban?

Genesis 29 THEN Jacob went on his journey, and came into the land of the people of the east.

2 And he looked, and behold a well in the field, and, lo, there *were* three flocks of sheep lying by it; for out of that well they watered the flocks: and a great stone *was* upon the well's mouth.

3 And thither were all the flocks gathered: and they rolled the stone from the well's mouth, and watered the sheep, and put the stone again upon the well's mouth in his place.

4 And Jacob said unto them, My brethren, whence *be* ye? And they said, Of Haran *are* we.

5 And he said unto them, Know ye Laban the son of Nahor? And they said, We know *him*.

6 And he said unto them, *Is* he well? And the said, *He is* well: and, behold, Rachel his daughter cometh with the sheep.

7 And he said, Lo, *it is* yet high day, neither *is it* time that the cattle should be gathered together: water ye sheep, and go *and* feed *them*.

8 And the said, We cannot, untill all the flocks be gathered together, and *till* they roll the stone from the well's mouth; then we water the sheep.

9 And while he yet spake with them, Rachel came with her father's sheep: for she kept them.

10 And it came to pass, when Jacob saw Rachel the daughter of Laban his mother's brother, and the sheep of Laban his mother's brother, that Jacob went near, and rolled the stone from the well's mouth, and watered the flock of Laban his mother's brother.

11 And Jacob kissed Rachel, and lifted up his voice, and wept.

12 And Jacob told Rachel that he *was* her father's brother, and that he *was* Rebekha's son: and she ran and told her father.

13 And it came to pass, when Laban heard the tidings of Jacob his sister's son, that he ran to meet him, and embraced him, and kissed him, and brought him to his house. And he told Laban all these things.

14 And Laban said to him, Surely thou *art* my bone and my flesh. And he abode with him the space of a month.

15 And Laban said unto Jacob, Because thou *art* my brother, shouldest thou therefore serve me for nought? tell me, what *shall* thy wages *be*?

16 And Laban had two daughters: the name of the elder *was* Leah, and the name of the younger *was* Rachel.

17 Leah *was* tender eyed; but Rachel was beautiful and well favoured.

18 And Jacob loved Rachel; and said, I will serve thee seven years for Rachel thy younger daughter.

19 And Laban said, *It is* better that I give her to thee, than that I should give her to another man: abide with me.

20 And Jacob served seven years for Rachel; and they seemed unto him *but* a few days, for the love he had to her.

21 And Jacob said unto Laban, Give *me* my wife, for my days are fulfilled, that I may go in unto her.

22 And Laban gathered together all the men of the place, and made a feast.

23 And it came to pass in the evening, that he took Leah his daughter, and brought her to him; and he went in unto her.

24 And Laban gave unto his daughter Leah Zilpah his maid *for* an handmaid.

25 And it came to pass, that in the morning, behold, it *was* Leah: and he said to Laban, What *is* this thou hast done unto me? did not I serve with thee for Rachel? wherefore then hast thou beguiled me?

26 And Laban said, It must not be so done in our country, to give the younger before the firstborn.

27 Fulfil her week, and we will give thee this also for the service which thou shalt serve with me yet seven other years.

28 And Jacob did so, and fulfilled her week: and he gave him Rachel his daughter to wife also.

29 And Laban gave to Rachel his daughter Bilhah his handmaid to be her maid.

30 And he went in also unto Rachel, and he loved also Rachel more than Leah, and served with him yet seven other years.

And it came to pass, when Laban heard the tidings of Jacob his sister's son, that he ran to meet him, and embraced him, and kissed him, and brought him to his house.
(Genesis 29:13)

Jacob's staff and his satchel are enough to remind us of the long journey he has made. Although the Bible text does not mention Rachel when Laban comes to greet his nephew, Rembrandt nevertheless showed the young shepherdess in the background tending her father's sheep. Her presence not only reminds us how happy Jacob was when he met her at the well, but also refers to the hard years of service which he will have to spend with Laban for her sake. Jacob the deceiver is shown here with the man who is soon to deceive him. Rembrandt deliberately drew Jacob as a very timid young man being embraced by his uncle. It is as though he already realizes that he will have a very hard time.

Rembrandt continually succeeds in clarifying a scene by depicting narrative elements in such a way that they interconnect with the rest of the story.

Laban Greets his Nephew, Jacob

Pen and brush drawing; 16.9 × 21.5 cm.
Ca. 1655.
Copenhagen, Kobberstiksamling.

Literature: Benesch V, no. 953 (*ca.* 1654-55); Slive II, no. 392 (*ca.* 1652-55)/Rotermund 1963, no. 44; Tümpel 1969, p. 138.

There wrestled a man with him

[After many years of service, Jacob finally decides, unknown to Laban, to return to Canaan with his family and the cattle he has craftily acquired. Laban pursues him, and when he has caught him up, the two men reach an agreement.]

Genesis 32 AND Jacob went on his way, and the angels of God met him

2 And when Jacob saw them, he said, This *is* God's host: and he called the name of that place Mahanaim.

3 And Jacob sent messengers before him to Esau his brother unto the land of Seir, the country of Edom.

4 And he commanded them, saying, Thus shall ye speak unto my lord Esau; Thy servant Jacob saith thus, I have sojourned with Laban, and stayed there until now:

5 And I have oxen, and asses, flocks, and menservants, and womenservants: and I have sent to tell my lord, that I may find grace in thy sight.

6 And the messengers returned to Jacob, saying, We came to thy brother Esau, and also he cometh to meet thee, and four hundred men with him.

7 Then Jacob was greatly afraid and distressed: and he divided the people that *was* with him, and the flocks, and herds, and the camels, into two bands;

8 And said, If Esau come to the one company, and smite it, then the other company which is left shall escape.

9 And Jacob said, O God of my father Abraham, and God of my father Isaac, the LORD which saidst unto me, Return unto thy country, and to thy kindred, and I will deal well with thee:

10 A am not worthy of the least of all the mercies, and of all the truth, which thou hast

shewed unto thy servant; for with my staff I passed over this Jordan; and now I am become two bands.

11 Deliver me, I pray thee, from the hand of my brother, from the hand of Esau: for I fear him, lest he will come and smite me, *and* and the mother with the children.

12 And thou saidst, I will surely do thee good, and make thy seed as the sand of the sea, which cannot be numbered for multitude.

13 And he lodged there that same night; [...]

22 And he rose up that night, and took his two wives, and his two womenservants, and his eleven sons, and passed over the ford Jabbok.

23 And he took them, and sent them over the brook, and sent over that he had.

24 And Jacob was left alone; and there wrestled a man with him until the breaking of the day.

25 And when he saw that he prevailed not against him, he touched the hollow of his thigh; and the hollow of Jacob's thigh was out of joint, as he wrestled with him.

26 And he said, Let me go, for the day breaketh. And he said, I will not let thee go, except thou bless me.

27 And he said unto him, What *is* thy name? And he said, Jacob.

28 And he said, Thy name shall be called no more Jacob, but Israel: for as a prince hast thou power with God and with men, and hast prevailed.

29 And Jacob asked *him,* and said, Tell *me,* I pray thee, thy name. And he said, Wherefore *is* it *that* thou dost ask after my name? And he blessed him there.

30 And Jacob called the name of the place Peniel: for I have seen God face to face, and my life is preserved.

31 And as he passed over Penuel the sun rose upon him, and he halted upon his thigh.

Jacob's Struggle with the Angel *And when he saw that he prevailed not against him, he touched the hollow of his thigh; and the hollow of Jacob's thigh was out of joint, as he wrestled with him.* (Genesis 32:25)

Just as God revealed himself to Jacob in the night before he left Canaan (see p. 44), he did so again in the night before Jacob returned to the Promised Land. The mysterious struggle, which lasts until daybreak, reveals how difficult was this longest night in Jacob's life. He fears the worst from his imminent meeting

with Esau. However, blessed with a new name, he feels strong enough to approach the confrontation with confidence when the sun rises.

Although the nocturnal duel is one of the most frequently depicted scenes from the stories about Jacob, it is rarely found in Dutch works of art. In his version of this subject, Rembrandt sublimated the struggle by showing it in the form of a duel in which there is no violence, and it is as though the opponents are embracing each other rather than fighting each other. The angel looks at Jacob with heavenly

mildness, and spreads his wings as though to bless him.

The painting is a fragment. Rembrandt's signature is at the bottom right on a piece of linen which was incorporated later; it probably comes from a part that was cut away from the original canvas.

Canvas; 137 × 116 cm.
Signed: *Rembrandt f.*
Ca. 1659-60.
Berlin, Gemäldegalerie der Staatlichen Museen.

Literature: Bredius, no. 528; Bauch, no. 36; Gerson, no. 346; Bredius-Gerson, no. 528/Hofstede de Groot, *Rembrandt Bijbel*, V.T.p.5; Tümpel 1969, p. 175V.

And Esau ran to meet him

Genesis 33 AND Jacob lifted up his eyes, and looked, and, behold, Esau came, and with him four hundred men. And he divided the children unto Leah, and unto Rachel, and unto the two handmaids.

2 And he put the handmaids and their children foremost, and Leah and her children after, and Rachel and Joseph hindermost.

3 And he passed over before them, and bowed himself to the ground seven times, until he came near to his brother.

4 And Esau ran to meet him, and embraced him, and fell on his neck, and kissed him: and they wept.

5 And he lifted up his eyes, and saw the women and the children; and said, Who *are* those with thee? And he said, The children which God hath graciously given thy servant.

6 Then the handmaidens came near, they and their children, and they bowed themselves.

7 And Leah also with her children came near, and bowed themselves: and after came Joseph near and Rachel, and they bowed themselves.

8 And he said, What *meanest* thou by all this drove which I met? And he said, *These are* to find grace in the sight of my lord.

9 And Esau said, I have enough, my brother; keep that thou hast unto thyself.

10 And Jacob said, Nay, I pray thee, if now I have found grace in thy sight, then receive my present at my hand: for therefore I have seen thy face, as though I had seen the face of God, and thou wast pleased with me.

11 Take, I pray thee, my blessing that is brought to thee; because God hath dealt graciously with me, and because I have enough. And he urged him, and he took *it*.

12 And he said, Let us take our journey, and let us go, and I will go before thee.

13 And he said unto him, My lord knoweth that the children *are* tender, and the flocks and herds with young *are* with me: and if men should overdrive them one day, all the flock will die.

14 Let my lord, I pray thee, pass over before his servant: and I will lead on softly, according as the cattle that goeth before me and the children be able to endure, until I come unto my lord unto Seir.

15 And Esau said, Let me now leave with thee *some* of the folk that *are* with me. And he said, What needeth it? let me find grace in the sight of my lord.

16 So Esau returned that day on his way unto Seir.

17 And Jacob journeyed to Succoth, and built him an house, and made booths for his cattle: therefore the name of the palace is called Succoth.

Esau's Reconciliation with Jacob

And Esau ran to meet him, and embraced him, and fell on his neck, and kissed him: and they wept.
(Genesis 33:4)

After so many years, the true Esau is the opposite of the frightening figure which Jacob had imagined in his fear and guilt. All his resentment and vengeance has disappeared and he does not say a word about the past.

The concise sketch in which Rembrandt showed the moving meeting of the twin brothers is one of the most striking examples of the simplification in his drawings in the course of the 1650s. Although the subject shown here was fairly popular with Dutch historical painters in the 17th century, there are no surviving works by Rembrandt based on this subject apart from this drawing.

Drawing in pen and ink; 20.8 × 30.3 cm.
Bottom right in later handwriting: *Rembrandt f.*
Ca. 1655.
Berlin, Kupferstichkabinett der Staatlichen Museen.

Literature: Benesch V, no. 966 (*ca.* 1655)/Rotermund 1963, no. 48; Tümpel 1970, no. 13.

Hear, I pray you, this dream which I have dreamed

Genesis 37

AND Jacob dwelt in the land wherein his father was a stranger, in the land of Canaan.

2 These *are* the generations of Jacob. Joseph, *being* seventeen years old, was feeding the flock with his brethren; and the lad *was* with the sons of Bilhah, and with the sons of Zilpah, his father's wives: and Joseph brought unto his father their evil report.

3 Now Israel loved Joseph more than all his children, because he *was* the son of his old age: and he made him a coat of *many* colours.

4 And when his brethren saw that their father loved him more than all his brethren, they hated him and could not speak peaceably unto him.

5 And Joseph dreamed a dream, and he told *it* his brethren: and they hated him yet the more.

6 And he said unto them, Hear, I pray you, this dream which I have dreamed:

7 For, behold, we *were* binding sheaves in the field, and, lo, my sheaf arose, and also stood upright; and, behold, your sheaves stood round about, and made obeisance to my sheaf.

8 And his brethren said to him, Shalt thou indeed reign over us or shalt thou indeed have dominion over us? And they hated him yet the more for his dreams, and for his words.

9 And he dreamed yet another dream, and told it his brethren, and said, Behold, I have dreamed a dream more; and, behold, the sun and the moon and the eleven stars made obeisance to me.

10 And he told *it* to his father, and to his brethren: and his father rebuked him, and said unto him, What *is* this dream that thou hast dreamed? Shall I and thy mother and the brothren indeed come to bow down ourselves to thee to the earth?

11 And his brethren envied him; but his father observed the saying.

Joseph Recounts his Dreams

For, behold, we were binding sheaves in the field, and, lo, my sheaf arose, and also stood upright; and, behold, your sheaves stood round about, and made obeisance to my sheaf. (Genesis 37:7)

The story of Joseph, which brings the book of Genesis to an end, is completely supported by a belief in God's providence. In contrast with previous stories, God does not openly intervene anywhere to bring about a sudden and unexpected turn of events. He works in hidden, but nevertheless irresistible, ways, as the commanding God who leads everything and can even use the evil of man to realize his plans. When Joseph has been put away by his brothers, it seems as though he is finished, but in reality his 'fall' was to be the salvation of God's people, for if Joseph had not been sold to Egypt, Jacob's family would have died of starvation.

It is not surprising that the story of Joseph has always reminded Christians of their own Saviour who, hated and rejected by his brothers, gave his life as 'a ransom for many' (Matthew 20:28). Therefore, in the Middle Ages, themes from the Passion of Christ were often accompanied by scenes from Joseph's life, for Joseph was seen as a precursor of Jesus. However, the story of Joseph has so many individual qualities that later on, when the textual link between Joseph and Jesus became less important, his story continued to fascinate artists more than any other Old Testament story. In Rembrandt's Biblical pictures the character of Joseph is very prominent.

In this brownish-grey sketch in oils, which is usually considered as the first draft for the etching dating from 1638 (see p. 56), Joseph stands opposite his father, recounting his dreams. The old man is listening with mixed feelings. Behind Joseph, trouble is brewing amongst his indignant brothers. The woman listening attentively from the bed in the background must be Joseph's mother, Rachel. She is always present in Rembrandt's representations of this subject, although it is clear from another point in the Bible that Rachel had already died (at the birth of Benjamin, Genesis 35:16-20). She can also be seen in the print by Lucas van Leyden on this subject, dating from 1512. This was the first of a series of five sketches devoted to Joseph's life. Presumably the reason for her presence at this scene is the words with which Jacob admonishes Joseph: 'What is this dream that thou hast dreamed? Shall I and thy mother and thy brethren indeed come to bow down ourselves to thee to the earth?' (Genesis 37:10).

Paper; 51 × 39 cm.
Signed and dated: *Rembrandt 163(...).*
Ca. 1637.
Amsterdam, Rijksmuseum.

Literature: Bredius, no. 504; Bauch, no. 19; Gerson, no. 86; Bredius-Gerson, no. 504/Hofstede de Groot, *Rembrandt Bijbel,* V.T.p.6; H.T. van Guldener, *Het Jozefverhaal bij Rembrandt en zijn school,* Utrecht 1947.

Joseph Recounts his Dreams

For, behold, we were binding sheaves in the field, and, lo, my sheaf arose, and also stood upright; and, behold, your sheaves stood round about, and made obeisance to my sheaf. (Genesis 37:7)

Despite the differences, it is clear that Rembrandt based this extremely delicate etching on the oil sketch depicted previously. (It should be noted that to print the etched copper plate, the representation on the plate appears on the paper in mirror image.) In the foreground a seated girl, Jacob's daughter Dina, has been added to the composition. The number of brothers has also increased and Joseph is not seen from the side, but from the front. Rembrandt beautifully expresses how the boy is completely immersed in recounting the contents of his dreams. He can see the whole dream before him again, but is blind to the bitterness he is provoking. Behind his back the brothers are whispering and planning animatedly, and the concern of the parents is understandable. The mother's face in the bed in the background reveals the full extent of the imminent drama.

Apart from the brownish-grey sketch in oils, Rembrandt's drawings also include several studies related to this etching. Even when he made the grisaille he used a red chalk study of an old man in an easy chair (Benesch I, no. 20), dating from 1631, for the figure of Jacob. For the girl seated in the foreground (who is missing on the grisaille) he did a separate preliminary study in pen and ink (Benesch I, no. 168). A composition sketch for the etching, which was unknown until recently, was published by J. Giltay, 'An Unknown Sketch by Rembrandt' in *De chroniek van het Rembrandtshuis* 29 (1977) no. 1, pp. 1-9, illus. 2.

Etching; 11 × 8.3 cm. Second state of three.
Signed and dated: *Rembrandt f. 1638.*
Amsterdam, Rijksprentenkabinet.

Literature: Bartsch, no. 37; Hind, no. 160; Münz, no. 175; Boon, no. 139; Filedt Kok, no. B 37/Hofstede de Groot, *Rembrandt Bijbel*, V.T.e.7; Rotermund 1963, no. 51; 'Bijbelse Inspiratie', no. 26; Tümpel 1970, no. 14.

And he told it to his father, and to his brethren: and his father rebuked him, and said unto him, What is this dream that thou hast dreamed? Shall I and thy mother and thy brethren indeed come to bow down ourselves to thee to the earth?
(Genesis 37:10)

In this beautiful drawing Rembrandt restricted himself to the main characters from the two preceding representations and concentrated above all on showing Jacob's reaction to Joseph recounting his dreams. For the first time young Benjamin, Joseph's younger brother, is also shown, standing between his old father's knees. The innocence of the ingenuous child forms a striking contrast with the concerned faces of the parents.

The composition is similar to the etching dating from 1638, and even more closely resembles the main group on the grisaille in the Rijksmuseum in Amsterdam. For this reason the drawing is often considered as one of the preparatory studies which eventually led to the print shown on the previous page.

Benesch ascribes a later date to the drawing (and Haak supports this view) and considers the study as a further development of the 1638 composition.

Pen and brush drawing; 17.5 × 24.5 cm.
Signed: *Rembrant f.*
Ca. 1642-45.
Vienna, Albertina.

Literature: Benesch III, no. 526 (*ca.* 1642-43); Haak, no. 38 (*ca.* 1642-43)/Rotermund 1963, no. 50; Tümpel 1970, under no. 20.

Joseph Recounts his Dreams

For twenty *pieces* of silver

12 And his brethren went to feed their father's flock in Shechem.

13 And Israel said unto Joseph, Do not thy brethren feed *the flock* in Shechem? come, and I will send thee unto them. And he said to him, Here *am I.*

14 And he said to him, Go, I pray thee, see whether it be well with thy brethern, and well with the flocks; and bring me word again. So he sent him out of the vale of Hebron, and he came to Shechem.

15 And a certain man found him, and, behold, *he was* wandering in the field: and the man aksed him, saying, What seekest thou?

16 And he said, I seek my brethren: tell me, I pray thee, where they feed *their flocks.*

17 And the man said, They are departed hence; for I heard them say, Let us go to Dothan. And Joseph went after his brethren, and found them in Dothan.

18 And when they saw him afar off, even before he came near unto them, they conspired against him to slay him.

19 And they said one to another, Behold, this dreamer cometh.

20 Come now therefore, and let us slay him, and cast him into some pit, and we will say, Some evil beast hath devoured him: and we shall see what will become of his dreams.

21 And Reuben heard *it,* and he delivered him out of their hands; and said, Let us not kill him.

22 And Reuben said unto them, Shed no blood, *but* cast him into this pit that *is* in the wilderness, and lay no hand upon him; that he might rid him out of their hands, to deliver him to his father again.

23 And it came to pass, when Joseph was come unto his brethren, that they stript Joseph out of his coat, *his* coat of *many* colours that *was* on him;

24 And they took him, and cast him into a pit: and the pit *was* empty, *there was* no water in it.

25 And they sat down to eat bread: and they lifted up their eyes and looked, and, behold, a company of Ishmeelites came from Gilead with their camels bearing spicery and balm and myrrh, going to carry *it* down to Egypt.

26 And Judah said unto his brethren, What profit *is it* if we slay our brother, and conceal his blood?

27 Come, and let us sell him to the Ishmeelites, and let not our hand be upon him; for he *is* our brother *and* our flesh. And his brethren were content.

28 Then there passed by Midianites merchantmen; and they drew and lifted up Joseph out of the pit, and sold Joseph to the Ishmeelites for twenty *pieces* of silver: and they brought Joseph into Egypt.

29 And Reuben returned unto the pit; and, behold, Joseph *was* not in the pit; and he rent his clothes.

30 And he returned unto his brethren, and said, The child *is* not; and I, whither shall I go?

31 And they took Joseph's coat, and killed a kid of the goats, and dipped the coat in the blood;

32 And they sent the coat of *many* colours, and they brought *it* to their father; and said, This have we found: know now whether it *be* thy son's coat or no.

33 And he knew it, and said, *It is* my son's coat; an evil beast hat devoured him; Joseph is without doubt rent in pieces.

34 And Jacob rent his clothes, and put sackcloth upon his loins, and mourned for his son many days.

35 And all his sons and all his daughters rose up to comfort him; but he refused to be comforted; and he said, For I will go down into the grave unto my son mourning. Thus his father wept for him.

Then there passed by Midianites merchantmen; and they drew and lifted up Joseph out of the pit, and sold Joseph to the Ishmeelites for twenty pieces of silver ... (Genesis 37:28)

Eventually the brothers decided on the most suitable manner to dispose of Joseph and prevent his dreams from coming true. In this way they did not have to spill his blood and, furthermore, they made some money from the transaction.

Rembrandt drew the scene very concisely, but extremely clearly. Weeping, the small child Joseph begs one of his brothers for mercy, but it is all to no avail. The bargain has been sealed and the pieces of silver for which they haggled are greedily taken. Joseph's plea for pity is only mentioned much later in the story. When the brothers come to Egypt to buy grain, they are so strictly treated by Joseph - whom they do not recognize - that their consciences prick them. Then they admit to each other: 'We are verily guilty concerning our brother, in that we saw the anguish of his soul when he besought us and we would not hear; therefore is distress come upon us' (Genesis 42:21). It is clear that in considering Joseph as a precursor of Jesus, the twenty silver pieces for which he was sold were comparable to the money received by Judas for delivering Jesus to his enemies (see Matthew 26:15).

Joseph is Sold by his Brothers

Drawing in pen and ink; 15.8 × 20.5 cm.
Ca. 1650.
Berlin, Kupferstichkabinett der Staatlichen Museen.

Literature: Benesch V, no. 876 (*ca.* 1651-52)/Hofstede de Groot, *Rembrandt Bijbel*, V.T.d.10; Rotermund 1963, no. 55; Tümpel 1970, no. 15.

Joseph's Coat is Shown to Jacob

And they took Joseph's coat, and killed a kid of the goats, and dipped the coat in the blood. And they sent the coat of many colours, and they brought it to their father; and said, This have we found: know now whether it be thy son's coat or no. And he knew it, and said, It is my son's coat; an evil beast hath devoured him; Joseph is without doubt rent in pieces.
(Genesis 37:31-33)

A long time previously, Rebecca had slaughtered two goats and, wearing their skins, Jacob had succeeded in deceiving his father. Now he is himself deceived by his sons with the blood of a slaughtered goat.

This theme is a common one in Dutch 17th-century historical painting. Seeing a painting of this subject by Jan Pynas, Joost van den Vondel was inspired to write his tragedy, *Joseph in Dothan* (1640), as he explained in the prologue to it. (This painting, dating from 1618, has survived and is now in the Hermitage in Leningrad.)

In this detailed print, dating from 1633, Rembrandt conveyed the consternation of the dramatic moment in a series of strongly evocative gestures. The two messengers of doom, instructed by Joseph's brothers, have gone right up to Jacob. One of them points into the distance where they say they found the garment.

The old man is beside himself with grief. Again Joseph's mother is shown (see the explanatory note on p. 54). Paralysed with shock, she also recognizes Joseph's coat.

Etching; 10.8 × 8.2 cm. First state of two.
Signed: *Rembrandt van Rijn fe.*
Ca. 1633.
Amsterdam, Rijksprentenkabinet.

Literature: Bartsch, no. 38; Hind, no. 104; Münz, no. 172; Boon, no. 88; Filedt Kok, no. B 38/Hofstede de Groot, *Rembrandt Bijbel*, V.T.e.8; Rotermund 1963, no. 58; Tümpel 1970, no. 16.

And they took Joseph's coat, and killed a kid of the goats, and dipped the coat in the blood. And they sent the coat of many colours, and they brought it to their father; and said, This have we found: know now whether it be thy son's coat or no. And he knew it, and said, It is my son's coat; an evil beast hath devoured him; Joseph is without doubt rent in pieces.
(Genesis 37:31-33)

The composition of this scene is broader, and except for one, contains all the same figures as the compact representation on the etching dating from about 1633. Again it is a beautiful example of the effective simplicity with which Rembrandt managed to express his imagination in the middle of the 1650s (cf. the drawing on p. 53). The young Benjamin is shown right next to the lamenting Jacob. He looks up at his father in consternation. Henceforth the old man will love the child, the only child remaining to him from his favourite wife, Rachel, with all his heart and soul. Benjamin's presence here so close to his father is a reference to the grief that Jacob will yet feel for his sake. For one day his sons will demand that he allow Benjamin to go with them to Egypt. Despite his fears that the boy will have an accident just like Joseph, he

finally feels forced to let the child go. '... If I am bereaved of children, I am bereaved' (Genesis 43:14, see pp. 74-75).

The fact that Rembrandt must have been familiar with the painting mentioned above which inspired Vondel to write his drama *Joseph in Dothan*, is clear from a drawing which he did later (Benesch V, no. 991; Rotterdam, Museum Boymans-van Beuningen), which was unmistakably influenced by Jan Pynas's composition.

Joseph's Coat is Shown to Jacob

Drawing in pen and ink; 16.2 × 24.1 cm.
Bottom in later handwriting: *R*.
Ca. 1655.
Amsterdam, Rijksprentenkabinet.

Literature: Benesch V, no. 971 (*ca.* 1655)/Rotermund 1963, no. 57; 'Bijbelse Inspiratie', no. 59; Tümpel 1970, under no. 16.

Lie with me

AND Joseph was brought down to Egypt; and Potiphar, an officer of Pharaoh, captain of the guard, an Egyptian, bought him of the hands of the Ishmeelites, which had brought him down thither.

2 And the LORD was with Joseph, and he was a prosperous man; and he was in the house of his master the Egyptian.

3 And his master saw that the LORD *was* with him, and that the LORD made all that he did to prosper in his hand.

4 And Joseph found grace in his sight, and he served him: and he made him overseer over his house, and all *that* he had he put into his hand.

5 And it came to pass from the time *that* he had made him overseer in his house, and over all that he had, that the LORD blessed the Egyptian's house for Joseph's sake; and the blessing of the LORD was upon all that he had in the house, and in the field.

6 And he left all that he had in Joseph's hand; and he knew not ought he had, save the bread which he did eat. And Joseph was *a* goodly *person,* and well favoured.

7 And it came to pass after these things, that his master's wife cast her eyes upon Joseph; and she said, Lie with me.

8 But he refused, and said unto his master's wife, Behold, my master wotteth not what *is* with me in the house, and he hath committed all that he hath to my hand;

9 *There is* none greater in this house than I; neither hath he kept back any things from me but thee, because thou *art* his wife: how then can I do this great wickedness, and sin against God?

10 And it came to pass, as she spake to Joseph day by day, that he hearkened not unto her, to lie by her, *or* to be with her.

11 And it came to pass about this time, that *Joseph* went into the house to do his business; and *there was* none of the men of the house there within.

12 And she caught him by his garment, saying, Lie with me: and he left his garment in her hand, and fled, and got him out.

13 And it came to pass, when she saw that he had left his garment in her hand, and was fled forth,

14 That she called unto the men of her house, and spake unto them, saying, See, he hath brought in an Hebrew unto us to mock us; he came in unto me to lie with me, and I cried with a loud voice:

15 And it came to pass, when he heard that I lifted up my voice and cried, that he left his garment with me, and fled, and got him out.

16 And she laid up his garment by her, until his lord came home.

17 And she spake unto him according to these words, saying, The Hebrew servant, which thou hast brought unto us, came in unto me to mock me:

18 And it came to pass, as I lifted up my voice and cried, that he left his garment with me, and fled out.

19 And it came to pass, when his master heard the words of his wife, which she spake unto him, saying, After this manner did thy servant to me; that his wrath was kindled.

20 And Joseph's master took him, and put him into the prison, a place where the king's prisoners *were* bound: and he was there in the prison.

21 But the LORD was with Joseph, and shewed him mercy, and gave him favour in the sight of the keeper of the prison.

22 And the keeper of the prison commited to Joseph's hand all the prisoners that *were* in the prison; and whatsoever they did there, he was the doer *of it.*

23 The keeper of the prison looked not to any thing *that was* under his hand; because the LORD was with him, and *that* which he did, the LORD made *it* to prosper.

And it came to pass, as she spake to Joseph day by day, that he hearkened not unto her, to lie by her, or to be with her. And it came to pass about this time, that Joseph went into the house to do his business; and there was none of the men of the house there within. And she caught him by the garment, saying, Lie with me: and he left his garment in her hand, and fled, and got him out.
(Genesis 39:10-12)

Joseph is described in the Bible as a wise, modest and virtuous young man, who, with God's grace, succeeds in everything and brings blessings to everyone who comes into contact with him. Nevertheless, he ends up in prison one day because he is falsely accused by his master's lecherous wife.

The scene in which Joseph flees from the temptress, leaving his coat behind, was particularly popular in Western European art during the Renaissance and baroque periods. Rembrandt used this subject once only, in this etching dating from 1634.

In his realistic portrayal of the subject, the woman's lack of shame and Joseph's repulsion are expressed very forcefully. Undoubtedly the sharp contrast between light and dark in this print has a symbolic significance, as well as an artistic function. Where light meets dark, Joseph chooses light.

Etching; 9 × 11.5 cm. First state of two.
Signed and dated: *Rembrandt f. 1634.*
Amsterdam, Rijksprentenkabinet.

Literature: Bartsch, no. 39; Hind, no. 118; Münz, no. 173; Boon, no. 107; Filedt Kok, no. B 39/Rotermund 1963, no. 60; Tümpel 1970, no. 18.

Joseph and Potiphar's Wife

Joseph is Accused by Potiphar's Wife

And she laid up his garment by her, until his lord came home. And she spake unto him according to these words, saying, The Hebrew servant, which thou hast brought unto us, came in unto me to mock me. And it came to pass, as I lifted up my voice and cried, that he left his garment with me, and fled out.
(Genesis 39:16-18)

In contrast with the previous scene of temptation, this episode in the story was rarely depicted, and then mainly in Dutch art. The subject can be found twice in Rembrandt's paintings: on the canvas reproduced here, which is in Berlin, and on a painting in Washington (Bredius, no. 523). Both works are dated 1655, and only differ from each other in detail.

Although the Biblical text states that Potiphar heard his wife's accusation in Joseph's absence, Rembrandt showed him in the painting. Appropriately, the scene takes place by the marriage bed which Joseph was accused of wanting to defile. The splendidly dressed woman seems to be in dishabille, and makes an accusing gesture towards the young man, who can barely conceal his amazement at so much falsehood. (X-rays have shown that Rembrandt initially depicted him with his hands covering his face.) In the foreground lies Joseph's coat, which was used as evidence. Potiphar, who is told that he is also to blame because he invited the boy into the house, silently listens to his wife's story.

In depicting Joseph, who was not mentioned as present in the Biblical text, as stated above, Rembrandt referred to the story in Flavius Josephus' *Jewish Histories*, which was very popular at the time, in which Joseph was said to be present in this particular scene. Previously, in 1629, Jan Pynas had depicted him in his painting of this subject. The three main characters also confront each other in Act V of Vondel's tragedy, *Joseph in Dothan*, written in 1639-40. With its splendid, warm colours, Rembrandt's canvas is a jewel in the art of painting, full of bewitching details such as the richly carved bedpost, which shines in the dark background. Nevertheless, the attention is not distracted for a moment from the offended woman in the middle, whose rejected love has turned to a destructive hatred.

Canvas; 110 × 87 cm.
Signed and dated: *Rembran(dt) f. 1655.*
Berlin, Gemäldegalerie der Staatlichen Museen.

Literature: Bredius, no. 524; Bauch, no. 32; Gerson, no. 274; Bredius-Gerson, no. 524/Hofstede de Groot, *Rembrandt Bijbel*, V.T.p.8; Ben Albach, 'Rembrandt en het toneel', in *De kroniek van het Rembrandthuis 31* (1979), no. 2, pp. 2-32, in particular pp. 24-28; Christian Tümpel, 'Beweeglijke historie', in *Openbaar Kunstbezit 25* (1981), no. 2, pp. 64-70.

We have dreamed a dream

Genesis 40 AND it came to pass after these things, *that* the butler of the king of Egypt and *his* baker had offended their lord the king of Egypt.

2 And Pharaoh was wroth against two *of* his officers, against the chief of the butlers, and against the chief of the bakers.

3 And he put them in ward in the house of the captain of the guard, into the prison, the place where Joseph *was* bound.

4 And the captain of the guard charged Joseph with them, and he served them: and they continued a season in ward.

5 And they dreamed a dream both of them, each man his dream in one night, each man according to the interpretation of his dream, the butler and the baker of the king of Egypt, which *were* bound in the prison.

6 And Joseph came in unto them in the morning, and looked upon them, and, behold, they *were* sad.

7 And he asked Pharaoh's officers that *were* with him in the ward of his lord's house, saying, Wherefore look ye *so* sadly to day?

8 And they said unto him, We have dreamed a dream, and *there is* no interpreter of it. And Joseph said unto them, *Do* not interpretations *belong* to God? tell me *them,* I pray you.

9 And the chief butler told his dream to Joseph, and said to him, In my dream, behold, a vine *was* before me;

10 And in the vine *were* three branches: and it *was* as though it budded, *and* her blossoms shot forth; and the clusters thereof brought forth ripe grapes:

11 And Pharaoh's cup *was* in my hand: and I took the grapes, and pressed them into Pharaoh's cup, and I gave the cup into Pharaoh's hand.

12 And Joseph said unto him, This *is* the interpretation of it: The three branches *are* three days:

13 Yet within three days shall Pharaoh lift up thine head, and restore thee unto thy place: and thou shalt deliver Pharaoh's cup into his hand, after the former manner when thou wast his butler.

14 But think on me when it shall be well with thee, and shew kindness, I pray thee, unto me, and make mention of me unto Pharaoh, and bring me out of this house:

15 For indeed I was stolen away out of the land of the Hebrews: and here also have I done nothing that they should put me into the dungeon.

16 When the chief baker saw that the interpretation was good, he said unto Joseph, I also *was* in my dream, and, behold, I *had* three white baskets on my head:

17 And in the uppermost basket *there was* of all manner of bakemeats for Pharaoh; and the birds did eat them out of the basket upon my head.

18 And Joseph answered and said, This *is* the interpretation thereof: The three baskets *are* three days:

19 Yet within three days shall Pharaoh lift up thy head from off thee, and shall hang thee on a tree; and the birds shall eat thy flesh from off thee.

20 And ik came to pass the third day, *which was* Pharaoh's birthday, that he made a feast unto all his servants: and he lifted up the head of the chief butler and of the chief baker among his servants.

21 And he restored the chief butler unto his butlership again; and he gave the cup into Pharaoh's hand:

22 But he hanged the chief baker: as Joseph had interpreted to them.

23 Yet did not the chief butler remember Joseph, but forgat him.

Joseph a le soin des prisonniers et les console   171

And he asked Pharaoh's officers that were with him in the ward of his lord's house, saying, Wherefore look ye so sadly today? And they said unto him: We have dreamed a dream, and there is no interpreter of it.
(Genesis 40:7-8)

Neither the French title, *Joseph a le soin des prisonniers et les console* (Joseph Looks After the Prisoners and Consoles Them), which dates from the 18th century, nor the usual title of this drawing which is based on that, *Joseph Serves His Two Fellow Prisoners*, really describes the true content of the drawing. As usual, Rembrandt has depicted a particular moment from the story, i.e., the morning on which Joseph, who is responsible for the two imprisoned courtiers, can see from the men's sombre faces that they are worried about something. They tell him that they each had a dream at the same time, of which they cannot understand the meaning. The gloomy place, a subterranean vault where the two prisoners are locked with their legs in stocks, has been suggestively depicted with very few details.

The drawing was once part of the huge collection of drawings and prints of the Parisian collector, Pierre Crozat (1665-1740), who had no fewer than 350 of Rembrandt's drawings. Presumably the French title came from him, and the number 171 in the bottom right probably referred to the number under which it was filed in his collection.

Drawing in pen and ink; 18 × 19.4 cm.
Ca. 1655.
London, British Museum.

Literature: Benesch V, no. 1001 (*ca.* 1656); Slive I, no. 110 (*ca.* 1655).

Joseph Asks his Two Fellow Prisoners the Reason for their Despondency

Joseph Explains the Dreams of his Fellow Prisoners

And Joseph said unto him, This is the interpretation of it: The three branches are three days. Yet within three days shall Pharaoh lift up thine head, and restore thee unto thy place: and thou shalt deliver Pharaoh's cup into his hand, after the former manner when thou wast his butler. (Genesis 40:12-13)

The dreams of the two courtiers, like the double dream of Joseph himself, had a prophetic meaning which the clairvoyant boy was able unerringly to unveil.

In this drawing from the early 1630s, Rembrandt showed in the lively style typical of his work at that time how Joseph explains the meaning of the dream to the butler. The fingers of his left hand represent the number of days which separate the man from having his honour restored. In the middle of the composition, the baker's sombre face indicates that the dream which he had presages another sort of raising: he will hang.

In a drawing of this subject made shortly afterwards (Benesch I, no. 109), the emphasis is on the baker's gesture of despair when Joseph predicts his fate.

Pen and brush drawing; 17.4 × 20.6 cm.
Ca. 1632-33.
Chicago, The Art Institute of Chicago.

Literature: Benesch I, no. 80 (*ca.* 1632-33).

And Joseph said unto him, This is the interpretation of it: The three branches are three days. Yet within three days shall Pharaoh lift up thine head, and restore thee unto his place: and thou shalt deliver Pharaoh's cup into his hand, after the former manner when thou wast his butler.
(Genesis 40:12-13)

The same story is told as in the previous drawing, using simiₗlar methods, but this time in the sublime simple images which Rembrandt used in the 1650s. Again Joseph turns to the butler and counts on his fingers the number of days it will be until he is freed. The man sitting on the straw listens in fascinaₜtion to the wise boy. In contrast, the baker dejectedly leans against the wall, portending the dreadful fate that Joseph will reveal to him in a moment. As in the drawing which he did twenty years earlier, there is a basket next to the boy to show that he has been

assigned to look after the prisoners (cf. the drawing on p. 67).

Rembrandt probably also did a painting of this subject. In the inventory of Ferdinand Bol, drawn up on 8 October 1659 in connection with his proposed marriage to Anna van Arckel, mention is made of a work now missing, 'Where Joseph explains the dream, by Rembrant', as well as of some other paintings by Rembrandt.

Drawing in pen and ink; 15.7 × 18.9 cm.
Ca. 1652.
Amsterdam, Rijksprentenkabinet.

Literature: Benesch V, no. 912 (*ca.* 1652); Slive I, no. 240 (*ca.* 1652)/Hofstede de Groot, *Rembrandt Bijbel*, V.T.d.II; Rotermund 1963, no. 63; 'Bijbelse Inspiratie', no. 60.

Joseph Explains the Dreams of his Fellow Prisoners

See, I have set thee over all the land of Egypt

Genesis 41 AND it came to pass at the end of two full years, that Pharaoh dreamed: and, behold, he stood by the river.

2 And, behold, there came up out of the river seven well favoured kine and fatfleshed; and they fed in a meadow.

3 And, behold, seven other kine came up after them out of the river, ill favoured and leanfleshed; and stood by the *other* kine upon the brink of the river.

4 And the ill favoured and leanfleshed kine did eat up the seven well favoured and fat kine. So Pharaoh awoke.

5 And he slept and dreamed the second time: and, behold, seven ears of corn came up upon one stalk, rank and good.

6 And, behold, seven thin ears and blasted with the east wind sprung up after them.

7 And the seven thin ears devoured the seven rank and full ears. And Pharaoh awoke, and, behold, *it was* a dream.

8 And it came to pass in the morning that his spirit was troubled; and he sent and called for all the magicians of Egypt, and all the wise men thereof; and Pharaoh told them his dream; but *there was* none that could interpret them unto Pharaoh.

9 Then spake the chief butler unto Pharaoh, saying, I do remember my faults this day:

10 Pharaoh was wroth with his servants, and put me in ward in the captain of the guard's house, *both* me and the chief baker.

11 And we dreamed a dream in one night, I and he; we dreamed each man according to the interpretation of his dream.

12 And *there was* there with us a young man, an Hebrew, servant to the captain of the guard; and we told him, and he interpreted to us our dreams; to each man according to his dream he did interpret.

13 And it came to pass, as he interpreted to us, so it was; me he restored unto mine office, and him he hanged.

14 Then Pharaoh sent and called Joseph, and the brought him hastily out of the dungeon: and he shaved *himself,* and changed his raiment, and came in unto Pharaoh.

15 And Pharaoh said unto Joseph, I have dreamed a dream, and *there is* none that can interpret it: and I have heard say of thee, *that* thou canst understand a dream to interpret it.

16 And Joseph answered Pharaoh, saying, It is not in me: God shall give Pharaoh an answer of peace.

17 And Pharaoh said unto Joseph, In my dream, behold, I stood upon the bank of the river:

18 And, behold, there came up out of the river seven kine, fatfleshed and well favoured; and the fed in a meadow:

19 And, behold, seven other kine came up after them, poor and very ill favoured and leanfleshed, such as I never saw in all the land of Egypt for badness:

20 And the lean and the ill favoured kine did eat up the first seven fat kine:

21 And when they had eaten them up, it could not be known that they had eaten them; but they *were* still ill favoured, as at the beginning. So I awoke.

22 And I saw in my dream, and, behold, seven ears came up in one stalk, full and good:

23 And, behold, seven ears, withered, thin, *and* blasted with the east wind, sprung up after them:

24 And the thin ears devoured the seven good ears: and I told *this* unto the magicians; but *there was* none that could declare *it* to me.

25 And Joseph sain unto Pharaoh, The dream of Pharaoh *is* one: God hath shewed Pharaoh what he *is* about to do.

26 The seven good kine *are* seven years; and the seven good ears *are* seven years: the dream *is* one.

27 And the seven thin and ill favoured kine that came up after them *are* seven years; and the seven empty ears blasted with the east wind shall be seven years of famine.

28 This *is* the thing which I have spoken unto Pharaoh: What God *is* about to do he sheweth unto Pharaoh.

29 Behold, there come seven years of great plenty throughout all the land of Egypt:

30 And there shall arise after them seven years of famine; and all the plenty shall be forgotten in the land of Egypt; and the famine shall consume the land;

31 And the plenty shall not be known in the land by reason of that famine following; for it *shall be* very grievous.

And Joseph said unto Pharaoh, The dream of Pharaoh is one: God hath shewed Pharaoh what he is about to do. (Genesis 41:25)

This time Joseph acts not only as an interpreter of dreams, but also reveals himself to be a wise counsellor, and this determines the rest of his life. Joseph's wisdom is all the more apparent because mention is first made of the failures of all the wise men and magicians from Egypt (verse 8).

Rembrandt depicts the ruler of Egypt in full regalia, with the royal ermine around his shoulders and a sceptre in his right hand. He radiates dignity. A scribe is seated on his haunches next to the throne, diligently noting what Joseph has to say. In the background the head of a bearded old man reminds us of the Egyptian magicians who did not know what to make of the dreams of their king.

Pen and brush drawing; 18.9 × 17.9 cm.
Ca. 1655-60.
Berlin, Kupferstichkabinett der Staatlichen Museen.

Literature: Benesch V, no. 989 (*ca.* 1655-56); Slive I, no. 31 (*ca.* 1655)/Rotermund 1963, no. 129 ('Haman is ordered by Ahasueros to destroy the Jews' (Esther 3:8-12)); Tümpel 1970, no. 19.

Joseph Before the Pharaoh

32 And for that the dream was doubled unto Pharaoh twice; *it is* because the thing *is* established by God, and God will shortly bring it to pass.

33 Now therefore let Pharaoh look out a man discreet and wise, and set him over the land of Egypt.

34 Let Pharaoh do *this,* and let him appoint officers over the land, and take up the fifth part of the land of Egypt in the seven plenteous years.

35 And let them gather all the food of those good years that come, and lay up corn under the hand of Pharaoh, and let them keep food in the cities.

36 And the food shall be for store the land against the seven years of famine, which shall be in the land of Egypt; that the land perish not through the famine.

37 And the thing was good in the eyes of Pharaoh, and in the eyes of all his servants.

38 And Pharaoh said unto his servants, Can we find *such a one* as this *is,* a man in whom the Spirit of God *is?*

39 And Pharaoh said unto Joseph, Forasmuch as God hath shewed thee all this, *there is* none so discreet and wise as thou *art*:

40 Thou shalt be over my house, and according unto thy word shall all my people be ruled: only in the throne will I be greater than thou.

41 And Pharaoh said unto Joseph, See, I have set thee over all the land of Egypt.

42 And Pharaoh took off his ring from his hand, and put it upon Joseph's hand, and arrayed him in vestures of fine linen, and put a gold chain about his neck;

43 And he made him to ride in the second chariot which he had; and they cried before him, Bow the knee: and he made him *ruler* over all the land of Egypt.

44 And Pharaoh said unto Joseph, I *am* Pharaoh, and without thee shall no man lift up his hand or foot in all the land of Egypt.

45 And Pharaoh called Joseph's name Zaphnathpaaneah; and he gave him to wife Asenath the daughter of Potipherah priest of On. And Joseph went out over *all* the land of Egypt.

46 And Joseph *was* thirty years old when he stood before Pharaoh king of Egypt. And Joseph went out from the presence of Pharaoh, and went throughout all the land of Egypt.

47 And in the seven plenteous years the earth brought forth by handfuls.

48 And he gathered up all the food of the seven years, which were in the land of Egypt, and laid up the food in the cities: the food of the field, which *was* round about every city, laid he up in the same.

49 And Joseph gathered corn as the sand of the sea, very much, until he left numbering: for *it was* without number.

50 And unto Joseph were born two sons before the years of famine came, which Asenath the daughter of Potipherah priest of On bare unto him.

51 And Joseph called the name of the firstborn Manasseh: For God, *said he,* hath made me forget all my toil, and all my father's house.

52 And the name of the second called he Ephraim: For God hath caused me to be fruitful in the land of my affliction.

53 And the seven years of plenteousness, that was in the land of Egypt, were ended.

54 And the seven years of dearth began to come, according as Joseph had said: and the dearth was in all lands; but in all the land of Egypt there was bread.

55 And when all the land of Egypt was famished, the people cried to Pharaoh for bread: and Pharaoh said unto all the Egyptians, Go unto Joseph; what he saith to you, do.

56 And the famine was over all the face of the earth: And Joseph opened all the storehouses, and sold unto the Egyptians; and the famine waxed sore in the land of Egypt.

57 And all countries came into Egypt to Joseph for to buy *corn*; because that the famine was *so* sore in all lands.

And when all the land of Egypt was famished, the people cried to Pharaoh for bread: and Pharaoh said unto all the Egyptians, Go unto Joseph; what he saith to you, do. And the famine was over all the face of the earth: And Joseph opened all the storehouses, and sold unto the Egyptians; and the famine waxed sore in the land of Egypt.
(Genesis 41:55-56)

In 1612 Rembrandt's teacher Pieter Lastman was the first to depict this subject in a painting; up to that time it had only been done in prints. In approximately 1635, Rembrandt made the drawing in chalks shown above, after Lastman's work, which is now in the National Gallery in Dublin. It is a faithful copy which shows that long after his apprenticeship he retained great admiration for the work of Lastman, who died in 1633. (Also see p. 26.)

The broad composition of the scene is largely based on the passage taken from further on (Genesis 47:13-26), where the story tells in detail how Joseph succeeded during the great famine in acquiring for the Pharaoh first the Egyptians' money and cattle, and later also the Egyptians themselves and all their land, in exchange for the food which he had stored during the years of plenty. The Bible story emphasizes Joseph's shrewdness as he serves his master so well without any concern for the social consequences of his monopolistic policy. In

Lastman's composition he supervises the sale of the grain from an elevated position in the middle of the work. On the Pharaoh's orders, no one in the whole land of Egypt will raise his hand or foot without Joseph's consent (verse 44). Below him, people are milling about, coming to him from far and wide with all their possessions, driven by hunger. Behind Joseph, soldiers guard the entrance to the barn from where the grain is taken in measured quantities. Scribes keep records and the buyers pay the collectors, jostling with each other to be first.

This Biblical theme was extremely topical in 17th-century Amsterdam, which was at the time the central storage depot in Europe. Grain which was imported from other places and stored in the city's high warehouses was the most important commodity. Failed harvests and famines in southern Europe more than once led to exorbitant profits in Amsterdam.

Drawing in black crayon; 31.3 × 42.6 cm.
Signed: *Rembrandt ft.*
Ca. 1635.
Vienna, Albertina.

Literature: Benesch II, no. 446 (*ca.* 1637)/Rotermund 1963, no. 66; Tümpel 1971, p. 24: 'Das seltene Thema'; C. Tümpel, *Rembrandt*, Reinbek bei Hamburg 1977, p. 18.

Joseph Sells Grain in Egypt

Take also your brother

[When Joseph's brothers also came to Egypt to buy grain they were recognized by him and he tested them: their youngest brother Benjamin was to come with them next time, and meanwhile Simeon was to stay as a hostage.]

Genesis 42 29 And they came unto Jacob their father unto the land of Canaan, and told him all that befell unto them; saying,

30 The man, *who is* the lord of the land, spake roughly to us, and took us for spies of the country.

31 And we said unto him, We *are* true *men*; we are no spies:

32 We *be* twelve brethren, sons of our father; one *is* not, and the youngest *is* this day with our father in the land of Canaan.

33 And the man, the lord of the country, said unto us, Hereby shall I know that ye *are* true *men*; leave one of your brethren *here* with me, and take *food for* the famine of your households, and be gone:

34 And bring your youngest brother unto me: then shall I know that ye *are* no spies, but *that* ye *are* true *men*: so will I deliver you your brother, and ye shall traffick in the land.

35 And it came to pass as they emptied their sacks, that, behold, every man's bundle of money *was* in his sack: and when *both* they and their father saw the bundles of money, they were afraid.

36 And Jacob their father said unto them, Me have ye bereaved *of my children*: Joseph *is* not, and Simeon *is* not, and ye will take Benjamin *away*: all these things are against me.

Genesis 43 AND the famine *was* sore in the land.

2 And it came to pass, when they had eaten up the corn which they had brought out of Egypt, their father said unto them, Go again, buy us a little food.

3 And Judah spake unto him, saying, The man did solemnly protest unto us, saying, Ye shall not see my face, except your brother *be* with you.

4 If thou wilt send our brother with us, we will go down and buy thee food:

5 But if thou wilt not send *him*, we will not go down: for the man said unto us, Ye shall not see my face, except your brother *be* with you.

6 And Israel said, Wherefore dealt ye *so* ill with me, *as* to tell the man whether ye had yet a brother?

7 And the said, The man asked us straitly of our state, and of our kindred, saying, *Is* your father alive? have ye *another* brother? and we told him according to the tenor of these words: could we centainly know that he would say, Bring your brother down?

8 And Judah said unto Israel his father, Send the lad with me, and we will arise and go; that we may live, and not die, both we, and thou, *and* also our little ones.

9 I will be surety for him; of my hand shalt thou require him: if I bring him not unto thee, and set him before thee, then let me bear the blame for ever:

10 For except we had lingered, surely now we had returned this second time.

11 And their father Israel said unto them, If *it must be* so now, do this; take of the best fruits in the land in your vessels, and carry down the man a present, al little balm, and a little honey, spices, and myrrh, nuts, and almonds:

12 And take double money in your hand; and the money that was brought again in the mouth of your sacks, carry *it* again in your hand; peradventure is *was* an oversight:

13 Take also your brother, and arise, go again unto the man:

14 And God Almighty give you mercy before the man, that he may send away your other brother, and Benjamin. If I be bereaved *of my children,* I am bereaved.

Take also your brother, and arise, go again unto the man: And God Almighty give you mercy before the man, that he may send away your other brother, and Benjamin. If I be bereaved of my children, I am bereaved.
(Genesis 43:13-14)

Initially Jacob flatly refused to allow Benjamin to go to Egypt: 'My son shall not go down with you; for his brother is dead, and he is left alone. If mischief befall him by the way in which ye go, then shall ye bring down my gray hairs with sorrow to the grave?' (Genesis 42:38). But finally he realizes that it is necessary, and entrusts the boy to his brothers. The drawing shows him giving his last instructions. On the right by the gate someone is waiting with a mule with the last baggage to be brought.

This Rembrandt-style composition is fairly generally considered to be an improved version by Rembrandt of a work by Barent Fabritius (1624-73), who is believed to have been taught by Rembrandt in about 1650. Earlier, in 1642, his older brother, Carel Fabritius (1622-54) had been taught by Rembrandt for a short while. The strong lines of the corrections by the master can most clearly be distinguished in the architecture on the right half of the drawing, but we can also recognize

Rembrandt's hand in many places in the contours of the figures. A painting in the Mauritshuis in The Hague, which corresponds to the left half of the drawing, is also ascribed to Barent Fabritius.

There are other drawings like this one, which showed that Rembrandt did not verbally criticize his pupils' work, but often redrew what had not been done properly, in his view. He was rarely concerned with improvements in the anatomy of a figure or with the perspective representation of an object. Virtually always the corrections were aimed at allowing the essence of a Biblical event to come into its own, or to make a gesture or pose by a figure more expressive.

Pen and brush drawing; 19 × 29 cm.
Ca. 1650.
Haarlem, Teylers Museum.

Literature: Benesch IV, no. 856 (Barent Fabritius; corrections *ca.* 1648-50); Slive II, no. 540/Hofstede de Groot, *Rembrandt Bijbel*, V.T.d.14; 'Bijbelse Inspiratie', no. 62. E. Haverkamp-Begemann, 'Rembrandt as Teacher', in Cat. *Rembrandt after Three Hundred Years*, Chicago 1969, pp. 21-30.

Jacob Allows Benjamin to Leave for Egypt

75

I *am* Joseph

[When they arrive in Egypt the brothers are hospitably enter¡tained in Joseph's house. Once again he tests them. He secretly tells his steward to hide his own silver cup in the top of Benjamin's sack. When the brothers have departed, the steward catches them up and accuses them of theft. The cup is discovered in Benjamin's sack and they return despondently to Joseph's house.]

Genesis 44 14 And Judah and his brethren came to Joseph's house; for he *was* yet there: and they fell before him on the ground.

15 And Joseph said unto them, What deed *is* this that ye have done? wot ye not that such a man as I can centainly divine?

16 And Judah said, What shall we say unto my lord? what shall we speak? or how shall we clear ourselves? God hath found out the iniquity of thy servants: behold, we *are* my lord's servants, both we, and *he* also with whom the cup is found.

17 And he said, God forbid that I should do so: *but* the man in whose hand the cup is found, he shall be my servant; and as for you, get you up in peace unto your father.

18 Then Judah came near unto him, and said, Oh my lord, let thy servant, I pray thee, speak a word in my lord's ears, and let not thine anger burn against thy servant; for thou *art* even as Pharaoh.

19 My lord asked his servants, saying, Have ye a father, or a brother?

20 And we said unto my lord, We have a father, an old man, and a child of his old age, a little one; and his brother is dead, and he alone is left of his mother, and his father loveth him.

21 And thou saidst unto thy servants, Bring him down unto me, that I may set mine eyes upon him.

22 And we said unto my lord, The lad cannot leave his father: for *if* he should leave his father, *his father* would die.

23 And thou saidst unto thy servants, Except your youngest brother come down with you, ye shall see my face no more.

24 And it came to pass when we came up unto thy servant my father, we told him the words of my lord.

25 And our father said, Go again, *and* buy us a little food.

26 And we said, We cannot go down: if our youngest brother be with us, then will we go down: for we may not see the man's face, except our youngest brother *be* with us.

27 And thy servant my father said unto us, Ye know that my wife bare me two *sons*:

28 And the one went out from me, and I said, Surely he is torn in pieces; and I saw him not since:

29 And if ye take this also from me, and mischief befall him, ye shall bring down my gray hairs with sorrow to the grave.

30 Now therefore when I come to thy servant my father, and the lad *be* not with us; seeing that his life is bound up in the lad's life;

31 It shall come to pass, when he seeth that the lad *is* not *with us,* that he will die: and thy servants shall bring down the gray hairs of thy servant our father with sorrow to the grave.

32 For thy servant became surety for the lad unto my father, saying, If I bring him not unto thee, then I shall bear the blame to my father for ever.

33 Now therefore, I pray thee, let thy servant abide instead of the lad a bondman to my lord; and let the lad go up with his brethren.

34 For how shall I go up to my father, and the lad *be* not with me? lest peradventure I see the evil that shall come on my father.

Genesis 45 THEN Joseph could not refrain himself before all them that stood by him; and he cried, Cause every man to go out from me. And there stood no man with him, while Joseph made himself known unto his brethren.

2 And he wept aloud: and the Egyptians and the house of Pharoah heard.

3 And Joseph said unto his brethren, I *am* Joseph; doth my father yet live? And his brethren could not answer him; for they were troubled at his presence.

4 And Joseph said unto his brethren, Come near to me, I pray you. And they came near. And he said, I *am* Joseph your brother, whom ye sold into Egypt.

5 Now therefore be not grieved, nor angry

And Joseph said unto his brethren, I am Joseph; doth my father yet live? And his brethren could not answer him; for they were all troubled at his presence. And Joseph said unto his brethren, Come near to me, I pray you. And they came near. And he said, I am Joseph your brother, whom ye sold into Egypt.
(Genesis 45:3-4)

Once the brothers had not been afraid to leave Joseph to his fate and return to their father without him. Now they refuse to abandon Benjamin and return to their father without him, and Judah says so. This is the irrefutable proof for Joseph that his brothers have changed profoundly since they mercilessly threw him into the pit. Now he no longer wishes to conceal his identity from them.

Rembrandt's drawing of the denouement, which evolves very slowly in the story, shows how the brothers fall back in shock and are unable to utter a word in their surprise at the words: 'I am Joseph.' The sharp contrasts between light and dark give the scene a theatrical character. Benjamin's special place at Joseph's feet is a reminder of what went before, for the 'stolen' cup had been found on Benjamin, and that is why Joseph had said he would have to remain behind alone as a slave.

Although Rembrandt generally had a preference for precisely those moments in the story at which a sudden and complete change occurs in the prevailing mood, as in this case, this episode from the story of Joseph is not represented in the work that has survived, except in this drawing.

Joseph Reveals Himself to his Brothers

Pen and brush drawing; 21 × 32.5 cm.
Bottom right in later handwriting: *Rembrandt Van Ry*(n).
Ca. 1640-42.
Paris, The Louvre.

Literature: Benesch III, no. 512 (*ca.* 1640-42)/Rotermund 1963, no. 67.

with yourselves, that ye sold me hither: for God did send me before you to preserve life.

6 For these two years *hath* the famine *been* in the land: and yet *there are* five years, in the which *there shall* neither *be* earing nor harvest.

7 And God sent me before you to preserve you a posterity in the earth, and to save your lives by a great deliverance.

8 So now *it was* not you *that* sent me hither, but God: and he hath made me a father to Pharaoh, and lord of all his house, and a ruler throughout all the land of Egypt.

9 Haste ye, and go up to my father, and say unto him, Thus saith thy son Joseph, God hath made me lord of all Egypt: come down unto me, tarry not:

10 And thou shalt dwell in the land of Goshen, and thou shalt be near unto me, thou, and thy children, and thy children's children, and thy flocks, and thy herds, and all that thou hast:

11 And there will I nourish thee; for yet *there are* five years of famine; lest thou, and thy household, and all that thou hast, come to poverty.

12 And, behold, your eyes see, and the eyes of my brother Benjamin, that *it is* my mouth that speaketh unto you.

13 And ye shall tell my father of all my glory in Egypt, and of all that ye have seen; and ye shall haste and bring down my father hither.

14 And he fell upon his brother Benjamin's neck, and wept; and Benjamin wept upon his neck.

15 Moreover he kissed all his brethren, and wept upon them: and after that his brethren talked with him.

16 And the fame thereof was heard in Pharaoh's house, saying, Joseph's brethren are come: and it pleased Pharaoh well, and his servants.

17 And Pharaoh said unto Joseph, Say unto thy brethren, This do ye; lade your beasts, and go, get you unto the land of Canaan;

18 And take your father and your households, and come unto me: and I will give you the good of the land of Egypt, and ye shall eat the fat of the land.

19 Now thou art commanded, this do ye; take you wagons out of the land of Egypt for your little ones, and for your wives, and bring your father, and come.

20 Also regard not your stuff; for the good of all the land of Egypt *is* your's.

21 And the children of Israel did so: and Joseph gave them wagons, according to the commandment of Pharaoh, and gave them provision for the way.

22 To all of them he gave each man changes of raiment; but to Benjamin he gave three hundred *pieces* of silver, and five changes of raiment.

23 And to his father he sent after this *manner*; ten asses laden with the good things of Egypt, and ten she asses laden with corn and bread and meat for his father by the way.

24 So he sent his brethren away, and they departed: and he said unto them, See that ye fall not out by the way.

25 And they went up out of Egypt, and came into the land of Canaan unto Jacob their father,

26 And told him, saying, Joseph *is* yet alive, and he *is* governor over all the land of Egypt. And Jacob's heart fainted, for he believed them not.

27 And they told him all the words of Joseph, which he had said unto them: and when he saw the wagons which Joseph had sent to carry him, the spirit of Jacob their father revived:

28 And Israel said, *It is* enough; Joseph my son *is* yet alive: I will go and see him before I die.

And they went up out of Egypt, and came into the land of Canaan unto Jacob their father, and told him, saying, Joseph is yet alive, and he is governor over all the land of Egypt. And Jacob's heart fainted, for he believed them not. (Genesis 45:25-26)

The focal point of this drawing is Jacob's suspicion. The old man, who had been deceived so often in his life, does not believe what his sons are telling him: that Joseph is alive and the governor of all of Egypt. He is too sensible simply to accept this straightaway. Referring to Joseph's last test, which had been concluded so fortunately, Rembrandt shows Benjamin standing next to Jacob, holding Joseph's cup, which had been found in his sack.

Hofstede de Groot, and others after him (including Benesch and Slive), saw this drawing in relation to another episode in the story of Joseph described in Genesis 43:3-10, which tells how Judah, on behalf of the other brothers, tried to explain to the old Jacob that without Benjamin a second journey to Egypt would be pointless (see the Bible text on p. 74). Seen in this light, the cup in Benjamin's hand is no more than an

attribute of Benjamin, and a way of identifying him as Benjamin. But Rembrandt never used this sort of motif for such a purpose in these Biblical scenes. There are always narrative elements which he used to pinpoint the moment that is represented by connecting it with related events.

Clearly Rembrandt was not satisfied with his first version of the brother seated in the foreground on the left. He stuck a piece of paper over it and drew the figure again. There is a second drawing of the same scene, viewed from a point further to the left, in the Louvre in Paris (Benesch III, no. 542).

Jacob Hears that Joseph is Alive

Pen and ink drawing; 17.6 × 23.1 cm.
Ca. 1640-45.
Amsterdam, Rijksprentenkabinet.

Literature: Benesch III, no. 541 (*ca*. 1643); Slive I, no. 300 (*ca*. 1638-40)/C. Hofstede de Groot, 'Rembrandts Bijbelsche en Historische Voorstellingen' in *Oud Holland* 41 (1923-24), pp. 106-08; Rotermund 1963, no. 68; 'Bijbelse Inspiratie', no. 61.

Jacob Blesses Joseph's Sons

And when Joseph saw that his father laid his right hand upon the head of Ephraim, it displeased him: and he held up his father's hand, to remove it from Ephraim's head unto Manasseh's head. And Joseph said unto his father, Not so, my father: for this is the firstborn; put thy right hand upon his head.
(Genesis 48:17-18)

As so often in the stories in the book of Genesis, the youngest son is preferred over the eldest. It is striking that in this famous painting Rembrandt ignores the unexpected way in which the strong-willed Jacob decided to bless the two children, according to Genesis 48:14. Furthermore, the gesture with which Joseph tries to correct the apparent mistake made by his father does not reveal the concern which he felt, according to the text in the Bible, but gives the impression that he wishes to support the old man's arm. Clearly Rembrandt would not accept any discord which might disturb the solemnity of this moment in his painting of the patriarch giving his blessing. The fair-haired Ephraim, who was depicted as the representative of later Christianity, in accordance with the traditional Christian interpretation of the story, respectfully bends forward with his hand crossed to receive the blessing. In order to characterize the scene as a family event, Rembrandt also showed Asmath, Joseph's Egyptian wife, although the Bible does not mention her in this context. Her beautiful appearance serves as a counterpart to the impressive figure of the old Jacob.

Canvas; 175.5 × 210.5 cm.
Signed and dated: *Rembran*(dt) *f. 1656.*
Kassel, Gemäldegalerie.

Literature: Bredius, no. 525; Bauch, no. 34; Gerson, no. 277; Bredius-Gerson, no. 525/Hofstede de Groot, *Rembrandt Bijbel*, V.T.p.9; Rotermund 1963, p. 24; Tümpel 1971, pp. 26-27.

Bring them, I pray thee, unto me, and I will bless them

27 And Israel dwelt in the land of Egypt, in the country of Goshen; and they had possessions therein, and grew, and multiplied exceedingly.

28 And Jacob lived in the land of Egypt seventeen years: so the whole age of Jacob was an hundred forty and seven years.

29 And the time drew night that Israel must die: and he called his son Joseph, and said

unto him, If now I have found grace in thy sight, put, I pray thee, thy hand under my thigh, and deal kindly and truly with me; bury me not, I pray thee in Egypt:

30 But I will lie with my fathers, and thou shalt carry me out of Egypt, and bury me in their buryingplace. And he said, I will do as thou hast said.

31 And he said, Swear unto me. And he sware unto him. And Israel bowed himself upon the bed's head.

AND it came to pass after these things, that *one* told Joseph, Behold, thy father *is* sick: and he took with him his two sons, Manasseh and Ephraim.

2 And *one* told Jacob, and said, Behold, thy son Joseph cometh unto thee: and Israel strengthened himself, and sat upon the bed. [...]

8 And Israel beheld Joseph's sons, and said, Who *are* these?

9 And Joseph said unto his father, They *are* my sons, whom God hath given me in this *place*. And he said, Bring them, I pray thee, unto me, and I will bless them.

10 Now the eyes of Israel were dim for age, *so that* he could not see. And he brought them near unto him; and he kissed them, and embraced them.

11 And Israel said unto Joseph, I had not thought to see thy face: and, lo, God hath shewed me also thy seed.

12 And Joseph brought them out from between his knees, and he bowed himself with his face to the earth.

13 And Joseph took them both, Ephraim in his right hand toward Israel's left hand, and Manasseh in his left hand toward Israel's right hand, and brought *them* near unto him.

14 And Israel stretched out his right hand, and laid *it* upon Ephraim's head, who *was* the younger, and his left hand upon Manasseh's head, guiding his hands wittingly; for Manasseh *was* the firstborn.

15 And he blessed Joseph, and said, God, before whom my father Abraham and Isaac did walk, the God which fed me all my life long unto this day.

16 The angel which redeemed me from all evil, bless the lads; and let my name be named on them, and the name of my fathers Abraham and Isaac; and let them grow into a multitude in the midst of the earth.

17 And when Joseph saw that his father laid his right hand upon the head of Ephraim, it displeased him: and he held op his father's hand, to remove it from Ephraim's head unto Manasseh's head.

18 And Joseph said unto his father, Not so, my father: for this *is* the firstborn; put thy right hand upon his head.

19 And his father refused, and said, I know *it*, my son, I know *it*: he also shall become a people, and he also shall be great: but truly his younger brother shall be greater than he, and his seed shall become a multitude of nations.

20 And he blessed them that day, saying, In thee shall Israel bless, saying, God make thee as Ephraim and as Manasseh: and he set Ephraim before Manasseh.

21 And Israel said unto Joseph, Behold, I die: but God shall be with you, and bring you again unto the land of your fathers.

I drew him out of the water

Exodus 1 6 And Joseph died, and all his brethren, and all that generation.

7 And the children of Israel were fruitful, and increased abundantly, and multiplied, and waxed exceeding mighty; and the land was filled with them.

8 Now there arose up a new king over Egypt, which knew not Joseph.

9 And he said unto his people, Behold, the people of the children of Israel *are* more and mightier than we:

10 Come on, let us deal wisely them; lest they multiply, and it come to pass, that, when there falleth out any war, they join also unto our enemies, and fight against us, and *so* get them up out of the land.

11 Therefore they did set over them taskmasters to afflict them with their burdens. And they built for Pharaoh treasure cities, Pithom and Raamses.

12 But the more they afflicted them, the more they multiplied and grew. And they were grieved because of the children of Israel.

13 And the Egyptians made the children of Israel to serve with rigour:

14 And they made their lives bitter with hard bondage, in morter, and in brick, and in all manner of service in the field: all their service, wherein they made them serve, *was* with rigour.

15 And the king of Egypt spake to the Hebrew midwives, of which the name of the one *was* Shiphrah, and the name of the other Puah:

16 And he said, When ye do the office of a midwife to the Hebrew women, and see *them* upon the stools; if it *be* a son, then ye shall kill him: but if it *be* a daughter, then she shall live.

17 But the midwives feared God, and did not as the king of Egypt commanded them, but saved the men children alive.

18 And the king of Egypt called for the midwives, and said unto them, Why have ye done this thing, and have saved the men children alive?

19 And the midwives said unto Pharaoh, Because the Hebrew women *are* not as the Egyptian women; for they *are* lively, and are delivered ere the midwives come in unto them.

20 Therefore God dealt well with the midwives: and the people multiplied, and waxed very mighty.

21 And it came to pass, because the midwives feared God, that he made them houses.

22 And Pharaoh charged all his people, saying, Every son that is born ye shall cast into the river, and every daughter ye shall save alive.

Exodus 2 AND there went a man of the house of Levi, and took *to wife* a daughter of Levi.

2 And the woman conceived, and bare a son: and when she saw him that he *was a* goodly *child,* she hid him three months.

3 And when she could not longer hide him, she took for him an ark of bulrushes, and daubed it with slime and with pitch, and put the child therein; and she laid *it* in the flags by the river's brink.

4 And his sister stood afar off, to wit what would be done to him.

5 And the daughter of Pharaoh came down to wash *herself* at the river; and her maidens walked along by the river's side; and when she saw the ark among the flags, she sent her maid to fetch it.

6 And when she had opened *it,* she saw the child: and, behold, the babe wept. And she had compassion on him, and said, This *is one* of the Hebrews' children.

7 Then said his sister to Pharaoh's daughter, Shall I go and call to thee a nurse of the Hebrew women, that she may nurse the child for thee?

8 And Pharaoh's daughter said to her, Go. And the maid went and called the child's mother.

9 And Pharaoh's daughter said unto her, Take this child away, and nurse it for me, and I will give *thee* thy wages. And the woman took the child, and nursed it.

10 And the child grew, and she brought him unto Pharaoh's daughter, and he became her son. And she called his name Moses: and she said, Because I drew him out of the water.

And the daughter of Pharaoh came down to wash herself at the river; and her maidens walked along by the river's side; and when she saw the ark among the flags, she sent her maid to fetch it. And when she had opened it, she saw the child: and, behold, the babe wept. And she had compassion on him, and said, This is one of the Hebrews' children. (Exodus 2:5-6)

The fascinating story of the birth of Moses, who was to lead the people of Israel out of the slavery of Egypt when the time came and take them through the desert to the borders of the Promised Land, serves to indicate that God was already working to free his oppressed people long before they had any intimation of this. Here, the saviour is saved, just as the other Saviour is saved from the hands of another child murderer later (see Matthew 2:13-18).

The discovery of Moses in a basket of reeds amongst the bulrushes on the banks of the River Nile was a favourite theme in northern Dutch art. In this painting dating from *ca.* 1635, Rembrandt illustrated the moment at which the tension in the story reaches a

climax. What will the Princess who has just got out of the water do with the little Hebrew boy who should already have been murdered, according to her father's commands? In the background, where the rich garments of the Egyptian Pharaoh's daughter are spread out, a parasol adds an exotic touch to the scene. This motif is also seen in the drawing of this subject which Rembrandt did in about 1655 (Benesch V, no. 592).

Canvas; 47 × 59 cm.
Signed: *Rembrandt.*
Ca. 1635.
Philadelphia, Philadelphia Museum of Art.
John G. Johnson Collection.

Literature: Bredius, no. 496; Bauch, no. 12; Bredius-Gerson, no. 496 (not by Rembrandt)/Hofstede de Groot, *Rembrandt Bijbel*, V.T.p.10.

The Discovery of Moses

Who *am* I, that I should bring forth the children of Israel out of Egypt?

Exodus 3   NOW Moses kept the flock of Jethro his father in law, the priest of Midian: and he led the flock to the backside of the desert, and came to the moutain of God, *even* tot Horeb.

2 And the angel of the LORD appeared unto him in a flame of fire out of the midst of a bush: and he looked, and, behold, the bush burned with fire, and the bush *was* not consumed.

3 And Moses said, I will now turn aside, and see this great sight, why the bush is not burnt.

4 And when the LORD saw that he turned aside to see, God called unto him out of the midst of the bush, and said, Moses, Moses. And he said, Here *am* I.

5And he said, Draw not nigh hither: put off thy shoes from off thy feet, for the place whereon thou standest *is* holy ground.

6 Moreover he said, I *am* the God of thy father, the God of Abraham, the God of Isaac, and the God of Jacob. And Moses hid his face; for he was afraid to look upon God.

7 And the LORD said, I have surely seen the affliction of my people which *are* in Egypt, and have heard their cry by reason of their taskmasters; for I know their sorrows;

8 And I come down to deliver them out of the hand of the Egyptians, and to bring them up out of that land unto a good land and a large, unto a land flowing with milk and honey; unto the place of the Canaanites, and the Hittites, and the Amorites, and the Perizzites, and the Hivites, and the Jebusites.

9 Now therefore, behold, the cry of the children of Israel is come unto me: and I have also seen the oppression wherewith the Egyptians oppress them.

10 Come now therefore, and I will send thee unto Pharaoh, that thou mayest bring forth my people the children of Israel out of Egypt.

11 And Moses said unto God, who *am* I, that I should go unto Pharaoh, and that I should bring forth the children of Israel out of Egypt?

12 And he said, Certainly I will be with thee: and this *shall be* a token unto thee, that I have sent thee: When thou hast brought forth the people out of Egypt, ye shall serve God upon this mountain.

13 And Moses said unot God. Behold, *when* I come unto the children of Israel, and shall say unto them. The God of your fathers hath sent me unto you; and they shall say to me, What *is* his name? what shall I say unto them?

14 And God said unto Moses, I AM THAT I AM: and he said, Thus shalt thou say unto the children of Israel, I AM hath sent me unto you.

15 And God said moreover unto Moses, Thus shalt thou say unto the children of Israel, The LORD God of your fathers, the God of Abraham, the God of Isaac, and the God of Jacob, hath sent me unto you: this *is* my name for ever, and this is my memorial unto all generations.

16 Go, and gather the elders of Israel together, and say unto them, The LORD God of your fathers, the God of Abraham, of Isaac, and of Jacob, appeared unto me, saying, I have surely visited you, and *seen* that which is done to you in Egypt:

17 And I have said, I will bring you up out of the affliction of Egypt unto the land of the Canaanites, and the Hittites, and the Amorites, and the Perizzites, and the Hivites, and the Jebusites, unto a land flowing with milk and honey.

18 And they shall hearken to thy voice: and thou shalt come, thou and the elders of Israel, unto the king of Egypt, and ye shall say unto him, The LORD God of the Hebrews hath met with us: and now let us go, we beseech thee, three days' journey into the wilderness, that we may sacrifice to the LORD our God.

19 And I am sure that the king of Egypt will not let you go, no, not by a mighty hand.

20 And I will stretch out my hand, and smite Egypt with all my wonders which I will do in the midst thereof: and after that he will let you go.

Now Moses kept the flock of Jethro his father in law, the priest of Midian: and he led the flock to the backside of the desert, and came to the mountain of God, even to Horeb. And the angel of the Lord appeared unto him in a flame of fire out of the midst of the bush: and he looked, and, behold, the bush burned with fire, and the bush was not consumed. (Exodus 3:1-2)

Not knowing where he is going, Moses, who has fled from the Pharaoh, thinks he has found peace in loneliness. One day he is called away from his sheep and, against his will, he is called to serve God to save the Israelites from the tyranny of their oppressors.

In this famous story of a mission, Rembrandt indicated the mysterious fire in which God reveals himself to Moses as a mere blaze of light. He reveals his awe for the mystery by restricting himself to drawing Moses' response to the strange phenomenon in order to indicate God's presence. The sublime composition, in which the concentration on the essential element is accompanied by a perfect illusion of light and space, is characteristic in every respect of Rembrandt's style of drawing in approximately the middle of the 1650s.

Pen and brush drawing; 17.5 × 24.7 cm.
Falsely signed and dated: *Rt. 1635.*
Ca. 1655.
Previously: London, Sir Max J. Bonn.

Literature: Benesch V, no. 951 (*ca.* 1654-55); Slive I, no. 254 (*ca.* 1655)/Hofstede de Groot, *Rembrandt Bijbel,* V.T.d.15; Rotermund 1963, no. 72.

*Moses and the
Burning Bush*

Moses went down from the mount

Exodus 32 AND when the people saw that Moses delayed to come down out of the mount, the people gathered themselves together unto Aaron, and said unto him, Up, make us gods, which shall go before us; for *as for* this Moses, the man that brought us up out of the land of Egypt, we wot not what is become of him.

2 And Aaron said unto them, Break off the golden earrings, which *are* in the ears of your wives, of your sons, and of your daughters, and bring *them* unto me.

3 And all the people brake off the golden earrings which *were* in their ears, and brought *them* unto Aaron.

4 And he received *them* at their hand, and fashioned it with a graving tool, after he had made it a molten calf: and they said, These *be* thy gods, O Israel, which brought thee up out of the land of Egypt.

5 And when Aaron saw *it,* he built an altar before it; And Aaron made proclamation, and said, To morrow *is* a feast to the LORD.

6 And they rose up early on the morrow, and offered burnt offerings, and brought peace offerings; and the people sat down to eat and to drink, and rose up to play.

7 And the LORD said unto Moses, Go, get thee down; for thy people, which thou broughtest out of the land of Egypt, have corrupted *themselves:*

8 They have turned aside quickly out of the way which I commanded them: they have made them a molten calf, and have worshipped it, and have sacrified thereunto, and said, These *be* thy gods, O Israel, which have brought thee up out of the land of Egypt. [...]

15 And Moses turned, and went down from the mount, and the two tables of the testimony *were* in his hand: the tables *were* written on both their sides; on the one side and on the other *were* they written.

16 And the tables *were* the work of God, and the writing *was* the writing of God, graven upon the tables.

17 And when Joshua heard the noise of the people as they shouted, he said unto Moses, *There is* a noise of war in the camp.

18 And he said, *It is* not the voice of *them that* shout for mastery, neither *is it* the voice of *them that* cry for being overcome: *but* the noise of *them that* sing do I hear.

19 And it came to pass, as soon as he came nigh unto the camp, that he saw the calf, and the dancing: ans Moses' anger waxed hot, and he cast the tables out of his hands, and brake them beneath the mount.

20 And he took the calf which they had made, and burnt *it* in the fire, and ground *it* to powder, and strawed *it* upon the water, and made the children of Israel drink of *it.* [...]

30 And it came to pass on the morrow, that Moses said unto the people. Ye have sinned a great sin: and now I will go unto the LORD; peradventure I shall make an atonement for your sin.

31 And Moses returned to the LORD, and said, Oh, this people have sinned a great sin, and have made them gods of gold.

32 Yet now, if thou wilt forgive their sin-; and if not, blot me, I pray thee, out of thy book which thou hast written.

33 And the LORD said unto Moses, Whosoever hath sinned against me, him will I blot out of my book.

34 Therefore now go, lead the people unto *the place* of which I have spoken unto thee: behold, mine Angel shall go before thee: nevertheless in the day when I visit I will visit their sin upon them.

Moses Smashes the Stone Tablets with the Text of the Covenant

And it came to pass, as soon as he came nigh unto the camp, that he saw the calf, and the dancing: and Moses' anger waxed hot, and he cast the tables out of his hands, and brake them beneath the mount.
(Exodus, 32:19)

The scene of Moses raising the stone tablets stating the Ten Commandments in order to smash them violently against the mountain was usually depicted in combination with the dance around the golden calf. In this work, Rembrandt concentrated exclusively on the figure of Moses. His face, framed by his raised arms, is the centre of the composition. The rugged rocks behind him merely serve to indicate the place where the event took place: Mount Sinai. Later in the story, Exodus 34:29 describes how Moses, when he descended Mount Sinai again with two stone tablets, did not know that his face was shining as a result of his talk with the Lord. Because Hieronymous had translated the Hebrew word for this shining by using the word

'cornuta' (horned) in his canonized Latin translation of the Bible, the Vulgate, it had long been customary to depict Moses in virtually every scene with horns on his head, often in the form of rays of light. Rembrandt followed this tradition, although he indicated the horns only vaguely, in the form of two horn-shaped locks of hair.

This large canvas, in which Moses' sorrow and anger are expressed in a very controlled way, without any attempt to create a theatrical effect, is remarkably similar to a painting dating from the same period, *Jacob Wrestling with the Angel* (see p. 51).

Canvas; 167 × 135 cm.
Signed and dated: *Rembrandt f. 1659.*
Berlin, Gemäldegalerie der Staatlichen Museen.

Literature: Bredius, no. 527; Bauch, no. 226; Gerson, no. 347; Bredius-Gerson, no. 527/Hofstede de Groot, *Rembrandt Bijbel*, V.T.d.12; Tümpel 1969, pp. 169-76.

Thou shalt not curse the people: for they *are* blessed

AND the children of Israel set forward, and pitched in the plains of Moab on this side Jordan *by* Jericho.

2 And Balak the son of Zippor saw all that Israel had done to the Amorites.

3 And Moab was sore afraid of the people, because they *were* many: and Moab was distressed because of the children of Israel.

4 And Moab said unto the elders of Midian, Now shall this company lick up all *that are* round about us, as the ox licketh up the grass of the field. And Balak the son of Zippor *was* king of the Moabites at that time.

5 He sent messengers therefore unto Balaam the son of Beor th Pethor, which *is* by the river of the land of the children of his people, to call him, saying, Behold, there is a people come out from Egypt: behold, they cover the face of the earth, and they abide over against me:

6 Come now therefore, I pray thee, curse me this people; for they are too mighty for me: peradventure I shall prevail, *that* we may smite them, and *that* I may drive them out of the land: for I wot that he whom thou blessed *is* blessed, and he whom thou cursest is cursed.

7 And the elders of Moab and the elders of Midian departed with the rewards of divination in their hand; and they came unto Balaam, and spake unto him the words of Balak.

8 And he said unto them, Lodge here this night, and I will bring you word again, as the LORD shall speak unto me: and the princes of Moab abode with Balaam.

9 And God became unto Balaam, and said, What men *are* these with thee?

10 And Balaam said unto God, Balak the son of Zippor, king of Moab, hath sent unto me, *saying,*

11 Behold, *there is* a people come out of Egypt, which covereth the face of the earth: come now, curse me them; peradventure I shall be able to overcome them, and drive them out.

12 And Gods said unto Balaam, Thou shalt not go with them; thou shalt not curse the people: for they *are* blessed.

13 And Balaan rose up in the morning, and said unto the princes of Balak, Get you into your land: for the LORD refuseth to give me leave to go with you.

14 And the princes of Moab rose up, and they went unto Balak, and said, Balaam refuseth to come with us.

15 And Balak sent yet again princes, more, and more honourable than they.

16 And they came to Balaam, and said to him, Thus saith Balak the son of Zippor, Let nothing, I pray thee, hinder thee from coming unto me:

17 For I will promote thee unto very great honour, and I will do whatsoever thou sayest unto me: come therefore, I pray thee, curse me this people.

18 And Balaam answered and said unto the servants of Balak, If Balak would give me his house full of silver and gold, I cannot go beyond the word of the LORD my God, to do less or more.

19 Now therefore, I pray you, tarry ye also here this night, that I may know what the LORD will say unto me more.

20 And Cod came unto Nalaam at night, and said unto him, If the men come to call thee, rise up, *and* go with them; but yet the word which I shall say unto thee, that shalt thou do.

21 And Balaam rose up in the morning, and saddled his ass, and went with the princes of Moab.

22 And God's anger was kindled because he went: and the angel of the LORD stood in the way for an adversary against him. Now he was riding upon his ass, and his two servants *were* with him.

23 And the ass saw the angel of the LORD standing in the way, and his sword drawn in his hand: and the ass turned aside out of the way, and went into the field: and Balaam smote the ass, to turn her into the way.

24 But the angel of the LORD stood in a path of the vineyards, a wall *being* on this side, and a wall on that side.

25 And when the ass saw the angel of the LORD, she thrust herself unto the wall, and crushed Balaam's foot against the wall: and he smote her again.

26 And the angel of the LORD went further, and stood in a narrow place, where *was* no way to turn either to the right hand or to the left.

But the angel of the Lord stood in a path of the vineyards, a wall being on this side, and a wall on that side. And when the ass saw the angel of the Lord, she thrust herself unto the wall, and crushed Balaam's foot against the wall: and he smote her again.
(Numbers 22:24-25)

Clearly Balaam had departed with the intention of ignoring God's prohibition on cursing Israel, but of acting in such a way that he would receive the reward promised him. From that moment, the journey which had been conditionally permitted (see verse 20) became a forbidden journey. When the avarice of all sorts of false prophets is denounced in the New Testament, they are said to have gone astray, following the way of Balaam, 'who loved the wages of unrighteousness; But was rebuked for his iniquity: the dumb ass speaking with man's voice forbad the madness of the prophet' (2 Peter 2:15-16).

Rembrandt painted the talking ass, the episode which has made the story so well known, in a work of the same scene dating from 1626 (see p. 91), based on a composition by his teacher, Pieter Lastman. In this drawing, dating from about 1660, the preceding event of the story is outlined, i.e., the moment at which the ass refuses to go on for the second time. Starting back from the angel, the creature fearfully presses against the wall of the road, no matter how cruelly her master urges her to walk on. Balaam's two young servants look on in consternation.

Pen and ink drawing; 20.7 × 25.7 cm.
Ca. 1660.
Vienna, Albertina.

Literature: Benesch V, no. 1063 (*ca.* 1660-62).

The Angel of the Lord Stands in Balaam's Path

27 And when the ass saw the angel of the LORD, she fell down under Balaam: and Balaam's anger was kindled, and he smote the ass with a staff.

28 And the LORD opened the mouth of the ass, and she said unto Balaam, What have I done unto thee, that thou hast smitten me these three times?

29 And Balaam said unto the ass, Because thou hast mocked me: I would there were a sword in mine hand, for now would I kill thee.

30 And the ass said unto Balaam, Am not I thine ass, upon which thou hast ridden ever since was thine unto this day? was I ever wont to do so unto thee? And he said, Nay.

31 The the LORD opened the eyes of Balaam, and he saw the angel of the LORD standing in the way, and his sword drawn in his hand: and

he bowed is head, and fell flat on his face.

32 And the angel of the LORD said unto him, Wherefore hast thou smitten thine ass these three times? behold, I went out to withstand thee, because thy way is perverse before me:

33 And the ass saw me, and turned from me these three times: unless she had turned from me, surely now also I had slain thee, and saved her alive.

34 And Balaam said unto the angel of the LORD, I have sinned; for I knew not that thou stoodest in the way against me: now therefore, if it displease thee, I will get me back again.

35 And the angel of the LORD said unto Balaam, Go with the men: but only the word that I shall speak unto thee, that thou shalt speak. So Balaam went with the princes of Balak.

Balaam and the Ass

And when the ass saw the angel of the Lord, she fell down under Balaam: and Balaam's anger was kindled, and he smote the ass with a staff. And the Lord opened the mouth of the ass, and she said unto Balaam, What have I done unto thee, that thou hast smitten me these three times?
(Numbers 22:27-28)

This painting, dating from 1626, is one of Rembrandt's earliest known works. The composition by Pieter Lastman dating from 1622, on which it is based, was possibly still in the latter's studio when the young Rembrandt was his pupil in 1624. Although most elements in Rembrandt's painting are clearly derived from Lastman's representation, he arranged and used them in such a way that he created a completely new composition. He transformed his teacher's scene, which had a horizontal layout, into a vertical composition in which the figures are condensed to form a single compact group. All the attention is focused on the 'blinded' prophet, who is grimly flailing his stick. Unlike Lastman, and departing from the Biblical text which indicates that the angel again stood in the path of the ass, Rembrandt showed Balaam's opponent descending from heaven behind the ass, with a drawn sword. Probably the vertical composition which he had decided to use also played a part in making this change. As in Lastman's work, though much more emphatically, the Moabite delegates of King Balak were depicted in the scene, as well as the two servants. According to the Bible story (verse 21), the prophet had left with them in the morning. The bright colours of the painting reveal the influence which Lastman's palette had on Rembrandt's early work.

The panel probably belonged to the art collection of the Spanish diamond merchant, art dealer and diplomat financier, Don Alfonso Lopez, who lived in Amsterdam. This collection was auctioned in Paris in December 1641. There is actually a letter dated November of that year, in which the French painter

Claude Vignon, a follower of Caravaggio from Paris, wrote to the French printer and art dealer, François Langlois: 'In Amsterdam, give my regards to Mr Rembrandt and bring back some of his work. Tell him that yesterday I valued his painting of the prophet Balaam, which Mr Lopez bought from him.'

The story of the behaviour of the prophet Balaam continues into chapter 24 of the book of Numbers. To the dismay of King Balak, he does not curse the Israelites, but blesses them, even four times. In his fourth blessing he speaks the well-known words:

I shall see him, but not now:
I shall behold him, but not nigh;
There shall come a Star out of Jacob,
And a Sceptre shall rise out of Israel.
(Numbers 24:17)

The ancient Jews viewed these words as a Messianic prophecy, and Christians from the earliest times have seen this text as a prediction which reached its highest fulfilment in Christ.

A painting on the wall in the Priscilla catacomb in Rome shows Balaam pointing to a star with his right hand, and to the Child on his mother's lap with his left hand.

Panel; 63.2 × 46.5 cm.
Signed and dated: *R f. 1626.*
Paris, Musée Cognacq-Jay.

Literature: Bredius, no. 487; Bauch, no. 1; Gerson, no. 6; Bredius-Gerson, no. 487/E.W. Moes, 'Een brief van kunsthistorische beteekenis' in *Oud Holland* 12 (1894), pp. 238-40; J.Bruyn, *Rembrandt's keuze van Bijbelse onderwerpen*, Utrecht 1959, p. 14; Franklin W. Robinson, 'A Note on the Visual Tradition of Balaam and his Ass' in *Oud Holland* 84 (1969, pp. 238-44); B.P.J. Broos, 'Rembrandt en zijn eeuwige leermeester Lastman' in *De kroniek van het Rembrandthuis* 26 (1972, pp. 76-84).

The LORD shall sell Sisera into the hand of a woman

[When the Israelites had taken over the Promised Land under the leadership of Joshua, Moses' successor, there was a new generation which was ignorant of the Lord and had no experience of what he had done for his people. It was not long before the Israelites increasingly practised idolatry. In order to punish them for their lack of fidelity, the Lord delivered them to their neighbouring enemies. But every time when the people were in the greatest distress and begged the Lord for deliverance, he gave them a saviour in the guise of a 'judge' who brought salvation, driven by the spirit of the Lord. The first two judges were Othniel and Ehud.]

Judges 4 AND the children of Israel again did evil in the sight of the LORD, when Ehud was dead.

2 And the LORD sold them into the hand of Jabin king of Canaan, that reigned in Hazor; the captain of whose host *was* Sisera, which dwelt in Harosheth of the Gentiles.

3 And the children of Israel cried unto the LORD: for he had nine hundred chariots of iron; and twenty years he mightily oppressed the children of Israel.

4 And Deborah, a prophetess, the wife of Lapidoth, she judged Israel at that time.

5 And she dwelt under the palm tree of Deborah between Ramah and Bethel in mount Ephraim: and the children of Israel came up to her for judgment.

6 And she sent and called Barak the son of Abinoam out of Kedeshnaphtali, and said unto hin, Hath not the LORD God of Israel commanded, *saying*, Go and draw toward mount Tabor, and take with thee ten thousand men of the children of Naphtali and the children of Zebulun?

7 And I will draw unto thee to the river Kishon Sisera, the captain of Jabin's army, with his chariots and his multitude; and I will deliver him into thine hand.

8 And Barak said unto her, If thou wilt go with me, then I will go: but if thou wilt not go with me, *then* I will not go.

9 And she said, I will surely go with thee: notwithstanding the journey that thou takest shall not be for thine honour; for the LORD shall sell Sisera into the hand of a woman. And Deborah arose, and went with Barak to Kedesh.

10 And Barak called Zebulun and Naphtali to Kedesh; and he went up with ten thousand men at his feet: and Deborah went up with him. [...]

12 And they shewed Sisera that Barak the son of Abinoam was gone up to mount Tabor.

13 And Sisera gathered together all his chariots, *even* nine hundred chariots of iron, and all the people that *were* with him, from Harosheth of the Gentiles unto the river of Kishon.

14 And Deborah said unto Barak, Up; for this *is* the day in which the LORD hath delivered Sisera into thine hand: is not the LORD gone out before thee? So Barak went down from mount Tabor, and ten thousand men after him.

15 And the LORD discomfited Sisera, and all *his* chariots, and all *his* host, with the edge of the sword before Barak; so that Sisera lighted down off *his* chariot, and fled away on his feet.

16 But Barak pursued after the chariots, and after the host, unto Harosheth of the Gentiles: and all the host of Sisera fell upon the edge of the sword; *and* there was not a man left.

17 Howbeit Sisera fled away on his feet to the tent of Jael the wife of Heber the Kenite: for *there was* peace between Jabin the king of Hazor and the house of Heber the Kenite.

18 And Jael went out to meet Sisera, and said unto him, Turn in, my lord, turn in to me; fear not. And when he had turned in unto her into the tent, she covered him with a mantle.

19 And he said unto her, Give me, I pray thee, a little water to drink; for I am thirsty. And she opened a bottle of milk, and gave him drink, and covered him.

20 Again he said unto her, Stand in the door of the tent, and it shall be, when any man doth come and enquire of thee, and say, Is there any man here? that thou shalt say, No.

21 Then Jael Heber's wife took a nail of the tent, and took an hammer in her hand, and went softly unto him, and smote the nail into his temples, and fastened it into the ground: for he was fast asleep and weary. So he died.

22 And, behold, as Barak pursued Sisera, Jael came out to meet him, and said unto him, Come, and I will shew thee the man whom thou seekest. And when he came into her *tent*, behold, Sisera lay dead, and the nail *was* in his temples.

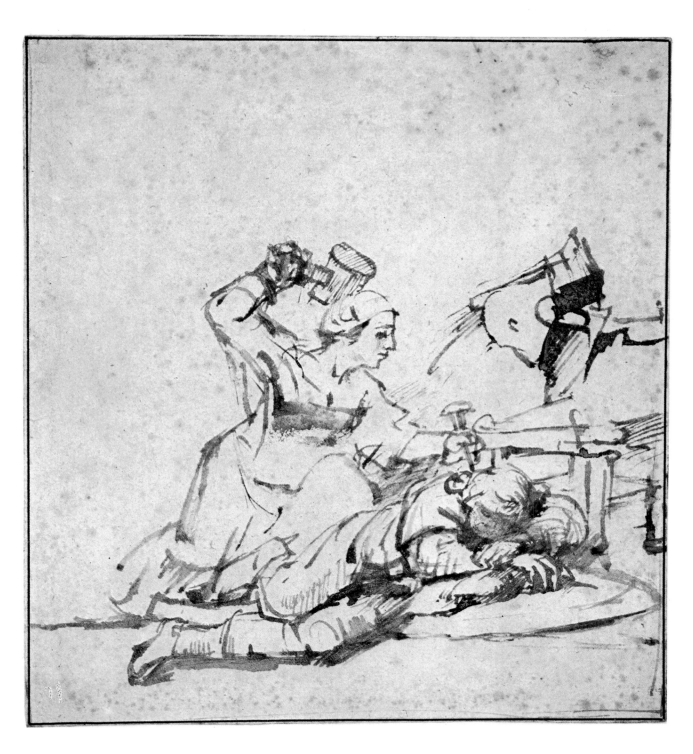

*Then Jael, Heber's wife, took a nail off the tent, and took an
hammer in her hand, and went softly unto him, and smote
the nail into his temples and fastened it into the ground.*
(Judges 4:21)

The captain delivered to Jael is completely exhausted
and sleeps like a log on his shield. His helmet hangs
from the arm of a chair behind him.

This drawing, inspired by a woodcut by Lucas van
Leyden on the same theme, is one of the most brilliant
examples of Rembrandt's concise and monumental
style of drawing in the second half of the 1650s. In
drawing Sisera's helmet, he was probably thinking of
the 'Japanese helmet' which was mentioned in his
inventory of 1656 (Hofstede de Groot, *Urkunden* 169, no.
158).

The Bible story does not make a judgment about
Jael's violation of hospitality. It merely rejoices in the
fact that with the death of Sisera, she chooses the side
of the oppressed Israel - in other words, God's side. In
the 'Song of Deborah', which follows this chapter in
the Bible, her deed is celebrated as follows:

*He asked water, and she gave him milk;
she brought forth butter in a lordly dish.
She put her hand to the nail,
And her right hand to the workmen's hammer;
And with the hammer she smote Sisera,
She smote off his head,
When she had pierced and stricken through his temples.*
(Judges 5:25-26)

Pen and brush drawing; 19 × 17.2 cm.
Ca. 1655-60.
Amsterdam, Rijksprentenkabinet.

Literature: Benesch V, no. 1042 (*ca.* 1659-60); Slive II, no.
437 (*ca.* 1657-60)/Hofstede de Groot, *Rembrandt Bijbel*,
V.T.d.17; Rotermund 1963, no. 78; 'Bijbelse Inspiratie',
no. 65.

The woman called his name Samson

Judges 13 AND the children of Israel did evil again in the sight of the LORD; and the LORD delivered them into the hand of the Philistines forty years.

2 And there was a certain man of Zorah, of the family of the Danites, whose name *was* Manoah; and his wife *was* barren, and bare not.

3 And the angel of the LORD appeared unto the woman, and said unto her, Behold now, thou *art* barren, and bearest not: but thou shalt conceive, and bear a son.

4 Now therefore beware, I pray thee, and drink not wine nor strong drink, and eat not any unclean *thing:*

5 For, lo, thou shalt conceive, and bear a son; and no razor shall come on his head: for the child shall be a Nazarite unto God from the womb: and he shall begin to deliver Israel out of the hand of the Philistines.

6 Then the woman came and told her husband, saying, A man of God came unto me, and his countenance *was* like the countenance of an angel of God, very terrible: but I asked him not whence he *was,* neither told he me his name:

7 But he said unto me, Behold, thou shalt conceive, and bear a son; and now drink no wine nor strong drink, neither eat any unclean *thing:* for the child shall be a Nazarite to God from the womb to the day of his death.

8 Then Manoah intreated the LORD, and said, O my LORD, let the man of God which thou didst send come again unto us, and teach us what we shall do unto the child that shall be born.

9 And God hearkened to the voice of Manoah; and the angel of God came again unto the woman as she sat in the field: but Manoah her husband *was* not with her.

10 And the woman made haste, and ran, and shewed her husband, and said unto him, Behold, the man hath appeared unto me, that came unto me the *other* day.

11 And Manoah arose, and went after his wife, and came to the man, and said unto him, *Art* thou the man that speakest unto the woman? And he said, I *am.*

12 And Manoah said, Now let thy words come to pass. How shall we order the child, and *how* shall we do unto him?

13 And the angel of the LORD said unto Manoah, Of all that I said unto the woman let her beware.

14 She may not eat of any *thing* that cometh of the vine, neither let her drink wine or strong drink, nor eat any unclean *thing:* all that I commanded her let her observe.

15 And Manoah said unto the angel of the LORD, I pray thee, let us detain thee, until we shall have made ready a kid for thee.

16 And the angel of the LORD said unto Manoah, Though thou detain me, I will not eat of thy bread: and if thou wilt offer a burnt offering, thou must offer it unto the LORD. For Manoah knew not that he *was* an angel of the LORD.

17 And Manoah said unto the angel of the LORD, What *is* thy name, that when thy sayings come to pass we may do thee honour?

18 And the angel of the LORD said unto him, Why askest thou thus after my name, seeing it *is* secret?

19 So Manuah took a kid with a meat offering, and offered *it* upon a rock unto the LORD: and *the angel* did wonderously; and Manoah and his wife looked on.

20 For it came to pass, when the flame went up toward heaven from off the altar, that the angel of the LORD ascended the flame of the altar. And Manoah and his wife looked on *it,* and fell on their faces to the ground.

21 But the angel of the LORD did no more appear to Manoah and to his wife. Then Manoah knew that he *was* an angel of the LORD.

22 And Manoah said unto his wife, we shall surely die, because we have seen God.

23 But his wife said unto him, If the LORD were pleased to kill us, he would not have received a burnt offering and a meat offering at our hands, neither would he shewed us all these *things,* nor would as at this time have told us *such things* as these.

24 And the woman bare a son, and called his name Samson: and the child grew, and the LORD blessed him.

25 And the Spirit of the LORD began to move him at times in the camp of Dan between Zorah and Eshtaol.

And Manoah and his wife looked on it, and fell on their faces to the ground. But the Angel of the Lord did no more appear to Manoah and to his wife.
(Judges 13:20-21)

At first sight, the story of Samson, which is dealt with extensively in Rembrandt's work (see pp. 98-105), seems to be little more than a series of adventures and crude jokes by a mighty figure who can barely control himself. However, the opening story about the announcement of his birth clearly shows that this Samson was nevertheless a saviour devoted to God, who was destined even before his birth to be instrumental in freeing Israel from the power of the Philistines by means of his powerful deeds.

The theme of Samson's parents, who suddenly realize that the bringer of the 'glad tidings' is heaven sent, was introduced in painting by Pieter Lastman, and was particularly popular with Rembrandt and his pupils. In this emotional drawing, dating from the end of the 1630s, Rembrandt placed the emphasis on the dismay with which Manoah and his wife observe the angel rising up in the blazing fire. The composition is related to Rembrandt's painting, *The Angel Leaves Tobias and his Family*, dating from 1637 (see p. 195). The woodcut by Maerten van Heemskerck, with a representation of the same subject, on which it was based, also served Rembrandt as an example for this drawing.

Pen and ink drawing; 17.5 × 19 cm.
Ca. 1637-40.
Berlin, Kupferstichkabinett der Staatlichen Museen.

Literature: Benesch I, no. 180 (*ca.* 1639); Slive I, no. 22 (*ca.* 1637-40); Haak, no. 27 (*ca.* 1639)/F. Saxl, *Rembrandt's Sacrifice of Manoach* (Studies of the Warburg Institute IX), London 1939; Rotermund 1963, no. 84; Tümpel 1970, no. 21.

The Angel Rises up in the Flame of Manoah's Sacrifice

The Angel Rises up in the Flame of Manoah's Sacrifice

Then Manoah knew that he was an angel of the Lord.
(Judges 13:21)

According to the view of the Old Testament, the sight of God was fatal to man, unless God was merciful to him. Therefore Manoah was afraid that he and his wife would die. On the other hand, his wife, joyful about the promise that she was to be the mother of a son, felt no fear at all. 'If the Lord were pleased to kill us, he would not have received a burnt offering and a meat offering at our hands, neither would he have shewed us all these things, nor would as at this time

have told us such things as these' (verse 23). In this, and even more clearly in the next drawing, Rembrandt wished to express in the position of Samson's parents' bodies the contrast between the husband's fear and the wife's trust.

Pen and ink drawing; 19.8 × 16 cm.
Ca. 1650-52.
Edinburgh, The National Gallery of Scotland.

Literature: Benesch V, no. 895 (*ca.* 1652).

L'ange quitte Manüé et sa femme, et s'élève au milieu de la flame quil auoir excitée 1807.

Then Manoah knew that he was an angel of the Lord. (Judges 13:21)

It is by no means impossible that this drawing played a part in the creation of the large painting of the same subject in Dresden (Bredius, no. 509), which most experts now consider to be a work by one of Rembrandt's pupils, designed and added to by Rembrandt himself.

The French title was presumably added by Crozat (see p. 67), and reads: *L'ange quitte Manüé et sa femme, et s'élève au milieu de la flame quil avoit excitée* (The angel leaves Manoah and his wife, and rises up in the flame he has lit). In the last part of the sentence, Manoah's sacrifice is confused with that of Gideon. For Gideon's sacrifice the fire was lit by the angel (Judges 6:21); Manoah lit the fire himself (see verses 19-20).

Pen and brush drawing; 23.3 × 20.3 cm.
Ca. 1655.
Stockholm, Nationalmuseum.

Literature: Benesch V, no. 975 (*ca.* 1655); Slive I, no. 132 (*ca.* 1655)/'Bijbelse Inspiratie', under no. 67.

The Angel Rises up in the Flame of Manoah's Sacrifice

Out of the eater came forth meat

AND Samson went down to Timnath, and saw a woman in Timnath of the daughters of the Philistines.

2 And he came up, and told his father and his mother, and said, I have seen a woman in Timnath of the daughters of the Philistines: now therefore get her for me to wife.

3 Then his father and his mother said unto him, *Is there* never a woman among the daughters of thy brethren, or among all my people, that thou goest to take a wife of the uncircumcised Philistines? And Samson said unto his father, Get her for me; for she pleaseth me well.

4 But his father and his mother knew not that it *was* of the LORD, that he sought an occasion against the Philistines: for at that time the Philistines had dominion over Israel.

5 Then went Samson down, and his father and his mother, to Timnath, and came to the vineyards of Timnath: and, behold, a young lion roared against him.

6 And the Spirit of the LORD came mightily upon him, and he rent him as he would have rent a kid, and *he had* nothing in his hand: but he told not his father or his mother what he had done.

7 And he went down, and talked with the woman; and she pleased Samson well.

8 And after a time he returned to take her, and he turned aside to see the carcase of the lion: and, behold, *there was* a swarm of bees and honey in the carcase of the lion.

9 And he took therof in his hands, and went on eating, and came to his father and mother, and he gave them, and they did eat : but he told not them that he had taken the honey out of the carcase of the lion.

10 So his father went down unto the woman: and Samson made there a feast; for so used the young men to do.

11 And it came to pass, when they saw him, that they brought thirty companions to be with him.

12 And Samson said unto them, I will now put forth a riddle unto you: if ye can certainly declare it me within the seven days of the feast, and find *it* out, then I will give you thirty sheets and thirty change of garments:

13 But if ye cannot declare *it* me, then shall ye give me thirty sheets and thirty change of garments. And they said unto him, Put forth thy riddle, that we may hear it.

14 And he said unto them, Out of the eater came forth meat, and out of the strong came forth sweetness. And they could not in three days expound the riddle.

15 And it came to pass on the seventh day, that they said unto Samson's wife, Entice thy husband, that he may declare unto us the riddle, lest we burn thee and thy father's house with fire: have ye called us to take that we have? *is it* not *so?*

16 And Samson's wife wept before him, and said, Thou dost but hate me, and lovest me not: thou hast put forth a riddle unto the children of my people, and hast not told *it* me. And he said unto her, Behold, I have not told *it* my father nor my mother, and shall I tell *it* thee?

17 And she wept before him the seven days, while their feast lasted: and it came to pass on the seventh day, that he told her, because she lay sore upon him: and she told the riddle to the children of her people.

18 And the men of the city said unto him on the seventh day before the sun went down, What *is* sweeter than honey? and what *is* stronger than a lion? And he said unto them, If ye had not plowed with my heifer, ye had not found out my riddle.

19 And the Spirit of the LORD came upon him, and he went down to Ashkelon, and slew thirty men of them, and took their spoil, and gave change of garments unto them which expounded the riddle. And his anger was kindled, and he went up to his father's house.

20 But Samson's wife was *given* to his companion, whom he had used as his friend.

... and Samson made there a feast .... And it came to pass, when they saw him, that they brought thirty companions to be with him. And Samson said unto them, I will now put forth a riddle unto you: .... And he said unto them, Out of the eater came forth meat, and out of the strong came forth sweetness.
(Judges 14:10-14)

In this work Rembrandt showed the moment at which Samson asked his companions a riddle. The men who had been appointed to keep an eye on the dangerous giant are very alert and full of suspicion. The wedding guests seated at the table to the left are more interested in other things. The dynamic tableau, with the mysterious Philistine bride as a static focal point, clearly reveals the influence of Leonardo da Vinci's *Last Supper*. Rembrandt had an engraving based on this work which had inspired him in 1635 to do a number of studies after the famous fresco (see pp. 368-69).

In 1641, only three years after this work was completed, it was lavishly praised by Philip Angel, a painter from Leyden, in his speech on St Lucas' Day (18 October), which was printed a year later under the title *In Praise of the Art of Painting*. Arguing that before starting on a work, a historical painter should thoroughly study the story he wishes to illustrate, Angel drew particular attention to Rembrandt's

painting of Samson's wedding feast, which he described at length as an excellent example of a well-thought-out historical work. For example, he praised the fact that Rembrandt had the guests lying on couches around the table, for, as he said, people in ancient times 'did not sit at the table as we do now, but lay on their elbows, as is still customary in those countries among the Turks, as he showed in a very realistic way. To make a distinction between this wedding and other weddings, he placed Samson in the foreground with long hair to show that his head had never succumbed to a razor.' Angel pointed out the effective gesture Samson makes with his hands, and concluded: 'See, this fruit of his own natural gift for representation is the result of thoroughly reading and studying the story and thinking about it at great length.'

Canvas; 126.5 × 175.5 cm.
Signed and dated: *Rembrandt f. 1638*.
Dresden, Staatliche Kunstsammlungen, Gemäldegalerie.

Literature: Bredius, no. 507; Bauch, no. 20; Gerson, no. 85; Bredius-Gerson, no. 507/Hofstede de Groot, *Rembrandt Bijbel*, V.T.p.14; J. Bruyn, *Rembrandt's keuze van Bijbelse onderwerpen*, Utrecht 1959, p. 17; Tümpel 1971, p. 24.

Samson's Wedding Feast

Now shall I be more blameless than the Philistines

Judges 15 BUT it came to pass within a while after, in the time of wheat harvest, that Samson visited his wife and kid; and he said, I will go in to my wife into the chamber. But her father would not suffer him to go in.

2 And her father said, I verily thought that thou hadst utterly hated her; therefore I gave her to thy companion: *is* not her younger sister fairer than she? take her, I pray thee, instead of her.

3 And Samson said concerning them, Now shall I be more blameless than the Philistines, though I do them a displeasure.

4 And Samson went and caught three hundred foxes, and took firebrands, and turned tail to tail, and put a firebrand in the midst between two tails.

5 And when he had set the brands on fire, he let *them* go into the standing corn of the Philistines, and burnt up both the shocks, and als the standing corn, with the vineyards *and* olives.

6 Then the Philistines said, Who hath done this? And they answered, Samson, the son in law of the Timnite. because he had taken his wife, and given her to his companion. And the Philistines came up, and burnt her and her father with fire.

7 And Samson said unto them, Though ye have done this, yet will I be avenged of you, and after that I will cease.

8 And he smote them hip and thigh with a great slaughter: and he went down and dwelt in the top of the rock Etam.

9 Then the Philistines went up, and pitched in Judah, and spread themselves in Lehi.

10 And the men of Judah said, Why are ye come up against us? And they answered, To bind Samson are we come up, tot do to him as he hath done to us.

11 Then three thousand men of Judah went to the top of the rock Etam, and said to Samson, Knowest thou not that the Philistines *are* rulers over us? what *is* this *that* thou hast done unto us? And he said unto them, As they did unto me, so have I done unto them.

12 And the said unto him, We are come down to bind thee, that we may deliver thee into the hand of the Philistines. And Samson said unto them, Swear unto me, that ye will not fall upon me yourselves.

13 And they spake unto him, saying, No; but we will bind thee fast, and deliver thee into their hand: but surely we will not kill thee. And they bound him with two new cords, and brought him up from the rock.

14 *And* when he came unto Lehi, the Philistines shouted against him: and the Spirit of the LORD came mightily upon him, and the cords that *were* upon his arms became as flax that was burnt with fire, and his bands loosed from off his hands.

15 And he found a new jawbone of an ass, and put forth his hand, and took it, and slew a thousand men therewith.

16 And Samson said, With the jawbone of an ass, heaps upon heaps, with the jaw of an ass have I slain a thousand men.

Samson Threatens his Father-in-law

But it came to pass within a while after, in the time of wheat harvest, that Samson visited his wife with a kid; and he said, I will go in to my wife into the chamber. But her father would not suffer him to go in. And her father said, I verily thought that thou hadst utterly hated her; therefore I gave her to thy companion.
(Judges 15:1-2)

Up to that time, this scene, painted life-size by Rembrandt, had only been done once as a print. In furious rage, Samson stands before the closed door of the house of his father-in-law, who refuses him entry. The last rays of the sun cast a golden glow on his damask outer garment and throw the shadow of his threateningly raised fist on to the wall.

Originally the painting must have been larger. On a 17th-century copy, illustrated in Bredius-Gerson, p. 413, the two negro boys to the left can both be seen, and beside them the kid that Samson had brought for his wife, as described in the Bible text.

Canvas; 156 × 129 cm.
Signed and dated: *Rembrandt ft. 163(5)*.
Berlin, Gemäldegalerie der Staatlichen Museen.

Literature: Bredius, no. 499; Bauch, no. 14; Gerson, no. 78; Bredius-Gerson, no. 499/Hofstede de Groot, *Rembrandt Bijbel*, V.T.p.15; J. Bruyn, *Rembrandt's keuze van Bijbelse onderwerpen*, Utrecht 1959, p. 17.

Tell me, I pray thee, wherein thy great strength *lieth*

Judges 16

4 And it came to pass afterward, that he loved a woman in the valley of Sorek, whose name *was* Delilah.

5 And the lords of the Philistines came up unto her, and said unto her, Entice him, and see wherein his great strength *lieth,* and by what *means* we may prevail against him, that we may bind him to afflict him: and we will give thee every one of us eleven hundred *pieces* of silver.

6 And Delilah said to Samson, Tell me, I pray thee, wherein thy great strength *lieth,* and wherewith thou mightest be bound to afflict thee.

7 And Samson said unto her, If they bind me with seven green withs that were never dried, then shall I be weak, and be as another man.

8 Then the lords of the Philistines brought up to her seven green withs which had not been dried, and she bound him with them.

9 Now *there were* men lying in wait, abiding with her in the chamber. And she said unto him, The Philistines *be* upon thee, Samson. And he brake the withs, as a thread of tow is broken when it toucheth the fire. So his strength was not known.

10 And Delilah said unto Samson, Behold, thou hast mocked me, and told me lies: now tell me, I pray thee, wherewith thou mightest be bound.

11 And he said unto her, If they bind me fast with new ropes that never were occupied, then shall I be weak, and be as another man.

12 Delilah therefore took new ropes, and bound him therewith, and said unto him, The Philistines *be* upon thee, Samson. And *there were* liers in wait abiding in the chamber. And he brake them from off his arms like a thread.

13 And Delilah said unto Samson, Hitherto thou hast mocked me, and told me lies: tell me wherewith thou mightest be bound. And he said unto her, If thou weavest the seven locks of my head with the web.

14 And she fastened *it* with the pin, and said unto him, The Philistines *be* upon thee, Samson. And he awaked out of his sleep, and went away with the pin of the beam, and with the web.

15 And she said unto him, How canst thou say, I love thee, when thine heart *is* not with me? thou hast mocked me these three times, and hast not told me wherein thy great strength *lieth.*

16 And it came to pass, when she pressed him daily with her words, and urged him, *so* that his soul was vexed unto death;

17 That he told her all his heart, and said unto her, There hath not come a razor upon mine head; fore I *have been* a Nazarite unto God from my mother's womb: if I be shaven, then my strength will go from me, and I shall become weak, and be like any *other* man.

18 And when Delilah saw that he had told her all his heart, she sent and called for the lords of the Philistines, saying, Come up this once, for he hath shewed me all his heart. Then the lords of the Philistines came up unto her, and brought money in their hand.

19 And she made him sleep upon her knees; and she called for a man, and she caused him to shave off the seven locks of his head; and she began to afflict him, and his strength went from him.

20 And she said, The Philistines *be* upon thee, Samson. And he awoke out of his sleep, and said, I will go out as at other times before, and shake myself. And he wist not that the LORD was departed from him.

21 But the Philistines took him, and put out his eyes, and brought him down to Gaza, and bound him with fetters of brass; and he did grind in the prison house.

And she made him sleep upon her knees; and she called for a man, and she caused him to shave off the seven locks off his head; and she began to afflict him, and his strength went from him.
(Judges 16:19)

After the woman from Timnath and a prostitute in Gaza (Judges 16:1-3), Delilah is the third Philistine woman who plays a prominent part in the story of Samson. Unlike the woman from Timnath, she is led to betray Samson not by a threat, but by the prospect of a great reward.

This subject is found repeatedly in late medieval prints and is one of the most famous examples of feminine trickery (see p. 22). The theme of the great hero who allows himself to be ensnared by a beautiful

woman was particularly popular in baroque art.

Rembrandt's early painting of Samson and Delilah is one of the most beautiful works from his Leyden period. The light shines ominously over the figures arranged diagonally towards the back. An oppressive silence is created around the victim between Delilah's knees, by means of wordless gestures and her furtive attempts to establish eye contact. Although older representations generally showed Delilah herself cutting Samson's hair, Rembrandt adhered to the text of the Bible, which says that she called someone to do this.

Samson and Delilah

Panel; 59.5 × 49.5 cm.
Signed and dated: *RHL van Rijn 1628*.
Berlin, Gemäldegalerie der Staatlichen Museen.

Literature: Bredius, no. 489; Bauch, no. 4; Gerson, no. 9; Bredius-Gerson, no. 489/Hofstede de Groot, *Rembrandt Bijbel*, V.T.p.16; 'Bijbelse Inspiratie', under no. 68.

Samson and Delilah

And she made him sleep upon her knees; and she called for a man, and she caused him to shave off the seven locks off his head; and she began to afflict him, and his strength went from him.
(Judges 16:19)

This drawing is rich in contrast and is a more broadly designed variation on the composition dating from 1628, reproduced on the previous page. Correcting the artistic tradition, Rembrandt again shows us that Delilah does not herself cut off Samson's long hair. As in the previous painting, she carefully raises a lock of the sleeping victim's hair in her right hand, waiting for the moment when she can call one of the Philistines standing ready to cut off all seven locks. The group of Samson and Delilah is made the dominant element in the drawing, not only because of its central position, but also by means of the accentuated contours and strong light.

Pen and brush drawing; 19 × 23.3 cm.
Ca. 1640.
Groningen, Groninger Museum.

Literature: Benesch III, no. 530 (*ca.* 1642-43)/Rotermund 1963, no. 87; 'Bijbelse Inspiratie', no. 68.

But the Philistines took him, and put out his eyes, and brought him down to Gaza, and bound him with fetters of brass.
(Judges 16:21)

In contrast with the previous scene, and the subsequent capture of Samson, the moment at which the enfeebled hero's eyes are put out is very rarely depicted. The painting in which Rembrandt showed this barbaric deed is by far the largest of the three canvases which he devoted to this story of Samson in the second half of the 1630s; and the extant copies reveal that the original must have been even larger. The breadth of scale with which the cruel deed by the armoured Philistine is depicted is in stark contrast to the simple words of the Bible text. The two components of the story are combined in a masterly way by means of the figure of Delilah, shown in the centre in the background, hurrying away with the trophies of her treachery.

It is generally assumed that this is the work which Rembrandt presented to the Stadtholder's secretary, Constantijn Huygens, in January 1639 in recognition of the part played by Huygens in the commission to paint a series of scenes from the Passion for Frederik Hendrik, which Rembrandt had recently completed (see p. 392). To indicate how he wished the painting to be hung, Rembrandt wrote a postscript to the letter he sent with the painting: 'Let my lord hang this work in strong light where you can stand a long way away from it to get the best effect.'

Canvas; 236 × 302 cm.
Signed and dated: *Rembrandt f. 1636.*
Frankfurt am Main, Städelsches Kunstinstitut.

Literature: Bredius, no. 501; Bauch, no. 15; Gerson, no. 76; Bredius-Gerson, no. 501/Hofstede de Groot, *Rembrandt Bijbel*, V.T.p.17.

The Blinding of Samson

All the earth may know that there is a God in Israel

I Samuel 17 NOW the Philistines gathered together their armies to battle, and were gathered together at Shochoh, which *belongeth* to Judah, and pitched between Shochoh and Azekah, in Ephesdammim.

2 And Saul and the men of Israel were gathered together, and pitched by the valley of Elah, and set the battle in array against the Philistines.

3 And the Philistines stood on a mountain on the one side, and Israel stood on a mountain on the other side: and *there was* a valley between them.

4 And there went out a champion out of the camp of the Philistines, named Goliath, of Gath, whose height *was* six cubits and a span.

5 And *he had* an helmet of brass upon his head, and he *was* armed with a coat of mail; and the weight of the coat *was* five thousand shekels of brass.

6 And *he had* greaves of brass upon his legs, and a target of brass between his shoulders.

7 And the staff of his spear *was* like a weaver's beam; and his spear's head *weighed* six hundred shekels of iron: and one bearing a hield went before him.

8 And he stood and cried unto the armies of Israel, and said unto them, Why are ye come out to set *your* battle in array? *am* not I a Philistine, and ye servants to Saul? choose a man for you, and let him come down to me.

9 If he be able to fight with me, and to kill me, then will we be your servants: but if I prevail against him, and kill him, then shall ye be our servants, and serve us.

10 And the Philistine said, I defy the armies of Israel this day; give me a man, that we may fight together.

11 When Saul and all Israel heard those words of the Philistine, they were dismayed, and greatly afraid.

12 Now David *was* the son of that Ephrathite of Bethlehemjudah, whose name *was* Jesse; and he had eight sons: and the man went among men *for* an old man in the days of Saul.

13 And the three eldest sons of Jesse went *and* followed Saul to the battle: and the names of his three sons that went to the battle *were* Eliab the firstborn, and next unto him Abinadab, and the third Shammah.

14 And David *was* the youngest: and the three eldest followed Saul. [...]

17 And Jesse said unto David his son, Take now for thy brethren an ephah of this parched *corn*, and these ten loaves, and run to the camp to thy brethren;

18 And carry these ten cheeses unto the captain of *their* thousand, and look how thy brethren fare, and take their pledge.

19 Now Saul, and they, and all the men of Israel, *were* in the valley of Elah, fighting with the Philistines.

20 And David rose up early in the morning, and left the sheep with a keeper, and took, and went, as Jesse had commanded him; and he came to the trench, as the host was going forth to the fight, and shouted for the battle.

21 For Israel and the Philistines had put the battle in array, army against army.

22 And David left his carriage in the hand of the keeper of the carriage, and ran into the army, and came and saluted his brethren.

23 And as he talked with them, behold, there came up the champion, the Philistine of Gath, Goliath by name out of the armies of the Philistines, and spake according to the same words: and David heard *them*.

24 And all the men of Israel, when they saw the man, fled from him, and were sore afraid.

25 And the men of Israel said, Have ye seen this man that is come up? surely to defy Israel is he come up: and it shall be, *that* the man who killeth him, the king will enrich him with great riches, and will give him his daughter, and make his father's house free in Israel.

26 And David spake to the men that stood by him, saying, What shall be done to the man that killeth this Philistine, and taketh away the reproach from Israel? for who *is* this uncircumcised Philistine, that he should defy the armies of the living God?

27 And the people answered him after this manner, saying, So shall it be done to the man that killeth him. [...]

31 And when the words were heard which David spake, they rehearsed *them* before Saul: and he sent for him.

32 And David said to Saul, Let no man's heart fail because of him; thy servant will go and fight with this Philistine.

And it came to pass, when the Philistine arose, and came and drew nigh to meet David, that David hasted, and ran toward the army to meet the Philistine. And David put his hand in his bag, and took thence a stone, and slang it, and smote the Philistine in his forehead, that the stone sunk into his forehead; and he fell upon his face to the earth.
(1 Samuel 17:48-49)

In order to oppose the pressure of the Philistines with more strength and to adapt to the states of the surrounding nations, the twelve tribes of Israel, which still had a large degree of independence under the local acting leaders, joined together to form a political unity under Saul, the first king of Israel. His main task was to liberate Israel from Philistine domination. However, Saul had a rather unbalanced character; he was saddled with a deep suspicion of everyone around him and was not equal to the task. The man who eventually succeeded in achieving true independent unity for Israel was David, whose qualities were so exceptional that after Saul's death he was recognized as king first by his own tribe of Judah and later by all of Israel.

David and Saul came across each other at an early stage. There are two traditional versions of their meeting. According to 1 Samuel 16:14-23, David was called to the court to dispel Saul's melancholy by playing his harp. In the other story, which follows this one, he is an unknown shepherd boy who brings food to his older brothers in Saul's army camp and attracts attention by being the only one with enough courage to engage in a fight against the raging giant in the Philistine ranks.

David Defeats Goliath

Of all the events in David's active life, the decisive duel with Goliath always appeals most to the imagination. In early Christian and medieval art, David's defeat of Goliath was viewed as anticipating Christ's victory over Satan. In Italian Renaissance art the beautiful figure of the young shepherd with his sword and the Philistine's head was used as the perfect symbol of the hero who shows that weakness combined with shrewdness is superior to brute force.

Rembrandt's only representation of this subject is in one of the four prints for the book *Piedra Gloriosa* (The Glorious Stone) by the Jewish scholar Menasseh ben Israel (see p. 47). In his view, the stone which killed Goliath is a symbol of the Messiah, upon whose arrival the nations of the world will bow to the kingdom of Israel. In this modest etching Rembrandt kept strictly to the text of the Bible. He shows us the young boy with the sling in action. As the giant reels with the impact of the stone and threatens to fall forwards, someone in the front line of the Israelite army behind David cheers and raises his hand. Rembrandt succeeded in portraying an astonishing number of men and weapons amongst the hills in the background of the print.

Etching; 10.6 × 7.4 cm. Fourth state of five.
Signed and dated: *Rembrandt f. 1655.*
Amsterdam, Rijksprentenkabinet.

Literature: Bartsch, no. 36C; Hind, no. 284; Münz, no. 183; Boon, no. 264; Filedt Kok, no. B. and B 36C/Hofstede de Groot, *Rembrandt Bijbel*, V.T.e.II; Rotermund 1963, no. 97; Tümpel 1970, no. 39.

33 And Saul said to David, Thou art not able to go against this Philistine to fight with him: for thou *art but* a youth, and he a man of war from his youth.

34 And David said unto Saul, Thy servant kept his hather's sheep, and ther came a lion, and a bear, and took a lamb out of the flock:

35 And I went out after him, and smote him, and delivered *it* out of his mouth: and when he arose against me, I caught *him* by his beard, and smote him, and slew him.

36 Thy servant slew both the lion and the bear: and this uncircumcised Philistine shall be as one of them, seeing he hath defied the armies of the living God.

37 David said moreover, The LORD that delivered me out of the paw of the lion, and out of the paw of the bear, he will deliver me out of the hand of this Philistine. And Saul said unto David, Go, and the LORD be with thee

38 And Saul armed David with his armour, and he put an helmet of brass upon his head; also he armed him with a coat of mail.

39 And David girded his sword upon his armour, and he assayed to go; for he had not proved *it*. And David said unto Saul, I cannot go with these; for I have not proved *them*. And David put them off him.

40 And he took his staff in his hand, and chose him five smooth stones out of the brook, and put them in a shepherd's bag which he had, even in a scrip; and his sling *was* in his hand: and he drew near to the Philistine.

41 And the Philistine came on and drew near unto David; and the man that bare the shield *went* before him.

42 And when the Philistine looked about, and saw David, he disdained him: for he was *but* a youth, and ruddy, and of a fair countenance.

43 And the Philistine said unto David, *Am* I a dog, that thou comest to me with staves? And the Philistine cursed David by his gods.

44 And the Philistine said to David, Come to me, and I will give thy flesh unto the fowls of the air, and to the beasts of the field.

45 Then said David to the Philistine, Thou comest to me with a sword, and with a spear, and with a shield: but I come to thee in the name of the LORD of hosts, the God of the armies of Israel, whom thou hast defied.

46 This day will the LORD deliver thee into mine hand; and I will smite thee, and take thine head from thee; and I will give the carcases of the host of the Philistines this day unto the fowls of the air, and to the wild beasts of the earth; that all the earth may know that there is a God in Israel.

47 And all this assembly shall know that the LORD saveth not with sword and spear: for the battle *is* the LORD's, and he will give you into our hands.

48 And it came to pass, when the Philistine arose, and came and drew nigh to meet David, that David hasted, and ran toward the army to meet the Philistine.

49 And David put his hand in his bag, and took thence a stone, and slang *it*, and smote the Philistine in his forehead; and he fell upon his face to the earth.

50 So David prevailed over the Philistine with a sling and with a stone, and smote the Philistine, and slew him; but *there was* no sword in the hand of David.

51 Therefore David ran, and stood upon the Philistine, and took his sword, and drew it out of the sheath thereof, and slew him, and cut off his head therewith. And when the Philistines saw their champion was dead, they fled.

52 And the men of Israel and of Judah arose, and shouted, and pursued the Philistines, until thou come to the valley, and to the gates of Ekron. And the wounded of the Philistines fell down by the way to Shaaraim, even unto Gath, and unto Ekron.

53 And the children of Israel returned from chasing after the Philistines, and they spoiled their tents. [...]

55 And when Saul saw David go forth against the Philistine, he said unto Abner, the captain of the host, Abner, whose son *is* this youth? And Abner said, *As* thy soul liveth, O king, I cannot tell.

56 And the king said, Enquire thou whose son the stripling *is*.

57 And as David returned from the slaughter of the Philistine, Abner took him, and brought him before Saul with the head of the Philistine in his hand.

58 And Saul said to him, Whose son *art* thou, *thou* young man? And David answered, *I am* the son of thy servant Jesse the Bethlehemite.

And as David returned from the slaughter of the Philistine, Abner took him, and brought him before Saul with the head of the Philistine in his hand.
And Saul said to him, Whose son art thou, thou young man? And David answered, I am the son of thy servant Jesse the Bethlehemite.
(1 Samuel 17:57-58)

This colourful panel, painted in a very free style, has a special place in Rembrandt's early work. Perhaps it should be viewed as a sketch for a larger painting intended to be shown to the person who commissioned the work before elaborating the composition to the desired size. If this is the case, the larger painting was either lost or never painted.

By situating the scene in the Israelite army camp where armed men have flocked together, Rembrandt reminds us of the recent victory over the Philistines. The scene is dominated by the heavy figure of King Saul, apparently no easy monarch. The train of his

royal gown is carried by two small pages who whisper their admiration for the young hero being presented to the King by Abner. In accordance with the traditional way in which this subject is represented, David shows Saul not only Goliath's head, as described in the Bible, but also the enormous sword of the slain giant. A red splash of paint over the left eye on the severed head indicates the place where the Philistine was felled with the stone from David's sling. The composition is flanked on the left by a seated horseman and on the right by the deliberately dark figures of a standing and a seated soldier, a group which also serves to strengthen the effect of depth in the painting.

Panel; 27.5 × 40 cm.
Signed and dated: *RH 1627.*
Basle, Öffentliche Kunstsammlung.

Literature: Bredius, no. 488; Bauch, no. 3; Gerson, no. 3; Bredius-Gerson, no. 488/Tümpel 1969, pp. 114-15.

David with Goliath's Head for Saul

And Saul eyed David from that day and forward

I Samuel 18

AND it came to pass, when he had made an end of speaking unto Saul, that the soul of Jonathan was knit with the soul of David, and Jonathan loved him as his own soul.

2 And Saul took him that day, and would let him go no more home to his father's house.

3 Then Jonathan and David made a covenant, because he loved him as his own soul.

4 And Jonathan stripped himself of the robe that *was* upon him, and gave it to David, and his garments, even to his sword, and to his bow, and to his girdle.

5 And David went out whithersoever Saul sent him, *and* behaved himself wisely: and Saul set him over the men of war, and he was accepted in the sight of all the people, and also in the sight of Saul's servants.

6 And it came to pass as they came, when David was returned from the slaughter of the Philistine, that the women came out of all cities of Israel, singing, and dancing, to meet king Saul, with tabrets, with joy, and with instruments of musick.

7 And the women answered *one another* as they played, and said, Saul hath slain his thousands, and David his ten thousands.

8 And Saul was very wroth, and the saying displeased him; and he said, They have ascribed unto David ten thousands, and to me they have ascribed *but* thousands: and *what* can he have more but the kingdom?

9 And Saul eyed David from that day and forward.

10 And it came to pass on the morrow, that the evil spirit from God came upon Saul, and he prophesied in the midst of the house: and David played with his hand, as at other times: and *there was* a javelin in Saul's hand.

11 And Saul cast the javelin; for he said, I will smite David even to the wall *with it*. And David avoided out of his presence twice.

12 And Saul was afraid of David, because the LORD was with him, and was departed from Saul.

13 Therefore Saul removed him from him, and made him his captain over a thousand; and he went out and came in before the people.

14 And David behaved himself wisely in all his ways; and the LORD *was* with him.

15 Wherefore when Saul saw that he behaved himself very wisely, he was afraid of him.

16 But all Israel and Judah loved David, because he went out and came in before them.

Saul and David

And it came to pass on the morrow, that the evil spirit from God came upon Saul, and he prophesied in the midst of the house: and David played with his hand, as at other times: and there was a javelin in Saul's hand. And Saul cast the javelin; for he said, I will smite David even unto the wall with it.
(1 Samuel 18:10-11)

The first book of Samuel describes twice - in almost the same words - how the jealous Saul attacks David with a javelin in a fit of madness while David tries to ease his melancholy with harp music. Rembrandt painted this subject in two of his works. Because of the similarities in the Biblical descriptions, it is not possible to assign either painting to a particular account.

There is no doubt that Rembrandt was familiar with Lucas van Leyden's engraving of this subject, dating from about 1508. As in Rembrandt's work, that print does not depict the actual attempted murder but the moment preceding Saul's outburst. As David plays his harp the melancholy Saul sits on his throne staring into space morosely and dejectedly, with a javelin in his hand. According to the painter and writer Carel van Mander in his *Schilder-boeck*, published in 1604, Lucas succeeded in expressing 'the essence of Saul, mindless of morals' in this print.

In the panel reproduced on the right, which was painted in Leyden, the young Rembrandt tried to achieve the same feeling. Saul's presence is one of pure aggression. The hand holding the javelin catches the full light and is exactly in the centre of the composition. David, playing his harp, is largely lost in the shadows. Only his hands touching the strings are illuminated. The painting has suffered to some extent as the result of progressive dissolving of the blue paint (Gerson).

Panel; 62 × 50 cm.
Ca. 1630.
Frankfurt am Main, Städelsches Kunstinstitut.

Literature: Bredius, no. 490; Bauch, no. 7; Gerson, no. 13; Bredius-Gerson, no. 490/Tümpel 1969, p. 138.

And the evil spirit from the Lord was upon Saul

AND Saul spake to Jonathan his son, and to all his servants, that they should kill David.

2 But Jonathan Saul's son delighted much in David: and Jonathan told David, saying, Saul my father seeketh to kill thee: now therefore, I pray thee, take heed to thyself until the morning, and abide in a secret *place,* and hide thyself:

3 And I will go out and stand beside my father in the field where thou *art,* and I will commune with my father of thee; and what I see, that I will tell thee.

4 And Jonathan spake good of David unto Saul his father, and said unto him, Let not the king sin against his servant, against David; because he hath not sinned against thee, and because his works *have been* to thee-ward very good:

5 For he did put his life in his hand, and slew the Philistine, and the LORD wrought a great

salvation for all Israel: thou sawest *it,* and didst rejoice: wherefore then wilt thou sin against innocent blood, to slay David without a cause?

6 And Saul hearkened unto the voice of Jonathan: and Saul sware, *As* the LORD liveth, he shall not be slain.

7 And Jonathan called David, and Jonathan shewed him all those things. And Jonathan brought David to Saul, and he was in his presence, as in times past.

8 And there was war again: and David went out, and fought with the Philistines, and slew them with a great slaughter; and they fled from him.

9 And the evil spirit from the LORD was upon Saul, as he sat in his house with his javelin in his hand: and David played with *his* hand.

10 And Saul sought to smite David even to the wall with the javelin; but he slipped away out of Saul's presence, and he smote the javelin into the wall: and David fled, and escaped that night.

I Samuel 19

And the evil spirit from the Lord was upon Saul, as he sat in his house with his javelin in his hand: and David played with his hand. And Saul sought to smite David even to the wall with the javelin; but he slipped out of Saul's presence, and he smote the javelin into the wall ...
(1 Samuel 19:9-10)

Despite Saul's promise to Jonathan, he made another attempt on David's life. It happened in virtually the same way as the previous attempt.

The suspicious potentate in Rembrandt's first work has given way in this large painting, dating from the second half of the 1650s, to a pitiable man who feels abandoned by God and everyone. Sinking into the deepest melancholy, Saul is at home surrounded by all the splendour of an Eastern ruler. The young harpist from Bethlehem kneels before him trying to cheer up the King with his music. But it is to no avail. The tortured man is impervious to his music and he grabs hold of the curtain to shut it out. It is fearful to see the malignancy shining in his one uncovered eye, a reflection of the 'evil spirit' which haunts Saul. It will

not be long before the slim hand, still loosely resting on his javelin, grips hold of the weapon to pin David to the wall.

The canvas was once cut in two with the intention of making two paintings. When it was restored, the section above David, which was lost, was replaced by a plain background. It is not unlikely that originally there were one or more figures observing events in the background.

Canvas; 130.5 × 164 cm.
Ca. 1655-60.
The Hague, Mauritshuis.

Saul and David

Literature: Bredius, no. 526; Bauch, no. 35; Bredius-Gerson, no. 526 (work by one or more pupils based on a design by Rembrandt)/Hofstede de Groot, *Rembrandt Bijbel,* V.T.p.18; H.E. van Gelder, *Rembrandt: Saul en David, Petrus verloochent Christus* (Saul and David, Peter denies Christ), Leiden 1948; Rotermund 1963, p. 97; Tümpel 1969, p. 138; Tümpel 1970, under no. 24.

113

The LORD *be* between thee and me for ever

I Samuel 20 AND David fled from Naioth in Ramah, and came and said before Jonathan, What have I done? what *is* mine iniquity? and what *is* my sin before thy father, that he seeketh my life?

2 And he said unto him, God forbid; thou shalt not die: behold, my father will do nothing either great or small, but that he will shew it me: and why should my father hide this thing from me? it *is* not *so*.

3 And David sware moreover, and said, Thy father certainly knoweth that I have found grace in thine eyes; and he saith, Let not Jonathan know this, lest he be grieved: but truly *as* the LORD liveth, and *as* thy soul liveth, *there is* but a step between me and death.

4 Then said Jonathan unto David, Whatsoever thy soul desireth, I will even do *it* for thee.

5 And David said unto Jonathan, Behold, to morrow *is* the new moon, and I should not fail to sit with the king at meat: but let me go, that I may hide myself in the field unto the third *day* at even.

6 If thy father at all miss me, then say, David earnestly asked *leave* of me that he might run to Bethlehem his city: for *there is* a yearly sacrifice there for all the family.

7 If he say thus, *It is* well; thy servant shall have peace: but if he be very wroth, *then* be sure that evil is determined by him.

8 Therefore thou shalt deal kindly with thy servant; for thou hast brought thy servant into a covenant of the LORD with thee: notwithstanding, if there be in me iniquity, slay me thyself; for why shouldest thou bring me to thy father?

9 And Jonathan said, Far be it from thee: for if I knew certainly that evil were determined by my father to come upon thee, then would not I tell it thee?

10 Then said David to Jonathan, Who shall tell me? or what *if* thy father answer thee roughly?

11 And Jonathan said unto David, Come, and let us go out into the field. And they went out both of them into the field. [...]

David's Parting from Jonathan

And as soon as the lad was gone, David arose out of a place toward the south, and fell on his face to the ground, and bowed himself three times: and they kissed one another, and wept one with another ...
(1 Samuel 20:41)

Unlike the jealous Saul, who felt threatened by David's success, Jonathan, his son, felt a great love and admiration for the young hero. Immediately after David's defeat of Goliath he made a covenant with him, '... because he loved him as his own soul. And Jonathan stripped himself of the robe that was upon him, and gave it to David, and his garments, even to his sword, and to his bow, and to his girdle' (1 Samuel 18:3-4). As the clothes a person wore in those days were regarded as a part of the person wearing them, this gesture of Jonathan's meant that he wished to bind himself wholly to David. In the conflict between Saul and his successor, the 'crown prince' from the very beginning chose the part of David, friendship with him being more important to him than the crown.

In the representations of David's parting from Jonathan, another Old Testament theme first depicted in a painting by Pieter Lastman, Jonathan is generally clearly older than David. This is also the case in Rembrandt's work. The youthful David with his yellow-gold hair has just appeared from his hiding place 'by the stone donkey'. Weeping, he throws himself into the arms of Jonathan, who not only embraces him in great friendship, but also supports him. In David's shining garments, the beautiful sword hanging at his side, the cloak, the bow and the bundle of arrows lying on the ground next to him, we recognize the gifts he received from Jonathan when they sealed their friendship. The dark, cloudy sky over the city in the background is a reminder of the danger threatening David from Saul, who hates him so much that he no longer even wants to say his name when talking to Jonathan about him and merely refers to 'the son of Jesse' (see verses 27 and 31).

The painting, which was in the past incorrectly interpreted as of Absalom's return to his father David (see 2 Samuel 14:33), was bought in 1760 at an auction in Amsterdam for Fl. 80 under the title *David and Jonathan* for the collection of Tsar Peter the Great who was visiting the Netherlands for the second time. It was the first of the many paintings by Rembrandt which went to Russia in the course of the 18th century.

Panel; 73 × 61.5 cm.
Signed and dated: *Rembrandt f. 1642.*
Leningrad, The Hermitage.

Literature: Bredius, no. 511; Bauch, no. 24; Gerson, no. 207; Bredius-Gerson, no. 511/Tümpel 1969, pp. 140-46.

18 Then Jonathan said to David, To morrow *is* the new moon: and thou shalt be missed, because thy seat will be empty.

19 And *when* thou hast stayed three days, *then* thou shalt go down quickly, and come to the place where thou didst hide thyself when the business was *in hand,* and shalt remain by the stone Ezel.

20 And I will shoot three arrows on the side *thereof,* as though I shot at a mark.

21 And, behold, I will send a lad, *saying,* Go, find out the arrows. If I expressly say unto the lad, Behold, the arrows *are* on this side of thee, take them; then come thou: for *there is* peace to thee, and no hurt; *as* the LORD liveth.

22 But if I say thus unto the young man, Behold, the arrows *are* beyond thee; go thy way: for the LORD hath sent thee away.

23 And *as thouching* the matter which thou and I have spoken of, behold, the LORD *be* between thee and me for ever.

24 So David hid himself in the field: and when the new moon was come, the king sat him down to eat meat.

25 And the king sat upon his seat, as at other times, *even* upon a seat by the wall: and Jonathan arose, and Abner sat by Saul's side, and David's place was empty.

26 Nevertheless Saul spake not any thing that day: for he thought, Something hath befallen him, he *is* not clean; surely he *is* not clean.

27 And it came to pass on the morrow, *which was* the second *day* of the month, that David's place *was* emtpy: and Saul said unto Jonathan his son, Wherefore cometh not the son of Jesse to meat, neither yesterday, nor to day?

28 And Jonathan answered Saul, David earnestly asked *leave* of me *to go* to Bethlehem:

29 And he said. Let me go, I pray thee; for our family hath a sacrify in the city; and my brother, he hath commanded me *to be there:* and now, if I have found favour in thine eyes, let met get away, I pray thee, and see my brethren. Therefore he cometh not unto the king's table.

30 Then Saul's anger was kindled against Jonathan, and he said unto him, Thou son of the perverse rebellious *woman,* do not I know that thou hast chosen the son of Jesse to thine own confusion, and unto the confusion of thy mother's nakedness?

31 For as long as the son of Jesse liveth upon the ground, thou shalt not be established, nor thy kingdom. Wherefore now send and fetch him unto me, for he shall surely die.

32 And Jonathan answered Saul his father, and said unto him, Wherefore shall he be slain? what hath he done?

33 And Saul cast a javelin at him to smite him: whereby Jonathan knew that it was determined of his father to slay David.

34 So Jonathan arose from the table in fierce anger, and did eat no meat the second day of the month: for he was grieved for David because his father had done him shame.

35 And it came to pass in the morning, that Jonathan went out into the field at the time appointed with David, and a little lad with him.

36 And he said unto his lad, Run, find out now the arrows which I shoot. *And* as the lad ran, he shot an arrow beyond him.

37 And when the lad was come to the place of the arrow which Jonathan had shot, Jonathan cried after the lad, and said, *is* not the arrow beyond thee?

38 And Jonathan cried after the lad, Make speed, haste, stay not. And Jonathan's lad gathered up the arrows, and came to his master.

39 But the lad knew not any thing: only Jonathan and David knew the matter.

40 And Jonathan gave his artillery unto his lad, and said unto him, Go, carry *them* to the city.

41 *And* as soon as the lad was gone, David arose out of *a place* toward the south, and fell on his face to the ground, and bowed himself three times: and they kissed one another, and wept one with another, until David exceeded.

42 And Jonathan said to David, Go in peace, forasmuch as we have sworn both of us in the name of the LORD, saying, The LORD be between me and thee, and between my seed and thy seed for ever.

And as soon as the lad was gone, David arose out of a place toward the south, and fell on his face to the ground, and bowed himself three times: and they kissed one another, and wept one with another ...
(1 Samuel 20:41)

This drawing, dating from the first half of the 1640s, is charged with the same emotional tension as the painting on the previous page, dating from 1642.

In this case the two friends meet on the banks of a peaceful river in a valley a long way from the town. Their figures are reflected in the water. The desolation of the wide landscape adds an extra dimension to the parting scene.

There are many indications that for his interpretations of this subject Rembrandt was inspired not only by the Bible text but also by the relevant story by Flavius Josephus. From his 1656 inventory we know that he had a Hochdeutsch edition of Josephus' writings 'illuminated with drawings by Tobias Timmerman' (Hofstede de Groot, *Urkunden* 169, no. 284). In this edition, which was published in 1574 and illustrated with prints by Tobias Stimmer, the relevant

passage describes how David threw himself at Jonathan's feet and called him a 'Protector and The Saviour of his Life'. However, Jonathan raised him up from the earth and fell about his neck. They kissed each other and bewailed their miserable fate.

David succeeded in escaping from Saul and in the desert he managed to assemble a band of four hundred men, all as free as he. He became their independent leader. In the skirmishes with Saul, who continued to pursue him, he twice had an opportunity to kill the King but he had too much respect for 'the anointed of the Lord' to slay him.

Pen and brush drawing; 18.2 × 23.5 cm.
Bottom left in later handwriting: *Rimbrant 1634.*
Ca. 1640-45.
Paris, The Louvre.

Literature: Benesch III, no. 552 (*ca.* 1643-44); Slive I, no. 187 (*ca.* 1642)/Rotermund 1963, no. 101 (the illustration is that of a copy which is also in the Louvre); Tümpel 1969, pp. 140-46.

David's Parting from Jonathan

God is departed from me, and answereth me no more

I Samuel 28 3 Now Samuel was dead, and all Israel had lamented him, and buried him in Ramah, even in his own city. And Saul had put away those that had familiar spirits, and the wizards, out of the land.

4 And the Philistines gathered themselves together, and came and pitched in Shunem: and Saul gathered all Israel together, and they pitched in Gilboa.

5 And when Saul saw the host of the Philistines, he was afraid, and his heart greatly trembled.

6 And when Saul enquired of the LORD, the LORD answered him not, neither by dreams, nor by Urim, nor by prophets.

7 Then said Saul unto his servants, Seek me a woman that hath a familiar spirit, that I may go to her, and enquire of her. And his servants said to him, Behold, *there is a* woman that hath a familiar spirit at Endor.

8 And Saul disguised himself, and put on other raiment, and he went, and two men with him, and they came to the woman by night: and he said, I pray thee, divine unto me by the familiar spirit, and bring me *him* up, whom I shall name unto thee.

9 And the woman said unto him, Behold, thou knowest what Saul hath done, how he hath cut off those that have familiar spirits, and the wizards, out of the land: wherefore then layest thou a snare for my life, to cause me to die?

10 And Saul sware to her by the LORD, saying, *As* the LORD liveth, there shall no punishment happen to thee for this king.

11 Then said the woman, Whom shall I bring up unto thee? And he said, Bring me up Samuel.

12 And when the woman saw Samuel, she cried with a loud voice: and the woman spake to Saul, saying, Why hast thou deceived me? for thou *art* Saul.

13 And the king said unto her, Be not afraid: for what sawest thou? And the woman said unto Saul, I saw gods ascending out of the earth.

14 And he said unto her, What form *is* he of? And she said, An old man cometh up; and he *is* covered with a mantle. And Saul perceived that is *was* Samuel, and het stopped with *his* face to the ground, and bowed himself.

15 And Samuel said to Saul, Why hast thou disquieted me, to bring me up? And Saul answered, I am sore distressed: for the Philistines make war against me, and God is departed from me, and answereth me no more, neither by prophets, nor by dreams: therefore I have called thee, that thou mayest make known unto me what I shall do.

16 Then said Samuel, Wherefore then dost thou ask of me, seeing the LORD is departed from thee, and is become thine enemy?

17 And the LORD hath done to him, as he spake by me: for the LORD hath rent the kingdom out of thine hand, and given it to thy neighbour, *even* tot David:

18 Because thou obeyedst not the voice of the LORD, nor executedst his fierce wrath upon Amalek, therefore hath the LORD done this thing unto thee this day.

19 Moreover the LORD will also deliver Israel with thee into the hand of the Philistines: and to morrow *shalt* thou and thy sons *be* with me: the LORD also shall deliver the host of Israel into the hand of the Philistines.

20 Then Saul fell straightway all along on the earth, and was sore afraid, because the words of Samuel: and there was no strength in him; for he had eaten no bread all the day, nor all the night.

21 And the woman came unto Saul, and saw that he was sore troubled, and said unto him, Behold, thine handmaid hath obeyed thy voice, and I have put my life in my hand, and have hearkened unto thy words which thou spakest unto me.

22 Now therefore, I pray thee, hearken thou also unto the voice of thine handmaid, and let me set a morsel of bread before thee; and eat, that thou mayest have strength, when thou goest on thy way.

23 But he refused, and said, I will not eat. But his servants, together with the woman, compelled him; and he hearkened unto their voice. So he arose from the earth, and sat upon the bed.

24 And the woman had a fat calf in the house; and she hasted, and killed it, and took flour, and kneaded *it,* and did bake unleavened bread thereof:

25 And she brought *it* before Saul, and before his servants; and they did eat. Then they rose up, and went away that night.

… *let me set a morsel of bread before thee; and eat, that thou mayest have strength, when thou goest on thy way. But he refused, and said, I will not eat. But his servants, together with the woman, compelled him; and he hearkened unto their voice. So he arose from the earth, and sat upon the bed. And the woman had a fat calf in the house; and she hasted and killed it, and took flour and kneaded it, and did bake unleavened bread thereof. And she brought it before Saul, and before his servants, and they did eat.*
(I Samuel 28:22-25)

The famous episode of Saul's secret visit to a woman who has powers of soothsaying is the only story in the Old Testament about contacting the dead, a practice which was strictly forbidden in Israel but did happen clandestinely. Saul is in such a desperate situation that, now that the Lord no longer answers him, he can see no other way than to contact Samuel, who had died some time before. In better times this prophet had often told him, on behalf of God, what he must do.

While the depictions of this story by other artists without exception show the dramatic scene in which the spirit of Samuel, summoned by Saul, predicts the latter's downfall, the two known drawings by Rembrandt, both dating from the 1650s, show the much more peaceful concluding scene. When Saul has revived, he and his men are given a big meal by their hospitable hostess.

The version shown here is the later one, with a richer content which reveals the total tragedy of Saul. While his two companions are enjoying the meal which has been served, he stares disconsolately into space and refuses to eat. Doomed to die on the battlefield with his sons the next day, he seems already to feel like a stranger in the land of the living.

Drawing in pen and ink; 15.6 × 23.5 cm.
Ca. 1655.
The Hague, Museum Bredius.

Literature: Benesch V, no. 1028 (*ca.* 1657); Slive II, no. 503 (*ca.* 1655)/Rotermund 1963, under no. 105.

Saul with his Servants Visits the Woman in Endor

How are the mighty fallen!

[In the fateful battle on Mount Gilboa the army of the Israelites suffers a heavy defeat against the Philistines. When Saul realizes he is lost, he takes his own life. Jonathan and his other two sons have already died in the battle.]

II Samuel 1 NOW it came to pass after the dead of Saul, when David was returned from the slaughter of the Amalekites, and David had abode two days in Ziklag;

2 It came even to pass on the third day, that, behold, a man came out of the camp from Saul with his clothes rent, and earth upon his head: and so it was, when he came to David, that he fell to the earth, and did obeisance.

3 And David said unto him, From whence comest thou? And he said unto him, Out of the camp of Israel am I escaped.

4 And David said to him, How went the matter? I pray thee, tell me. And he answered, That the people are fled from the battle, and many of the people also are fallen and dead; and Saul and Jonathan his son are dead also.

5 And David said unto the young man that told him, How knowest thou that Saul and Jonathan his son be dead?

6 And the young man that told him said, As I happened by chance upon mount Gilboa, behold, Saul leaned upon his spear; and, lo, the chariots and horsemen followed hard after him.

7 And when he looked behind him, he saw me, and called unto me. And I answered, Here *am* I.

8 And he said unto me. Who *art* thou? And I answered him, I *am* an Amalekite.

9 He said unto me again, Stand, I pray thee, upon me, and slay me: for anguish is come upon me, because my life *is* yet whole in me.

10 So I stood upon him, and slew him, because I was sure that he could not live after that he was fallen: and I took the crown that *was* upon his head, and the bracelet that *was* on his arm, and have brought them hither unto my LORD.

11 Then David took hold on his clothes, and rent them; and likewise all the men that *were* with him:

12 And they mourned, and wept, and fasted until even, for Saul, and for Jonathan his son, and for the people of the LORD, and for the house of Israel; because they were fallen by the sword.

13 And David said unto the young man that told him, Whence *art* thou? And he answered, I *am* the son of a stranger, an Amalekite.

14 And David said unto him, How wast thou not afraid to stretch forth thine hand to destroy the LORD's anointed?

15 And David called one of the young men, and said, Go near, *and* fall upon him. And he smote him that he died.

16 And David said unto him, Thy blood *be* upon thy head; for thy mouth hath testified against thee, saying, I have slain the LORD's anointed.

17 And David lamented with his lamentation over Saul and over Jonathan his son:

18 (Also he bade them teach the children of Judah *the use of* the bow: behold, *it is* written in the book of Jasher.)

19 The beauty of Israel is slain upon thy high places: how are the mighty fallen!

20 Tell *it* not in Gath, publish *it* not in the streets of Askelon; lest the daughters of the Philistines rejoice, lest the daughters of the uncircumcised triumph.

21 Ye mountains of Gilboa, *let there be* no dew, neither *let there be* rain, upon you, nor fields of offerings: for there the shield of the mighty is vilely cast away, the shield of Saul, *as though he had* not *been* anointed with oil.

22 From the blood of the slain, from the fat of the mighty, the bow of Jonathan turned not back, and the sword of Saul returned not empty.

23 Saul and Jonathan *were* lovely and pleasant in their lives, and in their death they were not divided: they were swifter than eagles, they were stronger than lions.

24 Ye daughters of Israel, weep over Saul, who clothed you in scarlet, with *other* delights, who put on ornaments of gold upon your apparel.

25 How are the mighty fallen in the midst of the battle! O Jonathan, *thou wast* slain in thine high places.

26 I am distressed for thee, my brother Jonathan: very pleasant hast thou been unto me: thy love to me was wonderful, passing the love of women.

27 How are the mighty fallen, and the weapons of war perished!

And David said unto the young man that told him, Whence art thou? And he answered, I am the son of a stranger, an Amalekite. And David said unto him, How wast thou not afraid to stretch forth thine hand to destroy the Lord's anointed? And David called one of the young men, and said, Go near, and fall upon him.
(2 Samuel 1:13-15)

In order to be out of Saul's reach, David had retreated to Philistine territory with his men some time before. When he was informed of Saul's death, he had just returned to his home there from a military expedition against the Amalekites. The bearer of the 'good' tidings no doubt expected to receive a large reward from this 'enemy of Saul', but in saying that he had personally killed the King, he uttered his own death sentence.

In Rembrandt's drawing of this scene the stark contours and heavy hanging drapes create a threatening atmosphere, suggesting the dire consequences of David's indignation. Contemptuously suppressing his rage, the future king looks down on the man bearing Saul's crown. We are waiting only for the sign from David to his servant, who stands next to the throne with a sword, ready to carry out the sentence.

Pen and brush drawing; 17 × 19.4 cm.
Ca. 1640-45.
Amsterdam, Rijksprentenkabinet.

Literature: Benesch III, no. 506 (*ca.* 1640-42); Slive II, no. 332 (*ca.* 1640-43)/Rotermund 1963, no. 106; 'Bijbelse Inspiratie', no. 72.

David Receives the Tidings of Saul's Death

Is not this Bathsheba, the wife of Uriah?

[When David was recognized as King, first by his own tribe of Judah and later by the other tribes of Israel, he moved his court from Hebron to the city of Jerusalem, which had been taken from the Jebusites and was not burdened by tribal traditions. When he also took the Ark of the Covenant to the new capital, he made Jerusalem the religious centre of the kingdom. Joab, David's best general, who had won one victory after another on the battlefield, was at the head of the army.]

II Samuel 11   AND it came to pass, after the yaer was expired, at the time when kings go forth *to battle,* that David sent Joab, and his servants with him, and all Israel; and they destroyed the children of Ammon, and besieged Rabbah. But David tarried still at Jerusalem.

2 And it came to pass in an eveningtide, that David arose from off his bed, and walked upon the roof of the king's house: and from the roof he saw a woman washing herself; and the woman *was* very beautiful to look upon.

3 And David sent and enquired after the woman. And *one* said, *Is* not this Bathsheba, the daughter of Eliam, the wife of Uriah the Hittite?

4 And David sent messengers, and took her; and she came in unto him, and he lay with her; for she was purified from her uncleanness: and she returned unto her house.

5 And the woman conceived, and sent and told David, and said, I *am* with child.

6 And David sent to Joab, *saying,* Send me Uriah the Hittite. And Joab sent Uriah to David.

7 And when Uriah was come unto him, David demanded of *him* how Joab did, and how the people did, and how the war prospered.

8 And David said to Uriah, Go down to thy house, and wash thy feet. And Uriah departed out of the king's house, and there followed him a mess *of meat* from the king.

9 But Uriah slept at the door of the king's house with all the servants of his lord, and went not down to his house.

10 And when they had told David, saying, Uriah went down unto his house, David said unto Uriah, Camest thou not from *thy* journey? why *then* didst thou not go down unto thine house?

11 And Uriah said unto David, The ark, and Israel, and Judah, abide in tents; and my lord Joab, and the servants of my lord, are encamped in the open fields; shall I then go into mine house, to eat and to drink, and to lie with my wife? *as* thou livest, and *as* thy soul liveth I will not do this thing.

12 And David said to Uriah, Tarry here to day also, and to morrow I will let thee depart. So Uriah abode in Jerusalem that day, and the morrow.

13 And when David had called him, he did eat and drink before him; and he made him drunk: and at even he went out to lie on his bed with the servants of his lord, but went not down to his house.

Bathsheba with the Letter from King David

... and from the roof he saw a woman washing herself; and the woman was very beautiful to look upon. And David sent and enquired after the woman. And one said, Is this not Bathsheba, the daughter of Eliam, the wife of Uriah the Hittite?
(2 Samuel 11:2-4)

As one of the few Bible stories in which it was possible to depict a female nude in her full beauty, the story of David and Bathsheba was a very popular theme with Renaissance and baroque artists. Usually these artists chose the moment at which King David, standing on the roof terrace of his palace, sees the beautiful woman sitting by the pool in her garden. In some versions there is even a messenger who has come to tell her what David wants of her.

In this large painting by Rembrandt, generally acknowledged as one of his finest works, this moment has already passed. Apart from a servant quietly doing her work, it shows only Bathsheba, deep in thought, holding in her hand the letter from the King, summoning her to tell her she has no choice. His fate is sealed. A sad calm surrounds the motionless woman, giving some indication of how much she must suffer.

X-rays have shown that Bathsheba's slightly bowed head was originally painted held higher. It was only when the painting was virtually completed that Rembrandt gave her the contemplative look which the observer finds so moving.

Canvas; 142 × 142 cm.
Signed and dated: *Rembrandt ft 1654.*
Paris, The Louvre.

Literature: Bredius, no. 521; Bauch, no. 31; Gerson, no. 271; Bredius-Gerson, no. 521.

14 And it came to pass in the morning, that David wrote a letter to Joab, and sent *it* by the hand of Uriah.

15 And he wrote in the letter, saying, Set ye Uriah in the forfront of the hottest battle, and retire ye from him, that he may be smitten, and die.

16 And it came to pass, when Joab observed the city, that he assigned Uriah unto a place where he knew that valiant men *were*.

17 And the men of the city went out, and fought with Joab: and there fell *some* of the people of the servants of David; and Uriah the Hittite died also.

18 Then Joab sent and told David all the things concerning the war;

19 And charged the messenger, saying, When thou hast made an end of telling the matters of the war unto the king,

20 And if so that be the king's wrath arise, and he say unto thee, Wherefore approached ye so nigh unto the city when ye did fight? knew ye not that they would shoot from the wall?

21 Who smote Abimelech the son of Jerubbesheth? did not a woman cast a piece of a millstone upon him from the wall, that he died in Thebez? Why went ye nigh the wall? then say thou, Thy servant Uriah the Hittite is dead also.

22 So the messenger went, and came and shewed David all that Joab had sent him for.

23 And the messenger said unto David, Surely the men prevailed against us, and came out unto us into field, and we were upon them even unto the entering of the gate.

24 And the shooters shot from off the wall upon thy servants; and *some* of the king's servants be dead, and thy servant Uriah the Hittite is dead also.

25 Then David said unto the messenger, Thus shalt thou say unto Joab, Let not this thing displease thee, for the sword devoureth one as well as another: make thy battle more strong against the city, and overthrow it: and encourage thou him.

26 And when the wife of Uriah heard that Uriah her husband was dead, she mourned for her husband.

27 And when the mourning was past, David sent and fetched her to his house, and she became his wife, and bare him a son. But the thing that David had done displeased the LORD.

David is Notified of Uriah's Death

And the messenger said unto David, Surely the men prevailed against us, and came out unto us into the field, and we were upon them even unto the entering of the gate. And the shooters shot from off the wall upon thy servants; and some of the king's servants be dead, and thy servant Uriah the Hittite is dead also.
(2 Samuel 11:23-24)

Out of solidarity with his comrades on the front, Uriah had twice refused to 'co-operate' in relieving David of his unwanted fatherhood. Finally the King saw no other way than to send Bathsheba's betrayed husband back to the front, bearing his own death sentence. David had no need to doubt Joab's help.

The drawing reproduced here brilliantly depicts the moment at which Joab's messenger comes to David to tell him Uriah has perished. He holds the proof in his hands, Uriah's armour. This is a device Rembrandt thought of himself which enabled him to show how the restless David, plagued by his bad conscience, is shocked when he is confronted with his terrible crime. To indicate that David's peace of mind is destroyed for ever, Rembrandt reveals the prophet Nathan behind Joab's messenger, anticipating the next episode in the story. He is to admonish David and declare the punishment for his crime.

Like the next two drawings, this drawing dates from the first half of the 1650s. Together with the painting dating from 1654 shown on the previous page and the etching of the penitent David dating from 1652 (p. 129), it shows how intensely concerned Rembrandt was with the drama of David and Bathsheba during this period.

Drawing in pen; 19.5 × 29 cm.
Underneath in two different later handwritings:
Rembrand van Rhijn and *Rembrant van Rein*.
Ca. 1650-55.
Amsterdam, Rijksprentenkabinet.

Literature: Benesch V, no. 890 (*ca.* 1652); Slive II, no. 432
(*ca.* 1650-52); Haak, no. 63 (*ca.* 1650-55)/Rotermund 1963,
no. 108; 'Bijbelse Inspiratie', no. 73.

Thou *art* the man

AND the Lord sent Hathan unto David. And he came unto him, and said unto him, There were two men in one city; the one rich, and the other poor.

2 The rich *man* had exceeding many flocks and herds:

3 But the poor *man* had nothing, save one little ewe lamb, which he had bought and nourished up: and it grew up together with him, and with his children; it did eat of his own meat, and drank of his own cup, and lay in his bosom, and was unto him as a daughter.

4 And there came a traveller unto the rich man, and he spared to take of his own flock and of his own herd, to dress for the wayfaring man that was come unto him; but took the poor man's lamb, and dressed it for the man that was come to him.

5 And David's anger was greatly kindled against the man; and he said to Nathan, *As* the Lord liveth, the man that hath done this *thing* shall surely die:

6 And he shall restore the lamb fourfold, because he did this thing, and because he had no pity.

7 And Nathan said to David, Thou *art* the man. Thus saith the Lord God of Israel, I anointed thee king over Israel, and I delivered thee out of the hand of Saul;

8 And I gave thee thy master's house, and thy master's wives into thy bosom, and gave thee the house of Israel and of Judah; and if *that had been* too little, I would moreover have given unto thee such and such things.

9 Wherefore hast thou despised the commandment of the Lord, to do evil in this sight? thou has killed Uriah the Hittite with the sword, and hast taken his wife *to be* thy wife, and hast slain him with the sword of the children of Ammon.

10 Now therefore the sword shall never depart from thine house; because thou hast despised me, and hast taken the wife of Uriah the Hittite to be thy wife.

11 Thus said the Lord, Behold, I will raise up evil against thee out of thine own house, and I will take thy wives before thine eyes, and give *them* unto thy neighbour, and he shall lie with thy wives in the sight of this sun.

12 For thou didst *it* secretly: but I will do this thing before all Israel, and before the sun.

13 And David said unto Nathan, I have sinned against the Lord. And Nathan said unto David, The Lord also hath put away thy sin; thou shalt not die.

14 Howbeit, because by this deed thou hast given great occasion to the enemies of the Lord to blaspheme, the child also *that is* born unto thee shall surely die.

15 And Nathan departed unto his house. And the Lord struck the child that Uriah's wife bare unto David, and it was very sick.

16 David therefore besought God for the child; and David fasted, and went in, and lay all night upon the earth.

17 And the elders of his house arose, *and went* to him, to raise him up from the earth: but he would not, either did he eat bread with them.

18 And it came to pass on the seventh day, that the child died. And the servants of David feared to tell him that the child was dead: for they said, Behold, while the child was yet alive, we spake unto him, and he would not hearken unto our voice: how will he then vex himself, if we tell him that the child is dead?

19 But when David saw that his servants whispered, David perceived that the child was dead: therefore David said unto his servants, Is the child dead? And they said, He is dead.

20 Then David arose from the earth, and washed, and anointed *himself,* and changed his apparel, and came into the house of the Lord, and worshipped: then he came to his own house; and when he required, they set bread before him, and he did eat.

21 Then said his servants unto him, What thing *is* this that thou hast done? thou didst fast and weep for the child, *while it was* alive; but when the child was dead, thou didst rise and eat bread.

22 And he said, While the child was yet alive, I fasted and wept: for I said, Who can tell *whether* God will be gracious to me, that the child may live?

23 But now he is dead, wherefore should I fast? can I bring him back again? I shall go to him, but he shall not return to me.

24 And David comforted Bathsheba his wife, and went in unto her, and lay with her: and she bare a son, and he called his name Solomon: and the Lord loved him.

And Nathan said to David, Thou art the man. Thus saith the Lord God of Israel ... thou hast killed Uriah the Hittite with the sword, and hast taken his wife to be thy wife, and hast slain him with the sword of the children of Ammon. Now therefore the sword shall never depart from thine house; because thou hast despised me, and hast taken the wife of Uriah the Hittite to be thy wife.
(2 Samuel 12:7,9-10)

By means of his story about a rich man who steals the only lamb of his poor neighbour in order to spare one of his own flock, Nathan succeeded in making the King pronounce his own judgment: 'As the Lord liveth, the man that hath done this thing shall surely die.' David is completely overwhelmed and does not know what to do.

In this drawing Rembrandt depicts the situation that has arisen in impressive images. When Nathan tells David the truth in simple terms, the King, in full regalia, deeply and sincerely repents.

Pen and brush drawing; 14.6 × 17.3 cm.
Ca. 1650-55.
Berlin, Kupferstichkabinett der Staatlichen Museen.

Literature: Benesch V, no. 947 (*ca.* 1654-55); Slive I, no. 211 (*ca.* 1655)/Hofstede de Groot, *Rembrandt Bijbel*, V.T.d.24; Rotermund 1963, no. 110; 'Bijbelse Inspiratie', under no. 73; Tümpel 1970, no. 24.

*Nathan Before
King David*

Nathan Before
King David

And David said unto Nathan, I have sinned against the
Lord. And Nathan said unto David, the Lord also hath put
away thy sin; thou shalt not die. Howbeit, because by this
deed thou hast given great occasion to the enemies of the
Lord to blaspheme, the child also that is born unto thee
shall surely die.
(2 Samuel 12:13-14)

The moment depicted here immediately follows on
from Rembrandt's previous version of this subject. The
King is ashamed as he admits his guilt and the prophet
comes to him with God's forgiveness.
   The way in which King David is characterized
reveals the influence of the 17th-century miniatures
which were the basis for a series of drawings by
Rembrandt in about 1655 (Benesch V, no. 1187-1206).

Pen and brush drawing; 18.3 × 25.2 cm.
Ca. 1650-55.
New York, The Metropolitan Museum of Art,
H.O. Havemeyer Collection.

Literature: Benesch V, no. 948 (*ca.* 1654-55); Slive I, no.
149 (*ca.* 1655-56)/Rotermund 1963, no. III; 'Bijbelse
Inspiratie', under no. 73; Tümpel 1970, under no. 24.

And the Lord struck the child that Uriah's wife bare unto David, and it was very sick. David therefore besought God for the child; and David fasted, and went in, and lay all night upon the earth. And the elders of his house arose, and went to him, to raise him up from the earth: but he would not ...
(2 Samuel 12:15-17)

The harp lying in the foreground clearly shows that this character is King David. Divested of all his splendour, he has shut himself in his bedchamber to fast and to pray for the life of his mortally ill child. He uses the words of Psalm 51:

Have mercy upon me, O God, according to thy loving-kindness; according unto the multitude of thy tender mercies blot out my transgressions.
Wash me thoroughly from mine iniquity, and cleanse me from my sin.
For I acknowledge my transgressions: and my sin is ever before me.
Against thee, thee only, have I sinned, and done this evil in thy sight; that thou mightest be justified when thou speakest, and be clear when thou judgest.
(Psalm 51:1-4)

The admirable simplicity with which the expressive scene has been composed makes this small etching one of Rembrandt's most perfect works of art.

The rest of the story of David is rarely represented in Rembrandt's surviving work, though there were some extremely dramatic moments in it. When David became old there was a fierce struggle between his sons for the throne. This power struggle shook David's kingdom to its very foundations, particularly when Absalom rebelled against his father. Peace was only restored when Solomon, the son of David and Bathsheba, was crowned king. 'So David slept with his fathers, and was buried in the city of David. And the days that David reigned over Israel were forty years: seven years reigned he in Hebron, and thirty and three years reigned he in Jerusalem. Then sat Solomon upon the throne of David his father; and his kingdom was established greatly' (1 Kings 2:10-12).

Etching; 14.3 × 9.3 cm. First state of three.
Signed and dated: *Rembrandt f. 1652.*
Amsterdam, Rijksprentenkabinet.

Literature: Bartsch, no. 41; Hind, no. 258; Münz, no. 182; Boon, no. 236; Filedt Kok, no. B 41/Hofstede de Groot, *Rembrandt Bijbel*, V.T.e.12; Rotermund 1963, no. 112; Tümpel 1970, no. 25.

David at Prayer

Whither thou goest, I will go

Ruth 1 NOW it came to pass in the days when the judges ruled, that there was a famine in the land. And a certain man of Bethlehem-judah went tot sojourn in the country of Moab, he, and his wife, and his two sons.

2 And the name of the man was Elimelech, and the name of his wife Naomi, and the name of his two sons Mahlon and Chilion, Ephrathites of Bethlehem-judah. And they came into the country of Moab, and continued there.

3 And Elimelech Naomi's husband died; and she was left, and her two sons.

4 And they took them wives of women of Moab; the name of the one *was* Orpah, and the name of the other Ruth: and they dwelled there about ten years.

5 And Mahlon and Chilion died also both of them; and the woman was left of her two sons and her husband.

6 Then she arose with her daughters in law, that she might return from the country of Moab: for she had heard in the country of Moab how that the LORD had visited his people in giving them bread.

7 Wherefore she went forth out of the place where she was, and her two daughters in law with her; and they went on the way to return unto the land of Judah.

8 And Naomi said unto her two daughters in law, Go, return each to her mother's house: the LORD deal kindly with you, as ye have dealt with the dead, and with me.

9 The LORD grant you that ye may find rest. each *of you* in the house of her husband. Then she kissed them; and they lifted up their voice, and wept.

10 And they said unto her, Surely we will return with thee unto thy people.

11 And Naomi said, Turn again, my daughters: why will ye go with me? *are* there yet *any more* sons in my womb, that they may be your husbands?

12 Turn again, my daughters, go *your way;* for I am too old to have an husband. If I should say, I have hope, *if* I should have an husband also to night, and should also bear sons;

13 Would ye tarry for them till they were grown? would ye stay for them from having husbands? nay, my daughters; for it grieveth me much for your sakes that the hand of the LORD is gone out against me.

14 And they lifted up their voice, and wept again: and Orpah kissed her mother in law; but Ruth clave unto her.

15 And she said, Behold, thy sister in law is gone back unto her people, and unto her gods: return thou after thy sister in law.

16 And Ruth said, Intreat me not to leave thee, *or* to return from following after thee: for whither thou goest, I will go; and where thou lodgest, I will lodge: thy people *shall be* my people, and thy God my God:

17 Where thou diest, will I die, and there will I be buried: the LORD do so to me, and more also, *if ought* but death part thee and me.

18 When she saw that she was stedfastly minded to go with her, then she left speaking unto her.

19 So they two went until they came to Bethlehem. And it came to pass, when they were come to Bethlehem, that all the city was moved about them, and they said, *is* this Naomi?

20 And she said unto them, Call me not Naomi, call me Mara: for the Almighty hath dealt very bitterly with me.

21 I went out full, and the LORD hath brought me home again empty: why *then* call ye me Naomi, seeing the LORD hath testified against me, and the Almighty hath afflicted me?

22 So Naomi returned, and Ruth the Moabitess, her daughter in law, with her, which returned out of the country of Moab: and they came to Bethlehem in the beginning of barley harvest.

And she said, Behold, thy sister in law is gone back unto her people, and unto her gods: return thou after thy sister in law. And Ruth said, Entreat me not to leave thee, ... for whither thou goest, I will go; and where thou lodgest, I will lodge: thy people shall be my people, and thy God my God. (Ruth 1:15-16)

The idyllic story of Ruth, the Moabite great-grandmother of King David, is one of the most attractive Old Testament stories because of its fascinating charm and profound humanity. Therefore it is not surprising that the edifying little story of Ruth attracted a great deal of attention when the choice of themes was made by 16th-century artists - more than it had done previously, on account of the moral content of the story, which was in accord with the new approach to the Old Testament. In northern Dutch 17th-century paintings it was particularly Rembrandt and his pupils, following Lastman and the historical painters in his circle, who regularly chose one or more episodes from this story as a subject for their work.

Although the story of Ruth was only dealt with by Rembrandt in drawings, the number of subjects which he derived from it was larger than those chosen by the majority of his predecessors and pupils. Most of them restricted themselves to the scene in which Ruth is addressed by the wealthy farmer Boaz, as she is gleaning ears of corn (see p. 133).

In the sketch shown above, which was probably done in about 1635 or slightly later, as suggested by the flowing style of drawing, Rembrandt depicts the emotional dialogue between Ruth and Naomi on the road to Bethlehem. We see how Ruth will not be persuaded, and assures her mother-in-law that she is determined to stay with her, no matter how insecure her own future may be as a result.

Pen and ink drawing; 18 × 12.5 cm.
Ca. 1635-38.
Rotterdam, Museum Boymans-van Beuningen.

Literature: Benesch I, no. 161 (*ca.* 1636).

Ruth and Naomi

So she gleaned in the field until even

Ruth 2 AND Naomi had a kinsman of her husband's, a mighty man of wealth, of the family of Elimelech; and his name *was* Boaz.

2 And Ruth the Moabitess said unto Naomi, Let me now go to the field, and glean ears of corn after *him* in whose sight I shall find grace. And she said unto her, Go, my daughter.

3 And she went, and came, and gleaned in the field after the reapers: and her hap was to light on a part of the field *belonging* unto Boaz, who *was* of the kindred of Elimelech.

4 And, Behold, Boaz came from Bethlehem, and said unto the reapers, The LORD *be* with you. And they answered him, The LORD bless thee.

5 Then said Boaz unto his servant that was set over the reapers, Whose damsel *is* this?

6 And the servant that was set over the reapers answered and said, It *is* the Moabitish damsel that came back with Naomi out of the country of Moab:

7 And she said, I pray you, let me glean and gather after the reapers among the sheaves: so she came, and hath continued even from the morning until now, that she tarried a little in the house.

8 Then said Boaz unto Ruth, Hearest thou not, my daughter? Go not to glean in another field, neither go from hence, but abide her fast by my maidens:

9 *Let* thine eyes *be* on the field that they do reap, and go thou after them: have I not charged the young men that they shall not touch thee? and when thou art athirst, go unto the vessels, and drink of *that* which the young men have drawn.

10 Then she fell on her face, and bowed herself to the ground, and said unto him, Why have I found grace in thine eyes, that thou shouldest take knowledge of me, seeing I *am* a stranger?

11 And Boaz answered and said unto her, It hath fully been shewed me, all that thou hast done unto thy mother in law since the death of thine husband: and *how* thou hast left thy father and thy mother, and the land of thy nativity, and art come unto a people which thou knewest not heretofore.

12 The LORD recompense thy work, and a full reward be given thee of the LORD God of Israel, under whose wings thou art come to trust.

13 Then she said, Let me find favour in thy sight, my lord; for that thou hast comforted me and for that thou hast spoken friendly unto thine handmaid, though I be not like unto one of thine handmaidens.

14 And Boaz said unto her, At mealtime come thou hither, and eat of the bread, and dip thy morsel in the vinegar. And she sat beside the reapers: and he reached her parched *corn*, and she did eat, and was sufficed, and left.

15 And when she was risen up to glean, Boaz commanded his young men, saying, Let her glean even among the sheaves, and reproach her not:

16 And let fall also *some* of the handfuls of purpose for her, and leave *them*, that she may glean *them*, and rebuke her not.

17 So she gleaned in the field until even, and beat out that she had gleaned: and it was about an ephah of barley.

18 And she took *it* up, and went into the city: and her mother in law saw what she had gleaned: and she brought forth, and gave to her that she had reserved after she was sufficed.

19 And her mother in law said unto her, Where hast thou gleaned to day? and where wroughtest thou? blessed be he that did take knowledge of thee. And she shewed her mother in law with whom she had wrought, and said, The man's name with whom I wrought to day *is* Boaz.

20 And Naomi said unto het daughter in law, Blessed *be* he of the LORD, who hath not left off his kindness to the living and to the dead. And Naomi said unto her, The man *is* near of kin unto us, one of our next kinsmen.

21 And Ruth the Moabitess said, He said unto me also, Thou shalt keep fast by my young men, until they have ended all my harvest.

22 And Naomi said unto Ruth her daughter in law, *It is* good, my daughter, that thou go out with his maidens, that they meet thee not in any other field.

23 So she kept fast by the maidens of Boaz to glean unto the end of barley harvest and of wheat harvest; and dwelt with her mother in law.

Then said Boaz unto Ruth, Hearest thou not, my daughter?
Go not to glean in another field, neither go from hence, but
abide here fast by my maidens: Let thine eyes be on the field
that they do reap, and go thou after them: have I not
charged the young men that they shall not touch thee? and
when thou art athirst, go unto the vessels, and drink of that
which the young men have drawn.
(Ruth 2:8-9)

According to the law of Moses, poor people and
strangers in Israel were permitted to glean the ears of
corn in a field that was being harvested. 'And when ye
reap the harvest of your land, thou shalt not make
clean riddance of the corners of thy field when thou
reapest, neither shalt thou gather any gleaning of thy
harvest: thou shalt leave them unto the poor, and to
the stranger: I am the Lord your God' (Leviticus 23:22).
The Israelite was never to forget that he himself had
once been a slave in Egypt, and that he owed his
freedom and prosperity only to God's mercy. This
realization was to encourage him in his turn to be
merciful to the weak and oppressed.

Rembrandt effectively depicted in the broad figure
of Boaz the gentleness with which the prosperous
farmer approached the young widow gleaning ears of
corn. As pointed out previously, this scene from the
story of Ruth was particularly popular with
17th-century Dutch historical painters. On the grounds
of the fact that the figures of Ruth and Boaz in the
drawing shown above look as if they have just been
lifted from a painting by Lastman, Tümpel considers it
possible that Rembrandt was inspired for this drawing
by one of his teacher's works that has now
disappeared.

Pen and brush drawing; 17.8 × 16.9 cm.
Ca. 1637-40.
Berlin, Kupferstichkabinett der Staatlichen Museen.

Literature: Benesch I, no. 162 (*ca.* 1638)/Hofstede de
Groot, *Rembrandt Bijbel*, V.T.d.19; Rotermund 1963, no.
90; Tümpel 1970, no. 23.

Boaz and Ruth

Go not empty unto thy mother in law

Ruth 3 THEN Naomi her mother in law said unto her, My daughter, shall I not seek rest for thee, that it may be well with thee?

2 And now *is* not Boaz of our kindred, with whose maidens thou wast? Behold, he winnoweth barley to night in the threshingfloor.

3 Wash thyself therefore, and anoint thee, and put thy raiment upon thee, and get thee down to the floor: *but* make not thyself known unto the man, until he shall have done eating and drinking.

4 And it shall be, when he lieth down, that thou shalt mark the place where he shall lie, and thou shalt go in, and uncover his feet, and lay thee down; and he will tell thee what thou shalt do.

5 And she said unto her, All that thou sayest unto me I will do.

6 And she went down unto the floor, and did acoording to all that her mother in law bade her.

7 And when Boaz had eaten and drunk, and his heart was merry, he went to lie down at the end of the heap of corn: and she came softly, and uncovered his feet, and laid her down.

8 And it came to pass at midnight, that the man was afraid, and turned himself: and, behold, a woman lay at his feet.

9 And he said, Who *art* thou? And she answered, I *am* Ruth thine handmaid: spread therefore thy skirt over thine handmaid; for thou *art* a near kinsman.

10 And he said, Blessed *be* thou of the LORD, my daughter: *for* thou hast shewed more kindness in the latter end than at the beginning, inasmuch as thou followedst not young men, whether poor or rich.

11 And now, my daughter, fear not; I will do to thee all that thou requirest: for all the city of my people doth know that thou *art* a virtuous woman.

12 And now it is true that I *am thy* near kinsman: howbeit there is a kinsman nearer than I.

13 Tarry this night, and it shall be in the morning, *that* if he will perform unto thee the part of a kinsman, well; let him do the kinsman's part: but if he will not do the part of the kinsman to thee, then will I do the part of a kinsman to thee, *as* the LORD liveth: lie down until the morning.

14 And she lay at his feet until the morning: and she rose up before one could know another. And he said, Let it not be known that a woman came into the floor.

15 Also he said, Bring the vail that *thou hast* upon thee, and hold it. And when she held it, he measured six *measures* of barley, and laid *it* on her: and she went into the city.

16 And when she came to her mother in law, she said, Who *art* thou, my daughter? And she told her all that the man had done to her.

17 And she said, These six *measures* of barley gave he me; for he said to me, Go not empty unto thy mother in law.

18 Then said she, Sit still, my daughter, until thou know how the matter will fall: for the man will not be in rest, until he have finished the thing this day.

Ruth 4 13 So Boaz took Ruth, and she was his wife: and when he went in unto her, the LORD gave her conception, and she bare a son.

14 And the women said unto Naomi, Blessed *be* the LORD, which hath not left thee this day without a kinsman, that his name may be famous in Israel.

15 And he shall be unto thee a restorer of *thy* life, and a nourisher of thine old age: for thy daughter in law, which loveth thee, which is better to thee than seven sons, hath born him.

16 And Naomi took the child, and laid it in her bosom, and became nurse unto it.

17 And the women her neighbours gave it a name, saying, There is a son born to Naomi; and they called his name Obed: he *is* the father of Jesse, the father of David.

Also he said, Bring the veil that thou hast upon thee, and hold it. And when she held it, he measured six measures of barley, and laid it on her ...
(Ruth 3:15)

The mutual attraction between Ruth and Boaz is very subtly expressed in the bold lines of the two figures bending towards each other.

   The scene depicted here was rarely used as a subject. Therefore we must assume that when he did this drawing, Rembrandt was not working from an example, but based it directly on the Bible text available to him. With regard to the still unanswered question of which Bible was meant by the 'Old Bible' referred to in Rembrandt's inventory of 1656, it is by no means insignificant that Miss L.C.V. Frerichs remarked that this drawing coincides remarkably closely to the text in the first edition (1526) of the so-called Liesveldt Bible, which states: 'Spread out your cloak which you are wearing and hold it with both hands.' The Liesveldt Bible was named after the Antwerp printer Jacob Van Liesveldt and was a highly esteemed adaption of the German Lutheran translation. It included many marginalia, and because one of these in the 1542 edition was considered heretical the printer was beheaded in Antwerp on 28 November 1545. A number of printers of that time paid with their lives for spreading the Bible.

Drawing in pen and ink; 12.6 × 14.3 cm.
Ca. 1650.
Amsterdam, Rijksprentenkabinet.

Literature: Benesch III, no. 643 (*ca.* 1649-50); Slive II, no. 431 (*ca.* 1648-50)/Hofstede de Groot, *Rembrandt Bijbel*, V.T.d.20; Rotermund 1963, no. 91; 'Bijbelse Inspiratie', no. 70.

Boaz Places Six Measures of Barley in Ruth's Veil

His wives turned away his heart

[Before David's monarchy divided into two separate kingdoms, it passed through a final golden autumn under King Solomon, who built the temple and was famous for his wisdom and wealth. A cultural and economic revolution took place in the centrally governed kingdom. The progressive policies of King Solomon may have aroused general admiration, but the machinery of government, the splendid edifices which were built and Solomon's sumptuous court all cost a great deal of money. The King imposed heavy taxes on the people and forced his subjects to carry out unpaid labour. While merchants and civil servants profited from the developments during this period, the common people became poorer. Moreover, the faithful followers of Israel's God were grieved to see that holy shrines were built for the gods of Solomon's foreign wives and that even the King himself participated in worshipping these gods. According to the Biblical historian, who assumed that loyalty to the covenant was rewarded with God's blessing and disloyalty punished with a curse, it was the latter that was, above all, responsible for the split in the nation.]

I Kings 11   BUT king Solomon loved many strange women, together with the daughter of Pharaoh, women of the Moabites, Ammonites, Edomites, Zidonians, *and* Hittites;

2 Of the nations *concerning* which the LORD said unto the children of Israel, Ye shall not go in to them, neither shall they come in unto you: *for* surely they will turn away your heart after their gods: Solomon clave unto these in love.

3 And he had seven hundred wives, princesses, and three hundred concubines: and his wives turned away his heart.

4 For it came to pass, when Solomon was old, *that* his wives turned away his heart after other gods: and his heart was not perfect with the LORD his God, as *was* the heart of David his father.

5 For Solomon went after Ashtoreth the goddess of the Zidonians, and after Milcom the abomination of the Ammonites.

6 And Solomon did evil in the sight of the LORD, and went not fully after the LORD as *did* David his father.

7 Then did Solomon build an high place for Chemosh, the abomination of Moab, in the hill that *is* before Jerusalem, and for Molech, the abomination of the children of Ammon.

8 And likewise did he for all his strange wives, which burnt incense and sacrified unto their gods.

9 And the LORD was angry with Solomon, because his heart was turned from the LORD God of Israel, which had appeared unto him twice,

10 And had commanded him concerning this thing, that he should not go after other gods: but he kept not that which the LORD commanded.

11 Wherefore the LORD said unto Solomon, Forasmuch as this is done of thee, and thou hast not kept my covenant and my statutes, which I have commanded thee, I will surely rend the kingdom from thee, and will give it to thy servant.

12 Notwithstanding in thy days I will not do it for David thy father's sake: *but* I will rend it out of the hand of thy son.

13 Howbeit I will not rend away all the kingdom; *but* will give one trible to thy son for David my servant's sake, and for Jerusalem's sake which I have chosen.

Solomon Worships Foreign Gods   *For Solomon went after Ashtoreth the goddess of the Zidonians, and after Milcom the abomination of the Ammonites. And Solomon did evil in the sight of the Lord ...* (1 Kings 11:5-6)

Among the studies that are known to have been done by Rembrandt as a young man, this large drawing in red chalk is a high point. It shows the interior of an enormous temple where incense is being burnt. King Solomon, surrounded and urged on by his wives, kneels in worship before the graven image of the mother goddess Astarte (known in the Bible text as Ashtoreth), who is represented as a mother suckling her child. The composition is similar to a painting dating from 1631, *The Song of Simeon*, in the Mauritshuis in The Hague (see p. 267). Benesch dates the drawing later, approximately 1637.

This subject was a popular one and in the late Middle Ages it often formed part of a series of feminine tricks (see p. 22). The representation of Solomon's idolatry is intended to show the extent to which a wise man can be fooled and tempted by a woman when his reason is taken over by his passions.

Drawing in red chalk, rounded at the top; 48.5 × 37.6 cm.
Ca. 1630.
Paris, The Louvre.

Literature: Benesch I, no. 136 (*ca.* 1637)/Rotermund 1963, no. 116.

For he went and dwelt by the brook Cherith

[Following Solomon's death, the western tribes broke away from Judah and did not choose Solomon's son, Rehoboam, but the Ephraimite Jeroboam to be their king. Henceforth there were two kingdoms: Israel in the north and Judah in the south. While Judah remained loyal to the house of David, Israel suffered a series of bloody revolutions in which one dynasty was ousted after another. The following stories about Elijah and Elisha took place in the northern kingdom of Israel of which Samaria, rebuilt by Omri, had become the new capital.]

I Kings 16 29 And in the thirty and eighth year of Asa king of Judah began Ahab the son of Omri to reign over Israel: and Ahab the son of Omri reigned over Israel in Samaria twenty and two years.

30 And Ahab the son of Omri did evil in the sight of the LORD above all that *were* before him.

31 And it came to pass, as if it had been a light thing for him to walk in the sins of Jeroboam the son of Nebat, that he took to wife Jezebel the daughter of Ethbaal king of the Zidonians, and went and served Baal, and worshipped him.

32 And he reared up an altar for Baal in the house of Baal, which he had built in Samaria.

33 And Ahab made a grove; and Ahab did more to provoke the LORD God of Israel to anger than all the king of Israel that were before him.

I Kings 17 AND Elijah the Tishbite, *who was* of the inhabitants of Gilead, said unto Ahab, *As* the LORD God of Israel liveth, before whom I stand, there shall not be dew nor rain these years, but according to my word.

2 And the word of the LORD came unto him, saying,

3 Get thee hence, and turn thee eastward, and hide thyself by the brook Cherith, that *is* before Jordan.

4 And it shall be, *that* thou shalt drink of the brook; and I have commanded the ravens to feed thee there.

5 So he went and did according unto the word of the LORD: for he went and dwelt by the brook Cherith, that *is* before Jordan.

6 And the ravens brought him bread and flesh in the morning, and bread and flesh in the evening; and he drank of the brook.

7 And it came to pass after a while, that the brook dried up, because there had been no rain in the land.

8 And the word of the LORD came unto him, saying,

9 Arise, get thee to Zarephath, which *belongeth* to Zidon, and dwell there: behold, I have commanded a widow woman there to sustain thee.

Elijah by the Cherith, Which Has Run Dry

So he went and did according to the word of the Lord; for he went and dwelt by the brook Cherith, that is before Jordan ... And it came to pass after a while, that the brook dried up, because there had been no rain in the land. And the word of the Lord came unto him, saying, Arise, get thee to Zarephath ...
(I Kings 17:5-9)

Elijah is one of those remarkable prophets in Israel who stood firm and unwavering for the purity of the old belief in the Lord at particularly critical moments. He was one of those men who, driven by the spirit of God, can bless and curse, kill and restore to life and are not afraid even to tell the King himself the truth. Elijah appeared from nowhere, and as suddenly as he arrived, he disappeared into heaven in a cloud of thunder (2 Kings 2:11).

After predicting a long drought to King Ahab, Elijah retreated to the distant valley of the Cherith at God's command. Unlike most representations of this subject, which usually show the prophet living in isolation and being fed by a raven, this drawing by Rembrandt depicts the moment at which Elijah is addressed by God a second time when the stream has run dry, and is told to rise and go to Zarephath. God's intervention is shown by a ray of light from heaven. The dry landscape with the little wilted tree on the bank of the stream shows the drought that has overtaken the land. We wonder how long it is since Elijah took a drink from the water bottle standing next to him. When he reaches the gates of Zarephath and encounters a woman collecting wood, his first request is: 'Fetch me, I pray thee, a little water in a vessel, that I may drink' (I Kings 17:10).

Pen and brush drawing; 20.5 × 23.3 cm.
Ca. 1655.
Berlin, Kupferstichkabinett der Staatlichen Museen.

Literature: Benesch V, no. 944 (*ca.* 1654-55); Slive I, no.
20 (*ca.* 1655)/Hofstede de Groot, *Rembrandt Bijbel*,
V.T.d.29; Hans-Martin Rotermund, 'The Motif of
Radiance in Rembrandt's Biblical Drawings' in *Journal
of the Warburg and Courtauld Institutes* XV (1952), pp. 104
and 106, note 3; Rotermund 1963, no. 120; Tümpel 1970,
no. 26.

And she, and he, and her house, did eat *many* days

I Kings 17 10 So he arose and went to Zarephath. And when he came to the gate of the city, behold, the widow woman *was* there gathering of sticks: and he called to her, and said, Fetch me, I pray thee, a little water in a vessel, that I may drink.

11 And as she was going to fetch *it*, he called to her, and said, Bring me, I pray thee, a morsel of bread in thine hand.

12 And she said, *As* the LORD thy God liveth, I have not a cake but an handful of meal in a barrel, and a little oil in a cruse: and, behold, I *am* gathering two sticks, that I may go in and dress it for me and my son, that we may eat it, and die.

13 And Elijah said unto her, Fear not; go *and* do as thou hast said: but make me thereof a little cake first, and bring *it* unto me, and after make for thee and for thy son.

14 For thus saith the LORD God of Israel, The barrel of meal shall not waste, neither shall the cruse of oil fail, until the day *that* the LORD sendeth rain upon the earth.

15 And she went and did according to the saying of Elijah: and she, and he, and her house, did eat *many* days.

16 *And* the barrel of meal wasted not, neither did the cruse of oil fail, according to the word of the LORD, which he spake by Elijah.

17 And it came to pass after these things' *that* the son of the woman, the mistress of the house, fell sick; and his sickness was so sore, that there was no breath left in him.

18 And she said unto Elijah, What have I to do with thee, O thou man of God? art thou come unto me to call my sin to remembrance, and to slay my son?

19 And he said unto her, Give me thy son. And he took him out of her bosom, and carried him up into a loft, where he abode, and laid him upon his own bed.

20 And he cried unto the LORD, and said, O LORD my God, hast thou also brought evil upon the widow with whom I sojourn, by slaying her son?

21 And he streched himself upon the child three times, and cried unto the LORD, and said, O LORD my God, I pray thee, let this child's soul come into him again.

22 And the LORD heard the voice of Elijah; and the soul of the child came into him again, and he revived.

23 And Elijah took the child, and brought him down out of the chamber into the house, and delivered him unto his mother: and Elijah said, See, thy son liveth.

24 And the woman said to Elijah, Now by this I know that thou *art* a man of God, *and* that the word of the LORD in thy mouth *is* truth.

Elijah and the Widow of Zarephath

And she went and did according to the saying of Elijah: and she, and he, and her house did eat many days. And the barrel of meal wasted not, neither did the cruse of oil fail, according to the word of the Lord, which he spake by Elijah.
(1 Kings 17:15-16)

The two groups composing this succinct drawing combine to give a striking impression of the miracle which occurs in the widow's family every day. No one in her household need fear anything from the prevailing famine because of the woman's faith; she had been prepared to give her last bit of oil and flour to the prophet. The little boy, wearing a kind of protective helmet and trying to keep his portion of food away from a demanding dog, serves to remind us of the widow's son, who dies after an illness and is brought back to life by Elijah.

The theme of a child being harassed by a dog while he is trying to eat is found in a virtually identical form in Rembrandt's etching *Woman Cooking Pancakes*, which dates from 1635 (Bartsch, no. 124). This drawing must have been done at roughly the same time, as well as another drawing of this subject which we now know only as a copy (Benesch II, no. C. 18).

Drawing in pen and ink; 11.6 × 15.8 cm.
Ca. 1635.
Paris, The Louvre.

Literature: Benesch I, no. 112 (*ca.* 1635)

The LORD, *he* is the God

I Kings 18 AND it came to pass *after* many days, that the word of the LORD came to Elijah in the third year, saying, Go, shew thyself unto Ahab; and I will send rain upon the earth.

2 And Elijah went to shew himself unto Ahab. And *there* was a sore famine in Samaria. [...]

17 And it came to pass, when Ahab saw Elijah, that Ahab said unto him, *Art* thou he that troubleth Israel?

18 And he answered, I have not troubled Israel; but thou, and thy father's house, in that ye have forsaken the commandments of the LORD, and thou hast followed Baalim.

19 Now therefore send, *and* gather to me all Israel unto mount Carmel, and the prophets of Baal four hundred and fifty, and the prophets of the groves four hundred, which eat at Jezebel's table.

20 So Ahab sent unto all the children of Israel, and gathered the prophets together unto mount Carmel.

21 And Elijah came unto all the people, and said, How long halt ye between two opinions? if the LORD *be* God, follow him: but if Baal, *then* follow him. And the people answered him not a word.

22 Then said Elijah unto the people, I, *even* I only, remain a prophet of the LORD; but Baal's prophets *are* four hundred and fifty man.

23 Let them therefore give us two bullocks; and let them choose one bullock for themselves, and cut it in pieces, and lay *it* on wood, and put no fire *under:* and I will dress the other bullock, and lay *it* on wood, and put no fire *under:*

24 And call ye on the name of your Gods, and I will call on the name of the LORD: and the God that answereth by fire, let him be God. And all the people answered and said, It is well spoken.

25 And Elijah said unto the prophets of Baal, Choose you one bullock for yourselves, and dress *it* first; for ye *are* many; and call on the name of your gods, but put no fire *under.*

26 And they took the bullock which was given them, and they dressed *it,* and called on the name of Baal from morning even until noon, saying, O Baal, hear us. But *there was* no voice, nor any that answered. And they leaped upon the altar which was made.

27 And it came to pass at noon, that Elijah mocked them, and said, Cry aloud: for he *is* a god; either he is talking, or he is pursuing, or he is in a journey, *or* peradventure he sleepeth, and must be awaked.

28 And they cried aloud, and cut themselves after their manner with knives and lancets, till the blood gushed out upon them.

29 And it came to pass, when midday was past, and the prophesied until the *time* of the offering of the *evening* sacrifice, that *there was* neither voice, nor any to answer, nor any that regarded.

30 And Elijah said unto all the people, Come near unto me. And all the people came near unto him. [...]

31 And Elijah took twelve stones, according to the number of the tribes of the sons of Jacob, unto whom the word of the LORD came, saying, Israel shall be thy name:

32 And with the stones he built an altar in the name of the LORD: and he made a trench about the altar. as great as would contain two measures of seed.

33 And he put the wood in order, and cut the bullock in pieces, and laid *him* on the wood, and said, Fill four barrels with water, and pour *it* on the burnt sacrifice, and on the wood.

34 And he said, Do *it* the second time. And they did *it* the second time. And he said, Do *it* the third time. And they did *it* the third time.

35 And the water ran round about the altar; and he filled the trench also with water.

36 And it came to pass at *the time of* the offering of the *evening* sacrifice, that Elijah the prophet came near, and said, LORD God of Abraham, Isaac, and of Israel, let it be known this day that thou *art* God in Israel, and *that* I *am* thy servant, and *that* I have done all these things at thy word.

37 Hear me, O LORD, hear me, that this people may know that hou *art* the LORD God, and *that* thou hast turned their heart back again.

38 Then the fire of the LORD fell, and consumed the burnt sacrifice, and the wood, and the stones, and the dust, and licked up the water that *was* in the trench.

39 And when all the people saw *it,* they fell on their faces: and they said, The LORD he *is* the God; the LORD, he *is* the God.

40 And Elijah said unto them, Take the prophets of Baal; let not one of them escape. And they took them: and Elijah brought them down to the brook Kishon, and slew them there.

And it came to pass at the time of the offering of the evening sacrifice, that Elijah the prophet came near, and said, Lord God of Abraham, Isaac, and of Israel, let it be known this day that thou art God in Israel ... Hear me, O Lord, hear me, that this people may know that thou art the Lord God, and that thou hast turned their heart back again. Then the fire of the Lord fell, and consumed the burnt sacrifice, and the wood, and the stones, and the dust, and licked up the water that was in the trench.
(1 Kings 18:36-38)

This subject requires a large number of figures and Rembrandt depicted it extremely clearly and expressively in this splendidly arranged composition. As the only remaining prophet of the Lord, Elijah stands alone facing a crowd of the prophets of Baal. But he is serving the strongest God, for while the sacrifice for the idol Baal lies untouched on the altar high in the background, the true God, the God of Abraham, Isaac and Jacob, reveals his power by making the burnt offering intended for him become set alight before everyone's eyes, at Elijah's command.

This theme can also be found in the work of some of Rembrandt's pupils, but their compositions cannot be compared with this drawing (for a drawing by Philips Koninck, see Cat. *Rembrandt after Three Hundred Years,* Chicago 1969, no. 185, illus., p. 263).

Pen and brush drawing; 20.4 × 31.5 cm.
Ca. 1645-50.
Constance, Städtische Wessenberg-Gemäldegalerie.

Literature: Benesch III, no. 593 (*ca.* 1647); Haak, no. 47 (*ca.* 1647)/Rotermund 1963, no. 123.

God's Judgment on Mount Carmel

Go forth, and stand upon the mount before the LORD

AND Ahab told Jezebel all that Elijah had done, and withal how he had slain all the prophets with the sword.

2 Then Jezebel sent a messenger unto Elijah, saying, So let the gods do *to me,* and more also, if I make not thy life of one of them by to morrow about this time.

3 And when he saw *that,* he arose, and went for his life, and came to Beersheba, which *belongeth* to Judah, and left his servant there.

4 But he himself went a day's journey into the wilderness, and came and sat down under a juniper tree: and he requested for himself that he might die; and said, I is enough; now, O LORD, take away my life; for I *am* not better than my fathers.

5 And as he lay and slept under a juniper tree, behold, then an angel touched him, and said unto him, Arise *and* eat.

6 And he looked, and behold, *there was* a cake baken on the coals, and a cruse of water at his head. And he did eat and drink, and laid him down again.

7 And the angel of the LORD came again the second time, and touched him, and said, Arise *and* eat; because the journey *is* too great for thee.

8 And he arose, and did eat and drink, and went in the strength of that meat forty days an forty nights unto Horeb the mount of God.

9 And he came thither unto a cave, and lodged there; and, behold, the word of the LORD *came* to him, and he said unto him, What doest thou here, Elijah?

10 And he said, I have been very jealous for the LORD God of hosts: for the children of Israel have forsaken thy covenant, thrown down thine altars, and slain thy prophets with the sword; and I, *even* I only, am left; and they seek my life, to take it away.

11 And he said, Go forth, and stand upon the mount before the LORD. And, behold, the LORD passed by, and a great and strong wind rent the mountains, and brake in pieces the rocks before the LORD; *but* the LORD *was* not in the wind: and after the wind an earthquake; *but* the LORD *was* not in the earthquake:

12 And after the earthquake a fire; *but* the LORD *was* not in the fire: and after the fire a still small voice.

13 And it was *so,* when Elijah heard *it,* that he wrapped his face in his mantle, and went out, and stood in the entering in of the cave. And, behold, *there came* a voice unto him, and said, What doest thou here, Elijah?

14 And he said, I have been very jealous for the LORD God of hosts: because the children of Israel have forsaken my covenant, thrown down thine altars, and slain thy prophets with the sword: and I, *even* I only, am left; and they seek my life, to take it away.

15 And the LORD said unto him, Go, return on thy way to the wilderness of Damascus: and when thou comest, anoint Hazael *to be* king over Syria:

16 And Jehu the son of Nimshi shalt thou anoint *to be* king over Israel: and Elisha the son of Shaphat of Abelmeholah shalt thou anoint *to be* prophet in thy room.

17 And it shall come to pass, *that* him that escapeth the sword of Hazael shall Jehu slay: and him that escapeth from the sword of Jehu shall Elisha slay.

18 Yet I have left *me* seven thousand in Israel, all the knees which have not bowed unto Baal, and every mouth which hath not kissed him.

And behold, there came a voice unto him, and said, What doest thou here, Elijah? And he said, I have been very jealous for the Lord God of hosts: because the children of Israel have forsaken thy covenant, thrown down thine altars, and slain thy prophets with the sword; and I, even I only, am left; and they seek my life, to take it away.
(1 Kings 19:13-15)

Although there are few indications in this drawing to enable determination of the subject with great certainty, it is likely that Rembrandt intended to show the prophet Elijah on Mount Horeb. After God passed him by there in 'a small, still wind of calm', he heard a voice calling: 'What doest thou here, Elijah?' In his reply the prophet complained bitterly to God. He has seen the general decline in Israel and in his own eyes he has fought for a lost cause. But God does not agree with him and sends him back with a new mission.

There are some in Israel who have remained loyal to the Lord and they will be spared in the downfall.

In the Fondation Custodia (Coll. Frits Lugt) in Paris, there is a drawing by Rembrandt dating from the early 1650s (Benesch V, no. 907) which shows the much more popularly depicted episode of the angel appearing to Elijah in the desert (verses 5-7).

Drawing in pen and ink; 19.1 × 12 cm.
Ca. 1655.
Rotterdam, Museum Boymans-van Beuningen.

Literature: Benesch V, no. 943 (*ca.* 1654)/H.-M. Rotermund, 'Unidentifizierte bzw. missverstandene Zeichnungen Rembrandts zu biblischen Szenen' in *Wallraf-Richartz-Jahrbuch* 21 (1959), pp. 192-93 (Elia); Rotermund 1963, no. 125.

Elijah on Mount Horeb

So she went and came unto the man of God

II Kings 4 8 And it fell on a day, that Elisha passed to Shunem, where *was* a great woman; and she constrained him to eat bread. And *so* it was, *that* as oft as he passed by, he turned in thither to eat bread.

9 And she said unto her husband, Behold now, I perceive that this *is* an holy man of God, which passeth by us continually.

10 Let us make a little chamber, I pray thee, on the wall; and let us set for him there a bed, and a table, and a stool, and a candlestick: and it shall be, when he cometh to us, that he shall turn in thither.

11 And it fell on a day, that he came thither, and he turned into the chamber, and lay there.

12 And he said to Gehazi his servant, Call this Shunammite. And when he had called her, she stood before him. [...]

16 And he said, About this season, according to the time of life, thou shalt embrace a son. And she said, Nay, my lord, *thou* man of God, do not lie unto thine handmaid.

17 And the woman conceived, and bare a son at that season that Elisha had said unto her, according to the time of life.

18 And when the child was grown, it fell on a day, that he went out to his father to the reapers.

19 And he said unto his father, My head, my head. And he said to a lad, Carry him to his mother.

20 And when he had taken him, and brought him to his mother, he sat on her knees till noon, and *then* died.

21 And she went up, and laid him on the bed of the man of God, and shut *the door* upon him, and went out.

22 And she called unto her husband, and said, Send me, I pray thee, one of the young men, and one of the asses, that I may run to the man of God, and come again.

23 And he said, Wherefore wilt thou go to him to day? *it is* neither new moon, nor sabbath. And she said, *It shall be* well.

24 Then he saddled an ass, and said to her servant, Drive, and go forward; slack not *thy* riding for me, except I bid thee.

25 So she went and came unto the man of God to mount Carmel. And it came to pass, when the man of God saw her afar off, that he said to Gehazi his servant, Behold, *yonder is* that Shunammite:

26 Run now, I pray thee, to meet her, and say unto her, *Is it* well with thee? *is it* well with thy husband? *is it* well with the child? And she answered, *It is* well.

27 And when she came to the man of God to the hill, she caught him by the feet: but Gehazi came naer to thrust her away. And the man of God said, Let her alone; for her soul *is* vexed within her: and the LORD hath hid *it* from me, and hath not told me.

28 Then she said, Did I desire a son of my lord? did I not say, Do not deceive me?

29 Then he said to Gehazi, Gird up thy loins, and take my staff in thine hand, and go thy way: if thou meet any man, salute him not, and if any salute thee, answer him not again: and lay my staff upon the face of the child.

30 And the mother of the child said, *As* the LORD liveth, and *as* thy soul liveth, I will not leave thee. And he arose, and followed her.

31 And Gehazi passed on before them, and laid the staff upon the face of the child; but *there was* neither voice, nor hearing. Wherefore he went again to meet him, and told him, saying, The child is not awaked.

32 And when Elisha was come into the house, behold, the child was dead, *and* laid upon his bed.

33 He went in therefore, and shut the door upon them twain, and prayed unto the LORD.

34 And he went up, and lay upon the child, and put his mouth upon his mouth, and his eyes upon his eyes, and his hands upon his hands: and he stretched himself upon the child; and the flesh of the child waxed warm.

35 Then he returned, and walked in the house to an fro; and went up, and stretched himself upon him: and the child sneezed seven times, and the child opened his eyes.

36 And he called Gehazi, and said, Call this Shunammite. So he called her. And when she was come in unto him, he said, Take up thy son.

37 Then she went in, and fell at his feet, and bowed herself to the ground, and took up her son, and went out.

And she called unto her husband, and said, Send me, I pray thee, one of the young men, and one of the asses, that I may run to the man of God, and come again. And he said, Wherefore wilt thou go to him today? It is neither new moon, nor sabbath. And she said, It shall be well. Then she saddled an ass, and said to her servant, Drive, and go forward; slack not thy riding for me, except I bid thee. (2 Kings 4:22-24)

According to the Bible, it was not only God who used the prophet to reveal his will to the people; conversely, the people, both rich and poor, turned to the prophet to summon his help. Apparently the best time to do this was on the sabbath or during a new moon, but the woman in this story needed the man of God straight away.

Rembrandt tried in the first place to express emotions and therefore he emphasized the woman's sorrow. She has just taken her dead child to the prophet's chambers to hide him. Nobody must know he is dead. Even her husband, whom she is leaving here as she rides away on an ass, is ignorant of the child's death and does not understand why she has to see the prophet so urgently. The prosperous home in the background, as well as the woman's clothes, shows that she is wealthy, as described in the introduction to the story.

It has been shown that Rembrandt was inspired to adopt this rarely depicted subject, which had never been used in a painting, by a few sheets from a 16th-century series of prints of this story by the Antwerp engraver, Hans Collaert, based on designs by Maerten de Vos. Before Tümpel pointed this out, the painting was called *The Expulsion of Hagar* (see pp. 24-27). X-rays have shown that the background, which is now a brownish black, was originally painted in light colours. The work was probably changed into a night-time scene in the 18th century, to comply with the expectations of a 'real' Rembrandt held at that time.

Panel; 39 × 53 cm.
Signed and dated: *Rembrandt f. 1640.*
London, Victoria and Albert Museum.

Literature: Bredius, no. 508; Bauch, no. 22; Gerson, no. 202; Bredius-Gerson, no. 508/Hofstede de Groot, *Rembrandt Bijbel*, V.T.p.2 (Hagar); Tümpel 1969, pp. 118-25.

The Departure of the Shunamite Woman

And the iron did swim

II Kings 6 AND the sons of the prophets said unto Elisha, Behold now, the place where we dwell with thee is too strait for us.

2 Let us go, we pray thee, unto Jordan, and take thence every man a beam, and let us make us a place there, where we may dwell. And he aswered, Go ye.

3 And one said, Be content, I pray thee, and go with thy servants. And he answered, I will go.

4 So he went with them. And when they came to Jordan, they cut down wood.

5 But as one was felling a beam, the ax head fell into the water: and he cried, and said, Alas, master! for it was borrowed.

6 And the man of God said, Where fell it? And he shewed him the place. And he cut down a stick, and cast *it* in thither; and the iron did swim.

7 Therefore said he, Take *it* up to thee. And he put out his hand, and took it.

Elisha Draws up the Axe

And he shewed him the place. And he cut down a stick, and cast it in thither; and the iron did swim. Therefore he said, Take it up to thee. And he put out his hand, and took it. (2 Kings 6:6-7)

In order to show this event as clearly as possible, Rembrandt combined in his drawing Elisha placing a stick in the water with the man who then takes the axe which has floated to the surface out of the water. The miracle itself is implicit. In the background we see the stump of the tree which was being felled when the head of the axe fell in the water. This subject was occasionally used, e.g. in a drawing from the circle of Nicolaes Maes (see *Tekeningen van Rembrandt en zijn school*, Catalogue of the Collection in the Museum Boymans-van Beuningen, Part I, illustrations, compiled by H.R. Hoetink, Rotterdam 1969, p. 63 and illus. 151).

Pen and brush drawing; 14.5 × 19.7 cm.
Ca. 1650-55.
The Hague, Bredius Museum.

Literature: Benesch V, no. 932 (*ca.* 1653); Slive II, no. 438 (*ca.* 1650-53)/Hofstede de Groot, *Rembrandt Bijbel*, V.T.d.31; Rotermund 1963, no. 126.

They burnt the house of God

[In 721 BC Samaria was captured by the Assyrians following a three-year siege, and this meant the end of the northern kingdom of Israel. A large proportion of the population was deported. It was partly because of the decline of Assyria that the downfall of the southern kingdom of Judah took another hundred years. In 598 BC the Babylonians took over power in Judah. Nebuchadnezzar replaced the reigning king in Jerusalem by another whose name he changed to Zedekiah, who became his vassal. The Babylonians did not wish the kingdom to collapse, but when King Zedekiah was tempted to revolt despite the warnings of the prophet Jeremiah, Jerusalem and Judah soon fell.]

II Chronicles 36 11 Zedekiah *was* one and twenty years old when he began to reign. [...].

12 And he did *that which was* evil in the sight of the LORD his God, *and* humbled not himself before Jeremiah the prophet *speaking* from the mouth of the LORD.

13 And he also rebelled against king Nebuchadnezzar, who had made him swear by God: but he stiffened his neck, and hardened his heart from turning unto the LORD God of Israel.

14 Moreover all the chief of the priests, and the people, transgressed very much after all the abominations of the heathen: and polluted the house of the LORD which he had hallowed in Jerusalem.

15 And the LORD God of their fathers sent to them by his messengers, rising up betimes, and sending; because he had compassion on his people, and on his dwelling place:

16 But they mocked the messengers of God, and despised his words, and misused his prophets, until the wrath of the LORD arose against his people, till *there was* no remedy.

17 Therefore he brought upon them the king of the Chaldees, who slew their young men with the sword in the house of their sanctuary, and had no compassion upon young man or maiden, old man, or him that stooped for age: he gave *them* all into his hand.

18 And all the vessels of the house of God, great and small, and the treasures of the house of the LORD, and the treasures of the king, and of his princes; all *these* he brought to Babylon.

19 And they burnt the house of God, and brake down the wall of Jerusalem, and burnt all the palaces thereof with fire, and destroyed all the goodly vessels thereof.

20 And them that had escaped from the sword carried he away to Babylon; where they were servants to him and his sons until the reign of the kingdom of Persia:

21 To fulfil the word of the LORD bu the mouth of Jeremiah, until the land had enjoyed her sabbaths: *for* as long as she lay desolate she kept sabbath, to fulfil threescore and ten years.

Jeremiah Laments the Devastation of Jerusalem

This panel was alternately painted very swiftly and with great precision and detail and is justifiably considered one of Rembrandt's first masterpieces. The figure of Jeremiah is placed diagonally across the painting, on the borders of light and dark. The downfall of Jerusalem can be seen in the background on the left. The round building, in danger of being engulfed by flames, represents the temple. Rembrandt was undoubtedly familiar with the many prints of views of Jerusalem which were around at the time and - like most of his contemporaries - he probably assumed that the Dome of the Rock, the Muslim holy shrine built on the old temple rock, shown on these prints, was the temple of Solomon. The grieving Jeremiah, leaning on a heavy tome (the word 'Bible' was probably added later) and surrounded by gold receptacles, is shown here in a posture which has been used since classical times to express despondency. In 1511 Michelangelo had painted the prophet in a similar posture of melancholy contemplation on the ceiling of the Sistine Chapel. In the Lamentations ascribed to Jeremiah on the devastation of Jerusalem, the prophet laments the fate of the city and its inhabitants in the following words:

Mine eyes do fail with tears, my bowels are troubled, my liver is poured upon the earth, for the destruction of the daughter of my people; because the children and the sucklings swoon in the streets of the city.

What thing shall I take to witness for thee? What thing shall I liken to thee, O daughter of Jerusalem? What shall I equal to thee, that I may comfort thee, O virgin daughter of Zion? For thy breach is great like the sea; who can heal thee?

All that pass by clap their hands at thee; they hiss and wag their head at the daughter of Jerusalem, saying, Is this the city that men call the perfection of beauty, the joy of the whole earth?

(Lamentations 2:11, 13 and 15)

Panel; 58 × 46 cm.
Signed and dated: *RHL 1630.*
Amsterdam, Rijksmuseum.

Literature: Bredius, no. 604; Bauch, no. 127; Gerson, no. 24; Bredius-Gerson, no. 604/Hofstede de Groot, *Rembrandt Bijbel*, V.T.p.23; Tümpel 1971, p. 20, note 2.

And the king loved Esther above all the women

[At the court of the Persian King Ahasuerus in Shushan, the mood is suddenly spoilt on the last day of a seven-day-long feast when Queen Vashti refuses to comply with the wish of her inebriated husband that she display her beauty to his guests, with the sole adornment of her royal diadem. On the advice of his counsellors, the King decides to deprive Vashti of her queenly title and give it to another woman. From all over the kingdom beautiful young girls are brought to the city where, after a beauty treatment in the harem of the palace, they will be presented to the King one by one so that he can make his choice.]

Esther 2   5 *Now* in Shushan the palace there was a certain Jew, whose name *was* Mordecai, the son of Jair, the son of Shimei, the son of Kish, a Benjamite;

6 Who had been carried away from Jerusalem with the captivity which had been carried away with Jeconiah king of Judah, whom Nebuchadnezzar the king of Judah, whom Nebuchadnezzar the king of Babylon had carried away.

7 And he brought up Hadassah, that *is,* Esther, his uncle's daughter: for she had neither father nor mother, and the maid *was* fair and beautiful; whom Mordecai, when her father and mother were dead, took his own daughter.

8 So it came to pass, when the king's commandment and his decree was heard, and when many maidens were gathered together unto Shushan the palace, to the custody of Hegai, that Esther was brought also unto the king's house, to the custody of Hegai, keeper of the women.

9 And the maiden pleased him, and she obtained kindness of him; and he speedily gave her her things for purification, with such things as belonged to her, and seven maidens, *which were* meet to be given her, out of the king's house: and he preferred her and her maids unto the best *place* of the house of the women.

10 Esther had not shewed her people nor her kindred: for Mordecai had charged her that she should not shew *it*.

11 And Mordecai walked every day before the court of the women's house, to know how Esther did, and what should become of her. [...]

15 Now when the turn of Esther, the daughter of Abihail the uncle of Mordecai, who had taken her for his daughter, was come to go in unto the king, she required nothing but what Hegai the king's chamberlain, the keeper of the women, appointed. And Esther obtained favour in the sight of all them that looked upon her.

16 So Esther was taken unto king Ahasuerus into the house royal in the tenth month, which *is* the month Tebeth, in the seventh year of his reign.

17 And the king loved Esther above all the women, and she obtained grace and favour in his sight more than all the virgins; so that he set the royal crown upon her head, and made her queen instead of Vashti.

18 Then the king made a great feast unto all his princes and his servants, *even* Esther's feast; and he made a release to the provinces, and gave gifts, according to the state of the king.

19 And when the virgins were gathered together the second time, then Mordecai sat in the king's gate.

20 Esther had not *yet* shewed her kindred nor her people; as Mordecai had charged her: for Esther did the commandment of Mordecai, like as when she was brought up with him.

21 In those days, while Mordecai sat in the king's gate, two of the king's chamberlains, Bigthan and Teresh, of those which kept the door, were wroth, and sought to lay hand on the king Ahasuerus.

22 And the king was known to Mordecai, who told *it* unto Esther the queen; and Esther certified the king *thereof* in Mordecai's name.

23 And when inquisition was made of the matter, it was found out; therefore they were both hanged on a tree: and it was written in the book of the chronicles before the king.

Now when the turn of Esther ... was come to go in unto the king, she required nothing but what Hegai the king's chamberlain, the keeper of the women, appointed. And Esther obtained favour in the sight of all them that looked upon her.
So Esther was taken unto king Ahasuerus into his house royal in the tenth month, which is the month Tebeth, in the seventh year of his reign.
(Esther 2:15-16)

As the moment arrives for Esther to appear before the King, she follows the advice, so we read, of Hegai, the keeper of the women, who, familiar as he is with the King's taste, clearly expects in her case the most success from simple apparel. In the above drawing (possibly a copy after a lost original), we see how with a slight bow the harem keeper presents the kneeling girl to the King. Ahasuerus, who has risen from his chair, immediately reaches out a gracious hand to her. Esther will become the new Queen.

Rounding off the account of Esther's elevation, the writer stresses that on the advice of her guardian Mordechai she keeps silent to the King and his direct entourage about her Jewish origins. A situation is thus created which will be vital to the development of the story.

Pen and brush drawing; 18.5 × 25 cm.
Ca. 1655.
Paris, The Louvre.

Literature: Not included in the catalogue by Benesch/Rotermund 1963, no. 128.

Esther is Presented to Ahasuerus

If I perish, I perish

[After presenting Mordechai and Esther, the writer introduces a third main character onto the scene in the person of the anti-Jewish Haman, a descendant of the Amalekite King Agag, whose people were Israel's enemies of old. When this Haman is promoted by the King to grand vizier, the self-assured Jew Mordechai refuses to bow to him in the prescribed manner. Enraged by this, Haman is not satisfied by simply laying hands on Mordechai, but sets his mind on annihilating all the Jewish subjects of the Persian Empire. After obtaining royal authorization, he produces a document in the name of the King in which it is decreed that throughout the kingdom on one and the same day, the 13th day of the 12th month, all Jews, both young and old, should be 'destroyed, killed and caused to perish'.]

Esther 4 WHEN Mordecai perceived all that was done, Mordecai rent his clothes, and put on sackcloth with ashes, and went out into the midst of the city, and cried with a loud and a bitter cry; [...]

4 So Esther's maids and her chamberlains came and told *it* her. Then was the queen exceedingly grieved; and she sent raiment to clothe Mordecai, and to take away his sackcloth from him: but he received *it* not.

5 Then called Esther for Hatach, *one* of the king's chamberlains, whom he had appointed to attend upon her, and gave him a commandment to Mordecai, to know what it *was,* and why it *was.*

6 So Hatach went forth to Mordecai unto the street of the city, which *was* before the king's gate.

7 And Mordecai told him all that had happened unto him, and of the sum of the money that Haman had promised to pay to the king's treasuries for the Jews, to destroy them.

8 Also he gave him the copy of the writing of the decree that was given at Shushan to destroy them, to shew *it* unto Eshter, and to declare *it* unto her, and to charge her that she should go in unto the king, to make supplication unto him, and to make request before him for her people.

9 And Hatach came and told Esther the words of Mordecai.

10 Again Esther spake unto Hatach, and gave him commandment unto Mordecai;

11 All the king's servants, and the people of the king's provinces, do know, that whosoever, whether man or woman, shall come unto the king into the inner court, who is not called, *there is* one law of his to put *him* to death, except such to whom the king shall hold out the golden sceptre, that he may live: but I have not been called to come in unto the king these thirty days.

12 And they told to Mordecai Esther's words.

13 Then Mordecai commanded to answer Esther, Think not with thyself that thou shalt escape in the king's house, more than all the Jews.

14 For if thou altogether holdest thy peace at this time, *then* shall there enlargement and deliverance arise to the Jews from another place; but thou and thy father's house shall be destroyed: and who knoweth whether thou art come to the kingdom for *such* a time as this?

15 Then Esther bade *them* return to Mordecai *this answer,*

16 Go, gather together all the Jews that are present in Shushan, and fast ye for me, and neither eat nor drink three days, night or day: I also and my maidens will fast likewise; and so will I go in unto the king, which *is* not according to the law: and if I perish, I perish.

17 So Mordecai went his way, and did according to all that Esther had commanded him.

Esther with the Decree for Destruction of the Jews In a convincing essay, Madlyn Kahr has advanced the theory that the young woman in this etching, which is known by the title *The Grand Jewish Bride*, represents Esther, who has withdrawn to prepare herself for her risky intercession with the King on behalf of her threatened people. In an apocryphal supplement to the book of Esther, which we also find for the most part in Flavius Josephus, it is related that, alerted by Mordechai, the Queen discards her court dress and puts on garments for mourning and lamentation, 'and all the places of her joy she filled with her torn hair' (Esther 14:2). The rolled-up document in her left hand is the decree for the destruction of the Jews prepared by Haman, a copy of which Mordechai has had brought to her. His tactics to avert the danger are based on the fact that Haman is unwittingly also after the blood of the King's consort. This is why Esther, in contrast with her previous behaviour, may no longer keep silent about her identity. For her intervention with the King to have the greatest chance of success, it must be shown that Haman's plan to annihilate all the Jews in the Persian Empire also threatens the Queen.

In the study for this etching which is preserved in

Stockholm (Benesch II, no. 292), the figure of Esther is depicted full-length. As she is only visible here to the knees, there is a far greater emphasis on the decree in her hand. In the above-mentioned supplement to this episode in the story, Esther beseeches God to let the warrant fall like a boomerang upon the head of the adversary: '... turn their device upon themselves, and make him an example, that has begun this against us' (Esther 14:11).

Etching; 21.9 × 16.8 cm. Fourth state of five.
Signed and dated: *R 1635*.
Amsterdam, Rijksprentenkabinet.

Literature: Bartsch, no. 340; Hind, no. 127; Münz, no. 90; Boon, no. 125; Filedt Kok, no. B 340/Madlyn Kahr, 'Rembrandt's Ester. A painting and an etching newly interpreted and dated', *Oud Holland 81* (1966), pp. 241VV.

What wilt thou, queen Esther?

NOW it came to pass on the third day, that Esther put on *her* royal *apparel*, and stood in the inner court of the king's house, over against the king's house: and the king sat upon his royal throne in the royal house, over against the gate of the house.

2 And it was so, when the king saw Esther the queen standing in the court, *that* she obtained favour in his sight: and the king held out to Esther the golden sceptre that *was* in his hand. So Esther drew near, and touched the top of the sceptre.

3 Then said the king unto her, What wilt thou, queen Esther? and what *is* thy request? it shall be even given thee to the half of the kingdom.

4 And Esther answered, If *it seem* good unto the king, let the king and Haman come this day unto the banquet that I have prepared for him.

5 Then the king said, Cause Haman to make haste, that he may do as Esther hath said. So the king and Haman came to the banquet that Esther had prepared.

6 And the king said unto Esther at the banquet of wine, What *is* thy petition? and it shall be granted thee: and what *is* thy request? even to the half of the kingdom it shall be performed.

7 Then answered Esther, and said, My petition and my request *is;*

8 If I have found favour in the sight of the king, and if it please the king to grant my petition, and to perform my request, let the king and Haman come to the banquet that I shall prepare for them, and I will do to morrow as the king hath said.

9 Then went Haman forth that day joyful and with a glad heart: but when Haman saw Mordecai in the king's gate, that he stood not up, nor moved for him, he was full of indignastion against Mordecai.

10 Nevertheless Haman refrained himself: and when he came home, he sent and called for his friends, and Zeresh his wife.

11 And Haman told them of the glory of his riches, and the multitude of his children, and all *the things* wherein the king had promoted him, and how he had advanced him above the princes and servants of the king.

12 Haman said moreover, Yea, Esther the queen did let no man come in with the king unto the banquet that she had prepared but myself; and to morrow am I invited unto her also with the king.

13 Yet all this availeth me nothing, so long as I see Mordecai the Jew sitting at the king's gate.

14 Then said Zeresh his wife and all his friends unto him, Let a gallows be made of fifty cubits high, and to morrow speak thou unto the king that Mordecai may be hanged thereon: then go thou in merrily with the king unto the banquet. And the thing pleased Haman; and he caused the gallows to be made.

Esther Faints Before the King After several days of praying and fasting in preparation for her intervention with the King, 'upon the third day' Esther makes her way to the throne room, well aware that anyone who dares to appear before the King without an invitation risks the death penalty. Moreover, she is no longer sure of her position as favourite in the palace. She has not been called to the King in thirty days, she has revealed to Mordechai (see Esther 4:11).

Rembrandt's drawing of her arrival in the King's chamber is a depiction of the apocryphal supplement to this part of the story, a text in which Esther's feelings are extensively considered, and in which the reader is left much longer in the dark than in the canonical Bible text about the outcome of her breach of unrelenting protocol. 'And upon the third day,

when she had ended her prayer, she laid away her mourning garments, and put on her glorious apparel. And being gloriously adorned, after she had called upon God, who is the beholder and saviour of all things, she took two maids with her: And upon the one she leaned, as carrying herself daintily; And the other followed, bearing up her train. And she was ruddy through the perfection of her beauty, and her countenance was cheerful and very amiable: but her heart was in anguish for fear. Then having passed through all the doors, she stood before the king, who sat upon his royal throne, and was clothed with all his robes of majesty, all glittering with gold and precious stones; and he was very dreadful. Then lifting up his countenance which shone with majesty, he looked very fiercely upon her: and the queen fell down, and was

pale, and fainted, and bowed herself upon the head of the maid that went before her. Then God changed the spirit of the king into mildness, who in a fear leaped from his throne, and took her in his arms, till she came to herself again, and comforted her with loving words, and said unto her, Esther, what is the matter?' (Esther 5:1-8).

In Rembrandt's representation, the King, descending from his throne, forms the central point of the composition. His stern gaze and the eyes of all the counsellors and court officials assembled round him are fixed on Esther, who swoons with terror and is supported by her maid. The drawing must have once been larger than it is now. In the two upper corners we can see that it was originally rounded off with an arch.

Pen drawing; 17.5 × 17.7 cm.
Ca. 1645.
Amsterdam, Rijksprentenkabinet.

Literature: Benesch III, no. 634 (*ca.* 1648-50); Slive II, no. 308 (*ca.* 1645-50)/Rotermund 1963, no. 130; 'Bijbelse Inspiratie', no. 77.

Make haste, and do even so to Mordecai the Jew

Esther 6 ON that night could not the king sleep, and he commanded to bring the book of records of the chronicles; and they were read before the king.

2 And it was found written, that Mordecai had told of Bigthana and Teresh, two of the king's chamberlains, the keepers of the door, who sought to lay hand on the king Ahasuerus.

3 And the king said, What honour and dignity hath been done to Mordecai for this? Then said the king's servants that ministered unto him, There is nothing done for him.

4 And the king said, Who *is* in the court? Now Haman was come into the outward court of the king's house, to speak unto the king to hang Mordecai on the gallows that he had prepared for him.

5 And the king's servants said unto him, Behold, Haman standeth in the court. And the king said, Let him come in.

6 So Haman came in. And the king said unto him, What shall be done unto the man whom the king delightet to honour? Now Haman thought in his heart, To whom would the king delight to do honour more than to myself?

7 And Haman answered the king, For the man whom the king delighteth to honour,

8 Let the royal apparel be brought which the king *useth* to wear, and the horse that the king rideth upon, and the crown royal which is set upon his head:

9 And let this apparel and horse be delivered to the hand of one of the king's most noble princes, that they may array the man *withal* whom the king delighteth to honour, and bring him on horseback through the street of the city, and proclaim before him, Thus shall it be done to the man whom the king delighteth to honour.

10 Then the king said to Haman, Make haste, *and* take the apparel and the horse, as thou hast said, and do even so to Mordecai the Jew, that sitteth at the king's gate: let nothing fail of all that thou hast spoken.

Haman Sets Forth to Honour Mordechai

Make haste, and take the apparel and the horse, as thou hast said, and do even so to Mordechai the Jew, that sitteth at the king's gate: let nothing fail of all that thou hast spoken. (Esther 6:10)

Esther's surprising decision to delay the revelation of her wish yet another day (see the previous chapter, verses 7-8) could have been almost fatal for Mordechai. Just in the nick of time coincidence gives another turn to the course of events. The scene in question ties in with the fact reported in chapter 2, that at that time Mordechai had saved the King from an assassination attempt without being rewarded for this (Esther 2:21-23).

Of the three life-size figures depicted in Rembrandt's painting, Haman has been made by far the most important. The self-important swaggerer finds himself suddenly compelled to do something at complete odds with his intentions. Arriving with the aim of bringing Mordechai to the gallows as quickly as possible, he must now make haste to honour the man publicly, and, what is more, in the manner he has had in mind for himself. Totally disillusioned, he sets forth, his eyes cast down, obviously anticipating what his wife and friends will soon be saying to him, after the tributes are over: 'If Mordechai be of the seed of the Jews, before whom thou hast begun to fall, thou shalt not prevail against him, but shalt surely fall before

him' (Esther 6:13). How painful the agony which Haman has to suffer will be can be read in particular on the face of the old chronicle reader in the left background - he knows about all court intrigues. The King, on the other hand, unaware of Haman's dispute with Mordechai, appears only to be asking himself how it is possible that a deserving man such as Mordechai should have remained unrewarded for so long.

With the figures seen from close to, sunk deep in thought, the painting is a characteristic example of the historical works from Rembrandt's very last creative period.

Canvas; 127 × 116 cm.
Signed: *Rembrandt.*
Ca. 1665.
Leningrad, Hermitage.

Literature: Bredius, no. 531; Bauch, no. 39; Gerson, no. 357; Bredius-Gerson, no. 531/Hofstede de Groot, *Rembrandt Bible*, V.T.p.21; Madlyn Kahr, 'A Rembrandt Problem: Haman or Uriah?' in *Journal of the Warburg and Courtauld Institutes* 28 (1965), pp. 258-73; Tümpel 1968, pp. 106-12; H. van de Waal, 'Rembrandt and the Feast of Purim' in *Oud Holland* 84 (1969), pp. 199-223; Tümpel 1970, under no. 19.

Haman brought him on horseback through the street of the city

Esther 6   11 Then took Haman the apparel and the horse, and arrayed Mordecai, and brought him on horseback through the street of the city, and proclaimed before him, Thus shall it be done unto the man whom the king delighteth to honour.

12 And Mordecai came again to the king's gate. But Haman hasted to his house mourning, and having his head covered.

13 And Haman told Zeresh his wife and all his friends every *thing* that had befallen him. Then said his wise men and Zeresh his wife unto him, If Mordecai *be* of the seed of the Jews, before whom thou hast begun to fall, thou shalt not prevail against him, but shalt surely fall before him.

14 And while they *were* yet talking with him, came the king's chamberlains, and hasted to bring Haman unto the banquet that Esther had prepared.

The Triumphal Procession of Mordechai

Then Haman took the apparel and the horse, and ... brought him on horseback through the street of the city, and proclaimed before him, Thus shall it be done unto the man whom the king delighteth to honour.
(Esther 6:11)

The accolade so unexpectedly given to Mordechai is here depicted by Rembrandt most imaginatively. The citizens have come onto the streets, and their lively expressions of respect, gratitude and admiration form a beautiful contrast with the calm which emanates from the imposing gateway in the middle distance. Preceded by Haman and his proclamations, Mordechai, seated on the King's horse and dressed in his mantle, with a sceptre in his hand, lets the accolades wash over him in a calm and dignified manner. In order to place the scene in its context, Rembrandt has the other two main characters in the story, Ahasuerus and Esther, witness the triumph of Mordechai from a balcony.

The etching was produced around 1640-41.

Rembrandt's principal source of inspiration was the engraving which Lucas van Leyden had made of the same subject in 1515. One significant detail, the fat man to the right respectfully removing his cap, is taken directly from that model. Lastman's painting of Haman and Mordechai from 1617, now in the Rembrandt House in Amsterdam, was probably an influence upon the composition as well. In the study which has been preserved (Benesch III, no. 487), the gateway which occupies such a dominant place in the etching is missing; it reappears a year later with a similar function in *The Nightwatch* (Bredius no. 410). The composition in question has other points of comparison with the painting, such as the grouping of the subsidiary figures left and right of the gateway in the centre. And who does not see the gesture with which Haman turns to the viewer without briefly thinking of the figure of Captain Frans Banning Cocq, who faces us in virtually the same attitude in Rembrandt's famous depiction of the citizens' militia?

Etching: 17.4 × 21.5 cm. Only state.
Ca. 1640-41.
Amsterdam, Rijksprentenkabinet.

Literature: Bartsch, no. 40; Hind, no. 172; Münz, no. 178;
Boon, no. 166; Filedt Kok, no. B 40/Hofstede de Groot,
Rembrandt Bijbel, V.T.e.13; J. Bruyn, *Rembrandt's keuze
van Bijbelse onderwerpen*, Utrecht 1959, p. 17; Rotermund
1963, no. 131; 'Bijbelse Inspiratie', no. 27; Tümpel 1970,
no. 27.

The adversary and enemy is this wicked Haman

Esther 7 SO the king and Haman came to banquet with Esther the queen.

2 And the king said again unto Esther on the second day at the banquet of wine, What *is* thy petition, queen Esther? and it shall be granted thee: and what *is* thy request? and it shall be performed, *even* to the half of the kingdom.

3 Then Esther the queen answered and said, If I have found favour in thy sight, O king, and if it please the king, let my life be given me at my petition, and my people at my request:

4 For we are sold, I and my people, to be destroyed, to be slain, and to perish. But if we had been sold for bondmen and bondwomen, I had held my tongue, although the enemy could not countervail the king's damage.

5 Then the king Ahasuerus answered and said unto Esther the queen, Who is he, and where is he, that durst presume in his heart to do so?

6 And Esther said, The adversary and enemy *is* this wicked Haman, Then Haman was afraid before the king and the queen.

7 And the king arising from the banquet of wine in his wrath *went* into the palace garden: and Haman stood up to make request for his life to Esther the queen; for he saw that there was evil determined against him by the king.

8 Then the king returned out of the palace garden into the place of the banquet of wine; and Haman was fallen upon the bed whereon Esther *was*. Then said the king, Will he force the queen also before me in the house? As the word went out of the king's mouth, they covered Haman's face.

9 And Harbonah, one of the chamberlains, said before the king, Behold also, the gallows fifty cubits high, which Haman had made for Mordecai, who had spoken good for the king, standeth in the house of Haman. Then the king said, Hang him thereon.

10 So the hanged Haman on the gallows that he had prepared for Mordecai. Then was the king's wrath pacified.

Esther 8 ON that day did the king Ahasuerus give the house of Haman the Jew's enemy unto Esther the queen. And Mordecai came before the king; for Esther had told what he *was* unto her.

2 And the king took off his ring, which he had taken from Haman, and gave it unto Mordecai. And Esther set Mordecai over the house of Haman.

Haman and Ahasuerus at Banquet with Esther

Then Esther the queen answered and said, If I have found favour in thy sight, O king, and if it please the king, let my life be given me at my petition, and my people at my request: For we are sold, I and my people, to be destroyed, to be slain and to perish ...
Then the king Ahasuerus answered and said unto Esther the queen, Who is he, and where is he, that durst to presume in his heart to do so?
And Esther said, The adversary and enemy is this wicked Haman. Then Haman was afraid before the king and queen.
(Esther 7:3-6)

At last Esther has answered the King's question; at last the truth has been told. The silence which follows is the real subject of this masterly painting. The three figures, each alone with their own thoughts, are placed against a neutral background. Anything which could detract from the tension of this dramatic moment is omitted. The light goes out for the unmasked Haman. Having already stumbled over Mordechai, he is brought down by Esther. The young Queen, ravishingly beautiful in her regal splendour, her hands still accusingly pointing to Haman, waits intently. Slowly the truth begins to dawn on the King.

The painting, dating from 1660, must have acquired a place shortly after its completion in the art collection of Jan Jacobsz Hinloopen, alderman and later mayor of Amsterdam. For amongst the poems by Amsterdam playwright and poet Jan Vos published in 1662 are a number of verses about several paintings from Hinloopen's collection, including 'Haman at banquet with Esther and Ahasuerus, painted by Rembrandt'. The poet writes about the canvas as follows:

Here we see Haman dining with Ahasuerus and Esther.
But it is to no avail, his breast is full of regret and hurt.
He bites into Esther's food: but deeper into her heart.
The King is possessed with revenge and fury.
The wrath of a monarch is terrible when it rages.
The one who threatens all men is confounded by a woman.
So does one fall from the heights to the depths of adversity.
The revenge which slowly comes employs the cruellest scourges.
(From *Alle gedichten van den Poeët Jan Vos*, Amsterdam
1662, p. 565)

For Haman's appearance Rembrandt has in all
probability drawn inspiration from several of his
drawings of Shah Jahan, after miniatures originating
from Moghul India (according to Benesch V, nos. 1193
and 1194). The composition as a whole has an affinity
with the etching *The Meal in Emmaus* from 1654 (see p.

428), and betrays, as do so many other of Rembrandt's
mealtime scenes, the profound and lasting effect of his
studies made after *The Last Supper* by Leonardo da
Vinci around 1635 (see pp. 368 - 69).

Canvas; 73 × 94 cm.
Signed and dated: *Rembrandt f. 1660.*
Moscow, Pushkin Museum.

Literature: Bredius, no. 530; Bauch, no. 37; Gerson, no.
351; Bredius-Gerson, no. 530/Joseph Gantner,
Rembrandt und die Verwandlung klassischer Formen,
Berne 1964, pp. 159-164.

Your feasts shall be turned into mourning

[Tobit, a pious Jew deported to Nineveh from the northern kingdom of Israel, has at first little to complain of as a buyer for the court. But political unrest causes the Jews' situation to deteriorate. Accused of secretly burying fellow Jews who have been killed, Tobit incurs the King's displeasure and takes flight, fearing for his life. All his possessions are confiscated. As soon as a change of monarch restores a more favourable climate for the Jews, he returns to Nineveh.]

Tobit 2 NOW when I was come home again, and my wife Anna was restored unto me, and my son Tobias, in the feast of Pentecost, which is the holy feast of the seven weeks, there was a good dinner prepared me, and I sat down to eat.

2 And I saw abundance of meat, and I said to my son, Go and bring what poor man soever thou shalt find of our brethren, who is mindful of the Lord; and, lo, I tarry for thee.

3 And he came, and said, Father, one of our race is strangled, and is cast out in the marketplace.

4 And before I had tasted aught, I sprang up, and took him up into a chamber until the sun was set.

5 And I returned, and washed myself, and ate my bread in heaviness.

6 And remembered the prophecy of Amos, as he said, Your feasts shall be turned into mourning, And all your mirth into lamentation.

7 And I wept: and when the sun was set, I went and made a grave, and buried him.

8 And my neighbours mocked me, and said, He is no longer afraid to be put to death for this matter: and yet he fled away: and, lo, he burieth the dead again.

9 And the same night I returned from burying him, and slept by the wall of my courtyard, being polluted; and my face was uncovered: and I knew not that there were sparrows in the wall;

10 And, mine eyes being open, the sparrows muted warm dung into mine eyes, and white films came in mine eyes; and I went to the physicians, and they helped me not: but Achiacharus did nourish me, until I went into Elymais.

11 And my wife Anna did spin in the women's chambers, and did send the work back to the owners.

12 And they on their part paid her wages, and gave her also besides a kid.

13 But when it came to my house, it began to cry, and I said unto her, From whence is this kid? is it stolen? render it to the owners; for it is not lawful to eat anything that is stolen.

14 But she said, It hath been given me for a gift more than the wages. And I did not believe her, and I bade her render it to the owners; and I was abashed at her. But she answered and said unto me, Where are thine alms, and thy righteous deeds? behold, thou and all thy works are known.

Tobit Spending the Night in the Courtyard of his House

And the same night I returned from burying him, and slept by the wall of my courtyard, being polluted; and my face was uncovered ...
(Tobit 2:9)

The story of Tobit and his son Tobias had been frequently depicted since the begining of the 16th century, particularly in etchings and engravings. For Rembrandt it was a constant and special source of inspiration, even more than the stories of the patriarchs. Referring back to the examples at hand by earlier artists, he illustrated virtually all the events in this moving family history in a large number of drawings, several etchings and a group of paintings. Although the greatest value was attached in the 16th century to an edifying presentation of the story, Rembrandt's principal intention was to highlight its emotional aspects, showing his awareness of moments to which little or no attention had been previously paid.

The book of Tobit has come down to us in a number of fairly divergent versions. As the original text is unknown, it is not clear which version merits preference. As in Rembrandt's time, the book of Tobit was best known in the Vulgate version (partly because Luther had also based his translation of Tobit upon it), only this text can in many cases sufficiently explain the manner in which Rembrandt has illustrated the various episodes.

This is immediately apparent in this beautifully composed drawing of Tobit spending the night in his

courtyard, having buried a murdered fellow Jew under cover of darkness. Differing from what is said in verse II of the version of the story printed here, we read in the Vulgate that Tobit fell asleep, after leaning against the wall to rest. 'And while he slept warm dung fell from a swallow's nest onto his eyes, so that he became blind.' On the basis of this text, Rembrandt has presented Tobit sleeping with a swallow's nest immediately above his head. The shovel lying next to him reminds us of his charitable deed which will cost him so dearly. The basket alludes in a more general fashion to his helpfulness (cf. pp. 68 and 69 the basket next to Joseph, now appointed a gaoler, who explains the dreams of the two imprisoned courtiers).

Drawing in pen; 17 × 19 cm.
Ca. 1650-52.
Rotterdam, Museum Boymans-van Beuningen.

Literature: Benesch V, no. 872 (*ca.* 1651)/J.S. Held, *Rembrandt and the Book of Tobit*, Northampton (Mass.) 1964; H.-M. Rotermund, *Das Buch Tobias. Erzählt und ausgelegt durch Zeichnungen und Radierungen Rembrandts*, Stuttgart (1962).

Tobit and Anna with the Kid

From whence is this kid? is it stolen? render it to the owners; for it is not lawful to eat anything that is stolen. But she said, It hath been given me for a gift more than the wages. And I did not believe her ... and I was abashed at her. But she answered and said unto me, Where are thine alms and thy righteous deeds? behold, thou and all thy works are known.
(Tobit 2:13-15)

In one of his earliest works, Rembrandt had already depicted the moment when, after his wife's violent outburst, Tobit in absolute desperation urgently begs God to be allowed to die (see pp. 168-69). Here he illustrates the altercation between Tobit and Anna which precedes this. The blind old man has heard the bleating of the kid which his wife has brought home, and to her great annoyance refuses to believe that she has obtained it honestly. 'Render it to the owners.'

   This pithy sketch is generally considered to be a preliminary study for the little panel from 1645 reproduced on the next page. Both are based on an engraving from one of the many series of prints of the Tobit story which were circulating during the 16th century, and which invariably contained a representation of the scene in question.

Drawing in pen; 14.6 × 18.5 cm.
Ca. 1645.
Berlin, Kupferstichkabinett der Staatlichen Museen.

Literature: Benesch III, no. 572 (*ca.* 1645)/Tümpel 1970, no. 28.

... render it to the owners; for it is not lawful to eat anything that is stolen. But she said, It hath been given me for a gift more than the wages. And I did not believe her, and I bade her render it to the owners; and I was abashed at her. But she answered and said unto me, Where are thine alms and thy righteous deeds? behold, thou and all thy works are known.
(Tobit 2:13-14)

The late light coming into the shabby home through the open window barely manages to separate the quarrelling couple by the fire from the darkness pressing from the other side.

The irritable Tobit is not open to reason, and his insinuating words finally cause Anna to retaliate violently and viciously: 'Where are thine alms and thy righteous deeds?' It has apparently all been hypocrisy, this charity of his. This is why he is now in misery. Behind her furious response hides the conviction, based on the old doctrine of retribution which only takes account of an earthly existence, that there has to be something wrong with someone who is pursued by misfortune, however pious he may appear to be. After all, God is just. He rewards good and punishes evil. The calamity which Tobit suffers can leave no other

conclusion than that his righteousness has only been an appearance. And in the eyes of Anna he has now also revealed his true nature through his suspiciousness. With her stinging response she recalls Job's wife, who concludes from the suffering with which he is overwhelmed that he must have been a secret sinner: 'Dost thou still retain thy integrity? curse God, and die' (Job 2:9).

The little painting forms a pair with the panel of the same size, dating from the same year, *The Angel Appears to Joseph in the Dream*, which is also in Berlin (see p. 249).

Panel; 20 × 27 cm.
Signed and dated: *Rembrandt f. 1645*.
Berlin, Gemäldegalerie der Staatlichen Museen.

Literature: Bredius, no. 514; Bauch, no. 26; Gerson, no. 209; Bredius-Gerson, no. 514/J. Bruyn, *Rembrandt's keuze van Bijbelse onderwerpen*, Utrecht 1959, p. 14V, Tümpel 1970, under no. 28.

Tobit and Anna with the kid

Command my spirit to be taken from me

Tobit 3 AND I was grieved and wept, and prayed in sorrow, saying,

2 O Lord, thou art righteous, and all thy works and all thy ways are mercy and truth, and thou judgest true and righteous judgement for ever.

3 Remember me, and look on me; take not vengeance on me for my sins and mine ignorances, and *the sins* of my fathers, which sinned before thee:

4 for they disobeyed thy commandments; and thou gavest us for a spoil, and for captivity, and for death, and for a proverb of reproach to all the nations among whom we are dispersed.

5 And now many are thy judgements, true are they; that thou shouldest deal with me according to my sins and *the sins* of my fathers: because we did not keep thy commandments, for we walked not in truth before thee.

6 And now deal with me according to that which is pleasing in thy sight, command my spirit to be taken from me, that I may be released, and become earth: for it is profitable for me to die rather than to live, because I have heard false reproaches, and there is much sorrow in me: command that I be now released from my distress, and go to the everlasting place: turn not thy face away from me.

Tobit and Anna with the Kid

And I was grieved and wept, and prayed in sorrow, ... command my spirit to be taken from me, that I may be released, and become earth: for it is profitable for me to die rather than to live, because I have heard false reproaches, and there is much sorrow in me:
(Tobit 3:1,6)

Although Tobit admits that his distress is a just punishment for the sins which he and his forefathers have committed, his wife's bitter reproach causes him such pain that he desires nothing more than to be released from his suffering, and beseeches God for death as if for a blessing.

In the small painting in which the 20-year-old Rembrandt has captured this moment, his talent for convincingly representing the emotions of his figures is already apparent. While Tobit, clothed in a worn reminder of better days, prays despairingly for death, Anna looks with amazement at the effect of her violent outburst. They are both equally upset. The distribution of the light, with the background left in shadow, reveals the first stage of the light and dark contrasts which Rembrandt will use in his later work in order to clarify a scene and increase its dramatic force.

The composition is based upon a print from *ca.* 1620,

made by Jan van de Velde after a drawing by Willem Buytewech (1591-1624). Several details are taken from this model, such as the birdcage, the string of garlic and the spool lying on the chair, an allusion to the handwork with which Anna is endeavouring to earn money. It is characteristic of the young Rembrandt that he has reduced the interior to a minimum and concentrated chiefly on the two figures. They precisely fill the picture area and demand the fullest attention. With the principal emphasis being laid upon the facial expressions of the two old people, the painting possesses a psychological tension which is alien to the picture on which Rembrandt has based it. Neither is the praying Tobit's weariness of life the subject in van de Velde's picture, but Anna's angry reaction to his groundless accusation.

Panel; 39.5 × 30 cm.
Signed and dated: *RH 1626.*
Amsterdam, Rijksmuseum.

Literature: Bredius, no. 486; Bauch, no. 2; Gerson, no. 4; Bredius-Gerson, no. 486/J. Bruyn, *Rembrandt's keuze van Bijbelse onderwerpen*, Utrecht 1959, p. 14; Tümpel 1969, p. 113.

May his angel go with you

Tobit 4 IN that day Tobit remembered concerning the money which he had left in trust with Gabael in Rages of Media,

2 and he said in himself, I have asked for death; why do I not call my son Tobias, that I may shew to him *of the money* before I die?

3 And he called him, and said, My child, when I die, bury me: and despise not thy mother; honour her all the days of thy life, and do that which is pleasing unto her, and grieve her not.

4 Remember, my child, that she hath seen many dangers for thee, *when thou wast* in her womb. When she is dead, bury her, by me in one grave.

5 My child, be mindful of the the LORD our God all thy days, and let not thy will be set to sin and to transgress his commandments: do righteousness all the days of thy life, and follow not the ways of unrighteousness. [...]

12 Beware, my child, of all whoredom, and take first a wife of the seed of thy fathers, and take not a strange wife, which is not of thy fathers tribe: for we are the sons of the prophets. Noah, Abraham, Isaac, Jacob, our fathers of old time, rememeber, my child, that they all took wives of their brethren, and we are blessed in their children, and their seed shall inherit the land. [...]

20 And now I shew thee of the ten talents of silver, which I left in trust with Gabael the son of Gabrias at Rages of Media.

21 And fear not, my child, because we are made poor: thou hast much wealth, if thou fear God, and depart from all sin, and do that which is pleasing in his sight.

Tobit 5 AND Tobias answered and said unto him, Father, I will do all things, whatsoever thou hast commanded me:

2 but how shall I be able to receive the money, seeing I know him not?

3 And he gave him the handwriting, and said unto him, Seek thee a man which shall go with thee, and I will give him wages, whiles I yet live: and go and receive the money.

4 And he went to seek a men,

5 and found Raphael which was an angel; and he kwew it not; and he said unto him, Can I go with thee to Rages of Media? and knowest thou the places well?

6 And the angel said unto him, I will go with thee, and I know the way well: and I have lodged with our brother Gabael.

7 And Tobias said unto him, Wait for me, and I will tell my father.

8 And he said unto him, Go, and tarry not. And he went in and said to his father, Behold, I have found one which will go with me. But he said, Call him unto me, that I may know of what tribe he is, and whether he be a trusty man to go with thee.

9 And he called him, and he came in, and they saluted one another.

10 And Tobit said unto him, Brother, of what tribe and of what family art thou? Shew me.

11 And he said unto him, Seekest thou a tribe and a family, or a hired man which shall go with thy son? And Tobit said unto him, I would know, brother, thy kindred and thy name.

12 And he said, I am Azarias, the son of Ananias the great, of thy brethren.

13 And he said unto him, Welcome, brother; and me not angry with me, because I sought to know thy tribe and family: and thou art my brother, of an honest and good lineage: for I knew Ananias and Jathan, the sons of Shemaiah the great, when we went together to Jerusalem to worship, and offered the firstborn, and the tenths of our increase: and they went not astry in the error of our brethren: my brother, thou art of a great stock.

14 But tell me, what wages shall I give thee? a drachma a day, and those things that be necessary for thee, as unto my son?

15 And moreover, if ye return safe and sound, I will add something to thy wages. And so they consented.

16 And he said to Tobias, Prepare thyself for the journey, and God prosper you. And his son prepared what was needful for the journey, and his father said unto him, Go thou with this man; but God, which dwelleth in heaven, shall prosper your journey; and may his angel go with you. And they both went forth to depart, and the young man's dog with them.

... and he came in and they saluted one another. And Tobit said unto him, Brother, of what tribe and of what family art thou? Shew me. And he said unto him, Seekest thou a tribe and a family, or a hired man which shall go with thy son? (Tobit 5:9-11)

True to tradition, Rembrandt represents Raphael, who is posing as an ordinary mortal, in the shape of an angel. He puts himself in the position of the viewer who already knows what is being hidden from Tobit and his family for the moment.

The drawing shows how the blind old man, characteristically suspicious, wants to know exactly who the person is that has agreed to be his son's travelling companion. In the left foreground Anna sits at her spinning wheel. Young Tobias' dog has already cottoned on to the fact that his master plans to leave, and jumps up him, tail wagging. Of course, he will be allowed to go with them.

Only when Tobias actually leaves with his guide, a little later, does Anna fully realize what the boy, their only child, means to them, and she bursts into tears. 'Why has thou sent away our child?' she snaps at Tobit. 'Is he not the staff of our hand, in going in and out before us? Be not greedy to add money to money: but let it be as refuse in respect of our child. For as the Lord has given us to live, so doth it suffice us.' Tobit is not daunted by his wife's harsh tone and sombre outlook, and retains his optimism. 'Take no care my sister; he shall return safe and sound, and thine eyes shall see him. For a good angel shall go with him, and his journey will be prospered and he shall return safe and sound. And she made an end of weeping.' (Tobit 5:17-22).

Drawing in pen; 17.2 × 22.3 cm.
Lower right in later handwriting: *Rembrand.*
Ca. 1645-50.
Vienna, Albertina.

Literature: Benesch III, no. 597 (*ca.* 1647-48).

Tobit Questioning the Angel

And a fish leaped out of the river

Tobit 6 NOW as they went on their journey, they came at eventide to the river Tigris, and they lodged there.

2 But the young man went down to wash himself, and a fish leaped out of the river, and would have swallowed up the young man.

3 But the angel said unto him, Take hold on the fish. And the young man caught hold of the fish, and cast it up on the land.

4 And the angel said unto him, Cut the fish open, and take the heart and the liver and the gall, and put them up safely.

5 And the young men did as the angel commanded him; but they roasted the fish, and ate it. And they both went on their way, till they drew near to Ecbatana.

6 And the young man said to the angel, Brother Azarias, to what use is the heart and the liver and the gall of the fish?

7 And he said unto him, Touching the heart and the liver, if a devil or an evil spirit trouble any, we must make a smoke thereof before the man or the woman, and the party shall be no more vexed.

8 But as for the gall, *it is good* to anoint a man that hath white films in his eyes, and he shall be healed.

9 But when they drew night unto Rages, the angel said to the young man,

10 Brother, to-day we shall lodge with Raguel, and he is thy kinsman; and he hath an only daughter, named Sarah. I will speak for her, that she should be given thee for a wife.

11 For to thee doth the inheritance of her appertain, and thou only art of her kindred: and the maid is fair and wise.

12 And now hear me, and I will speak to her father; and when we return from Rages we will celebrate the marriage: for I know that Raguel may in no wise marry her to another according to the law of Moses, or else he shall be liable to death, because it appertaineth unto thee to take the inheritance, rather than any other.

13 Then the young man said unto the angel, Brother Azarias, I have heard that this maid hath been given to seven men, and that they all perished in the bride-chamber.

14 And now I am the only son of my father, and I am afraid, lest I go in and die, even as those before me: for a devil loveth her, which hurteth no man, but those which come unto her: and now I fear lest I die, and bring my father's and my mother's life to the grave with sorrow because of me: and they have no other son to bury them.

15 But the angel said unto him, Dost thou not remember the words which thy father commanded thee, that thou shouldest take a wife of thine own kindred? and now hear me, brother; for she shall be thy wife; and make thou no reckoning of the devil; for this night shall she be given thee to wife.

16 And when thou shalt come into the bride-chamber, thou shalt take the ashes of incense, and shalt lay upon them some of the heart and liver of the fish, and shalt make a smoke *therewith:* and the devil shall smell it, and flee away, and never come again any more.

17 But when thou goest night unto her, rise up both of you, and cry to God which is merciful, and he shall save you, and have mercy on you. Fear not, for she was prepared for thee from the beginning; and thou shalt save her, and she shall go with thee. And I suppose that thou shalt have children of her. And when Tobias heard these things, he loved her, and his soul clave to her exceedingly.

Now as they went on their journey, they came at eventide to the river Tigris, and they lodged there. But the young man went down to wash himself ...
(Tobit 6:1-2)

This representation of Tobias, who is making ready to remove his footgear, is based upon the Vulgate version, which says that the boy goes to wash his feet. The dog who is travelling with them has already hastened down the bank to quench his thirst.

This beautifully structured drawing, dating from the beginning of the 1650s, was the model for a painting from the school of Rembrandt (Berlin Gemäldegalerie der Staatlichen Museen; see Cat. *Rembrandt after Three Hundred Years*, Chicago 1969, no. 25).

Drawing in pen; 17.9 × 26.3 cm.
Ca. 1650-52.
Paris, The Louvre.

Literature: Benesch V, no. 908 (*ca.* 1652); Slive I, no. 196 (*ca.* 1652).

Tobias and the Angel on the Banks of the Tigris

Tobias Frightened by the Fish

But the young man went down to wash himself, and a fish leaped out of the river, and would have swallowed up the young man. But the angel said unto him, Take hold on the fish.
(Tobit 6:2-3)

Differing from the version of the story reproduced here, the text of the Vulgate emphasizes the fright which the fish causes Tobias when it suddenly surfaces, so that the young man cries out to the Lord that he is being attacked. Raphael, of remarkably solid stature in comparison with the boyish Tobias, appears in this picture as a kind of guardian angel, who watches over the welfare of his youthful protégé (see also the drawing reproduced on the next page).

Pen and brush drawing; 20.5 × 27.3 cm.
Ca. 1645.
Berlin, Kupferstichkabinett der Staatlichen Museen.

Literature: Benesch III, no. 559 (*ca.* 1644); Haak, no. 42 (*ca.* 1644)/Tümpel 1970, no. 29 (school of Rembrandt).

174

But the young man went down to wash himself, and a fish leaped out of the river, and would have swallowed up the young man. But the angel said unto him, Take hold on the fish.
(Tobit 6:2-3)

The incident on the banks of the Tigris is illustrated here against the background of a sweeping mountain terrain, which contributes to the narrative and stimulates the viewer's imagination. From a copy kept in the Louvre in Paris, it appears that a section of the drawing has been cut off on the right-hand side.

Pen and brush drawing; 20.6 × 28.9 cm.
Ca. 1650.
Copenhagen, Kobberstiksamling.

Literature: Benesch III, no. 638 (*ca.* 1649-50).

*Tobias Frightened
by the Fish*

175

It appertaineth unto thee to take my child

Tobit 7 AND they came to Ecbatana, and arrived at the house of Raguel. But Sarah met them; and she saluted them, and they her; and she brought them into the house.

2 And he said to Edna his wife, How like is the young man to Tobit my cousin.

3 And Raguel asked them, From whence are ye, brethren? And they said unto him, We are of the sons of Naphtali, which are captives in Nineveh.

4 And he said unto them, Know ye Tobit our brother? But they said, We know him. And he said unto them, Is he in good health?

5 But they said, He is both alive, and in good health: and Tobias said, He is my father.

6 And Raguel sprang up, and kissed him, and wept, and blessed him, and said unto him, Thou art the son of an honest and good man.

7 And when he had heard that Tobit had lost his sight, he was grieved, and wept: and Edna his wife and Sarah his daughter wept.

8 And they received them gladly; and they killed a ram of the flock, and set store of meat before them. But Tobias said to Raphael, Brother Azarias, speak of those things of which thou didst talk in the way, and let the matter be finished.

9 And he communicated the thing to Raguel: and Raguel said to Tobias, Eat and drink, and make merry: for it appertaineth unto thee to take my child.

11 Howbeit I will shew thee the truth. I have given my child to seven men, and whensoever they came in unto her, they died in the night. But for the present be merry. And Tobias said, I will taste nothing here, until ye make covenants and enter into covenant with me.

12 And Raguel said, Take her to thyself from henceforth according to the manner: thou art her brother, and she is thine: but the merciful God shall give all good success to you.

13 And he called his daughter Sarah, and took her by the hand, and gave her to be wife to Tobias, and said, Behold, take her to thyself after the law of Moses, and lead her away to thy father.

14 And he blessed them; and he called Edna his wife, and took a book, and wrote an instrument, and sealed it.

15 And the began to eat.

16 And Raguel called his wife Edna, and said unto her, Sister, prepare the other chamber, and bring her in thither.

17 And she did as he bade her, and brought her in thither: and she wept, and she received the tears of her daughter, and said unto her,

18 Be of good comfort, my child; the Lord of heaven and earth give thee favour for this thy sorrow: be of good comfort, my daughter.

Raguel Embraces the Young Tobias

And Raguel sprang up, and kissed him, and wept, and blessed him, and said unto him, Thou art the son of an honest and good man. And when he heard that Tobit had lost his sight, he was grieved, and wept; and Edna his wife and Sarah his daughter wept.
(Tobit 7:7-8)

The Vulgate version does not mention, unlike verse 1 of the version used here, an initial encounter with Sarah, the daughter of Raguel, who invites the travellers to enter. In the Vulgate it is Raguel himself who welcomes them delightedly. The hospitable man, struck by the strong likeness between the youngest of the two and his cousin Tobit, then begins to question them about where they have come from. He soon learns that the young man is the son of his cousin in Nineveh, and there follows the moving scene, here depicted by Rembrandt. While Raguel embraces his blood relation with great fervour, his wife and daughter show their compassion for the lot of Tobit, who has gone blind. It is wonderful to see how Raphael (who is here, very exceptionally, represented without wings) keeps a discreet distance from this tender family scene. In a few moments the company will go up the winding staircase into the house, where the reception will be finished off with a meal.

The drawing dates from the beginning of the 1650s, a period in which - as the drawings on pages 165 and 173 already discussed, and the etching to follow on page 185, dated 1651, show - Rembrandt was intensively occupied with the story of Tobit.

Drawing in pen; 19.2 × 27.1 cm.
Ca. 1650-52.
Amsterdam, Rijksprentenkabinet.

Literature: Benesch V, no. 871 (*ca.* 1651); Slive II, no. 320
(*ca.* 1650-52)/'Bijbelse Inspiratie', no. 82 [as *The
Departure of Tobias from Raguel's House* (Tobit 10:9-13)].

Blessed art thou, O God of our fathers

Tobit 8 AND when they had finished their supper, they brought Tobias in unto her.

2 But as she went, he remembered the words of Raphael, and took the ashes of the incense, and put the heart and the liver of the fish thereupon, and made a smoke *therewith*.

3 But when the devil smelled the smell, he fled into the uppermost parts of Egypt, and the angel bound him.

4 But after they were both shut in together, Tobias rose up from the bed, and said, Sister, arise, and let us pray that the Lord may have mercy on us.

5 And Tobias began to say, Blessed art thou, O God of our fathers, and blessed is thy holy and glorious name for ever; let the heavens bless thee, and all thy creatures.

6 Thou madest Adam, and gavest him Eve his wife for a helper and a stay: of them came the seed of men: thou didst say, It is not good that the man should be alone; let us make him a helper like unto him.

7 And now, O Lord, I take not this my sister for lust, but in truth: command that I may find mercy and grow old with her.

8 And she said with him, Amen.

9 And they slept both that night.

10 And Raguel arose, and went and digged a grave, saying, Lest he also should die.

11 And Raguel came into his house, and said to Edna his wife,

12 Send one of the maidservants, and let them see whether he be alive: but if not, that we may bury him, and no man know it.

13 So the maidservant opened the door, and went in, and found them both sleeping,

14 and came forth, and told them that he was alive.

15 And Raguel blessed God, saying, Blessed art thou, O God, with all pure and holy blessing; and let thy saints bless thee, and all thy cratures; and let all thine angels and thine elect bless thee for ever.

16 Blessed art thou, because thou hast made me glad; and it hath not befallen me as I suspected; but thou hast dealt with us according to thy great mercy.

17 Blessed art thou, because thou hast had mercy on two that were the only begotten children of their parents: shew them mercy, O Lord; accomplish their life in health with gladness and mercy.

18 But he commanded his servants to fill the grave.

19 And he kept the wedding feast for them fourteen days.

20 And before the days of the wedding feast were finished, Raguel sware unto him, that he should not depart till the fourteen days of the wedding feast were fulfilled;

21 and that then he should take the half of his goods, and go in safety to his father; and the rest, *said he*, when I and my wife shall die.

Tobit 9 AND Tobias called Raphael, and said unto him,

2 Brother Azarias, take with thee a servant, and two camels, and go to Rages of Media to Gabael, and receive the money for me, and bring him to the wedding feast:

3 because Raguel hath sworn that I shall not depart;

4 and my father counteth the days; and if I tarry long, he will be sorely grieved.

5 And Raphael went on his way, and lodged with Gabael, and gave him the handwriting: but he brought forth the bags with their seals, and gave them to him.

6 And they rose up early in the morning together, and came to the wedding feast: and Tobias blessed his wife.

But when the devil smelled the smell, he fled into the uppermost parts of Egypt, and the angel bound him. But after they were both shut in together, Tobias rose up from the bed, and said, Sister, arise, and let us pray that the Lord may have mercy upon us.
(Tobit 8:3-4)

After Tobias has done with the heart and liver of the fish as the angel told him, the event predicted by the angel promptly occurs: 'The devil shall smell it, and flee away, and never come again any more' (Tobit 6:17). Tied down in Upper Egypt, far away on the other side of the world, he will not be able to harm anyone any more. Then Tobias begins to pray. He sings God's praises and ends with a supplication to which Sarah heartily assents in the pronouncement of the Amen.

In the drawing in question, Rembrandt has combined the prayer of Tobias and Sarah with the flight of the Devil which precedes it. In the door opening to the left, we have a glimpse of old Raguel who has just brought the young bridegroom to his daughter's chamber in fear and anxiety, and will soon dig a grave for him, because after all that has happened to Tobias's predecessors he scarcely dares to hope any longer for a happy outcome.

In 1611 Pieter Lastman depicted this episode for the first time in a painting (Boston, Museum of Fine Arts). Until then it had only been illustrated in prints. Although his version restricts itself to the moment when the Devil is rendered harmless, while Rembrandt here lays the emphasis upon the prayer of the young couple which follows, the connection between the two is unmistakable. There is a copy after this Rembrandt drawing in the Museum Boymans-van Beuningen in Rotterdam (see H.R. Hoetink, *Tekeningen van Rembrandt en zijn school*, Rotterdam 1969, pl. 196).

Drawing in pen; 17.4 × 23.7 cm.
Ca. 1648-50.
New York, The Metropolitan Museum of Art, Rogers Fund.

Literature: Benesch III, no. 633 (*ca.* 1648-50)/Tümpel 1969, pp. 176-78, ill. 56 (as copy after Rembrandt).

The Wedding Night of Tobias and Sarah

The child hath perished

Tobit 10 AND Tobit his father made his count every day: and when the days of the journey were expired, and they came not, he said,

2 Is he perchance detained? or is Gabael perchance dead, and there is no man to give him the money?

3 And he was sorely grieved.

4 But his wife said unto him, The child hath perished, seeing he tarrieth long; and she began to bewail him, and said,

5 I care for nothing, my child, since I have let thee go, the light of mine eyes.

6 And tobit said unto her, Hold thy peace, take no care; he is in good health.

7 And she said unto him, Hold thy peace, deceive me not; my child hath perished. And she went out every day into the way by which they went, and did eat no bread in the day-time, and ceased not whole nights to bewail her son Tobias, until the fourteen days of the wedding feast were expired, which Raguel had sworn that he should spend there. But Tobias said unto Raguel, Send me away, for my father and my mother look no more to see me.

Tobit and Anna Awaiting the Return of their Son

And Tobit his father made his count every day: and when the days of the journey were expired, and they came not, he said, Is he perchance detained ... And he was sorely grieved. But his wife said unto him, The child hath perished, seeing he tarrieth long; and she began to bewail him. (Tobit 10:1-4)

The story takes us briefly back to Tobias' parents in Nineveh, where anxiety and sorrow contrast sharply with the joy and youthful happiness in the house of Raguel and Edna.

Rembrandt has based the painting of this rarely illustrated moment upon the drawing from the second half of the 1640s, reproduced on p. 171. We find the old couple in the same attitudes in which we left them: Anna at her spinning wheel, Tobit in his chair by the fire, with his back to the light. At the window we once again see a birdcage, as in the little painting from 1626 (see p. 169).

A gloomy atmosphere prevails in the bare, gradually darkening room. The torturing uncertainty about the fate of their child has driven the couple apart. Tobit no longer ventures any attempt to cheer up his wife. 'Hold thy peace,' is what he hears, 'deceive me not; my child hath perished.' *My* child! Anna has disagreed with her husband from the outset about the value of the wretched journey, and now that the boy not come back, she is less ready than ever to listen to him.

While the painting was being cleaned in 1947, it emerged that the date was not 1650, as had been read up till then, but 1659. This makes it Rembrandt's last work with a theme from the book of Tobit.

Panel; 40.3 × 54 cm.
Signed and dated: *Rembrandt f. 1659.*
Rotterdam, Museum Boymans-van Beuningen,
Collection Willem van der Vorm.

Literature: Bredius, no. 520; Bauch, no. 30; Gerson, no.
348; Bredius-Gerson, no. 520.

But take in thy hand the gall of the fish

Tobit 10 8 But his father in law said unto him, Abide with me, and I will send to thy father, and they shall declare unto him how things go with thee.

9 And Tobias saith, No; but send me away to my father.

10 But Raguel arose, and gave him Sarah his wife, and half his goods, servants and cattle and money;

11 and he blessed them, and sent them away,

Tobit 11 AFTER these things Tobias also went his way, blessing God because he had prospered his journey; and he blessed Raguel and Edna his wife. And he went on his way till they drew near unto Nineveh.

2 And Raphael said to Tobias, Knowest thou

saying The God of heaven shall prosper you, my children, before I die.

12 And he said to his daugher, Honour thy father and thy mother in law; they are now thy parents; let me hear a good report of thee. And he kissed her. And Edna said to Tobias, The Lord of heaven restore thee, dear brother, and grant to me that I may see thy children of my daughter Sarah, that I may rejoice before the Lord: and, behold, I commit my daughter unto thee in special trust: vex her not.

not, brother, how thou didst leave thy father? 3 Let us run forward before thy wife, and prepare the house.

4 But take in thy hand the gall of the fish. And they went their way, and the dog went after them.

Tobias and Sarah with the Angel on the Way to Nineveh

And he went on his way till they drew near unto Nineveh. And Raphael said to Tobias, Knowest thou not, brother, how thou didst leave thy father? Let us run forward before thy wife, and prepare the house. But take in thy hand the gall of the fish.
(Tobit 11:1-4)

At last Raguel has allowed Tobias to leave. And happiness is finally at hand for the house of Tobit as well.

In this lively drawing, dating from the middle of the 1650s, Rembrandt has confined himself to the main characters. Of the animals and slaves which Raguel presented to Tobias along with his daughter, we only see the donkey on which the young man is conveying his wife homewards. Tobias's face is radiant with happiness. How surprisingly differently everything has turned out than expected! The fish from the Tigris and the bride from Ecbatana have reduced Gabael's money, for which he originally undertook the journey, to a barely relevant side issue. Now the company is approaching Nineveh, Raphael proposes to Tobias that they run ahead together and return to his parents the way they left them: a twosome accompanied by the dog. After all, his mother and father are not yet equal in their destitution to receiving his bride.

Drawing in pen, rounded at the top; 21.1 × 18.8 cm.
Ca. 1655.
Edinburgh, The National Gallery of Scotland.

Literature: Benesch V, no. 985 (*ca.* 1654-55).

Be of good cheer, my father

Tobit 11 5 And Anna sat looking about toward the way for her son.

6 And she espied him coming, and said to his father, Behold, thy son cometh, and the man that went with him.

7 And Raphael said, I know, Tobias, that thy father will open his eyes.

8 Do thou therefore anoint his eyes with the gall, and being pricked therewith, he shall rub, and shall make the white films to fall away, and he shall see thee.

9 And Anna ran unto him, and fell upon the neck of her son, and said unto him, I have seen thee, my child; from henceforth I will die. And the wept both.

10 And Tobit went forth toward the door, and stumbled: but his son ran unto him, and took hold of his father:

11 and he strake the gall on his father's eyes, saying, Be of good cheer, my father.

12 But when his eyes began to smart, he rubbed them; and the white films scaled away from the corners of his eyes; and he saw his son, and fell upon his neck.

14 And he wept, and said, Blessed art thou, O God, and blessed are thy holy angels; for thou didst scourge, and didst have mercy on me: behold, I see my son Tobias.

15 And his son went in rejoicing, and told his father the great things that had happened to him in Media.

16 And Tobit went out to meet his daughter in law at the gate of Nineveh, rejoicing, and blessing God: and they which saw him go marvelled, because he had received his sight.

17 And Tobit gave thanks before them, because God had shewed mercy on him. And when Tobit came near to Sarah his daughter in law, he blessed her, saying, Welcome, daughter: blessed is God which hath brought thee unto us, and *blessed are* thy father and thy mother. And there was joy to all his brethren which were at Nineveh.

The Blind Tobit Goes to Meet his Son

And Tobit went forth toward the door and stumbled. (Tobit 11:10)

In representations of the moment when Tobias returns to his parents, we generally find ourselves outside and see how the boy is embraced by his mother in front of the house, while old Tobit appears in the doorway. Even in his early print from around 1629, Rembrandt opts for a different approach to this subject. He is not interested by what is going on outside, but what is happening in the house to the blind father. Caught off guard by Anna's joyous news - 'Behold, thy son cometh, and the man that went with him' - the stiff old greybeard feels his way towards the door, to meet his son. Rembrandt probably intended originally to give an impression through the door opening of Tobias being greeted by his mother, but at an early stage he made this group virtually indecipherable with hatching, and restricted the scene to Tobit.

Etching; 7.9 × 5.5 cm. Second state of five.
Ca. 1629.
Amsterdam, Rijksprentenkabinet.

Literature: Bartsch, no. 153; Hind, no. 74; Münz, no. 171; Boon, no. 18/Tümpel 1970, no. 30.

And Tobit Went Forth Toward the Door, and Stumbled (Tobit 11:10)

In this etching from 1651, Rembrandt once more focuses full attention on Tobit's consternation at the news of his son's approach. How touchingly is the old man drawn, both in his joy and yet in his misery. He has risen hastily from his chair by the large open hearth. So agitated is he, so yearning for his son, that he has knocked over the spinning wheel on his way outside, and is now disoriented and no longer knows where to find the door. According to the Vulgate version, young Tobias's dog has run ahead of the two homeward bound travellers as messenger of the joyful news, merrily wagging its tail. Here the animal has already leaped through the open door and is pressing himself in greeting against Tobit's legs. Not only for its profound human content, but also for the technical mastery with which the simplest devices have been employed, this is one of the loveliest examples of Rembrandt's etchings.

Etching; 16.1 cm × 12.9 cm. First state of two.
Signed and dated: *Rembrandt f. 1651.*
Amsterdam, Rijksprentenkabinet.

Literature: Bartsch, no. 42; Hind, no. 252; Münz, no. 181; Boon, no. 232; Filedt Kok, no. B 42/'Bijbelse Inspiratie', no. 28; Tümpel 1968, p. 115; Tümpel 1970, no. 32.

The Healing of Tobit   *And after waiting for about half an hour, the whiteness*
peeled away from his eyes like the membrane of an egg.
Tobias took hold of it and pulled it from his father's eyes. At
the same moment, his sight was returned to him.
(Translation from Dutch Vulgate, Tobias 11:14-15)

The group of four figures, bunched together by the
open window, shows many points of similarity to the
group on the little panel from 1636. Probably the
drawing was made as a preliminary study for the
painting, but it is also possible that it was produced
somewhat later, as a design for a similar scene, but
with the direction reversed.

   Anna is represented here kneeling. Judging by the
drawings on pp. 190 and 191, what she is holding in her
hands is a dish with on it the fish gall that Tobias has
used to treat his father's eyes. In the background,
roughly indicated, is her spinning wheel. The dog,
tired out from the long journey, but quite at home
once again, has stretched himself out contentedly at
Tobit's feet.

Drawing in pen; 20.8 × 20.2 cm.
Ca. 1636-40.
Amsterdam, Amsterdams Historisch Museum.

Literature: Benesch III, no. 548 (*ca.* 1642-44); Slive II, no.
419 (*ca.* 1640)/'Bijbelse Inspiratie', no. 84.

And after waiting for about half an hour, the whiteness peeled away from his eyes like the membrane of an egg. Tobias took hold of it and pulled it from his father's eyes. At the same moment, his sight was returned to him.
(Translation from Dutch Vulgate, Tobias 11:14-15)

In comparison with the previous and following representations of Tobit's healing, we see here a far less crowded arrangement of the four figures. Particularly noticeable is the angel's aloofness in the background. Anna's spinning wheel is once again present, standing by the hearth which finishes off the composition on the right side. And Tobias's dog has not been forgotten this time, either.

Pen and brush drawing; 16 × 15.5 cm.
Ca. 1640.
Copenhagen, Kobberstiksamling.

Literature: Benesch III, no. 546, (*ca.* 1642-44)/'Bijbelse Inspiratie', under no. 84.

The Healing of Tobit

The healing of Tobit

Then Tobias took some of the gall from the fish, and he strake it on his father's eyes. And after waiting for about half an hour, the whiteness peeled away from his eyes like the membrane of an egg. Tobias took hold of it and pulled it from his father's eyes. At the same moment, his sight was returned to him.
(Translation from Dutch Vulgate, Tobias 11:13-15)

Where the healing of Tobit in particular is concerned, we have to refer to the description which the Vulgate gives for a good understanding of Rembrandt's representations. This is why the text above, and accompanying the other drawings of this theme, is not quoted from the version of the story used for this edition, but has been chosen from the relevant section in the Dutch Vulgate. Only there do we read how, after about half an hour of waiting, the young Tobias goes into action again and removes the white fleck from his father's eye, like the loosened membrane of an egg. And that is precisely the moment which Rembrandt has repeatedly illustrated. His representations are different from older depictions of this theme, which invariably involve the earlier moment when Tobias smears his father's blind eyes with the fish gall.

Ophthalmologists have pointed out that this painting, and the many drawings in which Rembrandt has illustrated the healing of Tobit, in each case depict the medically correct performance of a cataract operation. We may therefore assume that the painter did once attend such an operation, in order to be able to give the most accurate impression of it. His illustrations are some of the earliest portrayals known of a cataract operation, and show that even then they were carried out with the aid of scalpel angled above the head of the patient. The answer to the question of why Rembrandt chose to use a cataract operation for

this theme can be found in the Dutch Bible translation from the 16th century, which was influenced by Luther's translation and describes Tobit's eye affliction as 'film'.

Just as in the other drawings with the same theme, we here see old Tobit sitting in a large chair, which has been pushed close to the window so Tobias can take the greatest possible advantage of the daylight for his operation. Under the protective, outspread wings of the Angel Raphael, the old man, supported by his wife, gives himself over in full confidence to the skilful hands of his son. It is wonderful how Rembrandt brings it to mind that through his marriage with Sarah Tobias has now become a prosperous man. This is clear from his appearance. We are moved when we look at Anna, who has clasped Tobit's hands in her own. During the course of the story we have come to know her as a caustic woman, who has found it increasingly difficult during the past days to get on with her husband, who is so different in temperament. But now that it's kill or cure time, they once again form a close-knit pair. For Rembrandt this reconciliation is also part of Tobit's healing. At some point the painting has been considerably reduced in size on the right edge. Its original form is known from an old copy which is kept in the Herzog-Anton-Ulrich-Museum in Brunswick (reproduced in Bredius-Gerson, p. 417).

Panel; 48 × 39 cm.
Signed and dated: *Rembrandt f. 1636.*
Stuttgart, Staatsgalerie.

Literature: Bredius, no. 502; Bauch, no. 16; Gerson, no. 75; Bredius-Gerson, no. 502/R. Greeff, *Rembrandts Darstellungen der Tobiasheilung*, Stuttgart 1907; Tümpel 1970, under no. 33.

The Healing of Tobit

And after waiting for about half an hour, the whiteness peeled away from his eyes like the membrane of an egg. Tobias took hold of it and pulled it from his father's eyes. At the same moment, his sight was returned to him.
(Translation from Dutch Vulgate, Tobias 11:14-15)

Yet again Rembrandt manages to portray the same subject in a different way. Here his representation is more absorbing than ever. Tensely, the aged patient grips the arms of his chair. The Angel Raphael follows Tobias' actions very carefully. Anna too, with a pince-nez on her nose, is totally absorbed. Judging from her face, the operation is going splendidly. As in many 16th-century representations of this theme, Sarah, Tobias's young bride, is also present at Tobit's healing, although according to the story she will only arrive later in his house. She was the first to derive benefit from the insides of the fish from the Tigris.

Pen and brush drawing; 21.1 × 17.7 cm.
Ca. 1640-45.
Cleveland, The Cleveland Museum of Art.

Literature: Benesch III, no. 547 (*ca.* 1642-44); Slive II, no. 501 (*ca.* 1640-45)/'Bjbelse Inspiratie', under no. 84; Tümpel 1970, under no. 33.

And after waiting for about half an hour, the whiteness peeled away from his eyes like the membrane of an egg. Tobias took hold of it and pulled it from his father's eyes. At the same moment, his sight was returned to him.
(Translation from Dutch Vulgate, Tobias 11:14-15)

The arrangement of the figures is pretty much the same as in the previous drawing. Young Sarah has been left out, however, and her place in the composition is occupied by Anna.

The clean, bold drawing style points to a date around 1650. It appears from a copy (Benesch, under no. 646) that the drawing is the left section of a sheet that was twice as broad in its original form. The copy shows the rest of the interior on the right with a door and an armchair, in which Tobias's dog has laid down to sleep.

Pen and brush drawing; 17.5 × 13.3 cm. Fragment.
Ca. 1650.
Berlin, Kupferstichkabinett der Staatlichen Museen.

Literature: Benesch III, no. 646 (*ca.* 1649-50)/Tümpel 1970, no. 33.

The Healing of Tobit

Be not afraid, ye shall have peace

Tobit 12 AND Tobit called his son Tobias, and said unto him, See, my child, that the man which went with thee have his wages, and thou must give him more.

2 And he said unto him, Father, it is no harm to me to give him the half of those things which I have brought:

3 for he hath led me for thee in safety, and he cured my wife, and brought my money, and likewise cured thee.

4 And the old man said, It is due unto him.

5 And he called the angel, and said unto him, Take the half of all that ye have brought.

6 Then he called them, Bless God, and give him thanks, and magnify him, and give him thanks in the sight of all that live, for the things which he hath done with you. It is good to bless God and exalt his name, shewing forth with honour the works of God; and be not slack to give him thanks.

7 It is good to keep close the secret of a king, but to reveal gloriously the works of God [...]

12 And now, when thou didst pray, and Sarah thy daughter in law, I did bring the memorial of your prayer before the Holy One: and when thou didst bury the dead, I was with thee likewise.

13 And when thou didst not delay to rise up, and leave thy dinner, that thou mightest go and cover the dead, thy good deed was not hid from me: but I was with thee.

14 And now God did send me to heal thee and Sarah thy daughter in law.

15 I am Raphael, one of the seven holy angels, which present the prayers of the saints, and go in before the glory of the Holy One.

16 And they were both troubled, and fell upon their faces; for they were afraid.

17 And he said unto them, Be not afraid, ye shall have peace; but bless God for ever.

18 For not of any favour of mine, but by the will of your God I came: wherefore bless him for ever.

19 All these days did I appear unto you; and I did neither eat or drink, but ye saw a vision.

20 And now give God thanks: because I ascend to him that sent me: and write in a book all the things which have been done.

21 And they rose up, and saw him no more.

22 And they confessed the great and wonderful works of God, and how the angel of the Lord had appeared unto them.

The Angel Leaves Tobit and his Family

And they were both troubled, and fell upon their faces; for they were afraid. And he said unto them, Be not afraid, ye shall have peace ... and now give God thanks: because I ascend to him that sent me ... And they rose up, and saw him no more.
(Tobit 12:16-17, 20-21)

In the representations which Rembrandt has devoted to the end of the story, mother Anna and Tobias's wife Sarah are always witnesses to the angel's departure, in addition to Tobit and Tobias. And the state of amazement in which Raphael leaves them, having revealed his true being, is in each case the real theme of the painting. We see the same expressions of reverence and amazement in Rembrandt's depictions of *The angel rises up in the flame of Manoch's offering* (pp. 95-97) and *The Meal in Emmaus* (pp. 423-29), two kindred subjects for which he had a special predilection all his life.

The painting in question, dating from 1637, appears quite clearly to have drawn its inspiration from a woodcut by Maerten van Heemskerck. The points of similarity in the rendering of the rising angel and the attitudes of Tobit and Tobias are so striking that it can even be said that Rembrandt has seldom followed his models so faithfully as he does in this instance. However, Heemskerck's version lacks the figure of Sarah and the dog, who looks no less amazed here than the humans.

Panel; 68 × 52 cm.
Signed and dated: *Rembrandt f. 1637*.
Paris, The Louvre.

Literature: Bredius, no. 503; Bauch, no. 17; Gerson, no. 81; Bredius-Gerson, no. 503/J. Bruyn, *Rembrandt's keuze van Bijbelse onderwerpen*, Utrecht 1959, pp. 16-17; Tümpel 1970, under no. 34.

The Angel Leaves
Tobit and his Family

And they were both troubled, and fell upon their faces; for they were afraid. And he said unto them, Be not afraid, ye shall have peace ... And now give God thanks: because I ascend to him that sent me ... And they rose up and saw him no more.
(Tobit 12:16-21)

The vertical representation of the painting from 1637 has been transformed in this etching of four years later into a horizontal composition, in which, in addition to a few figures, the scene has been enriched with several motifs alluding to previous events. The pack mule looking sideways in astonishment and the man holding him are a reminder of the caravan in which Sarah travelled to Tobias's family house. And the open casket with valuables, one of which has already been brought out for inspection, alludes to the gifts which the young Tobias, with his father's agreement, had wanted to give to his travelling companion. The angel, flying up to heaven in a stream of dazzling light, has already half disappeared from the picture. This time the dog does not share the amazement in which the angel leaves the family. Anna drops her stick from shock. And just as in the painting in the Louvre, Rembrandt draws it falling.

Etching; 10.3 × 15.4 cm. Second state of four.
Signed and dated: *Rembrandt f. 1641.*
Amsterdam, Rijksprentenkabinet.

Literature: Bartsch, no. 43; Hind, no. 185; Münz, no. 179; Boon, no. 169; Filedt Kok, no. B 43/O. Benesch, 'Über den Werdegang ener Komposition Rembrandts' in *Bulletin du Musée Hongrois des Beaux-Arts* 22 (1963), pp. 71-87 (Collected Writings I, pp. 235-43); Tümpel 1970, no. 34.

And they were both troubled, and fell upon their faces; for they were afraid. And he said unto them, Be not afraid, ye shall have peace ... And now give God thanks: because I ascend to him that sent me ... And they rose up and saw him no more.
(Tobit 12:16-21)

This carefully executed drawing, dating from the second half of the 1640s, is in a certain sense a synthesis of the two previous portrayals of this subject. The motifs which it incorporates are the same as in the etching from 1641, but as far as composition is concerned, there is a return to the painting from 1637. Of the disappearing angel only the legs can still just be seen in the upper left corner. In the left foreground is

the casket with Tobias's possessions. However, here it is the dish the boy is holding in his hands which chiefly alludes to the gifts which he had offered Raphael. The mule and his astonished driver are now in the background. We find Rembrandt's last version of this subject in a drawing from the beginning of the 1650s (Benesch V, no. 893).

Pen and brush drawing; 20.5 × 18.5 cm.
Lower right in later handwriting: *Rembrant.*
Ca. 1645-50.
Oxford, Ashmolean Museum.

Literature: Benesch III, no. 638a (*ca.* 1649-50.

The Angel Leaves Tobit and his Family

A stone smote the image upon his feet *that were* of iron and clay

[On the order of Nebuchadnezzar, the King of Babylon, several notable young men with an all-round education are chosen out of the exiles from Judah to do service at the court after three years of training. Amongst these are Daniel and his friends, Jews steadfast in the law, who in these foreign surroundings remain true to the faith of their fathers. Daniel is gifted with exceptional wisdom and the ability to interpret dreams.]

Daniel 2 AND in the second year of the reign of Nebuchadnezzar Nebuchadnezzar dreamed dreams, wherewith his spirit was troubled, and his sleep brake from him.

2 Then the king commanded to call the magicians, and the astrologers, and the sorcerers, and the Chaldeans, for to shew the king his dreams. So they came and stood before the king.

3 And the king said unto them, I have dreamed a dream, and my spirit was troubled to know the dream.

4 Then spake the Chaldeans to the king in Syriack, O king, live for ever: tell thy servants the dream, and we will shew the interpretation.

5 The king answered and said to the Chaldeans, The thing is gone from me: if ye will not make known unto me the dream, with the interpretation thereof, ye shall be cut in pieces, and your houses shall be made a dunghill.

6 But if ye shew the dream, and the interpretation thereof, ye shall receive of me gifts and rewards and great honour: therefore shew me the dream, and the interpretation thereof.

7 They answered again and said, Let the king tell his servants the dream, and we will shew the interpretation of it.

8 The king answered and said, I know of certainty that ye would gain the time, because ye see the thing is gone from me.

9 But if ye will not make known unto me the dream, *there is but* one decree for you: for ye have prepared lying and corrupt words to speak before me, till the time be changed: therefore tell me the dream, and I shall know

that ye can shew me the interpretation thereof.

10 The Chaldeans answered before the king, and said, There is not a man upon the earth that can shew the king's matter: therefore *there is* no king, lord, nor ruler, *that* asked such things at any magician, or astrologer, or Chaldean.

11 And *it is* a rare thing that the king requireth, and there is none other that can shew it before the king, except the gods, whose dwelling is not with flesh.

12 For this cause the king was angry and very furious, and commanded to destroy all the wise *men* of Babylon. [...]

24 Therefore Daniel went in unto Arioch, whom the king had ordained to destroy the wise *men* of Babylon: he went and said thus unto him; Destroy not the wise *men* of Babylon: bring me in before the king, and I will shew unto the king the interpretation.

25 Then Arioch brought in Daniel before the king in haste, and said thus unto him, I have found a man of the captives of Judah, that will make known unto the king the interpretation.

26 The king answered and said to Daniel, whose name *was* Belteshazzar, Art thou able to make known unto me the dream which I have seen, and the interpretation thereof?

27 Daniel answered in the presence of the king, and said, The secret which the king hath demanded cannot the wise *men*, the astrologers, the magicians, the soothsayers, shew unto the king;

28 But there is a God in heaven that revealeth secrets, and maketh known to the king Nebuchadnezzar what shall be in the latter days. Thy dream, and the visions of thy head upon thy bed, are these;

29 As for thee, O king, thy thoughts came *into thy mind* upon thy bed, what should come to pass hereafter: and he that revealeth secrets maketh known to thee what shall come to pass.

30 But as for me, this secret is not revealed to me for *any* wisdom that I have more than any living, but for *their* sakes that shall make known the interpretation to the king, and that thou mightest know the thoughts of thy heart.

31 Thou, O king, sawest, and behold a great image. this great image, whose brightness *was* excellent, stood before thee; and the form thereof *was* terrible.

Thou, O king, sawest and behold a great image. This great image, whose brightness was excellent, stood before thee; and the form thereof was terrible.
This image's head was of fine gold, his breast and arms of silver, his belly and thighs of brass,
His legs of iron, his feet part of iron and part of clay.
Thou sawest till that a stone was cut out without hands, which smote the image upon his feet that were of iron and clay, and brake them to pieces.
Then was the iron, the clay, the brass, the silver, and the gold, broken to pieces together, and became like the chaff of the summer threshingfloors; and the wind carried them away, that no place was found for them: and the stone that smote the image became a great mountain, and filled the whole earth.
(Daniel 2:31-35)

The image seen by Nebuchadnezzar, made of four metals whose value progressively decreases but whose hardness progressively increases, is, so Daniel reveals, the symbol of the successive world powers who become increasingly cruel, inhuman and ungodly. But there comes a day when God breaks these powers and clears the land of them for an everlasting kingdom. The stone cut out without the agency of human hands which, after crushing the terrible image, grows into a great mountain covering the entire earth, is the Messianic kingdom.

This etching dating from 1655 in which Rembrandt has attempted to depict the fall of the image, belongs, along with *Jacob's Dream* (p. 47), *David Defeats Goliath* (p. 107) and *Daniel's dream of the four beasts* (p. 205), to the illustrations for the book previously mentioned, written in Spanish, by the Jewish theologian Menasseh ben Israel, entitled *Piedra Gloriosa o de la estatua de Nebuchadnezzar* (The Glorious Stone, or About the Image of Nebuchadnezzar). Based on Daniel's Messianic interpretation of the dream of Nebuchadnezzar, Menasseh's mystical treatise contends that the stone which shatters the image is the stone on which Jacob rested his head when he dreamed of a ladder connecting heaven and earth (Genesis 28:11-15), and also the stone with which David brings down Goliath (1 Samuel 17:1-54). For this 'glorious stone' is the symbol of the coming Messiah, who finally, in Daniel's dream of the four beasts, appears before the throne of God in the mysterious form of the son of man and then, after the destruction of the four beasts (who, like the image made of four metals in the dream of Nebuchadnezzar, symbolize the ungodly world powers), receives dominion over an everlasting kingdom. According to Menasseh ben Israel, that never-ending kingdom of the coming Messiah will be the kingdom of Israel.

The learned rabbi was apparently very set on a meticulous reproduction of his interpretation. The reasons why at a later stage Rembrandt lengthened the ladder in *Jacob's Dream* have already been discussed (see p. 47). In order to satisfy the wishes of his client, he had to change this first of the four illustrations several times. In the first version, printed above, we see how the legs of the image - and not the feet, as the Bible text says - are shattered by the stone. In the third version (p. 199, left) this has been corrected, and in the fifth version, the version finally included in the book, the names of the empires cited by Menasseh have also been put on the statue by way of clarification (see p. 199, right).

Etching; 9.6 × 7.6 cm. First, third and fifth stage of five.
Signed and dated: *Rembrandt f. 1655*.
Amsterdam, Rijksprentenkabinet.

Literature: Bartsch, no. 36; Hind, no. 284; Münz, no. 183; Boon, no. 264; Filedt Kok, no. B 36A/Hofstede de Groot, *Rembrandt Bijbel*, V.T.e.14; H. van de Waal, 'Rembrandts Radierung zur Piedra Gloriosa des Menasseh ben Israel' in *Imprimatur, ein Jahrbuch für Bücherfreunde* 12 (1954-55), pp. 52-61; Tümpel 1970, no. 39.

32 This image's head *was* of fine gold, his breast and his arms of silver, his belly and his thighs of brass,

33 His legs of iron, his feet part of iron and part of clay.

34 Thou sawest till that a stone was cut out without hands, which smote the image upon his feet *that were* of iron and clay, and brake them to pieces.

35 Then was the iron, the clay, the brass, the silver, and the gold, broken in pieces together, and became like the chaff of the summer threshingfloors; and the wind carried them away, that no place was found for them: and the stone that smote the image became a great mountain, and filled the whole earth.

36 This *is* the dream; and we will tell the interpretation thereof before the king.

37 Thou, O king, *art* a king of kings: for the God of heaven hath given thee a kingdom, power, and strength, and glory.

38 And wheresoever the children of men dwell, the beasts of the field and the fowls of the heaven hath he given into thine hand, and hath made thee ruler over them all. Thou *art* this head of gold.

39 And after thee shall arise another kingdom inferior to thee, and another third kingdom of brass, which shall bear rule over all the earth.

40 And the fourth kingdom shall be strong as iron: forasmuch as iron breaketh all these, shall it break in pieces and bruise.

41 And whereas thou sawest the feet and toes, part of potters' clay, and part of iron, the kingdom shall be divided; but there shall be in it of the strength of the iron, forasmuch as thou sawest the iron mixed with miry clay.

42 And *as* the toes of the feet *were* part of iron, and part of clay, *so* the kingdom shall be partly strong, and partly broken.

43 And whereas thou sawest iron mixed with miry clay, they shall mingle themselves with the seed of men: but they shall not cleave one to another, even as iron is not mixed with clay.

44 And in the days of these kings shall the God of heaven set up a kingdom, which shall never be destroyed: and the kingdom shall not left to other people, *but* it shall break in pieces and consume all these kingdoms, and it shall stand for ever.

45 Forasmuch as thou sawest that the stone was cut out of the mountain without hands, and that it brake in pieces the iron, the brass, the clay, the silver, and the gold; the great God hath made known to the king what shall come to pass hereafter: and the dream *is* certain, and the interpretation thereof sure.

46 Then the king Nebuchadnezzar fell upon his face, and worshipped Daniel, and commanded that they should offer an oblation and sweet odours unto him.

47 The king answered unto Daniel, and said, Of a truth *it is,* that your God *is* a God of gods, and a Lord of kings, and a revealer of secrets, seeing thou couldest reveal this secret.

48 Then the king made Daniel a great man, and gave him many great gifts, and made him ruler over the whole province of Babylon, and chief of the governors over all the wise *men* of Babylon.

The king saw the part of the hand that wrote

Daniel 5 BELSHAZZAR the king made a great feast fo a thousand of his lords, and drank wine before the thousand.

2 Belshazzar, whiles he tasted the wine, commanded to bring the golden and silver vessels which his father Nebuchadnezzar had taken out of the temple which *was* in Jerusalem; that the king, and his princes, his wives, and his concubines, might drink therein.

3 Then they brought the golden vessels that were taken out of the temple of the house of God which *was* at Jerusalem; and the king, and his princes, his wives, and his concubines, drank in them.

4 They drank wine, and praised the gods of gold, and of silver, of brass, of iron, of wood, and of stone.

5 In the same hour came forth fingers of a man's hand, and wrote over against the candlestick upon the plaister of the wall of the king's palace: and the king saw the part of the hand that wrote.

6 Then the king's countenance was changed, and his thoughts troubled him, so that the joints of his loins were loosed, and his knees smote one against another.

7 The king cried aloud to bring in the astrologers, the Chaldeans, and the soothsayers. *And* the king spake, and said to the wise *men* of Babylon, Whosoever shall read this writing, and shew me the interpretation thereof, shall be clothed with scarlet, and *have* a chain of gold about his neck, and shall be the third ruler in the kingdom.

8 Then came in all the king's wise *men*: but they could not read the writing, nor make known to the king the interpretation thereof. [...]

13 Then was Daniel brought in before the king. *And* the king spake and said unto Daniel, *Art* thou that Daniel, which *art* of the children of the captivity of Judah, whom the king my father brought out of Jewry?

14 I have even heard of thee, that the spirit of the gods *is* in thee, and *that* light and understanding and excellent wisdom is found in thee.

15 And now the wise *men*, the astrologers, haven been brought in before me, that they should read this writing, and make known unto me the interpretation thereof: but they could not shew the interpretation of the thing:

16 And I have heard of thee, that thou canst make interpretations, and dissolve doubts: now if thou canst read the writing, and make known to me the interpretation thereof, thou shalt be clothed with scarlet, and *have* a chain of gold about thy neck, and shalt be the third ruler in the kingdom.

17 Then Daniel answered and said before the king, Let thy gifts be to thyself, and give thy rewards to another; yet I will read the writing unto the king, and make known to him the interpretation.

18 O thou king, the most high God gave Nebuchadnezzar thy father a kingdom, and majesty, and glory, and honour: [...]

20 But when his heart was lifted up, and his mind hardened in pride, he was deposed from his kingly throne, and they took his glory from him: [...]

22 And thou his son, O Belshazzar, hast not humbled thine heart, though thou knewest all this;

23 But hast lifted up thyself against the Lord of heaven; and they have brought the vessels of his house before thee, and thou, and thy lords, thy wives and thy concubines, have drunk wine in them; and thou hast praised the gods of silver, and gold, of brass, iron, wood, and stone, which see not, nor hear, nor know: and the God in whose hand thy breath *is*, and whose *are* all thy ways, hast thou not glorified:

24 Then was the part of the hand sent from him; and this writing was written.

25 And this *is* the writing that was written, MENE, MENE, TEKEL, UPHARSIN.

26 This *is* the interpretation of the thing: MENE; God hath numbered thy kingdom, and finished it.

27 TEKEL; Thou art weighed in the balances, and art found wanting.

28 PERES; Thy kingdom is divided, and given to the Medes and Persians.

29 Then commanded Belshazzar, and they clothed Daniel with scarlet, and *put* a chain of gold about his neck, and made a proclamation concerning him, that he should be the third ruler in the kingdom.

30 In that night was Belshazzar the king of the Chaldeans slain.

... *and the king saw the part of the hand that wrote.*
Then the king's countenance was changed, and his thoughts
troubled him, so that the joints of his loins were loosed, and
his knees smote one against another.
(Daniel 5:5-6)

Rembrandt's painting of the moment when
Belshazzar's sacrilegious feast is suddenly disrupted by
the appearance of the *mene tekel* belongs to the group
of large-scale historical pieces from the middle of the
1630s, when the ambitious artist gave free rein to his
craving for violent drama and movement. Contrary to
the custom with this subject in Western art,
Rembrandt has reproduced the cryptic words which
appear on the wall in Hebrew characters. He was
probably furnished with the notation by Rabbi
Menasseh ben Israel, already referred to, who, it
seems, published the enigmatic script in the same form
in his book *De termino vito* of 1639. In this the Jewish
scholar advances the conjecture that King Belshazzar's
experts were at an utter loss because the words *Mené,*
Mené, Tekél, Upharsin were not - as is usual in Hebrew -

written horizontally from right to left, but vertically.
This is how they appear in the painting by Rembrandt.

It may be assumed that the large canvas was painted
after 1635, although not necessarily not until 1639, the
year in which Menasseh ben Israel produced his book.
In 1636 Rembrandt made an etched portrait of the
illustrious rabbi (Bartsch, no. 269), so it is quite possible
that he consulted this expert (who lived in the
Breestraat, diagonally opposite Hendrick van
Uylenburgh) before the publication of the rabbi's book
about the *mene tekel*.

Canvas; 16.6 × 209.2 cm.
Signed and dated: *Rembrandt f. 163...*
London, National Gallery.

Literature: Bredius, no. 497; Bauch, no. 21; Gerson, no.
77; Bredius-Gerson, no. 497/Hofstede de Groot,
Rembrandt Bijbel, V.T.p.25; R. Haussherr, 'Zur
Menetekel-Inschrift auf Rembrandts Belsazarbild' in
Oud Holland 78 (1963), pp. 142-49; C. Tümpel,
Rembrandt, Reinbek 1977, pp. 74-75.

Belshazzar's Feast

Is thy God able to deliver thee from the lions?

[As one of the three governors of the kingdom appointed by King Darius, Daniel excites the envy of his colleagues and the other magistrates through his exceptional ability, and they fear that the King will entrust him with control of the entire kingdom because of his singular qualities. They cannot manage to bring any kind of charge against him because Daniel meticulously observes the prevailing laws and the King's commands. He could only be brought down, they realize, if a decree of the King were to conflict with the law of his God. So they urge the King to issue a written decree in which everyone is strictly forbidden for thirty days to address a prayer to any god or man apart from the King. Darius, not suspecting any evil, does so and sets the prohibition down in writing, as a law of the Medes and Persians.]

Daniel 6   10 Now when Daniel knew that the writing was signed, he went into his house; and his windows being open in his chamber toward Jerusalem, he kneeled upon his knees three times a day, and prayed, and gave thanks before his God, as he did aforetime.

11 Then these men assembled, and found Daniel praying and making supplication before his God.

12 Then they came near, and spake before the king concerning the king's decree; Hast thou not signed a decree, that every man that shall ask *a petition* of any God or man within thirty days, save of thee, O king, shall be cast into the den of lions? The king answered and said, The thing *is* true, according to the law of the Medes and Persians, which altereth not.

13 Then answered they and said before the king, That Daniel, which *is* of the children of the captivity of Judah, regardeth not thee, O king, nor the decree that thou hast signed, but maketh his petition three times a day.

14 Then the king, when he heard *these* words, was sore displeased with himself, and set *his* heart on Daniel to deliver him: and he laboured till the going down of the sun to deliver him.

15 Then these men assembled unto the king, and said unto the king, Know, O king, that the law of the Medes and Persians *is,* That no decree nor statute which the king establisheth may be changed.

16 Then the king commanded, and they brought Daniel, and cast *him* into the den of lions. *Now* the king spake and said unto Daniel, Thy God whom thou servest continually, he will deliver thee.

17 And a stone was brought, and laid upon the mouth of the den; and the king sealed it with his own signet, and with the signet of his lords; that the purpose might not be changed concerning Daniel.

18 Then the king went to his palace, and passed the night fasting: neither were instruments of musick brought before him: and his sleep went from him.

19 Then the king arose very early in the morning, and went in haste unto the den of lions.

20 And when he came to the den, he cried with a lamentable voice unto Daniel: *and* the king spake and said to Daniel, O Daniel, servant of the living God, is thy God, whom thou servest continually, able to deliver thee from the lions?

21 Then said Daniel unto the king, O king, live for ever.

22 My God hath sent his angel, and hath shut the lions' mouths, that they have not hurt me: forasmuch as before him innocency was found in me; and also before thee, O king, have I done no hurt.

23 Then was the king exceeding glad for him, and commanded that they should take Daniel up out of the den. So Daniel was taken up out of the den, and no manner of hurt was found upon him, because he believed in his God.

24 And the king commanded, and they brought those men which had accused Daniel, and they cast *them* into the den of lions, them, their children, and their wives; and the lions had the mastery of them, and brake all their bones in pieces or ever they came at the bottom of the den.

Then the king arose very early in the morning, and went in haste unto the den of lions.
And when he came to the den, he cried with a lamentable voice unto Daniel: and the king spake and said unto Daniel, O Daniel, servant of the living God, is thy God, whom thou servest continually, able to deliver thee from the lions?
(Daniel 6:19-20)

We see the King looking tensely down through the bars of the grating along the upper wall of the lions' den. Depicted in various attitudes, the lions, who refuse to harm Daniel, reveal how fascinated Rembrandt was by the character of this imposing

predator. Studies of lions occupy the greatest place amongst those of his drawings of 'beasts from life' which have been preserved.

Pen and brush drawing; 22.3 × 18.3 cm.
Ca. 1652.
Amsterdam, Rijksprentenkabinet.

Literature: Benesch V, no. 887 (*ca.* 1652); Slive II, no. 379 (*ca.* 1652); Haak, no. 71 (*ca.* 1652)/Hofstede de Groot, *Rembrandt Bijbel*, V.T.d.33; Rotermund 1963, no. 135; 'Bijbelse Inspiratie', no. 79.

Daniel in the Lions' Den

The visions of my head troubled me

In the first year of Belshazzar king of Babylon Daniel had a dream and visions of his head upon his bed: then he wrote the dream, *and* told the sum of the matters.

2 Daniel spake and said, I saw in my vision by night, and, behold, the four winds of the heaven strove upon the great sea.

3 And four great beasts came up from the sea, diverse one from another.

4 The first *was* like a lion, and had eagle's wings: I beheld till the wings thereof were plucked, and it was lifted up from the earth, and made stand upon the feet as a man, and a man's heart was given to it.

5 And behold another beast, a second, like to a bear, and it raised up itself on one side, and *it had* three ribs in the mouth of it between the teeth of it: and they said thus unto it, Arise, devour much flesh.

6 After this I beheld, and lo another, like a leopard, which had upon the back of it four wings of a fowl; the beast had also four heads; and dominion was given to it.

7 After this I saw in the night visions, and behold a fourth beast, dreadful and terrible, and strong exceedingly; and it had great iron teeth: it devoured and brake in pieces, and stamped the residue with the feet of it: and it *was* diverse from all the beasts that *were* before it; and it had ten horns.

8 I considered the horns, and, behold, there came up among them another little horn, before whom there were three of the first horns plucked up by the roots: and, behold, in this horn *were* eyes like the eyes of man, and a mouth speaking great things.

9 I beheld till the thrones were cast down, and the Ancient of days did sit, whose garment *was* white as snow, and the hair of his head like the pure wool: his throne *was like* the fiery flame, *and* his wheels *as* burning fire.

10 A fiery stream issued and came forth from before him: thousand thousands ministered unto him, and ten thousand times ten thousand stood before him: the judgment was set, and the books were opened.

11 I beheld then because of the voice of the great words which the horn spake: I beheld *even* till the beast was slain, and his body destroyed, and given to the burning flame.

12 As concerning the rest of the beasts, they had their dominion taken away: yet their lives were prolonged for a season and time.

13 I saw in the night visions, and, behold, *one* like the Son of man came with the clouds of heaven, and came to the Ancient of days, and they brought him near before him.

14 And there was given him dominion, and glory, and a kingdom, that all people, nations, and languages, should serve him: his dominion *is* an everlasting dominion, which shall not pass away, and his kingdom *that* which shall not be destroyed.

15 I Daniel was grieved in my spirit in the midst of *my* body, and the visions of my head troubled me.

16 I came near unto one of them that stood by, and asked him the truth of all this. So he told me, and made me know the interpretation of the things.

17 These great beasts, which are four, *are* four kings, *which* shall arise out of the earth.

18 But the saint of the most High shall take the kingdom, and possess the kingdom for ever, even for ever and ever.

This little etching is the last of the four illustrations which Rembrandt made for the book *Piedra Gloriosa* by the Jewish theologian Menasseh ben Israel, published in 1655 (see the commentary on p. 197). Using other images, Daniel's dream of the four beasts, which is extensively described, has the same significance as Nebuchadnezzar's much briefer dream about the destruction of a terrifying statue made of four metals: sooner or later, the increasingly brutal and godless powers on earth will have to make way for the everlasting dominion of the Messianic kingdom to which all nations will be subject.

Despite the small format at his disposal, Rembrandt has succeeded admirably in doing justice to virtually all the elements in Daniel's vision. Out of the dark ocean, which is agitated by the four winds (left and right of centre), four beasts emerge one after the other (verses 2-3). In the lead is a lion with eagle's wings, standing on two feet like a man (verse 4); then a bear with three ribs in its teeth (verse 5); next a four-headed leopard with bird's wings on its back (verse 6) and finally the unnamed fourth beast with great fangs and ten horns on its head (in two branches of five), between which an eleventh horn sprouts up, small, with human eyes and 'a mouth speaking great things' (verses 7-8). The four beasts symbolize the successive world powers, and just like the four metals from which the image is made in Nebuchadnezzar's dream, they decrease in value but increase in cruelty. Above in the heavens 'the Ancient of days' is enthroned, surrounded by millions of angels who serve him. While two beams of light, emanating from the Almighty, scorch the beasts, the 'son of man' is led before God's throne and receives eternal dominion (verses 11-14).

There are only four copies known of Menasseh ben Israel's book in which Rembrandt's etchings appear. In the fourth edition of the book, which appeared after the death of the author in 1657, the etchings, whose plates were almost certainly worn out by then, were replaced with crude imitations by an unknown engraver. In accordance with the second of the Ten Commandments, forbidding the making of images of gods, the figure of God is omitted from Daniel's dream of the four beasts. Apparently this later publisher wished to observe this Biblical commandment more strictly than Menasseh ben Israel had done.

Etching; 9.7 × 7.6 cm. Third state of three.
Signed and dated: *Rembrandt f. 1655.*
Amsterdam, Rijksprentenkabinet.

Literature: Bartsch, no. 36; Hind, no. 284; Münz, no. 183; Boon, no. 264; Filedt Kok, no. B 36 and B 36D/Hofstede de Groot, *Rembrandt Bijbel*, V.T.e.15; Rotermund 1963, no. 134; Tümpel 1970, no. 39.

Daniel's Dream of the Four Beasts

Understand, O son of man

Daniel 8   IN the third year of the reign of king Belshazzar a vision appeared unto me, *even unto* me Daniel, after that which appeared unto me at the first.

2 And I saw in a vision; and it came to pass, when I saw, that I *was* at Shushan *in the* palace, which *is* in the province of Elam; and I saw in a vision, and I was by the river of Ulai.

3 Then I lifted up mine eyes, and saw and, behold, there stood before the river a ram which had *two* horns: and the *two* horns *were* high; but one *was* higher than the other, and the higher came up last.

4 I saw the ram pushing westward, and northward, and southward; so that no beasts might stand before him, neither *was there any* that could deliver out of his hand; but he did according to his will, and became great.

5 And as I was considering, behold, an he goat came from the west on the face of the whole earth, and touched not the ground: and the goat *had* a notable horn between his eyes.

6 And he came to the ram that had *two* horns, which I had seen standing before the river, and ran unto him in the fury of his power.

7 And I saw him come close unto the ram, and he was moved with choler against him, and smote the ram, and brake his two horns: and there was no power in the ram to stand before him, but he cast him down to the ground, and stamped upon him: and there was none that could deliver the ram out of his hand.

8 Therefore the he goat waxed very great: and when he was strong, the great horn was broken; and for it came up four notable ones toward the four winds of heaven.

9 And out of one of them came forth a little horn, which waxed exceeding great, toward the pleasant *land.*

10 And it waxed great, *even* to the host of heaven; and it cast down *some* of the host and of the stars to the ground, and stamped upon them.

11 Yea, he magnified *himself* even to the prince of the host, and by him the daily *sacrifice* was taken away, and the palace of his sanctuary was cast down.

12 And an host was given *him* against the daily *sacrifice* by reason of transgression, and it cast down the truth to the ground; and it practised, and prospered.

15 And it came to pass, when I, *even* I Daniel, had seen the vision and sought for the meaning, then, behold, there stood before me as the appearance of a man.

16 And I heard a man's voice between *the banks of* Ulai, which called, and said, Gabriel, make this *man* to understand the vision.

17 So he came near where I stood: and when he came, I was afraid, and fell upon my face: but he said unto me, Understand, O son of man: for at the time of the end *shall be* the vision.

18 Now as he was speaking with me, I was in a deep sleep on my face toward the ground: but he touched me, and set me upright.

19 And he said, Behold, I will make thee know what shall be in the last end of the indignation: for at the time appointed the end *shall be.*

20 The ram which thou sawest having *two* horns *are* the kings of Media and Persia.

21And the rough goat *is* the king of Grecia: and the great horn that *is* between his eyes *is* the first king.

22 Now that being broken, whereas four stood up for it, four kingdoms shall stand up out of the nation, but not in his power.

23 And in the latter time of their kingdom, when the transgressors are come to the full, a king of fierce countenance, and understanding dark sentences, shall stand up.

24 And his power shall be mighty, but not by his own power: and he shall destroy wonderfully, and shall prosper, and practise, and shall destroy the mighty and the holy people.

25 And through his policy also he shall cause craft to prosper in his hand; and he shall magnify *himself* in his heart, and by peace shall destroy many: he shall also stand up against the Prince of princes; but he shall be broken without hand.

26 [...] wherefore shut thou up the vision; for it *shall be* for many days.

And I heard a man's voice between the banks of Ulai, which called, and said, Gabriel, make this man to understand this vision.
So he came near where I stood: and when he came, I was afraid, and fell upon my face: but he said unto me, Understand, O son of man: for at the time of the end shall be the vision.
Now as he was speaking with me, I was in a deep sleep on my face toward the ground: but he touched me ...
(Daniel 8:16-18)

The fearsome vision of the bitter struggle between a sovereign ram and an even more formidable billygoat once more contains the message that the growing and apparently unstoppable power of God's adversaries will one day be broken without the intervention of a hand (verse 25).

In this unsigned painting from *ca.* 1650, the details of the vision are limited to the ram which Daniel sees standing before the river (verse 3). The major theme is the appearance of the Angel Gabriel. While he is explaining the vision, the heavenly interpreter soothingly places his right hand on the shoulder of the young seer, who slowly begins to rise to his feet, as if waking from a bad dream. The mysterious character of the picture is accentuated by the gloomy atmosphere of the strangely lit, rocky landscape which surrounds the two figures. In the Louvre in Paris there is a preparatory drawing for the painting (Benesch V, no. 901).

The English painter Sir Joshua Reynolds (1723-92), once the proud owner of this canvas, called it 'Rembrandt's most beautiful work'. More and more contemporary connoisseurs are casting doubts on the attribution to Rembrandt and consider the painting to be the work of a pupil after a subject by Rembrandt, who possibly assisted his pupil in its execution.

Canvas; 98.5 × 119 cm.
Berlin, Gemäldegalerie der Staatlichen Museen.

Literature: Bredius, no. 519; Bauch, no. 29;
Bredius-Gerson, no. 519 (school of Rembrandt); Hak,
pp. 14-15/Hofstede de Groot, *Rembrandt Bijbel* V.T.p.26.

The Vision of Daniel on the Banks of the River Ulai

No man can see us

Daniel 13 THERE dwelt a man in Babylon, and his name was Joakim:

2 and he took a wife, whose name was Susanna, the daughter of Helkias, a very fair woman, and one that feared the Lord.

3 Her parents also were righteous, and taught their daughter according to the law of Moses.

4 Now Joakim was a great rich man, and had a fair garden joining unto his house: and to him resorted the Jews; because he was more honourable that all others.

5 And the same year there were appointed two of the ancients of the people to be judges, such as the Lord spake of, that wickedness came from Babylon from ancient judges, who were accounted to govern the people.

6 These kept much at Joakim's house: and all that had any suits in law came unto them.

7 Now when the people departed away at noon, Susanna went into her husband's garden to walk.

8 And the two elders beheld her going in every day, and walking; and they were inflamed with love for her.

9 And they perverted their own mind, and turned away their eyes, that they might not look unto heaven, nor remember just judgements.

10 And albeit they both were wounded with her love, yet durst not one shew another his grief.

11 For they were ashamed to declare their lust, that they desired to have to do with her.

12 Yet they watched jealously from day to day to see her. And the one said to the other, Let us now go home: for it is dinner time.

14 So when they were gone out, they parted the one from the other, and turning back again they came to the same place; and after that they had asked one another the cause, they acknowledged their lust: and then appointed they a time both together, when they might find her alone.

15 And it fell out, as they watched a fit day, she went in as aforetime with two maids only, and she was desirous to wash herself in the garden: for it was hot.

16 And there was nobody there save the two elders, that had hid themselves, and watched her.

17 Then she said to her maids, Bring me oil and washing balls, and shut the garden doors, that I may wash me.

18 And they did as she bade them, and shut the garden doors, and went out themselves at the side doors to fetch the things that she had commanded them: and they saw not the elders, because they were hid.

19 Now when the maids were gone forth, the two elders rose up, and ran unto her, saying,

20 Behold, the garden doors are shut, that no man can see us, and we are in love with thee; therefore consent unto us, and lie with us.

21 If thou wilt not, we will bear witness against thee, that a young man was with thee: and therefore thou didst send away thy maids from thee.

Susanna and the Two Elders

Then Susanna sighed, and said, I am straightened on every side: For if I do this thing, it is death unto me: and if I do it not, I cannot escape your hands.
It is better for me to fall into your hands, and not do it, than to sin in the sight of the Lord.
(Daniel 13:22-23)

In this lovely little panel from 1637, Rembrandt's chief concern was to portray the terror which seizes Susanna when the two elders approach. In the bushes behind her the spying head of one of her attackers can be seen. Suddenly feeling herself threatened on all sides, the girl looks the viewer right in the eyes, as if his curiosity also alarms her.

The figure of Susanna virtually matches the figure in the Berlin painting already mentioned (see p. 213). So it is certain that the panel played a part in the creation of the ultimate version of this work.

Panel; 47.5 × 39 cm.
Signed and dated: *Rembrandt f. 1637.*
The Hague, Mauritshuis.

Literature: Bredius, no. 505; Bauch, no. 18; Gerson, no. 84; Bredius-Gerson, no. 505/Tümpel 1970, under no. 35.

22 Then Susanna sighed, and said, I am straitened on every side: for if I do this thing, it is death unto me: and if I do it not, I cannot escape your hands.

23 It is better for me to fall into your hands, and not do it, than to sin in the sight of the Lord.

24 With that Susanna cried with a loud voice: and the two elders cried out against her.

25 Then ran the one, and opened the garden doors.

26 So when the servants of the house heard the cry in the garden, they rushed in at the side door, to see what had befallen her.

27 But when the elders had told their tale, the servants were greatly ashamed: for there was never such a report made of Susanna.

28 And it came to pass on the morrow, when the people assembled to her husband Joakim, the two elders came full of their wicked intent against Susanna to put her to death;

29 and said before the people, Send for Susanna, the daughter of Helkias, Joakim's wife.

30 So they sent; and she came with her father and mother, her children, and all her kindred.

31 Now Susanna, was a very delicate woman, and beauteous to behold.

32 And these wicked men commanded her to be unveiled, (for she was veiled) that they might be filled with her beauty.

33 Therefore her friends and all that saw her wept.

34 Then the two elders stood up in the midst of the people, and laid their hands upon her head.

35 And she weeping looked up toward heaven: for her heart trusted in the Lord.

36 And the elders said, As we walked in the garden alone, this *woman* came in with two maids, and shut the garden doors, and sent the maids away.

37 Then a young man, who there was hid, came unto her, and lay with her.

38 And we, being in the corner of the garden, saw this wickedness, and ran unto them.

39 And when we saw them together, the man we could not hold: for he was stronger than we, and opened the doors, and leaped out.

40 But having taken this *woman,* we asked who the young man was, but she would not tell us: these things do we testify.

41 Then the assembly believed them, as those that were elders of the people and judges: so they condemned her to death.

42 Then Susanna cried out with a loud voice, and said, O everlasting God, that knowest the secrets, that knowest all things before they be:

43 thou knowest that they have borne false witness against me, and, behold, I must die; whereas I never did such things as these men have maliciously invented against me.

44 And the Lord heard her voice.

Susanna and the Two Elders

Now when the maids were gone forth, the two elders rose up, and ran unto her, saying,

Behold, the garden doors are shut, that no man can see us, and we are in love with thee; therefore consent unto us, and lie with us.

If thou wilt not, we will bear witness against thee, that a young man was with thee: and therefore thou didst send away thy maids from thee.

(Daniel 13:19-21)

The Susanna story, a later addition to the book of Daniel, is one of the most popular Biblical subjects in Renaissance and baroque painting. In by far the majority of cases, painters have chosen the moment when Susanna, suspecting nothing, is about to bathe in the pool in the courtyard, while the two elders spy on her from their hiding place, or when they have already approached her and are attempting to seduce her. Just like the frequently illustrated scene of Bathsheba bathing (2 Samuel 11:2; see p. 123), this scene offered painters a welcome opportunity to indulge themselves by painting the loveliest female nude possible. For, as the story says, Susanna 'was very beautiful'.

Rembrandt's principal representations of this theme show a clear affinity with the 1614 painting by Pieter Lastman on the same subject (Berlin, Gemäldegalerie der Staatlichen Museen). He produced a fairly precise copy of this in red pencil around 1635 (Benesch II, no. 448). In the pen drawing reproduced here, which must have been made not long after that, he presents his

own vision of the subject, which is closely connected
with his master's composition. The violence with which
the two men make clear their intentions is greater than
in Lastman's painting, and the terror in the attitude of
Susanna, driven into a corner, is much more explicit.

Presumably the drawing is one of the first
preliminary studies for Rembrandt's painting of this
subject, now in Berlin (see p. 213). The painting bears
the date 1647, it is true, but it has emerged that the
present paint surface conceals an older, more
dramatically formulated version, which was painted
around 1635.

Drawing in pen; 14.9 × 17.7 cm.
Ca. 1635.
Berlin, Kupferstichkabinett der Staatlichen Museen.

Literature: Benesch I, no. 159 (*ca.* 1637-38); Haak, no. 22
(*ca.* 1637-38)/J. Bruyn, *Rembrandt's keuze van Bijbelse
onderwerpen*, Utrecht 1959, p. 10; Tümpel 1970, no. 36.

Susanna and the Two Elders

Now when the maids were gone forth, the two elders rose up, and ran unto her, saying,
Behold, the garden doors are shut, that no man can see us, and we are in love with thee; therefore consent unto us, and lie with us.
If thou wilt not, we will bear witness against thee, that a young man was with thee: and therefore thou didst send away thy maids from thee.
(Daniel 13:19-21)

It is probable that this study, dating from the second half of the 1640s, is connected with the preparatory work for the painting from 1647 reproduced on the next page. But it is also possible that the drawing was made after completion of the painting. Perhaps Rembrandt toyed with the idea of painting the scene in approximately the same style, but in the opposite direction, as he had done in 1646 with *The Adoration of the Shepherds* (see pp. 233 and 237). The drawing has been added to in grey ink by a later hand.

Drawing in pen; 20 × 18.8 cm.
Ca. 1645-50.
Amsterdam, Rijksprentenkabinet.

Literature: Benesch III, no. 592 (*ca.* 1647).

Then Susanna sighed, and said, I am straightened on every side: For if I do this thing, it is death unto me: and if I do it not, I cannot escape your hands.
It is better for me to fall into your hands, and not do it, thatn to sin in the sight of the Lord.
(Daniel 13:22-23)

This painting, consisting of two different layers of paint (a discovery made by Kauffman in 1924 and confirmed by X-rays) is, in the version now visible with its warm colours and gently glowing chiaroscuro, one of Rembrandt's loveliest works from the second half of the 1640s. Susanna, the beautiful wife of the rich Joacim, has just removed her splendid garments and is already standing with one foot in the water, when the villain who has come closest to her seizes the linen

cloth with which she is still partially covered. Once again, as she looks at the viewers, the girl creates the impression that she not only feels cornered by the apprearance of the elders but by our gazes as well.

Two of the drawings stemming from the 1650s show that Rembrandt was repeatedly interested in this theme.

Panel; 76.6 × 92.7 cm.
Signed and dated: *Rembrandt F. 1647.*
Berlin, Gemäldegalerie der Staatliche Museen.

Literature: Bredius, no. 516; Bauch, no. 28; Gerson, no. 221; Bredius-Gerson, no. 516/H. Kauffmann, 'Rembrandts Berliner Susanna' in *Jahrbuch der preussischen Kunstsammlungen* 45 (1924), pp. 72-80.

Susanna and the Two Elders

These have borne false witness against her

Daniel 13 45 Therefore when she was led away to be put to death, God raised up the holy spirit of a young youth, whose name was Daniel:

46 and he cried with a loud voice, I am clear from the blood of this woman.

47 Then all the people turned them toward him, and said, What mean these words that thou hast spoken?

48 So he standing in the midst of them said, Are ye such fools, ye sons of Israel, that without examination or knowledge of the truth ye have concemned a daughter of Israel?

49 Return again to the place of judgement: for these have borne false witness against her.

50 Wherefore all the people turned again in haste, and the elders said unto him, Come, sit down among us, and shew it us, seeing God hath given thee the honour of an elder.

51 Then said Daniel unto them, Put them asunder one far from another, and I will examine them.

52 So when they were put asunder one from another, he called one of them, and said unto him, O thou that art waxen old in wickedness, now are thy sins come *home to thee* which thou hast committed aforetime,

53 in pronouncing unjust judgement, and condemning the innocent, and letting the guilty go free; albeit the Lord saith, The innocent and righteaous shalt thou not slay.

54 Now then, if thou sawest her, tell me, Under what tree sawest thou them companying together? Who answered, Under a mastick tree.

55 And Daniel said, Right well hast thou lied against thine own head; for even now the angel of God hath received the sentence of God and shall cut thee in two.

56 So he put him aside, and commanded to bring the other, and said unto him, O thou seed of Canaan, and not Judah, beauty hath deceived thee, and lust hath perverted thine heart.

57 Thus have ye dealt with the daughters of Israel, and they for fear companied with you: but the daughter of Judah would not abide your wickedness.

58 Now therefore tell me, Under what tree didst thou take them companying together? Who answered, Under a holm tree.

59 Then said Daniel unto him, Right well hast thou also lied against thine own head: for the angel of God waiteth with the sword to cut thee in two, that he may destroy you.

60 With that all the assembly cried out with a loud voice, and blessed God, who saveth them that hope in him.

61 And they arose against the two elders, for Daniel had convicted them of false witness out of their own mouth:

62 and according to the law of Moses the did unto them in such sort as they maliciously intended to do to their neighbour: and they put them to death, and the innocent blood was saved the same day.

63 Therefore Helkias and his wife praised God for their daughter Susanna, with Joakim her husband, and all the kindred, because there was no dishonesty found in her.

Condemned to Death
Susanna is Saved
by Daniel

So he standing in the midst of them said, are ye such fools, ye sons of Israel, that without examination or knowledge of the truth ye have condemned a daughter of Israel? (Daniel 13:48-49)

We are here witnesses to the turning point in Susanna's story. The assembly held in Joacim's house has just been terminated. Preceded by her judges, who have also been her accusers, the condemned Susanna is led away between two guards to be put to death. But Daniel suddenly appears on the scene and cries: I am clear from the blood of this woman. He makes the procession turn around and convenes a second sitting in order to unmask the lies and save an innocent from death. Above the corrupt judges the statue of blind Justice with scales and sword rises very significantly.

Drawing in pen; 23.8 × 19.6 cm.
Ca. 1655.
Oxford, Ashmolean Museum.

Literature: Benesch V, no. 942 (*ca.* 1654).

The Lord smote him by the hand of a woman

[The story of the book of Judith begins with a show of power by the arrogant Nebuchadnezzar, who marches from Nineveh against the King of the Medes, and then sends Holofernes, the commander in chief of his army, on a punitive expedition to the west. All the peoples there, Israel included, are to be compelled to destroy their native gods and acknowledge only Nebuchadnezzar as god. When the character of Judith, a God-fearing Jewish widow, enters the story, the devastating army of the Assyrians has already marched up to the gates of the Jewish city of Bethulia, where a state of emergency has arisen on account of this siege. At the moment when everyone, including the city's governors, has lost heart, Judith, as wise as she is beautiful, emerges from the seclusion of her widow's state and offers to force a solution: how - that is her secret. After an earnest prayer for God's blessing, she proceeds in the company of her maidservant to the enemy's camp, strikingly beautiful and decked with all her jewellery. When she arrives, she pretends to be a turncoat who seeks contact with Holofernes in order to be of service to him in her conquest of the city. Thanks to her charms and her eloquence, she manages to talk the Assyrian general into a promising 'battle plan'.]

Judith 12

5 And the servants of Holofernes brought her into the tent, and she slept till midnight, and she rose up toward the morning watch,

6 and sent to Holofernes, saying, Let my lord now command that they suffer thy servant to go forth unto prayer.

7 And Holofernes commanded his guards that they should not stay her: and she abode in the camp three days, and went out every night into the valley of Bethulia, and washed herself at the fountain of water in the camp.

8 And when she came up, she besought the Lord God of Israel to direct her way to the raising up of the children of his people.

9 And she came in clean, and remained in the tent, until she took her meat toward evening.

10 And it came to pass on the fourth day, Holofernes made a feast to his own servants only, and called none of the officers to the banquet.

11 And he said to Bagoas the eunuch, who had charge over all that he had, Go now, and persuade this Hebrew woman which is with thee, that she come unto us, and eat and drink with us.

12 For, lo, it is a shame for our person, if we shall let such a woman go, not having had her company; for if we draw her not unto us, she shall laugh us to scorn.

13 And Bagoas went from the presence of Holofernes, and came in to her , and said, Let not this fair damsel fear to come to my lord, and to be honoured in his presence, and to drink wine and be merry with us, and to be made this day as one of the daughters of the children of Asshur, which wait in the house of Nebuchadnezzar.

14 And Judith said unto him, And who am I, that I should gainsay my lord? for whatsoever shall be pleasing in his eyes I will do speedily, and this shall be my joy unto the day of my death.

15 And she arose, and decked herself with her apparel and all her woman's attire; and her servant went and laid fleeces on the ground for her over against Holofernes, which she had received of Bagoas for her daily use, that she might sit and eat upon them.

16 And Judith came in and sat down, and Holofernes heart was ravished with her, and his soul was moved, and he desired exceedingly her company: and he was watching for a time to deceive her, from the day that he had seen her.

17 And Holofernes said unto her, Drink now, and be merry with us.

18 And Judith said, I will drink now, my lord, because my life is magnified in me this day more than all the days since I was born.

19 And she took and ate and drank before him what her servant had prepared.

20 And Holofernes took great delight in her, and drank exceeding much wine, more than he had drunk at any time in one day since he was born.

And she came to the rail of the bed, which was at
Holofernes' head, and took down his scimitar from thence,;
and she drew near unto the bed, and took hold of the hair of
his head, and said, Strengthen me, O Lord God of Israel,
this day. And she smote twice upon his neck with all her
might, and took away his head from him ...
(Judith 13:7-9)

The cunning Judith, who does not flinch at the critical
moment and in the strength of her faith manages to
destroy the enemy of her people, belongs with
Deborah, Jael and Esther among the great women of
the Old Testament. In the Middle Ages she was seen
as a prefiguration of the Virgin Mary: just as Judith
had freed the Israelites from the hands of Holofernes,
so did Mary in Christ release humankind from the
power of Satan. In the Renaissance, with its
predilection for valiant men and women, she was seen
principally as a heroine, and the theme of Judith with
the head of Holofernes was scarcely less popular at
that time than David with the head of Goliath.

Whenever the artists did not restrict themselves to a
more or less isolated representation of Judith with the
head of Holofernes, they opted in most cases when
depicting this story for the moment immediately after
the beheading, when Judith hands over the hacked-off
head to her maidservant, who hides it in her bag.
Rembrandt too, who as far as we know only bothered
with the book of Judith in several drawings, opts for
this episode in a lively sketch from the middle of the
1630s (see p. 219). In the drawing of some twenty years
later, reproduced above, we see a rendering of the
beheading itself, which is just as terse and suggestive as
the description in the text.

Drawing in pen; 18.2 × 15 cm.
Ca. 1652-55.
Naples, Museo di Capodimonte.

Literature: Benesch V, no. 897 (*ca.* 1652).

*Judith Beheads
Holofernes*

BUT when the evening was come, his servants made haste to depart, and Bagoas shut the tent without, and dismissed them that waited from the presence of his lord; and they went away to their beds: for they were all weary, because the feast had been long.

2 But Judith was left alone in the tent, and Holofernes lying along upon his bed: for he was overflown with wine.

3 And Judith had said to her servant that she should stand without her bedchamber, and wait for her coming forth, as she did daily: for she said she would go forth to her prayer; and she spake to Bagoas according to the same words.

4 And all went away from her presence, and none was left in the bedchamber, neither small nor great. And Judith, standing by his bed, said in her heart, O Lord God of all power, look in this hour upon the works of my hands for the exaltation of Jerusalem.

5 For now is the time to help thine inheritance, and to do the thing that I have purposed to the destruction of the enemies which are risen up against us.

6 And she came to the rail of the bed, which was at Holofernes' head and took down his scimitar from thence;

7 and she drew near unto the bed, and took hold of the hair of his head, and said, Strengthen me, O Lord God of Israel, this day.

8 And she smote twice upon his neck with all her might, and took away his head from him, and tumbled his body down from the bed, and took down the canopy from the pillars;

9 and after a little while she went forth, and gave Holofernes' head to her maid; and she put it in her bag of victuals:

10 and they twain went forth together unto prayer, according to their custom: and they passed through the camp, and compassed that valley, and went up to the mountain of Bethulia, and came to the gates thereof.

11 And Judith said afar off to the watchmen at the gates, Open, open now the gate: God is with us, even our God, to shew his power yet in Israel, and his might against the enemy, as he hath done even this day.

12 And it came to pass, when the men of her city heard her voice, they made haste to go down to the gate of their city, and they called together the elders of the city.

13 And they ran all together, both small and great, for it was strange unto them that she was come: and they opened the gate, and received them, making a fire to give light, and compassed them round about.

14 And she said to them with a loud voice, Praise God, praise him: praise God, who hath not taken away his mercy from the house of Israel, but hath destroyed our enemies by my hand this night.

15 And she took forth the head out of the bag, and shewed it, and said unto them, Behold, the head of Holofernes, the chief captain of the host of Asshur, and behold, the canopy, wherein he did lie in his drunkenness; and the Lord smote him by the hand of a woman.

16 And as the Lord liveth, who preserved me in my way that I went, my countenance deceived him to his destruction, and he did not commit sin with me, to defile and shame me.

17 And all the people were exceedingly amazed, and bowed themselves and worshipped God, and said with one accord, Blessed art thou, O our God, which hast this day brought to nought the enemies of thy people.

18 And Ozias said unto her, Blessed art thou, daughter, in the sight of the Most High God, above all the women upon the earth; and blessed is the Lord God, who created the heavens and the earth, who directed thee to the smiting of the head of the prince of our enemies.

19 For thy hope shall not depart from the heart of men that remember the strength of God for ever.

20 And God turn these things to thee for a perpetual praise, to visit thee with good things, because thou didst not spare thy life by reason of the affliction of our race, but didst avenge our fall, walking a straight way before our God. And all the people said, So be it, so be it.

And after a little while she went forth and gave Holofernes' head to her maid; and she put it in her bag of victuals. (Judith 13:9-10)

This speedily sketched composition displays the baroque play of lines which is characteristic of Rembrandt's drawing from the mid-1630s. Judith, placed centre front, still holds in her hand the sword with which she has beheaded Holofernes.

When the Assyrians see the next morning that their general has been murdered, they flee in panic. Bethulia and the whole of Israel have been saved, and with Judith in their midst the people celebrate for three months before the sanctuary in Jerusalem.

Drawing in pen; 17.8 × 21.2 cm.
Ca. 1635.
Paris, The Louvre.

Literature: Benesch I, no. 176 (*ca.* 1638-39); Slive II, no. 346 (*ca.* 1632-34).

Judith's Maidservant Putting the Head of Holofernes in a Bag

The New Testament

Hail, *thou that art* highly favoured

Luke 1

26 And in the sixth month the angel Gabriel was sent from God unto a city of Galilee, named Nazareth.

27 To a virgin espoused to a man whose name was Joseph, of the house of David; and the virgin's name *was* Mary.

28 And the angel came in unto her, and said, Hail, *thou that art* highly favoured, the Lord *is* with thee: blessed *art* thou among women.

29 And when she saw *him,* she was troubled at his saying, and cast in her mind what manner of salutation this should be.

30 And the angel said unto her, Fear not, Mary: for thou hast found favour with God.

31 And, behold, thou shalt conceive in thy womb, and bring forth a son, and shalt call his name JESUS.

32 He shall be great, and shall be called the Son of the Highest: and the Lord God shall give unto him the throne of his father David:

33 And he shall reign over the house of Jacob for ever; and of his kingdom there shall be no end.

34 Then said Mary unto the angel, How shall this be, seeing I know not a man?

35 And the angel answered and said unto her, The Holy Ghost shall come upon thee, and the power of the Highest shall overshadow thee: therefore also that holy thing which shall be born of thee shall be called the Son of God.

36 And, behold, thy cousin Elisabeth, she hath also conceived a son in her old age: and this is the sixth month with her, who was called barren.

37 For with God nothing shall be impossible.

38 And Mary said, Behold the handmaid of the Lord; be it unto me according to thy word. And the angel departed from her.

The Annunciation of the Angel Gabriel to Mary

Fear not, Mary: for thou hast found favour with God (Luke 1:30)

Gabriel's annunciation to Mary, the moment at which God's plan for salvation through his incarnation as a man began, had been one of the most important themes in Christian art since the earliest times. During the late Middle Ages this scene was invariably part of the traditional series of pictures of the life of Jesus or of Mary. During the 16th century, when the Reformation opposed the prevailing cult of the Virgin Mary, the popularity of this theme declined considerably in the northern Netherlands. Rembrandt's treatment of the subject is restricted to a few drawings.

In this extremely dramatic version, we see the Angel Gabriel with wings outspread, bending over Mary and trying to calm her as she slides off her chair in shock. There is no indication of the presence of the Holy Ghost, which was virtually always shown in older pictures in the form of a dove above Mary's head.

This drawing is a typical example of the way in which Rembrandt was working in the years around 1635, his most baroque period.

Pen and ink drawing; 14.4 × 12.4 cm.
Ca. 1635.
Besançon, Musée des Beaux-Arts.

Literature: Benesch I, no. 99 (*ca.* 1635)/Sumowski 1963, no. 3.

Blessed *art* thou among women

Luke 1 39 And Mary arose in those days, and went into the hill country with haste, into a city of Juda;

40 And entered into the house of Zacharias, and saluted Elisabeth.

41 And it came to pass, that, when Elisabeth heard the salutation of Mary, the babe leaped in her womb; and Elisabeth was filled with the Holy Ghost:

42 And she spake out with a loud voice, and said, Blessed *art* thou among women, and blessed *is* the fruit of thy womb.

43 And whence *is* this to me, that the mother of my Lord should come to me?

44 For, lo, as soon as the voice of thy salutation sounded in mine ears, the babe leaped in my womb for joy.

45 And blessed *is* she that believed: for there shall be a performance of those things which were told her from the Lord.

46 And Mary said, My soul doth magnify the Lord,

47 And my spirit hath rejoiced in God my Saviour.

48 For he hath regarded the low estate of his handmaiden: for, behold, from henceforth all generations shall call me blessed.

49 For he that is mighty hath done to me great things; and holy *is* his name.

50 And his mercy *is* on them that fear him from generation to generation.

51 He hath shewed strength with his arm; he hath scattered the proud in the imagination of their hearts.

52 He hath put down the mighty from *their* seats, and exalted them of low degree.

53 He hath filled the hungry with good things; and the rich he hath sent empty away.

54 He hath holpen his servant Israel, in remembrance of *his* mercy;

55 As he spake to our fathers, to Abraham, and to his seed for ever.

56 And Mary abode with her about three months, and returned to her own house.

Mary's Visit to Elizabeth

And Elizabeth was filled with the Holy Ghost: and she spake out with a loud voice, and said, Blessed art thou among women, and blessed is the fruit of thy womb. And whence is this to me, that the mother of my Lord should come to me? (Luke 1:41-43)

Following artistic tradition rather than the Biblical text, Rembrandt painted this scene, a work of extensive detail, not inside, but outside the house of the priest Zachariah. While the remarkably young Mary is greeted by her elderly cousin as dusk falls, a negress removes her travelling cloak and another servant takes the donkey on which she has made the journey. Old Zachariah has also come outside to welcome Mary. He comes down the steps with some difficulty, leaning on the shoulder of a young boy.

Rembrandt's composition clearly shows that he was familiar with the woodcut made by Albrecht Dürer of this subject in about 1504. In the woodcut the welcome also takes place in front of the house, against a background of a mountainous landscape, the 'hill country' mentioned in the Bible (Luke 1:39). Rembrandt changed this into a view of the 'city of Juda', to which Mary had hastily departed.

Apart from two later sketches, this theme, which was a popular subject in medieval art, is not found again in Rembrandt's work.

Panel, rounded at the top; 57 × 48 cm.
Signed and dated: *Rembrandt 1640.*
Detroit, The Detroit Institute of Art.

Literature: Bredius, no. 562; Bauch, no. 70; Gerson, no. 203; Bredius-Gerson, no. 562/Hofstede de Groot, *Rembrandt Bijbel*, N.T.p.4; Sumowski 1963, no. 5.

His name is John

Luke 1 57 Now Elisabeth's full time came that she should be delivered; and she brought forth a son.

58 And her neighbours and her cousins heard how the Lord had shewed great mercy upon her; and they rejoiced with her.

59 And it came to pass, that on the eight day they came to circumcise the child; and they called him Zacharias, after the name of his father.

60 And his mother answered and said, Not *so;* but he shall be called John.

61 And they said unto her, There is none of thy kindred that is called by this name.

62 And they made signs to his father, how he would have him called.

63 And he asked for a writing table, and wrote, saying, His name is John. And they marvelled all.

64 And his mouth was opened immediately, and his tongue *loosed,* and he spake, and praised God.

65 And fear came on all that dwelt round about them: and all these sayings were noised abroad throughout all the hill country of Judæa.

66 And all they that heard *them* laid *them* up in their hearts, saying, What manner of child shall this be! And the hand of the Lord was with him.

67 And his father Zacharias was filled with the Holy Ghost, and prophesied, saying,

68 Blessed *be* the Lord God of Israel; for he hath visited and redeemed his people,

69 And hath raised up an horn of salvation for us in the house of his servant David;

70 As he spake by the mouth of his holy prophets, which have been since the world began:

71 That we should be saved from our enemies, and from the hand of all that hate us;

72 To perform the mercy *promised* to our fathers, and to remember his holy covenant;

73 The oath which he sware to our father Abraham,

74 That he would grant unto us, that we being delivered out of the hand of our enemies might serve him without fear,

75 In holiness and righteousness before him, all the days of our life.

76 And thou, child, shalt be called the prophet of the Highest: for thou shalt go before the face of the Lord to prepare his ways;

77 To give knowledge of salvation unto his people by the remission of their sins,

78 Through the tender mercy of our God; whereby the dayspring from on high hath visited us,

79 To give light to them that sit in darkness and *in* the shadow of death, to guide our feet into the way of peace.

80 And the child grew, and waxed strong in spirit, and was in the deserts till the day of his shewing unto Israel.

The Naming of
St John the Baptist

And they made signs to his father, how he would have him called. And he asked for a writing table, and wrote, saying, His name is John, and they marvelled all.
(Luke 1:62-63)

This fascinating composition, executed in the monumental style of drawing used by Rembrandt in the middle of the 1650s, comprises three interconnected scenes. In the background on the right, preparations are being made for the Child's circumcision and the writing down of his name, while one of the servants is waiting between the curtains of the bed where the Child was born to take him from his mother's hands. However, Elizabeth delays handing him over for a moment until Zachariah has announced his decision regarding the dispute about the name. This last scene, showing the old man writing - he had been struck dumb when John was born because he did not believe the words of the Angel Gabriel (Luke 1:5-20) - is the central part of the composition. Three women attentively follow the movements of his hand, curious to know what name will appear on the writing table.

This incident concerning the birth of St John the Baptist was a popular subject with artists for a long time, but in Rembrandt's work this drawing is the only version of the subject.

Pen and brush drawing; 19.9 × 31.4 cm.
Bottom right in later handwriting: *Rembrant.*
Ca. 1655.
Paris, The Louvre.

Literature: Benesch V, no. 1007 (*ca.* 1656); Slive II, no. 335 (*ca.* 1655)/Hofstede de Groot, *Rembrandt Bijbel*, N.T.d.3; Rotermund 1963, no. 139; 'Bijbelse Inspiratie', no. 86.

For unto you is born this day a Saviour

Luke 2 AND it came to pass in those days, that there went out a decree from Cæsar Augustus, that all the world should be taxed.

2 (*And* this taxing was first made when Cyrenius was governor of Syria.)

3 And all went to be taxed, every one into his own city.

4 And Joseph also went up from Galilee, out of the city of Nazareth, into Judæa, unto the city of David, which is called Bethlehem; (because he was of the house and lineage of David:)

5 To be taxed with Mary his espoused wife, being great with child.

6 And so it was, that, while they were there, the days were accomplished that she should be delivered.

7 And she brought forth her firstborn son, and wrapped him in swaddling clothes, and laid him in a manger; because there was no room for them in the inn.

8 And there were in the same country shepherds abiding in the field, keeping watch over their flock by night.

9 And, lo, the angel of the Lord came upon them, and the glory of the Lord shone round about them: and they were sore afraid.

10 And the angel said unto them, Fear not: for, behold, I bring you good tidings of great joy, which shall be to all people.

11 For unto you is born this day in the city of David a Saviour, which is the Christ the Lord.

12 And this *shall be* a sign unto you; Ye shall find the babe wrapped in swaddling clothes, lying in a manger.

13 And suddenly there was with the angel a multitude of the heavenly host praising God, and saying,

14 Glory to God in the highest, and on earth peace, good will toward men.

The Angel Appears to the Shepherds — *And the angel said unto them, Fear not: for, behold, I bring you good tidings of great joy, which shall be to all people.* (Luke 2:10)

This subject was depicted only as an independent scene towards the end of the 16th century. Before that time the announcement to the shepherds was virtually always depicted in combination with the scene of Jesus' birth, as an additional feature in the background.

In this etching dating from 1634, Rembrandt interpreted the story from the Gospel according to St Luke as dramatically as possible. In the middle of the night the heavens open and a forgotten corner of the world is suddenly illuminated with the 'glory of the Lord': a crown of light surrounded by angels with a dove, the traditional symbol of the Holy Ghost, at the centre. The angel, who has stepped out of the light, raises his hand to bring the glad tidings, but for the moment he succeeds only in sowing confusion and panic among the shepherds.

Because of the poetic way in which nature is depicted and the strong contrast between light and dark, this impressive print, Rembrandt's first etching of a night scene, is reminiscent of the night scenes by the German painter Adam Elsheimer (1578-1610), who worked in Rome at the beginning of the 17th century. His works were known in the Netherlands through the engravings based on them made between 1610 and 1614 by Hendrick Goudt (*ca.* 1582-1648), and had a great influence on the development of Dutch landscape painting during the 17th century.

Etching; 26.2 × 21.8 cm. Third state of three.
Signed and dated: *Rembrandt f. 1634.*
Amsterdam, Rijksprentenkabinet.

Literature: Bartsch, no. 44; Hind, no. 120; Münz, no. 199; Boon, no. 106 Filedt Kok, no. B 44/Hofstede de Groot, *Rembrandt Bijbel*, N.T.e.1; J.G. van Gelder, 'Rembrandt: *De verkondiging aan de herders*, in: *Openbaar Kunstbezit* 7 (1963), no. 40; Sumowski 1963, no. 7; 'Bijbelse Inspiratie', no. 29; Tümpel 1970, no. 41.

The Angel Appears to the Shepherds

Fear not: for, behold, I bring you good tidings of great joy, which shall be to all people. For unto you is born this day in the city of David, a Saviour, which is Christ the Lord. (Luke 2:10-11)

The appearance of the angel who rents asunder the darkness of night with a light shining around him is closely related to the etching dating from 1634 (p. 229), which Rembrandt elaborated. However, this time the emphasis is not on the confusion sown by the heavenly messenger, but on the 'glad tidings of great joy' which the shepherds receive with a mixture of awe and dread.

This charming drawing is one of a group in which attempts were made to achieve a strong contrast between light and dark in the same way.

Pen and brush drawing; 17.6 × 20 cm.
Ca. 1640-42.
Hamburg, Kunsthalle.

Literature: Benesch III, no. 501 (*ca.* 1640-42).

Fear not: for, behold, I bring you good tidings of great joy, which shall be to all people. For unto you is born this day in the city of David, a Saviour, which is Christ the Lord. (Luke 2:10-11)

In this composition, dating from the middle of the 1650s, the scene has great breadth. The angel penetrates the picture with his light from the side. His sudden appearance only sows fear and panic among the shepherds, though the cattle do not respond.

In 17th-century Dutch art this theme was not infrequently depicted in combination with cattle, so that the sheep traditionally shown in this subject were increasingly replaced by cows. This tendency is also found in Rembrandt's work.

Pen and brush drawing; 18.8 × 28 cm.
Ca. 1655.
Amsterdam, Rijksprentenkabinet.

Literature: Benesch V, no. 1023 (*ca.* 1656-57); Slive II, no. 321 (*ca.* 1655)/Rotermund 1963, no. 143; 'Bijbelse Inspiratie', no. 88.

The Angel Appears to the Shepherds

As it was told unto them

Luke 2 15 And it came to pass, as the angels were gone away from them into heaven, the shepherds said one to another, Let us now go even unto Bethlehem, and see this thing which is come to pass, which the Lord hath made known unto us.

16 And they came with haste, and found Mary, and Joseph, and the babe lying in a manger.

17 And when they had seen *it,* they made known abroad the saying which was told them concerning this child.

18 And all they that heard *it* wondered at those things which were told them by the shepherds.

19 But Mary kept all these things, and pondered *them* in her heart.

20 And the shepherds returned, glorifying and praising God for all the things that they had heard and seen, as it was told unto them.

The Shepherds Worship the Child

And they came with haste, and found Mary, and Joseph, and the babe lying in a manger.
(Luke 2:16)

The shepherds worshipping the Child is a much more recent theme as an independent subject than the Adoration of the Magi. In the earliest works showing this scene, which date from the 15th century, the shepherds are little more than observers in the background as the Child is worshipped by his mother Mary. It was only in the course of the 16th century that they were involved in the scene as main characters in their own right, and the worshipping shepherds became as significant a subject as the three kings.

The human aspect, which affects the age-old representation of the mystery of the Nativity in the West, achieves a high point in Rembrandt's work. There are no angels and no heavenly music - only the earthly reality of ordinary people in the dark stable. And yet all this realism does not detract from the dignity of the subject in any way. All the faces, lit up by the warm glow of a stable lantern and the candle in Joseph's hands, are turned towards the newborn Child, and the shepherds are ecstatic because He is 'wrapped in swaddling clothes, lying in a manger', just as the angel said (Luke 2:12).

Together with the *Circumcision of Jesus,* which has disappeared, this painting was commissioned by Stadtholder Frederik Hendrik, the Prince of Orange, in the same size as the series of scenes from the Passion which Rembrandt had made for him in the 1630s.

Canvas rounded at the top; 97 × 71.5 cm.
Signed and dated: *...ndt f. 1646.*
Munich, Alte Pinakothek.

Literature: Bredius, no. 574; Bauch, no. 79; Gerson, no. 215; Bredius-Gerson, no. 574/Hofstede de Groot, *Rembrandt Bijbel,* N.T.p.5.

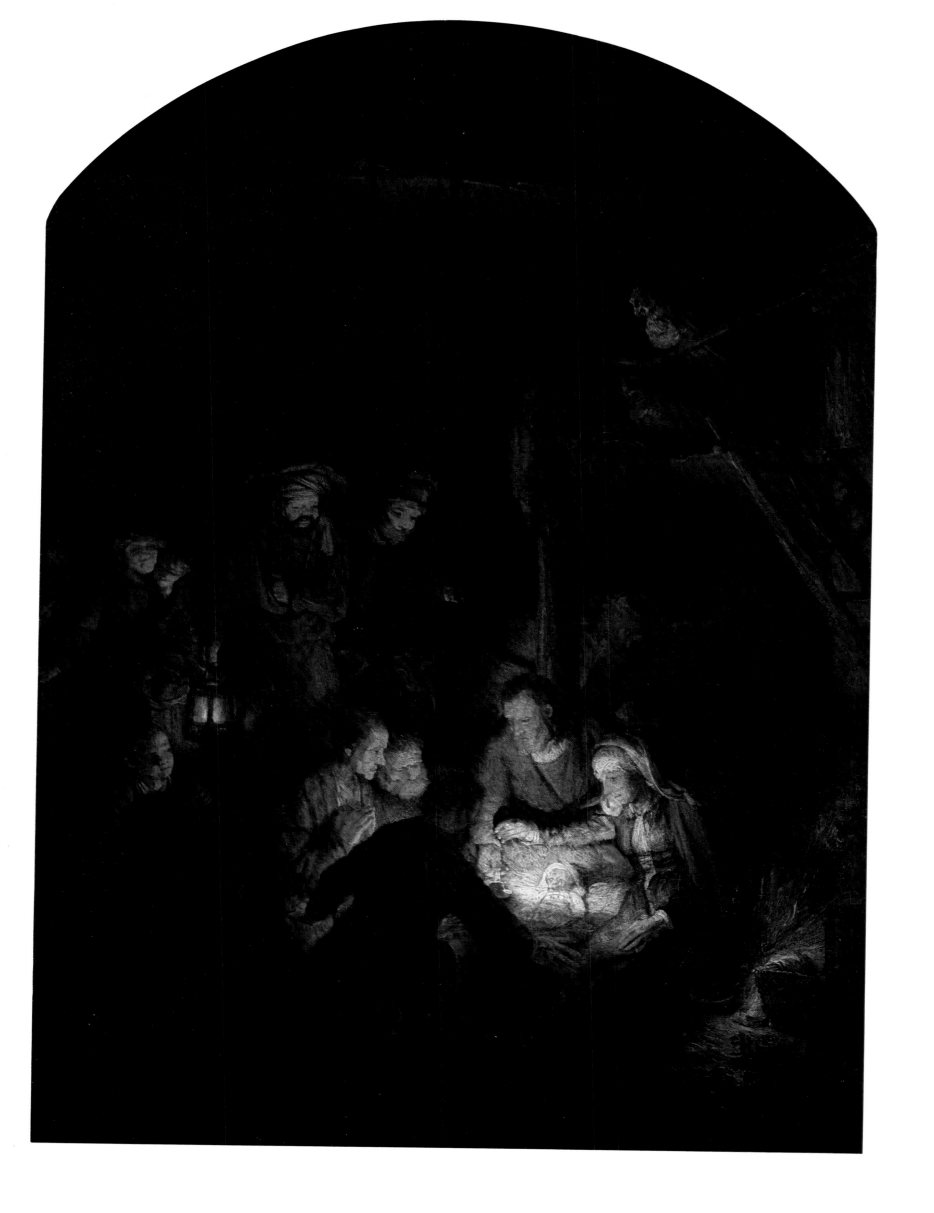

The Shepherds
Worship the Child

And they came with haste, and found Mary, and Joseph,
and the babe lying in a manger.
(Luke 2:16)

In about 1652, when Rembrandt first portrayed the
shepherds worshipping the Child in an etching, he
showed a night-time scene 'in which no figure is
distinct, no form is accentuated, no gesture stands out,
and everything is a matter of appearances' (Jan Veth).
This time he completely departed from the traditional
way of depicting this subject, and makes it seem as
though the parents of the Child are unexpectedly
surprised by the visit from the shepherds. Wrapped in
a blanket, Mary lays down to rest next to the Child,
and Joseph looks up in surprise from the book he is
reading. The faint glow of the stable lantern, which
the shepherds have brought with them, lights up the
vague silhouettes of some cows on the left.

Etching; 14.8 × 19.8 cm. Eighth state of eight.
Ca. 1652.
Amsterdam, Rijksprentenkabinet.

Literature: Bartsch, no. 46; Hind, no. 255; Münz, no. 237;
Boon, no. 234; Filedt Kok, no. B 46/Hofstede de Groot,
Rembrandt Bijbel, N.T.e.3; Sumowski 1963, no. 6;
Tümpel 1970, no. 42.

And they came with haste, and found Mary, and Joseph, and the babe lying in a manger.
(Luke 2:16)

In this etching, Mary and the Child in the manger are in the centre of the composition against a plain wall outlined with an arch and illuminated by a small oil lamp. On the left, the shepherds - including a traditional shepherd with a bagpipe - are crowding each other to see the Child, and on the right the circle of light finishes with Joseph seated on an upturned wheelbarrow. Two cows serve to make it clear that this is a byre.

This etching, together with five others (*The Circumcision*, p. 242; *The Flight into Egypt*, p. 259; *The Holy Family*, p. 284; *The Twelve-year-old Jesus in the Temple*, p. 294; and *Jesus Returns from the Temple with his Parents*, p. 295) forms a cycle about the childhood of Jesus which includes what must be considered some of Rembrandt's finest etchings because of their moving simplicity and the accuracy with which the simplest methods are used.

Etching; 10.5 × 12.9 cm. First state of two.
Signed: *Rembrandt f.*
Ca. 1654.
Amsterdam, Rijksprentenkabinet.

Literature: Bartsch, no. 45; Hind, no. 273; Münz, no. 226; Boon, no. 250; Filedt Kok, no. B 45/Hofstede de Groot, *Rembrandt Bijbel*, N.T.e.2; Rotermund 1963, no. 146; Sumowski 1963, no. 8; 'Bijbelse Inspiratie', no. 30; Tümpel 1970, no. 43.

The Shepherds
Worship the Child

The Shepherds
Worship the Child

And they came with haste, and found Mary, and Joseph,
and the babe lying in a manger.
(Luke 2:16)

This painting is a mirror-image variation of the
somewhat larger canvas in the Alte Pinakothek in
Munich (see p. 233), executed in a slightly freer style.
The two works are dated the same year: 1646.

In Rembrandt's works of the shepherds worshipping
the Child, there is no sign of the ox and the ass, the
two 'dumb creatures' which had been depicted next to
the manger since early Christian times although they
are not mentioned in the story of the Nativity in the
Gospels. The origin of their faithful presence in the
stable of Bethlehem can be found in the Old
Testament in the words of the prophet Isaiah:

The ox knoweth his owner,
And the ass his master's crib:
But Israel doth not know,
My people doth not consider.
(Isaiah 1:3)

These words of the prophet, which refer to the words
of St John in the prologue to his Gospel: 'He came
unto his own, and his own received him not' (John 1:11)
were explained as early as the first half of the 3rd
century AD as a prediction of the birth of Jesus, and it
was not long before the ox and ass assumed a
permanent place next to the manger. Rembrandt
probably did not know of their Old Testament origin
and, keeping to the text of the Gospels, he depicted
the animals which are usually found in a stable.

Canvas; 65.5 × 55 cm.
Signed and dated: *Rembrandt f. 1646.*
London, National Gallery.

Literature: Bredius, no. 575; Bauch, no. 78; Gerson, no.
216; Bredius-Gerson, no. 575/Tümpel 1970, under no. 42.

His name was called JESUS

Luke 2 21 And when eight days were accomplished for the circumcising of the child, his name was called JESUS, which was so named of the angel before he was conceived in the womb.

The Circumcision   According to Jewish law, every Jewish boy had to be circumcised on the eighth day after his birth. The circumcision was a sign that the child became part of the covenant which God had sealed with Israel.

The circumcision of St John the Baptist took place in his parents' house (Luke 1:59, see pp. 226-27). The Gospel according to St Luke does not mention where Jesus was circumcised. In general, the apocryphal scriptures state that the Circumcision took place in the stable in Bethlehem. It is not possible that the ceremony took place in the temple in Mary's presence, for, according to Mosaic law, a mother was unclean for seven days after the birth of a son, and then had to remain away from the temple for another thirty-three days (Leviticus 12:2-4; cf. Luke 2:22).

Nevertheless, it was common for Western artists to depict the Circumcision of Jesus in the temple of Jerusalem in Mary's presence. In this way, the ritual to which the infant Jesus was submitted was characterized as anticipating the sacrament of baptism, the spiritual circumcision of the new covenant. Up to 1646, Rembrandt also depicted the Circumcision as taking place in the temple in accordance with tradition. It was only in 1654, when he realized this was not correct, that he first showed the ceremony being performed in the stable in Bethlehem (see p. 242).

This etching, which was rejected for a long time, is now generally recognized as an authentic work by Rembrandt. The print probably dates from the year 1626, and together with *The Rest on the Flight into Egypt* (p. 261), it is one of Rembrandt's very first etchings.

Etching; 21.4 × 16 cm. Second state of two.
Caption (not in his own hand): *Rembrant fecit I.P. Berendrech ex.*
Ca. 1626.
Amsterdam, Rijksprentenkabinet.

Literature: Gersaint, no. 48; Hind, no. 388; Münz, no. 187; Boon, no. 1; Filedt Kok, p. 53/Sumowski 1963, no. 10; Tümpel 1970, under no. 44.

Rembrant fe.   I. P. Berendrecb. ex.

The Circumcision   In accordance with the customary view, Rembrandt
shows the Circumcision of Jesus in the temple of
Jerusalem (see explanatory note on p. 238). The High
Priest has the Child on his lap, while the circumcisor
carries out the ritual. In the front on the right, Mary
(kneeling) and Joseph watch in awe with their hands
folded. The frankincense burning on the high altar
emphasizes the solemn nature of the event.

Etching; 8.8 × 6.4 cm. Only state.
Ca. 1630.
Amsterdam, Rijksprentenkabinet.

Literature: Bartsch, no. 48; Hind, no. 19; Münz, no. 194;
Boon, no. 55; Filedt Kok, no. B 48/Hofstede de Groot,
Rembrandt Bijbel, N.T.e.4; Tümpel 1970, no. 44.

In common with the etching dating from 1654, this painting, dating from 1661, shows the Circumcision of Jesus being performed in the stable in Bethlehem. However, this time it is not Joseph but Mary who is holding the baby. Next to the priest who is performing the ritual, the modest Madonna and the divine Child form a triangle of glowing colour in the centre of the composition. The painting is a splendid example of Rembrandt's late style of painting, in which the forms are never sharply outlined, but are only indicated with broad brushstrokes.

Canvas; 56.5 × 75 cm.
Signed and dated: *Rembrandt f. 1661.*
Washington, National Gallery of Art, Widener Collection.

Literature: Bredius, no. 596; Bauch, no. 93; Gerson, no. 350; Bredius-Gerson, no. 596.

The Circumcision

The Circumcision

In this etching, which forms part of the cycle of the childhood of Jesus mentioned on p. 235, Rembrandt first shows the Circumcision being performed in the stable at Bethlehem, instead of in the temple. The Child is circumcised lying on Joseph's lap. Mary lies next to him, with her hands meekly folded, and caught with Joseph and the Child in the light falling from above.

When Rembrandt used this subject again in 1661, he again showed the ceremony taking place in the stable. From this, Christian Tümpel concluded that after 1646 - when he still showed the Circumcision being performed in the temple - and before 1654, the year in which he did this etching, Rembrandt must have realized, either of his own accord or because he was told, that a correct interpretation of the Biblical text does not allow for the Circumcision of Jesus to be shown in the temple in Mary's presence. It is possible that Rembrandt heard that the way in which the Circumcision was popularly represented in the Middle Ages was considered to be incorrect by the Biblical scholars of his time. Influenced by this criticism, the Antwerp engraver Antoon Wierix had already shown the Circumcision of Jesus in the stable in Bethlehem. Rembrandt was probably familiar with this engraving, and therefore wondered which interpretation of the text in the Gospels was correct.

Etching; 9.5 × 14.4 cm. First state of two.
Signed and dated (twice): *Rembrandt f. 1654.*
Amsterdam, Rijksprentenkabinet.

Literature: Bartsch, no. 47; Hind, no. 274; Münz, no. 227; Boon, no. 251; Filedt Kok, no. B 47/Hofstede de Groot, *Rembrandt Bijbel*, N.T.e.5; Rotermund 1963, no. 151; Sumowski 1963, no. 11; Tümpel 1970, no. 46.

In 1646 Rembrandt was commissioned by Prince
Frederik Hendrik to do two paintings, *The Shepherds
Worshipping the Child* (p. 233) and a *Circumcision of Jesus*,
to supplement the scenes of the Passion he had done
for the Prince in the 1630s. The painting of the
Circumcision is now lost. However, an old copy of it
which is in the Herzog-Anton-Ulrich Museum in
Brunswick suggests that this drawing, dating from
about 1645, may have played a role in the creation of
the painting.

Again the scene is set in the temple, in accordance
with tradition, in a sort of priests' choir, enclosed at
the back by a semicircular balustrade. Mary and Joseph
are kneeling in the foreground on the right.

Pen and brush drawing; 20.3 × 28.7 cm.
Ca. 1645.
Berlin, Kupferstichkabinett der Staatlichen Museen.

Literature: Benesch III, no. 574 (*ca*. 1645-46); Slive I, no.
19 (*ca*. 1645)/Tümpel 1970, no. 45.

The Circumcision

Gold, and frankincense, and myrrh

Matthew 2 NOW when Jesus was born in Bethlehem of Judæa in the days of Herod the king, behold, there came wise men from the east to Jerusalem,

2 Saying, Where is he that is born King of the Jews? for we have seen his star in the east, and are come to worship him

3 When Herod the king had heard *these things,* he was troubled, and all Jerusalem with him.

4 And when he had gathered all the chief priests and scribes of the people together, he demanded of them where Christ should be born.

5 And they said unto him, In Bethlehem of Judæa: for thus is written by the prophet,

6 And thou Bethlehem, *in* the land of Juda, art not the least among the princes of Juda: for out of thee shall come a Governor, that shall rule my people Israel.

7 Then Herod, when he had privily called the wise men, enquired of them diligently what time the star appeared.

8 And he sent them to Bethlehem, and said, Go and search diligently for the young child; and when ye have found *him,* bring me word again, that I may come and worship him also.

9 When they had heard the king, they departed; and, lo, the star, which they saw in the east, went before them, till it came and stood over where the young child was.

10 When they saw the star, they rejoiced with exceeding great joy.

11 And when they were come into the house, they saw the young child with Mary his mother, and fell down, and worshipped him: and when they had opened their treasures, they presented unto him gifts; gold, and frankincense, and myrrh.

12 And being warned of God in a dream that they should not return to Herod, they departed into their own country another way.

The Adoration of the Magi

And when they were come into the house, they saw the young child with Mary his mother, and fell down, and worshipped him.
(Matthew 2:11)

Even in the oldest catacombs of the first Roman Christians, there was a picture of the Adoration of the Magi. They were seen as the first to be called outside Israel, as the beginning of the Church among the heathens. They wore Persian garments, not regal robes. The latter only became popular during the Middle Ages when legends changed the wise men from the East into kings, on the grounds of their royal gifts, and also harking back to a text in the Book of Psalms:

The kings of Tarshish and of the isles
Shall bring presents:
The kings of Sheba and Seba
Shall offer gifts.
Yea, all kings shall fall down before him:
All nations shall serve him.
(Psalms 72:10-11)

Their number (invariably the reference is to three kings) is undoubtedly based on the number of gifts mentioned in the Gospel according to St Matthew: gold, frankincense and myrrh. The three represent the continents known in the Middle Ages - Europe, Asia and Africa - and as characters with different ages they also symbolize the three stages in the life of man: youth, middle age and old age.

This subject can only be found a few times in Rembrandt's known work, and then only in the work dating from his first Amsterdam period. In this greyish-brown sketch in oils on paper, a so-called 'grisaille', which was possibly intended as a preliminary study or a design for an etching (which was never executed), he uses his own style to depict the wise men from the East as three kings of different races and ages, accompanied by a large retinue. The oldest, who is kneeling in worship in the foreground, has removed his turban to show that he recognizes the Child on Mary's lap as the highest king.

The painting, which came into the possession of the Hermitage in Leningrad in 1923, was only officially recognized as a work signed and dated by Rembrandt in 1968. A slightly larger version of the same composition executed in the early Rembrandt style has been known for a long time, and is in Göteborg (Bredius, no. 541).

Paper on canvas; 45 × 39 cm.
Signed and dated: *Rembrandt f. 1632.*
Leningrad, Hermitage.

Literature: Irina Linnik: 'Die Anbetung der Könige von Rembrandt', in: *Pantheon*, XXVII (1969), pp. 36-41; Bredius-Gerson, p. 604, under no. 541.

Study for an Adoration of the Magi

And when they were come into the house, they saw the young child with Mary his mother, and fell down, and worshipped him.
(Matthew 2:11)

This powerful sketch expresses only the essence of the theme: the manifestation of God in a helpless human child, recognized by the wise men as the Lord of creation. The figures form a tight unit because of the diagonal structure of the composition.

Pen and ink drawing; 17.8 × 16 cm.
Ca. 1635.
Amsterdam, Rijksprentenkabinet.

Literature: Benesch I, no. 115 (*ca.* 1635); Slive II, no. 324 (*ca.* 1635); Haak, no. 13 (1634-35)/Rotermund 1963, no. 145; Sumowski 1963, no. 9; 'Bijbelse Inspiratie', no. 89.

246

And when they were come into the house, they saw the young child with Mary his mother, and fell down, and worshipped him.

(Matthew 2:11)

This drawing was probably done in the second half of the 1630s. Again the wise men from the East are depicted in the traditional form of three kings with a large retinue. Mary is sitting under the roof of the stable on the left in the foreground, with Jesus on her lap. Behind her stands Joseph, looking at the oldest king, who kneels to worship the Child and offer his gift. The middle of the composition is dominated by the second king, who enters the scene with the self-consciousness of an Eastern potentate. The train of his regal gown is carried by a child behind him. In the foreground on the right, the youngest king approaches, attired like a warrior with a sabre, bow and quiver of arrows.

Pen and ink drawing; 17.4 × 22.8 cm.
Ca. 1638.
Berlin, Kupferstichkabinett der Staatlichen Museen.

Literature: Benesch I, no. 160 (*ca.* 1638)/Tümpel 1970, no. 47; Peter Schatborn, 'Twee Aanbiddingen van de Koningen' in: *De kroniek van het Rembrandthuis*, 26 (1972), pp. 97-106.

The Adoration of the Magi

Arise, and flee into Egypt

Matthew 2   13 And when they were departed, behold, the angel of the Lord appeareth to Joseph in a dream, saying, Arise, and take the young child and his mother, and flee into Egypt, and be thou there until I bring thee word: for Herod will seek the young child to destroy him.

14 When he arose, he took the young child and his mother by night, and departed into Egypt:

15 And was there until the death of Herod: that it might be fulfilled which was spoken of the Lord by prophet, saying, Out of Egypt have I called my son.

The Angel Appears to Joseph in a Dream

Arise, and take the young child and his mother, and flee into Egypt, and be thou there until I bring thee word: for Herod will seek the young child to destroy him.
(Matthew 2:13)

Rembrandt has depicted this apparition, which is rarely found in Dutch art, in the stable in Bethlehem. It shows the parents, who have fallen into an exhausted sleep after the visit of the wise men. They are sitting on the bare floor, next to the stalls. Mary's arms protectively hold the Child wrapped in a red cloth in the manger. In order to show that Joseph did not see and hear the angel in reality, but only in a dream, as described in the Gospel according to St Matthew, Rembrandt has placed the warning angel behind Joseph as he sleeps on peacefully, and only hears and sees the warning inwardly (cf. the drawings of this theme on pp. 250 and 251).

Panel; 20 × 27 cm.
Signed and dated: *Rembrandt f. 1645.*
Berlin, Gemäldegalerie der Staatlichen Museen.

Literature: Bredius, no. 569; Bauch, no. 76; Gerson, no. 210; Bredius-Gerson, no. 569/Hofstede de Groot, *Rembrandt Bijbel*, N.T.p.8.

The Angel Appears to Joseph in a Dream

Arise, and take the young child and his mother, and flee into Egypt, and be thou there until I bring thee word: for Herod will seek the young child to destroy him.
(Matthew 2:13)

The passionate style of drawing gives this quick sketch an energy which is appropriate for the angel's alarming message. The donkey in the background is a reference to the flight which Joseph is being urged to take.

Judging by a copy of this drawing, the sheet was considerably reduced at the top. This composition served as a model for a painting by Barent Fabritius which is in Budapest and which has the same diagonal composition.

Pen and brush drawing; 14.5 × 18.7 cm.
Ca. 1650.
Berlin, Kupferstichkabinett der Staatlichen Museen.

Literature: Benesch V, no. 879 (*ca.* 1651-52); Slive I, no. 17 (*ca.* 1648-50)/Rotermund 1963, no. 156; Sumowski 1963, no. 18; Tümpel 1970, no. 53.

Arise, and take the young child and his mother, and flee into Egypt, and be thou there until I bring thee word: for Herod will seek the young child to destroy him.
(Matthew 2:13)

This drawing of Joseph's dream is one of the most beautiful Biblical scenes drawn by Rembrandt in the early 1650s, because of its quiet intimacy and its execution, which is at the same time both restrained and very effective. The saddle on the ground next to Joseph serves as a reference to the angel's warning to flee.

Pen and ink drawing; 17.9 × 18.1 cm.
Ca. 1652.
Amsterdam, Rijksprentenkabinet.

Literature: Benesch V, no. 915 (*ca.* 1652); Slive II, no. 327 (*ca.* 1652)/Rotermund 1963, no. 155; 'Bijbelse Inspiratie', no. 93.

The Angel Appears to Joseph in a Dream

251

The Flight into Egypt

When he arose, he took the young child and his mother by night, and departed into Egypt.
(Matthew 2:14)

This theme has been popular for centuries, and in Rembrandt's Biblical work it has a special place, particularly in his etchings portraying Jesus' childhood. The Gospel according to St Matthew is very brief on the subject of the Flight into Egypt, unlike the apocryphal gospels and medieval elaborations of these. They describe in great detail all sorts of wonderful events which supposedly took place on the way. According to a legend, the Holy Family was accompanied on the journey by an angel, the trees bowed down their crowns before God's Son, a palm tree even offered its fruits to the refugees and the graven images in the temple of Hermopolis fell off their pedestals when the Virgin entered the land of Egypt with her child. In the many late medieval works portraying the Flight into Egypt, these stories, the product of devout religious imagination, not infrequently played an important role. Their influence gradually diminished in the course of the 16th century, and themes were introduced which appealed to a sense of empathy with the couple driven to flee in the middle of the night.

This night scene by the young Rembrandt is a moving example of the more affective approach to the scene. The small panel only came to light in 1954, and is also the earliest example of his magical use of chiaroscuro, which was to become one of his main means of expression from 1627. '... Virtually none of the surroundings can be distinguished in the pale light of the moon, but how poetically this enriches the age-old theme of the Flight into Egypt! The attention is wholly focused on the group, and an impression is created of mystery, of immeasurable space and uncertainty regarding the future of this small family entering the loneliness of night' (Jacques Foucart, in the catalogue for the exhibition *Le Siècle de Rembrandt*, Paris 1970-71, no. 168). The donkey is a traditional feature of depictions of the Flight into Egypt, though the text in the Bible does not mention any beast of burden. Rembrandt makes a reference to Joseph's profession as a carpenter through the tools carried on the back of the donkey - a hand drill and the blade of a saw can be seen.

Panel; 26.5 × 24 cm.
Signed and dated: *RHL, 1627*.
Tours, Musée des Beaux-Arts.

Literature: Bauch, no. 43; Gerson, no. 8; Bredius-Gerson, no. 532A/Sumowski 1963, no. 20.

The Flight into Egypt

When he arose, he took the young child and his mother by night, and departed into Egypt.
(Matthew 2:14)

This early etching, which was probably done shortly after the painting dating from 1627 on the previous page, shows the refugees at a spot where there is a sharp bend in the road; while the donkey and Mary and the Child are still coming towards us, Joseph, in his humble garments, already has his back to us.

After the first state, of which there are only two known prints, Rembrandt reworked the plate. Clearly he was not satisfied with the result, and did not see any possibility of making improvements. He only elaborated the successful part with the figure of Joseph.

Etching; 14.6 × 12.2 cm. First state of six.
Ca. 1627.
Amsterdam, Rijksprentenkabinet.

Literature: Bartsch, no. 54; Hind, no. 17; Münz, no. 189; Boon, no. 3/Tümpel 1970, no. 54.

254

*When he arose, he took the young child and his mother by
night, and departed into Egypt.*
(Matthew 2:14)

Without looking up or round, Joseph leads the donkey
on with its precious burden, away from Bethlehem,
where Herod threatened to murder all infants. Again,
there are some tools among the baggage carried by the
donkey to refer to Joseph's profession as a carpenter.

It is clear that when he made this finely detailed
etching dating from 1633, Rembrandt based it on the
first state of the etching shown on the previous page,
dating from 1627, which was never completed. The
large number of 17th-century copies which are known
of this etching, the earliest of which dates from 1643,
show how popular this little print was even during
Rembrandt's own lifetime. (See Tümpel 1970, under no.
55.)

Etching; 8.9 × 6.2 cm. First state of two.
Signed and dated: *Rembrandt inventor et fecit, 1633.*
Amsterdam, Rijksprentenkabinet.

The Flight into Egypt

Literature: Bartsch, no. 52; Hind, no. 105; Münz, no. 195;
Boon, no. 87; Filedt Kok, no. B 52/Tümpel 1970, no. 55.

The Flight into Egypt

When he arose, he took the young child and his mother by night, and departed into Egypt.
(Matthew 2:14)

In the years between this etching, dating from 1651, and the previous one, dating from 1633, Rembrandt only used the theme of the Flight into Egypt once, in a painting that is probably dated 1634 (Bredius-Gerson, no. 552A). A comparison of the two prints shows the extent of the improvement in direct expression and concentration on the essential aspect of the theme which took place in the intervening period as a result of the simplification of the work. In the six successive states of this night scene, which are similar in nature to the night-time worship of the shepherds, dating from *ca.* 1652 (see p. 234), he shrouded all the details in darkness, attempting to create as strong as possible an effect of night, until the areas of light were finally so small that in the sixth state it is only possible to discern Joseph finding his way with great difficulty through the dead of night, holding a lantern.

Pastor's son Vincent Van Gogh, who had a profound admiration for Rembrandt's work, was referring to this etching among others, when he wrote to his brother Theo about his father in a letter dated 18 September 1877: 'How much someone like father would have felt for the etchings by Rembrandt, such as the Flight into Egypt by Night, or the Burial of Jesus, as he so often made trips, also by night, holding a lantern, for example, to visit the sick or dying, to talk to them about him whose word is also a light in the night of suffering and mortal fear.'

Etching; 12.8 × 11 cm. First, third and sixth state of six.
Signed and dated: *Rembrandt f. 1651.*
Amsterdam, Rijksprentenkabinet.

Literature: Bartsch, no. 53; Hind, no. 253; Münz, no. 221; Boon, no. 225; Filedt Kok, no. B 53/Hofstede de Groot, *Rembrandt Bijbel*, N.T.e.8; 'Bijbelse Inspiratie', no. 31; Tümpel 1970, no. 56.

The Flight into Egypt

When he arose, he took the young child and his mother by night, and departed into Egypt.
(Matthew 2:14)

For this print Rembrandt used an etching plate by Hercules Seghers (1590-1640), which he probably acquired after the etcher's death. The few prints of the original etching by Seghers which have survived show that it depicted a landscape with Tobias and the angel, a free copy after an engraving by Hendrick Goudt, dated 1613, which in turn was based on a painting by Adam Elsheimer, now in the National Gallery in London. Rembrandt removed the group of Tobias and the angel and replaced them with a Flight into Egypt with smaller figures and a group of trees behind them. He changed little of the landscape on the left, so that the print retains the characteristic aspects of Seghers's work: a rocky terrain going up to the left and right, overgrown with all sorts of trees and a view into the distance from the centre.

Rembrandt was a great admirer of Seghers and had eight of his paintings, which have left their impression on Rembrandt's own imaginative landscapes painted between 1636 and 1640.

Etching; 21.2 × 28.4 cm. Fourth state of seven.
Ca. 1653.
Amsterdam, Rijksprentenkabinet.

Literature: Bartsch, no. 56; Hind, no. 266; Münz, no. 216 (*ca.* 1643-44); Boon, no. 246; Filedt Kok, no. B 56/Tümpel 1970, no. 57.

When he arose, he took the young child and his mother by night, and departed into Egypt.
(Matthew 2:14)

By showing the fleeing couple in the etching, as they wade through a stream, Rembrandt clearly revealed the difficulties and dangers of the long journey through an inhospitable wilderness in a very original way.

This etching forms part of the series on the childhood of Jesus referred to on p. 235.

Etching; 9.3 × 14.4 cm. Only state.
Signed and dated: *Rembrandt f. 1654.*
Amsterdam, Rijksprentenkabinet.

Literature: Bartsch, no. 55; Hind, no. 276; Münz, no. 228; Boon, no. 253; Filedt Kok, no. B 55/Hofstede de Groot, *Rembrandt Bijbel*, N.T.e.9; Sumowski 1963, no. 21; Tümpel 1970, no. 58.

The Flight into Egypt

The Rest on the
Flight into Egypt

Late medieval artists liked to depict all sorts of
episodes from the Flight into Egypt of which there is
no mention at all in the Gospel according to St
Matthew. These are based on the apocryphal
scriptures, and even more on the popular literature
derived from them. Pictures of the rest during the
flight - a theme which originated in the apocryphal
gospel of the pseudo-Matthew - were very popular,
particularly in Dutch art. There are versions of this
subject in Rembrandt's work.

This print, in many respects rather clumsily
executed, is among Rembrandt's earliest etchings,
together with that of the Circumcision, dating from *ca.*
1626 (see p. 239). The peaceful scene takes place in a
shady spot along the road. Joseph has prepared some
food on a wood fire, and holds a dish for Mary from
which she feeds the Child with a spoon. The baby's
holiness is shown by an aura around his head. We can
imagine that Mary has just said to Joseph something on
the lines of one of the verses of an old Dutch
Christmas poem:

Joseph make us some sweet gruel,
Hurry, make it quickly.
Let me feed this innocent babe
He is God's holy son.

A number of features from this etching, such as the
donkey's head and Joseph's wide-brimmed straw hat in
the foreground next to the basket with the saw, were
used again by Rembrandt in the small painting of the
Flight into Egypt which he made a year later (see p. 253).

Etching; 21.7 × 16.5 cm. Only state.
Ca. 1626.
Amsterdam, Rijksprentenkabinet.

Literature: Bartsch, no. 59; Hind, no. 307; Münz, no. 186;
Boon, no. 2/J. Mak, *Middeleeuwse Kerstliederen*,
Utrecht-Brussels 1948, Psalm no. XXIX, 5, 1-4; 'Bijbelse
Inspiratie', no. 32.

260

The Rest on the Flight into Egypt

Rembrandt's works depicting this topical subject were mostly created during the 1640s, when he was also particularly interested in the related theme of the Holy Family in Nazareth (see pp. 283-87).

In the minute detail of this etching of a night scene, the warm light of Joseph's stable lantern glints between the leaves of the trees, under which the weary couple are resting for a while from their exhausting journey through the night.

Etching; 9.2 × 5.9 cm. Third state of four.
Ca. 1644.
Amsterdam, Rijksprentenkabinet.

Literature: Bartsch, no. 57; Hind, no. 208; Münz, no. 337 (Ferdinand Bol); Boon, no. 188; Filedt Kok, no. B 57.

This small panel, probably inspired by an engraving by Hendrick Goudt, itself based on a painting by Adam Elsheimer of the Flight into Egypt, is one of Rembrandt's most sublime masterpieces. Joseph and Mary, with the Child in her arms, are on the shore of a pool in which they are reflected, enjoying the warm glow of a wood fire lit by shepherds. The enchanting landscape outlined against a softly illuminated sky, in which the moon is just concealed behind a thin veil of cloud, exudes the mystery of night.

Panel; 34 × 47 cm.
Signed and dated: *Rembrandt f. 1647.*
Dublin, National Gallery of Ireland.

Literature: Bredius, no. 576; Bauch, no. 80; Gerson, no. 220; Bredius-Gerson, no. 576/Hofstede de Groot, Rembrandt Bijbel, N.T.p.9.

The Rest on the Flight into Egypt

The Rest on the Flight into Egypt

Rembrandt's source of inspiration for this etching is the engraving made by Lucas van Leyden of the same subject in about 1506, which had also served as a model for the first etching of this theme, dating from *ca.* 1626 (see p. 261). Therefore it is no coincidence that the two versions by Rembrandt evoke the same feelings of tenderness. In this etching we see how Mary raises the wrap for a moment to give Joseph an opportunity to take a look at the sleeping child on her lap as he is peeling a piece of fruit. This time there is no donkey, though it is referred to by the saddle lying in the foreground on the right. 'The subtle simplicity with which the scene is etched into the copper accords perfectly with its peaceful character' (Filedt Kok).

Etching; 13 × 11.5 cm. Only state.
Signed and dated: *Rembrandt f. 1645.*
Amsterdam, Rijksprentenkabinet.

Literature: Bartsch, no. 58; Hind, no. 216; Münz, no. 219; Boon, no. 190; Filedt Kok, no. B 58/Rotermund 1963, no. 158; Sumowski 1963, no. 22; Tümpel 1970, no. 59.

In this drawing Rembrandt depicts the scene following the actual rest: Joseph and Mary have been resting in a secluded spot, and now leave to resume their journey to Egypt. Joseph lovingly leads his wife to the donkey which is standing ready to go.

Rembrandt corrected the position of Joseph's right arm, for which he first did a small sketch in the top right-hand corner of the drawing (Tümpel).

Pen and brush drawing; 19.3 × 24.1 cm.
Ca. 1652.
Berlin, Kupferstichkabinett der Staatlichen Museen.

Literature: Benesch V, no. 902 (*ca.* 1662)/Rotermund 1963, no. 157; Sumowski 1963, no. 19; Tümpel 1970, no. 60.

Resuming the Journey after the Rest on the Flight into Egypt

265

Mine eyes have seen thy salvation

Luke 2

22 And when the days of her purification according to the law of Moses were accomplished, they brought him to Jerusalem, to present *him* to the Lord;

23 (As it is written in the law of the Lord, Every male that openeth the womb shall be called holy to the Lord;)

24 And to offer a sacrifice according to that which is said in the law of the Lord, A pair of turtledoves, or two young pigeons.

25 And, behold, there was a man in Jerusalem, whose name *was* Simeon; and the same man *was* just and devout, waiting for the consolation of Israel: and the Holy Ghost was upon him.

26 And it was revealed unto him by the Holy Ghost, that he should not see death, before he had seen the Lord's Christ.

27 And he came by the Spirit into the temple: and when the parents brought in the child Jesus, to do for him after the custom of the law,

28 Then took he him up in his arms, and blessed God, and said,

29 Lord, now lettest thou thy servant depart in peace, according to thy word:

30 For mine eyes have seen thy salvation,

31 Which thou hast prepared before the face of all people;

32 A light to lighten the Gentiles, and the glory of thy people Israel.

33 And Joseph and his mother marvelled at those things which were spoken of him.

34 And Simeon blessed them, and said unto Mary his mother, Behold, this *child* is set for the fall and rising again of many in Israel; and for a sign which shall be spoken against;

35 (Yea, a sword shall pierce through thy own soul also,) that the thoughts of many hearts may be revealed.

36 And there was one Anna, a prophetess, the daughter of Phanuel, of the tribe of Aser: she was a great age, and had lived with an husband seven years from her virginity;

37 And she *was* a widow of about fourscore and four years, which departed not from the temple, but served *God* with fastings and prayers night and day.

38 And she coming in that instant gave thanks likewise unto the Lord, and spake of him to all them that looked for redemption in Jerusalem.

39 And when they had performed all things according to the law of the Lord, they returned into Galilee, to their own city of Nazareth.

The Song of Simeon

And when the parents brought in the child Jesus, to do for him after the custom of the law, then he took him up in his arms, and blessed God ...
(Luke 2:27-28)

The incident involving Simeon and the prophetess Anna preceded the actual Presentation in the Temple. As the apocryphal scriptures incorrectly elevated Simeon to the position of High Priest - in fact, as Zachariah's successor - though he was actually a devout layman, according to St Luke, it was customary in works of art to interweave the story of the encounter with Simeon with the Presentation of Jesus in the temple. Thus the old man would be presented as the High Priest taking the infant Jesus from Mary by the altar. Christian Tümpel pointed out that Rembrandt corrected this iconographic tradition, and from the very beginning depicted the encounter taking place in the middle of the temple and not in front of the altar. Therefore it is not correct to give to Rembrandt's many versions of this subject the title *The Presentation in the Temple*.

In this painting dating from 1631, one of Rembrandt's earliest masterpieces, the scene is set at the foot of broad stairs leading up to the High Priest's throne. The light entering the building is concentrated on the grey-haired Simeon with the Child in his arms, and on Mary looking on in surprise. Joseph is kneeling to her left, holding the two doves for a sacrifice, as prescribed by the law of the Lord. The most prominent character is the figure seen from the back, whom we must assume to be the prophetess Anna. Like Simeon, she recognizes the Child who has been brought in to be the long-awaited Messiah.

The composition of this painting broadly corresponds with the small etching dating from 1630 shown on p. 276, though that does not depict the Song of Simeon but Simeon's subsequent prophecy to Mary. The same scene is shown on the panel dating from *ca.* 1628 (see p. 275), now in Hamburg.

Panel; 61 × 48 cm.
Signed and dated: *RHL 1631*.
The Hague, Mauritshuis.

Literature: Bredius, no. 543; Bauch, no. 52; Gerson, no. 17; Bredius-Gerson, no. 543/Hofstede de Groot, *Rembrandt Bijbel*, N.T.p.7; Sumowski 1963, no. 13; Tümpel 1970, under no. 48.

The Song of Simeon

And when the parents brought in the child Jesus, to do for him after the custom of the law, then he took him up in his arms, and blessed God ...
(Luke 2:27-28)

Simeon is kneeling, completely absorbed in the infant Jesus. He has bared his head - his turban is lying at Mary's feet. Joseph holds the doves he has brought in both hands. A fourth figure, only partially elaborated, is listening attentively to Simeon's words. In the top right-hand corner there is an incomplete sketch of a head and profile.

This study, drawn on two pieces of paper stuck together, probably served as a preliminary study for the etching shown on the next page.

Pen and ink drawing; 18 × 19 cm.
Ca. 1640.
Amsterdam, Amsterdams Historisch Museum.

Literature: Benesch III, no. 486 (*ca.* 1640-41); Slive II, no. 420 (*ca.* 1640)/'Bijbelse Inspiratie', no. 90.

And when the parents brought in the child Jesus, to do for him after the custom of the law, then he took him up in his arms, and blessed God ... And there was one Anna, a prophetess ... And she coming in that instant gave thanks likewise unto the Lord, and spake of him to all them that looked for redemption in Jerusalem.
(Luke 2:27-28, 36-38)

The prophetess Anna is the dominant figure here, even more than in the painting dating from 1631 (p. 267). Her gesture is the same as that in the painting. It is not a blessing, as is often suggested, but a gesture often used in Rembrandt's Biblical scenes to reveal a sudden awareness of the presence of God (cf. the works on p. 233, 237, 245 and 275). The Holy Ghost floats over Anna's head in the form of a dove surrounded by a radiant crown. With this motif, Rembrandt departs from the text in the Bible which states that it was Simeon, not Anna, who was driven to the temple by the Holy Ghost (Luke 2:27). It is not certain which of the two women next to and opposite Simeon represents Mary. Joseph can again be identified by the two doves he is holding.

Etching; 21.3 × 29 cm. Second state of three.
Ca. 1640.
Amsterdam, Rijksprentenkabinet.

Literature: Bartsch, no. 49; Hind, no. 162; Münz, no. 210; Boon, no. 154; Filedt Kok, no. B 49/Sumowski 1963, no. 14; 'Bijbelse Inspiratie', no. 33; Tümpel 1970, no. 49.

The Song of Simeon

The Song of Simeon *Lord, now lettest thou thy servant depart in peace,*
according to thy word:
For mine eyes have seen thy salvation,
Which thou hast prepared before the face of all people;
A light to lighten the Gentiles,
and the glory of thy people Israel.
(Luke 2:29-32)

Canvas; 99 × 78.5 cm.
1669.
Stockholm, Nationalmuseum.

Literature: Bredius, no. 600; Bauch, no. 95; Gerson, no. 358; Bredius-Gerson, no. 600/Sumowski 1963, no. 17.

In concentrating on the essential element of this theme, which fascinated him throughout his life, Rembrandt went even further in this unfinished painting - from the last year of his life - than in the drawing dating from 1661. The place where the action occurs is not indicated in any way; Joseph, who was always present in other depictions of this subject, is not shown; and it is fairly certain that the Mary in the background was not painted by Rembrandt but was added later by someone else. Only the grey-haired old man with the Child in his stiff arms is important to Rembrandt.

In 1949 many layers of paint added later were removed, and the painting is now in very poor condition. It is assumed that it was one of the canvases which were found in Rembrandt's house on 5 October 1669, the day following his death. A document dated 12 May 1671 reveals that several months before Rembrandt's death, the artists Allaert and Cornelis van Everdingen, a father and son, had seen a painting in his studio of 'Simeon, made and painted by Rembrandt van Rhijn, though it has not yet been completed'. The painting concerned was owned by the Amsterdam art dealer Dirck van Cattenburgh, who had evidently paid Rembrandt in advance for the work he had commissioned. Nothing is known about the fate of the other unfinished works, so this muted *Song of Simeon* is Rembrandt's last known painting.

The Song of Simeon   *And when the parents brought in the child Jesus, to do for him after the custom of the law, then he took him up in his arms, and blessed God ...*
(Luke 2:27-28)

In the foreground Joseph and Mary are kneeling next to Simeon, who is singing praises with the Child in his arms. The décor, an enormous temple with wide stairs leading up to the High Priest, is reminiscent of the painting in The Hague (see p. 267). Once again the soaring architecture serves to increase the solemnity of

the scene taking place in the foreground.

In this scene the figure of the prophetess Anna assumes a subordinate role. The aged woman is approaching with difficulty up the stairs at the front, leaning on a young companion. Earlier, in the painting of Mary's visit to Elizabeth (see p. 225), Rembrandt used the same motif to express the advanced age of the priest Zachariah.

Lord, now lettest thou thy servant depart in peace,
according to thy word:
For mine eyes have seen thy salvation,
Which thou hast prepared before the face of all people;
A light to lighten the Gentiles,
and the glory of thy people Israel.
(Luke 2:29-32)

In this small, picturesque drawing, which is
characterized by the greatest simplicity, Rembrandt
restricts himself to a close-up view of the figures of
Simeon, the infant Jesus, Mary and Joseph. The halo
over Mary's head is a striking detail. Rembrandt's
signature and the year 1661 are underneath the
drawing, which is a memento in the *Album Amicorum*
(Book of Friends) of Jacobus Heyblock, the preacher

and headmaster of the Latin School in Amsterdam. On
the opposite page, a certain A.L. wrote a poem
relating to the drawing, which starts with the words:

The Song of Simeon

Here Rembrandt shows us how old Simeon
Joyfully takes his Redeemer and Messiah into his arms
And is ready to die because His merciful Son
Has appeared ...

Pen and brush drawing; 12 × 8.9 cm.
Signed and dated: *Rembrandt f. 1661.*
The Hague, Koninklijke Bibliotheek.

Literature: Benesch V, no. 1057; Haak, no.
90/Rotermund 1963, no. 150; Sumowski 1963, no. 16;
'Bijbelse Inspiratie', no. 92.

Pen and brush drawing; 23.8 × 20.8 cm.
Ca. 1647.
Paris, The Louvre.

Literature: Benesch III, no. 589 (*ca.* 1647); Slive I, no. 197
(*ca.* 1647)/Tümpel 1969, pp. 190 *et seq*.

Simeon's Prophecy to Mary

And Simeon blessed them, and said unto Mary his mother, Behold, this child is set for the fall and rising again of many in Israel; and for a sign which shall be spoken against; (Yea, a sword shall pierce through thy own soul also,) that the thoughts of many hearts may be revealed. (Luke 2:34-35)

Panel; 55.5 × 44 cm.
Signed: *Rembrandt f.*
Ca. 1628.
Hamburg, Kunsthalle.

Literature: Bredius, no. 535; Bauch, no. 46; Gerson, no. 10; Bredius-Gerson, no. 535/Sumowski 1963, no. 12.

This is probably the painting which was described in the inventory of Prince Frederik Hendrik, drawn up in 1632, as 'A Simeon in the Temple holding Christ in his arms by Rembrants or Jan Lievensz'.

This early panel, dating from 1628, is one of the first of many versions of this subject which Rembrandt did in the course of his life. However, unlike most of the other versions, this work does not portray the Song of Simeon, but Simeon's prophecy to Mary, which followed immediately upon it. All the attention is focused on the main characters; the surroundings hardly play a part. Only a massive pillar in the background indicates that the scene takes place in a temple. Mary has folded her hands and is looking at the Child, her eyes wide open in astonishment. The figure of the prophetess Anna rises behind them, showing more clearly than ever that she also recognizes the Child in Simeon's arms as the Messiah, the bringer of salvation.

In the late Middle Ages Simeon's prophecy to Mary formed the first scene in the popular series of Mary's Seven Sorrows. Not infrequently these scenes are arranged around a picture of Mary seated under the Cross holding the lifeless body of Jesus on her lap. That moment was the fulfilment of Simeon's prophecy that her soul would be pierced by a sword.

274

Simeon's Prophecy to Mary

And Simeon blessed them, and said unto Mary his mother, Behold, this child is set for the fall and rising again of many in Israel; and for a sign which shall be spoken against; (Yea, a sword shall pierce through thy own soul also,) that the thoughts of many hearts may be revealed. (Luke 2:34-35)

Indicating the Child in his arms, Simeon turns to Mary, who is kneeling opposite him, so that the subject of this etching, like that of the painting in Hamburg shown on the previous page, can best be described as 'Simeon's prophecy to Mary'. There is a very strange detail of an angel drawing the attention of the prophetess Anna to the infant Jesus. On the far left, a crippled beggar disappears from the picture on his crutches.

The composition of this etching served as a starting point for Rembrandt's painting of the Song of Simeon, dating from 1631, now in The Hague (p. 267).

Etching; 10.3 × 7.8 cm. Second state of two.
Signed and dated: *RHL 1630*.
Amsterdam, Rijksprentenkabinet.

Literature: Bartsch, no. 51; Hind, no. 18; Münz, no. 191; Boon, no. 54; Filedt Kok, no. B 51/Tümpel 1970, no. 48.

The Presentation in the Temple

It is not until this etching dating from *ca.* 1654, in which the scene is shown at the feet of the High Priest, that Rembrandt confronts us with an image of the actual Presentation in the temple. The Gospel according to St Luke, which begins by listing the legal obligations with which parents must comply (Luke 2:22-24), goes on to describe the incident with Simeon and the prophetess Anna in great detail, and concludes with only one sentence about the story of the actual Presentation of the infant Jesus: 'And when they had performed all things according to the law of the Lord, they returned into Galilee, to their own city Nazareth' (Luke 2:39). The strange aspect of Rembrandt's version of this solemn occasion is that the infant Jesus is not presented to the High Priest by Joseph and Mary, but by Simeon. This is why the scene is so reminiscent of the Song of Simeon that one could say that even Rembrandt has merged the two events, though in a completely new way. The inner transportation of the devout old man contrasts with the rigid and unmoving High Priest seated above him and the temple overseer looming in the background. By portraying their reserve, Rembrandt expresses the future refusal of the Jewish priesthood to recognize Jesus of Nazareth as the Messiah.

Etching; 21 × 16.2 cm. Only state.
Ca. 1654.
Amsterdam, Rijksprentenkabinet.

Literature: Bartsch, no. 50; Hind, no. 279; Münz, no. 240;
Boon, no. 258; Filedt Kok, no. B 50/Hofstede de Groot,
Rembrandt Bijbel, N.T.e.6; Rotermund 1963, no. 152;
Sumowski 1963, no. 15; 'Bijbelse Inspiratie', no. 34;
Tümpel 1970, no. 52.

The Holy Family　Rembrandt's numerous works depicting the Holy Family, in which he emphasized the figure of Mary in the role of the caring mother, are characterized by an atmosphere of intimate, domestic happiness. The subject is not based on a particular passage in the New Testament, but probably developed from the theme of the Rest on the Flight into Egypt, which had been extremely popular in the late Middle Ages and in the 16th century. In fact, initially the parents and Child were usually portrayed against a background of an imaginary landscape. In contrast, Rembrandt always portrayed this scene in the privacy of a contemporary Dutch interior.

In this monumental painting from the beginning of his most baroque period, the interior still played a fairly subordinate role, and the life-size figures take up virtually the whole canvas. The colour and composition are reminiscent of the art of Rubens and Van Dijck. Joseph bends lovingly over the Child, who has fallen asleep in Mary's lap, sated, while Mary settles into a comfortable position with the infant. The red of her skirt contrasts beautifully with the green of the shawl in which the Child is wrapped. The cradle, with the coverlet thrown back, is also emphasized. Joseph's carpentry tools are hanging on the back wall of the room.

Canvas; 183.5 × 123 cm.
Signed and dated: *Rembrandt f. 163...*
Munich, Alte Pinakothek.

Literature: Bredius, no. 544; Bauch, no. 53; Gerson, no. 63; Bredius-Gerson, no. 544/Sumowski 1963, no. 23.

The Holy Family   This print was unusually freely executed for Rembrandt's work in the early 1630s. For the composition, Rembrandt used a print of this subject by Annibale Carracci, 'but he transcended his model in the figures of Joseph engrossed in his reading, and Mary gazing absent-mindedly' (K.J. Boon, in: Cat. Exhibition *Rembrandt: Etchings*, Amsterdam/Rotterdam 1956, no. 16). The open basket of napkins in the foreground on the right emphasizes the domestic atmosphere of this peaceful scene.

Etching; 9.6 × 7 cm. Only state.
Signed: *RHL.*
Ca. 1632.
Amsterdam, Rijksprentenkabinet.

Literature: Bartsch, no. 62; Hind, no. 95; Münz, no. 193; Boon, no. 82; Filedt Kok, no. B 62/Tümpel 1970, no. 61.

In this serene drawing of Mary with her child, the human element is based on day-to-day life in such a realistic and direct way that it must be assumed that Rembrandt did not do the drawing from his imagination, but drew it from nature. Perhaps he used his wife Saskia with one of their children as a model. If so, on the basis of the most probable dating of the drawing (*ca.* 1635-37), the baby could only have been Rumbartus, Saskia's first child, who was baptized on 15 December 1635. However, the little boy lived for only two months. The two girls who followed, both called Cornelia, were born after 1637, in July 1638 and July 1640. They lived even less long: the first Cornelia died after three weeks, the second after only two. Only the fourth child of Rembrandt and Saskia, Titus, born in September 1641, survived. The fact that Rembrandt was particularly fascinated by the theme of the Holy Family in the following years is undoubtedly related to the presence of a growing child in his home.

Pen and brush drawing; 15.5 × 13.7 cm.
Ca. 1635-37.
London, British Museum.

Literature: Benesch I, no. 113 (*ca.* 1635); Slive I, no. 116 (*ca.* 1635-37).

Mary with the Child by a Window

The Holy Family In his paintings of this subject, Rembrandt always showed Joseph as a carpenter, except in his painting in Amsterdam (p. 289). On this panel, dating from 1640, he is shown working on a piece of wood by the window. Broadly speaking, the beautifully illuminated group of Mary and the Child is a repetition of the group in the print of this subject dating from *ca.* 1632 (p. 280). In this work the Holy Family also includes grandmother Anna. Seated next to her daughter, she has interrupted her reading of the Bible for a moment to admire her grandson. Rembrandt derived this motif of St Anne, together with Mary and the infant Jesus, from the Christian tradition of the late Middle Ages, when St Anne was one of the most revered saints, particularly in the Netherlands and in Germany. She was therefore depicted very often, usually together with Mary and the infant Jesus. Initially she was shown standing up with Mary on her arm, who in turn carried the infant Jesus. Later on, she was usually shown seated. After the Council of Trent (1545-63), works depicting Anna with Mary and the infant Jesus, which actually represent a greatly abbreviated family tree of Jesus, became much less important because the Roman Catholic Church objected; it was considered that too much emphasis was placed on St Anne, though there was no objection to the veneration of St Anne herself. The mother of Mary is not mentioned in the Gospels. The legendary details of her life are derived from the apocryphal scriptures, and could be found, *inter alia*, in the *Legenda Aurea*, the most widespread book of devotions in the late Middle Ages.

Panel; 41 × 34 cm.
Signed and dated: *Rembrandt f. 1640.*
Paris, The Louvre.

Literature: Bredius, no. 563; Bauch, no. 71; Gerson, no. 205; Bredius-Gerson, no. 563.

The Holy Family In this study of light and dark, the scene with the Holy
Family exudes the same atmosphere of harmony and
peace as Rembrandt's paintings of this subject. Again
the group of the Mother and Child is joined by the
figure of grandmother Anna, in a way that is
reminiscent of the panel in the Louvre, reproduced on
the previous page. The motif of an outsider peering in
through the window is also found in a famous etching
of the Holy Family, dating from 1654, in which it is
Joseph who appears outside by the window (see p. 285).

Pen and brush drawing; 18.4 × 24.6 cm.
Ca. 1640-42.
London, British Museum.

Literature: Benesch III, no. 516 (*ca.* 1640-42); Slive II, no.
511 (*ca.* 1640-43).

284

Rembrandt's most mysterious representation of this theme is found in this etching dating from 1654, which forms part of the cycle mentioned on p. 235, with scenes from the childhood of Jesus. He expresses the intimate relationship between Mary and her child in a very moving way; an intimacy from which Joseph, standing watching by the window, is excluded. The rays of the rising sun, entering through the window, are the symbol of Christ, 'the Sun of righteousness', with healing in his wings (Malachi 4:2) and surround Mary's head like a halo. According to Van Regteren Altena (cf. Filedt Kok), it is probable that by placing Mary on the ground with an empty chair behind her on a raised platform, Rembrandt deliberately used a depiction of Mary which derived from the 15th century, 'the Virgin of Humility', with Mary sitting on the ground rather than on the chair behind her. Mary's humility was strongly emphasized in the late Middle Ages: her meekness supposedly led God the Son to descend to earth from heaven.

The snake under Mary's feet serves as a reference to Genesis 3:15, where God speaks to the snake after Adam and Eve have sinned:

And I will put enmity between thee and the woman,
And between thy seed and her seed;
It shall bruise thy head,
And thou shalt bruise his heel.

The Church Fathers had applied this text, the so-called proto or original Gospel, to Mary, the 'second Eve', who vanquished the snake with her child, in contrast with the first Eve, who allowed herself to be tempted by the snake.

The symbolism contained in this etching does not in any way detract from the domestic atmosphere of the scene. The cat playing with the hem of Mary's dress, the open basket of napkins next to Mary and the wood fire burning on the hearth lend an air of great intimacy to the scene as a whole. It is generally assumed that for this group of Mary and her child, Rembrandt was inspired by an engraving of the Madonna by Mantegna.

Etching; 9.5 × 14.5 cm. Second state of two.
Signed and dated: *Rembrandt f. 1654.*
Amsterdam, Rijksprentenkabinet.

Literature: Bartsch, no. 63; Hind, no. 275; Münz, no. 229; Boon, no. 252; Filedt Kok, no. B 63/Hofstede de Groot, *Rembrandt Bijbel*, N.T.e.13; Rotermund 1963, no. 154; Sumowski 1963, no. 27; Tümpel 1970, no. 64.

The Holy Family with a Cat and a Snake

This subject particularly fascinated Rembrandt during the middle of the 1640s. In this poetic painting dating from 1645, he devotes all his attention to the group of Mary and the Child. Just as grandmother Anna stops reading the Bible for a moment to enjoy looking at her grandson in the panel dating from 1640 (p. 283), Mary stops reading to peep into the cradle and reassure herself that the baby is all right. Her left foot rests on a hot stove and a wood fire burns on the tiles in the fireplace. In the background, Joseph is carving a yoke at his workbench. The charm of this everyday scene is barely disturbed by the supernatural light falling on the Mother and Child, with the angels above.

Canvas; 117 × 91 cm.
Signed and dated: *Rembrandt f. 1645.*
Leningrad, The Hermitage.

Literature: Bredius, no. 570; Bauch, no. 73; Gerson, no. 211; Bredius-Gerson, no. 570/Sumowski 1963, no. 25.

The Holy Family

This much smaller panel dating from 1646 is no less charming than the large canvas from 1645. It is painted deceptively in a frame with a curtain that looks as though it has just been drawn aside. In the 17th century it was customary to protect paintings with little curtains that could be drawn. The curtain actually painted on the painting (a *trompe-l'oeil* curtain) was a motif which was often used and served to strengthen the illusion of depth. In this work it particularly emphasizes the domestic intimacy of the Holy Family, which should really remain concealed from outsiders behind the curtain.

Panel; 45 × 67 cm.
Signed and dated: *Rembrandt ft. 1646.*
Kassel, Gemäldegalerie.

Literature: Bredius, no. 572; Bauch, no. 77; Gerson, no. 212; Bredius-Gerson, no. 572/Hofstede de Groot, *Rembrandt Bijbel*, N.T.p.1; Sumowski 1963, no. 26.

The Holy Family The everyday character of all Rembrandt's versions of this theme is particularly pronounced in this drawing dating from the beginning of the 1650s. Nevertheless, such a devout silence hangs over this domestic scene that there is no possible doubt regarding the subject. As usual, Rembrandt places the figure of Joseph slightly in the background. He silently sits and watches from behind the table between him and Mary. He is outside the holy secret which connects her with the infant Jesus.

Pen and brush drawing; 22 × 19.1 cm.
Ca. 1652.
Vienna, Albertina.

Literature: Benesch V, no. 888 (*ca.* 1652); Haak, no. 69 (*ca.* 1652).

The central group in this interior shut away from the outside world again consists of old Anna with Mary and the Child, who is peacefully sleeping in the cradle which is standing by Anna's feet. Her hands are still holding the cord with which she rocked the baby to sleep. Joseph is shown in a very inconspicuous way, concealed in the dark under the staircase to the door. The light shining into the room draws the eye to Mary, as she sits reading. It sharply outlines her profile and casts a ghostly shadow of Anna on to the wall where a map is hanging. 'Rembrandt never achieved such a fascinating effect with shadows as with this large shadow cast on the wall, which gives a tremendous added dimension to the figure of Anna. At the same time - and certainly not by coincidence - it repeats the silhouette of Mary on a larger scale, so that the figures of the two women appear to flow together in the dark form which rises up above the Child like a protecting spirit' (Van Thiel, p. 146).

Panel; 66.5 × 78 cm.
Ca. 1644.
Amsterdam, Rijksmuseum.

Literature: Bredius, no. 568; not included in Bauch and Gerson; Bredius-Gerson, no. 568/P.J.J. Van Thiel, 'Rembrandts Heilige Familie bij avond', in: *Bulletin van het Rijksmuseum* 13 (1965), pp. 145-59; J.G. van Gelder, 'Rembrandt: *De Heilige Familie bij avond*' in: *Openbaar Kunstbezit* 10 (1966), no. 36.

The Holy Family in the Evening

And all that heard him were astonished

Luke 2

41 Now his parents went to Jerusalem every year at the feast of the passover.

42 And when he was twelve years old, they went up to Jerusalem after the custom of the feast.

43 And when they had fulfilled the days, as they returned, the child Jesus tarried behind in Jerusalem; and Joseph and his mother knew not *of it*.

44 But they, supposing him to have been in the company, went a day's journey; and they sought him among *their* kinsfolk and acquaintance.

45 And when they found him not, they turned back again to Jerusalem, seeking him.

46 And it came to pass, that after three days they found him in the temple, sitting in the midst of the doctors, both hearing them, and asking them questions.

47 And all that heard him were astonished at his understanding and aswers.

48 And when they saw him, they were amazed: and his mother said unto him, Son, why hast thou thus dealt with us? behold, thy father and I have sought thee sorrowing.

49 And he said unto them, How is it that ye sought me? wist ye not that I must be about my Father's business?

50 And they understood not the saying which he spake unto them.

51 And he went down with them, and came to Nazareth, and was subject unto them: but his mother kept all these sayings in her heart.

52 And Jesus increased in wisdom and stature, and in favour with God and man.

The Twelve-year-old Jesus in the Temple

And it came to pass, that after three days they found him in the temple, sitting in the midst of the doctors, both hearing them, and asking them questions. And all that heard him were astonished at his understanding and answers.
(Luke 2:46-47)

In the late Middle Ages this theme formed part of the traditional cycle in which the life of Jesus or of Mary was depicted. In addition, the scene was part of the popular series of Mary's Seven Sorrows, as *The Loss of the Twelve-year-old Jesus*, so that older versions of this scene usually assign a prominent place to the figure of Mary (in the company of Joseph).

Rembrandt always focused on the twelve-year-old Jesus as the central figure. In this small print dating from 1630, he used the light entering the building to focus the attention on him. The teachers of Israel are arranged round the precocious boy in a semicircle, and listen to him with both astonishment and scepticism. The small figure of the Child is almost drowned in the large space of the temple, of which the dimensions are indicated by means of an imposing pillar. In the background on the right the small figures of Jesus' parents can be seen entering the temple in search of their child.

Etching; 8.9 × 6.8 cm. Third state of three.
1630.
Amsterdam, Rijksprentenkabinet.

Literature: Bartsch, no. 66; Hind, no. 20; Münz, no. 190; Boon, no. 40; Filedt Kok, no. B 66/Tümpel 1970, no. 65.

The Twelve-year-old Jesus in the Temple

And all that heard him were astonished at his understanding and answers.
(Luke 2:47)

This subject particularly fascinated Rembrandt during the first half of the 1650s. In this hastily executed etching dating from 1652, the twelve-year-old teacher forms the focal point of the picture. His frail figure is separate from the crowd of people, in front and behind him, and is clearly outlined against the wall of the balustrade. The scribes are all ears.

C. White noted that it is possible that Rembrandt intended to elaborate this plate further, but when he did a test print he was justifiably so satisfied with its suggestive quality that in the end he merely decided to work on a few places with a dry needle. In his pragmatic way he was led by results rather than holding on to the realization of his original idea. This approach forms the basis of his later etchings in which there is no standard finish (C. White, *Rembrandt as an Etcher*, p. 71).

Etching; 12.6 × 21.4 cm. First state of three.
Signed and dated: *Rembrandt f. 1652.*
Amsterdam, Rijksprentenkabinet.

Literature: Bartsch, no. 65; Hind, no. 257; Münz, no. 222; Boon, no. 239; Filedt Kok, no. B 65/Hofstede de Groot, *Rembrandt Bijbel*, N.T.e.11; Rotermund 1963, no. 161; Tümpel 1970, no. 66.

And it came to pass, that after three days they found him in the temple, sitting in the midst of the doctors, both hearing them, and asking them questions. And all that heard him were astonished at his understanding and answers. (Luke 2:46-47)

The main scene is shown on the right half of the drawing. On the left, Joseph and Mary are entering the temple.

In drawing the figures, Rembrandt kept to the very minimum, and yet each and every one is full of life. The architecture is only indicated by a few lines, which suggest spacious dimensions.

Pen and ink drawing; 18.8 × 22.5 cm.
Ca. 1652-54.
Stockholm, Nationalmuseum.

Literature: Benesch V, no. 936 (*ca.* 1653-54); Slive I, no. 236 (*ca.* 1654); Haak, no. 72 (*ca.* 1652-54).

The Twelve-year-old Jesus in the Temple

The Twelve-year-old Jesus in the Temple

And it came to pass, that after three days they found him in the temple, sitting in the midst of the doctors, both hearing them, and asking them questions. And all that heard him were astonished at his understanding and answers. (Luke 2:46-47)

The young Jesus unselfconsciously explains his ideas to the scribes sitting around him. In the foreground on the right his tired, anxious father approaches to take the boy back to Nazareth.

This sublime print belongs to the series about the childhood of Jesus, mentioned on p. 235.

Etching; 9.5 × 14.4 cm. Only state.
Signed and dated: *Rembrandt f. 1654*.
Amsterdam, Rijksprentenkabinet.

Literature: Bartsch, no. 64; Hind, no. 277; Münz, no. 230; Boon, no. 254; Filedt Kok, no. B 64/Hofstede de Groot, *Rembrandt Bijbel*, N.T.e.10; Sumowski 1963, no. 28; 'Bijbelse Inspiratie', no. 35; Tümpel 1970, no. 67.

*And he said unto them, How is it that ye sought me? Wist ye
not that I must be about my Father's business? And they
understood not the saying which he spake unto them. And he
went down with them, and came to Nazareth, and was
subject unto them.*
(Luke 2:49-51)

The etching of this subject, which is rarely depicted, is
the last in the series of six scenes from the childhood
of Jesus. 'The seriousness with which the mother
considers the words which the young Christ has just
spoken, and the ecstatic face of the young boy, remain
unforgettable images through the centuries' (Boon, p.
30).

In the past this print was unjustifiably entitled *The
Return from Egypt*. Depictions of that subject always
reveal the donkey, and Joseph is always shown with his
carpenter's tools (Tümpel). It is probable that
Rembrandt made use of a print by Schelte & Bolswert,
based on a painting by Rubens. That print is subtitled:
'*Et irat subditus*' ('And he was subject unto them').

Etching; 9.5 × 14.4 cm. Only state.
Signed and dated: *Rembrandt f. 1654.*
Amsterdam, Rijksprentenkabinet.

Literature: Bartsch, no. 60; Hind, no. 278; Münz, no. 231;
Boon, no. 255; Filedt Kok, no. B 60/Hofstede de Groot,
Rembrandt Bijbel, N.T.e.12; Rotermund 1963, no. 162;
Sumowski 1963, no. 29; 'Bijbelse Inspiratie', no. 36;
Tümpel 1970, no. 68.

*Jesus Returns from
the Temple with
his Parents*

Prepare ye the way of the Lord

Luke 3 NOW in the fifteenth year of the reign of Tiberius Cæsar, Pontius Pilate being governor of Judæa, and Herod being tetrarch of Galilee, and his brother Philip tetrarch of Ituræa and of the region of Trachonitis, and Lysanias the tetrarch of Abilene,

2 Annas and Caiaphas being the high priests, the word of God came unto John the son of Zacharias in the wilderness.

3 And he came into all the country about Jordan, preaching the baptism of repentance for the remission of sins,

4 As it is written in the book of the words of Esaias the prophet, saying, The voice of one crying in the wilderness, Prepare ye the way of the Lord, make his paths straight

5 Every valley shall be filled, and every mountain and hill shall be brought low; and the crooked shall be made straight, and the rough ways *shall be* made smooth;

6 And all flesh shall see the salvation of God.

7 Then said he to the multitude that came forth to be baptized of him, O generation of vipers, who hath warned you to flee from the wrath to come?

8 Bring forth therefore fruits worthy of repentance, and begin not to say within yourselves, We have Abraham to *our* father: for I say unto you, That God is able of these stones to raise up children unto Abraham.

9 And now also the axe is laid unto the root of the trees: every tree therefore which bringeth not forth good fruit is hewn down, and cast into the fire.

10 And the people asked him, saying, What shall we do then?

11 He answereth and saith unto them, He that hath two coats, let him impart to him that hath none; and he that hath meat, let him do likewise.

12 Then came also publicans to be baptized, and said unto him, Master, what shall we do?

13 And he said unto them, Exact no more than that which is appointed you.

14 And the soldiers likewise demanded of him, saying, And what shall we do? And he said unto them, Do violence to no man, neither accuse *any* falsely; and be content with your wages.

15 And as the people were in expectation ,and all men mused in their hearts of John, whether he were the Christ, or not;

16 John answered, saying unto *them* all, I indeed baptize you with water; but one mightier than I cometh, the latchet of whose shoes I am not worthy to unloose: he shall baptize you with the Holy Ghost and with fire:

17 Whose fan *is* in his hand, and he will throughly purge his floor, and will gather the wheat into his garner; but the chaff he will burn with fire unquenchable.

18 And many other things in his exhortation preached he unto the people [...]

21 Now when all the people were baptized, it came to pass, that Jesus also being baptized, and praying, the heaven was opened,

22 And the Holy Ghost descended in a bodily shape like a dove upon him, and a voice came from heaven, which said, Thou art my beloved Son; in thee I am well pleased.

The Sermon of St John the Baptist

And he came into all the country about Jordan, preaching the baptism of repentance for the remission of sins.
(Luke 3:3)

The sermon of St John the Baptist was a regularly recurring theme in 16th- and 17th-century art in north-west Europe. It is not surprising that depictions of St John the Baptist exhorting people to be converted were very popular, particularly in the 16th century: at that time there was increasing opposition to all sorts of abuses in the Church and in society, and humanists and followers of the Reformation argued in favour of restoring the original purity of the doctrines and customs of the Christian Church. This was particularly evident in the art of the northern and southern Netherlands. In connection with this, it was undoubtedly significant that since the beginning of the 16th century landscape painting had gradually developed as an individual autonomous genre, although the landscape for the time being usually remained a subordinate component in works with a narrative Biblical theme. The sermon of St John the Baptist was a perfect subject for the inclusion of a landscape.

In this fascinating sketch in oils, painted in about 1634-36, the crowded scene is dominated by an impressive pillar with the bust of the Roman Emperor. This is a masterful representation of the beginning of the solemn sentence with which the Gospel according to St Luke introduces the acts of the man paving the way for Jesus in the historical context of the time (Luke 3:1-2). The gesturing preacher of penitence stands in full light on the sloping bank of a river, and we can see the water crashing down through a ruined structure. The crowd pressing around John consists of people from every walk of life: young and old, rich and poor, citizens, authorities and armed soldiers. Most are listening attentively, but some are distracted by crying or romping children, and others pay no attention at all to the preacher. The Pharisees in the foreground, dressed in long cloaks, turn away from John in deep discussion, forming the most prominent group. St Luke does not explicitly mention the presence of Pharisees while John the Baptist is preaching; Rembrandt bases them on the Gospel according to St Matthew. However, John's sharp words, 'O generation of vipers, who hath warned you to flee from the wrath to come?' (Luke 3:7) are aimed at the Pharisees and Sadducees who come to him to be baptized (see Matthew 3:7).

Since the 17th century this grisaille, in which the greyish browns and soft greens merge almost indistinguishably, has been one of Rembrandt's most admired works. Some of the sketches in oils which he painted on paper are known to have served as preliminary studies for an etching. Probably this sketch, painted on a canvas which was enlarged on all sides with strips about 10 cm. wide, was also initially intended as a preliminary study for an etching, though Rembrandt never actually executed it.

Canvas on panel; 62 × 80 cm.
Ca. 1634-36.
Berlin, Gemäldegalerie der Staatlichen Museen.

Literature: Bredius, no. 555; Bauch, no. 63; Gerson, no. 71; Bredius-Gerson, no. 555/Hofstede de Groot, *Rembrandt Bijbel*, N.T.p.10; Sumowski 1963, no. 30.

And when the tempter came to him

Matthew 4 THEN was Jesus led up of the spirit into the wilderness to be tempted of the devil.

2 And when he had fasted forty days and forty nights, he was afterward an hungred.

3 And when the tempter came to him, he said, if thou be the Son of God, command that these stone be made bread.

4 But he answered and said, It is written, Man shall not live by bread alone, but by every word that proceedeth out of the mouth of God.

5 Then the devil taketh him up into the holy city, and setteth him on a pinnacle of the temple,

6 And saith unto him, If thou be the Son of God, cast thyself down: for it is written, He shall give his angels charge concerning thee: and in *their* hands they shall bear thee up, lest at any time thou dash thy foot against a stone.

7 Jesus said unto him, It is written again, Thou shalt not tempt the Lord thy God.

8 Again, the devil taketh him up into an exceeding high mountain, and sheweth him all the kingdoms of the world, and the glory of them;

9 And saith unto him, All these things will I give thee, if thou wilt fall down and worship me.

10 Then saith Jesus unto him, Get thee hence, Satan: for it is written, Thou shalt worship the Lord thy God, and him only shalt thou serve.

11 Then the devil leaveth him, and, behold, angels came and ministered unto him.

The Devil Shows Jesus all the Riches of the World

Again, the devil taketh him up into an exceeding high mountain, and sheweth him all the kingdoms of the world, and the glory of them; and saith unto him, All these things will I give thee, if thou wilt fall down and worship me. (Matthew 4:8-9)

In this drawing Rembrandt depicted the third of the three temptations in the desert, the traditional place for the conflict with evil mentioned in the Gospel according to St Matthew. Jesus has been taken by the Devil to a high mountain, and he sits on the edge of a ravine, looking out in bewilderment under the spell of the delights of all the kingdoms of the world, which Satan has conjured up for him. The two circles which were drawn around the figures of Jesus and the Devil at a later date led some scholars to suppose that the composition was intended as a design for decorating an embossed metal dish or a Delftware plate. However, nothing is known of any designs being produced by Rembrandt for craft products. Perhaps the aura around the double circle actually suggests an attempt on the part of the artist to indicate the vision of all the earthly splendours which the Devil summoned up in Jesus' mind (Tümpel).

In a number of pen and ink drawings done at an earlier date, Rembrandt depicted the much more common first temptation. As was customary in the Middle Ages, the Devil was represented as a satyr-like creature, with goat's legs, a tail and bat wings. It is strange that here Rembrandt depicted the Devil as a skeleton, a form usually reserved for representing Death. However, the tail and the bat wings are still incorporated.

Pen and brush drawing; 23.2 × 19.9 cm.
Ca. 1650.
Berlin, Kupferstichkabinett der Staatlichen Museen.

Literature: Benesch III, no. 635 (*ca.* 1649)/Rotermund 1963, no. 166; Tümpel 1970, no. 69.

Living water

John 4 WHEN therefore the Lord knew how the Pharisees had heard that Jesus made and baptized more disciples than John,

2 (Though Jesus himself baptized not, but his disciples,)

3 He left Judæa, and departed again into Galilee.

4 And he must needs go through Samaria.

5 Then cometh he to a city of Samaria, which is called Sychar, near to the parcel of ground that Jacob gave to his son Joseph.

6 Now Jacob's well was there, Jesus therefore, being wearied with *his* journey, sat thus on the well: *and* it was about the sixth hour.

7 There cometh a woman of Samaria to draw water: Jesus saith unto her, Give me to drink.

8 (For his disciples were gone away unto the city to buy meat.)

9 Then saith the woman of Samaria unto him, How is that thou, being a Jew, askest drink of me, which am a woman of Samaria? for the Jews have no dealings with the Samaritans.

10 Jesus answered and said unto her, If thou knewest the gift of God, and who it is that saith to thee, Give me to drink; thou wouldest have given thee living water.

11 The woman saith unto him, Sir, thou hast nothing to draw with, and the well is deep: from whence then hast thou that living water?

12 Art thou greater than our father Jacob, which gave us the well, and drank thereof himself, and his children, and his cattle?

13 Jesus answered and said unto her, Whosoever drinketh of this water shall thirst again:

14 But whosoever drinketh of the water that I shall give him shall never thirst; but the water that I shall give him shall be in him a well of water springing up into everlasting life.

15 The woman saith unto him, Sir, give me this water, that I thirst not, neither come hither to draw.

16 Jesus saith unto her, Go, call thy husband, and come hither.

17 The woman answered and said, I have no husband. Jesus said unto her, Thou hast well said, I have no husband:

18 For thou hast had five husbands; and he whom thou now hast is not thy husband: in that saidst thou truly.

19 The woman saith unto him, Sir, I perceive that thou art a prophet.

20 Our fathers worshipped in this mountain; and ye say, that in Jerusalem is the place where men ought to worship.

21 Jesus saith unto her, Woman, believe me, the hour cometh, when ye shall neither in this mountain, nor yet at Jerusalem, worship the Father.

22 Ye worship ye know not what: we know what we worship: for salvation is of the Jews.

23 But the hour cometh, and now is, when the true worshippers shall worship the Father in spirit and in truth: for the Father seeketh such to worship him.

24 God *is* a Spirit: and they that worship him must worship *him* in spirit and in truth.

25 The woman saith unto him, I know that Messias cometh, which is called Christ: when he is come, he will tell us all things.

26 Jesus saith unto her, I that speak unto thee am *he*.

27 And upon this came his disciples, and marvelled that he talked with the woman: yet no man said, What seekest thou? or, Why talkest thou with her?

28 The woman then left her waterpot, and went her way into the city, and saith to the men,

29 Come, see a man, which told me all things that ever I did: is not this the Christ?

30 Then they went out of the city, and came unto him. [...]

Jesus and the Samaritan Woman — The wealth of colour and detail in this painting, clearly reveal Rembrandt's admiration for 16th-century Venetian art. This time it is the figure of Jesus which is in the centre facing us. The gesture of pointing his hand may be considered as an illustration of his words: 'Woman, believe me, the hour cometh, when ye shall neither in this mountain, nor yet at Jerusalem, worship the Father' (John 4:21).

Panel; 63.5 × 48.9 cm.
Signed and dated: *Rembrandt f. 1655.*
New York, The Metropolitan Museum of Art.

Literature: Bredius, no. 589; Bauch, no. 87; Gerson, no. 273; Bredius-Gerson, no. 589/Hofstede de Groot, *Rembrandt Bijbel*, N.T.p.11.

39 And many of the Samaritans of that city believed on him for the saying of the woman, which testified, He told me all that ever I did. 40 So when the Samaritans were come unto him, they besought him that he would tarry with them: and he abode there two days.

41 And many more believed because of his own word;

42 And said unto the woman, Now we believe, not because of thy saying: for we have heard *him* ourselves, and know that this is indeed the Christ, the Saviour of the world.

Jesus and the Samaritan Woman

Rembrandt repeatedly used the subject of this story - which is only found in the Gospel according to St John - particularly between 1655 and 1660, when he did no fewer than three paintings and one etching of the meeting by Jacob's well.

The etching shown here, dated 1634, is Rembrandt's earliest version of this subject, a lively and purely narrative depiction in which Jesus is talking to the woman, with a picturesque ruin in the background. Jesus' gesture, as he sits on the edge of the well, does not make it clear which passage of the constantly changing dialogue is shown here. In the background on the right we see Jesus' disciples returning from the city of Sichar. This detail, which is almost always shown in Rembrandt's works on this subject, was traditionally a feature of depictions of this theme; it cannot simply be interpreted as an indication that the moment which is expressed in this work is that when Jesus reveals himself to the woman as the Messiah (see John 4:26-27).

According to the inventory dating from 1656,

Rembrandt had a large work of the Samaritan woman by 'Sjorjon' (Giorgione), one of the great Venetian masters of the beginning of the 16th century. The note stating that Pieter de la Tombe shared the ownership of the painting (Hofstede de Groot, *Urkunden* 169, no. 109) indicates that it was one of the works of art which Rembrandt had in store to sell. But it is striking that in his works of Jesus and the Samaritan woman the figures are always placed against a background of a gently undulating landscape and monumental architecture, as is characteristic of 16th-century Venetian art.

Etching; 12.3 × 10.6 cm. First state of two.
Signed and dated: *Rembrandt f. 1634.*
Amsterdam, Rijksprentenkabinet.

Literature: Bartsch, no. 71; Hind, no. 122; Münz, no. 201; Boon, no. 105; Filedt Kok, no. B 71/Rotermund 1963, no. 205; Tümpel 1970, no. 77.

Jesus and the Samaritan Woman

In this drawing, and in later works on this subject, Rembrandt placed the conversation by the well as near to the foreground as possible. He tried to express the physical tension of the dialogue and to involve the observer in the encounter as far as possible.

We are opposite the woman, who is completely overwhelmed because this Jew appears to know everything about her past. When she dares look up again, she says: 'Sir, I perceive that thou art a prophet' (John 4:19). As usual, Jesus' disciples are shown in the background.

Pen and ink drawing; 20.7 × 18.7 cm.
Ca. 1648-49.
University of Birmingham, Barber Institute of Fine Arts.

Literature: Benesch III, no. 611 (*ca.* 1648-49); Haak, no. 51 (*ca.* 1648-49)/Rotermund 1963, no. 207.

Jesus and the Samaritan Woman

In his second etching of this subject, Rembrandt again sets the scene by the well against the background of an undulating Italian-style landscape. The city of Sichar lies high up in the distance.

It is probable that Rembrandt wished to depict the last stage of the conversation. Responding to the woman's words about the Messiah whom she is awaiting, Jesus points at himself and says to her: 'I that speak unto thee am he' (John 4:26). The two figures standing to the right behind them express the Gospel text about the returning disciples: '... They marvelled that he talked with the woman' (John 4:27). According to the morals and customs of the time, it was certainly inappropriate for a rabbi to talk to a woman at any length. However, from the very beginning, Jesus deliberately adopted a different attitude towards women than that which was then customary for a rabbi.

Etching: 12.5 × 16 cm. Third state of three.
Signed and dated: *Rembrandt f. 1658.*
Amsterdam, Rijksprentenkabinet.

Literature: Bartsch, no. 70; Hind, no. 294; Münz, no. 238; Boon, no. 273; Filedt Kok, no. B 70/Hofstede de Groot, *Rembrandt Bijbel*, N.T.e.14; Rotermund 1963, no. 206; 'Bijbelse Inspiratie', no. 38; Tümpel 1970, no. 78.

It has been shown that this colourful painting is not dated 1655, as was formerly believed, but 1659. The composition is reminiscent of the drawing now in Birmingham, which was done about ten years earlier (see p. 303). Between Jesus and the woman, we see the head of a little boy looking over the edge of the well, a detail which can also be seen in Rembrandt's painting of this subject in Leningrad, also painted in 1659 (Bredius-Gerson, no. 592A). The darkness of the rocky wall of the well in the foreground contrasts with the background bathed in light, a contrast which reinforces the illusion of depth, but also expresses an atmospheric contrast: the coolness by the well compared with the searing heat of the midday sun. (See the time indicated in John 4:6: 'and it was about the sixth hour', i.e., around midday.) Again in relation to this subject, we see Rembrandt's sensitivity to the characteristic aspects of the Venetian School. The great Venetian artists, particularly those of the 16th century, enriched their art with poetic translations of the constantly changing moods in the atmosphere created by light and temperature.

Panel; 48 × 40.5 cm.
Signed and dated: *Rembran(dt) f.(1)659.*
Berlin, Gemäldegalerie der Staatlichen Museen.

Literature: Bredius, no. 588; Bauch, no. 86; Gerson, no. 272; Bredius-Gerson, no. 588/Sumowski 1963, no. 48.

Repent: for the kingdom of heaven is at hand

Matthew 4 12 Now when Jesus had heard that John was cast into prison, he departed into Galilee;
13 And leaving Nazareth, he came and dwelt in Capernaum, which is upon the sea coast, in the borders of Zabulon and Nephthalim:
14 That it might be fulfilled which was spoken by Esaias the porphet, saying,

15 The land of Zabulon, and the land of Nephthalim, *by* the way of the sea, beyond Jordan, Galilee of the Gentiles;
16 The people which sat in darkness saw great light; and to them which sat in the region and shadow of death light is sprung up.
17 From that time Jesus began to preach, and to say, Repent: for the kingdom of heaven is at hand.

The Sermon of Jesus (La petite Tombe)

The subject of this etching is related to that in *The Hundred Guilder Print* completed a few years earlier (see p. 341), with the difference that the scene depicted here does not contain any clear references to a particular passage in the Bible, but concentrates on the preaching of Jesus and its effect on his listeners in general. The figures surrounding Jesus as he is preaching are characterized in a masterly way, and altogether they form an image of the faith and expectation, as well as the doubt and criticism, provoked in the people to whom he is talking.

In the 18th century the print was given the strange title *La petite Tombe* in France because it was thought that the name *Latombisch plaatjen* - under which the etching plate appears in the inventory of the Amsterdam publisher and print dealer, Clement de Jonghe, drawn up in 1679 - was related to the raised platform, rather like a tomb, on which Jesus is standing. In fact, this title referred to the name of the art dealer, Pieter de la Tombe, mentioned on p. 302, a business friend of Rembrandt who may have commissioned the print or perhaps owned the copper plate for some time.

Etching; 15.5 × 20.6 cm. Only state.
Ca. 1652.
Amsterdam, Rijksprentenkabinet.

Literature: Bartsch, no. 67; Hind, no. 256; Münz, no. 236; Boon, no. 237; Filedt Kok, no. B 67/Hofstede de Groot, *Rembrandt Bijbel*, N.T.e.20; Rotermund 1963, no. 187; Sumowski 1963, no. 35; Tümpel 1970, no. 88.

From henceforth thou shalt catch men

Luke 5 AND it came to pass, that, as the people pressed upon him to hear the word of God, he stood by the lake of Gennesaret,

2 And saw two ships standing by the lake: but the fishermen were gone out of them, and were washing *their* nets.

3 And he entered into one of the ships, which was Simon's, and prayed him that he would thrust out a little from the land. And he sat down, and taught the people out of the ship.

4 Now when he had left speaking, he said unto Simon, Launch out into the deep, and let down your nets for a draught.

5 And Simon answering said unto him, Master, we have toiled all the night, and have taken nothing: nevertheless at thy word I will let down the net.

6 And when they had this done, they inclosed a great multitude of fishes: and their net brake.

7 And they beckoned unto *their* partners, which were in the other ship, that they should come and help them. And they came, and filled both the ships, so that they began to sink.

8 When Simon Peter *saw it*, he fell down at Jesus' knees, saying, Depart from me; for I am a sinful man, O Lord.

9 For he was astonished, and all that were with him, at the draught of the fishes which they had taken:

10 And so *was* also James, and John, the sons of Zebedee, which were partners with Simon. And Jesus said unto Simon, Fear not; from henceforth thou shalt catch men.

11 And when they had brought their ships to land, they forsook all, and followed him.

A Miraculous Draught of Fishes

When Simon Peter saw it, he fell down at Jesus' knees, saying, Depart from me; for I am a sinful man, O Lord. (Luke 5:8)

This simple drawing is the only treatment of this subject in Rembrandt's work.

Peter's reaction is the central theme. The miracle is depicted merely by indicating the net hanging over the side of the boat and several men who are engaged in hauling in the catch. A copy in the British Museum in London shows that part of the drawing was cut off on the right.

It is only in the Gospel according to St Luke that the miraculous draught of fish is related to Peter and his companions becoming disciples. Matthew (4:18-22) and Mark (1:16-20) describe only how Jesus, as he was walking along the shores of the lake of Galilee, first called on the fishermen brothers Peter and Andrew to follow him, and shortly afterwards called on the sons of Zebedee, James and John, as they were drawing in their nets.

Pen and brush drawing; 18 × 19.2 cm.
Ca. 1655.
Paris, The Louvre.

Literature: Benesch V, no. 930 (*ca.* 1653); Slive II, no. 397 (*ca.* 1655)/Hofstede de Groot, *Rembrandt Bijbel*, N.T.d.10; Rotermund 1963, no. 167; Sumowski 1963, no. 34.

If thou wilt, thou canst make me clean

Mark 1 40 And there came a leper to him, beseeching him, and kneeling down to him, and saying unto him, If thou wilt, thou canst make me clean.

41 And Jesus, moved with compassion, put forth *his* hand, and touched him, and saith unto him, I will; be thou clean.

42 And as soon as he had spoken, immediately the leprosy departed from him, and he was cleansed.

43 And he straitly charged him, and forthwith sent him away;

44 And saith unto him, See thou say nothing to any man: but go thy way, shew thyself to the priest, and offer for thy cleansing those things which Moses commanded, for a testimony unto them.

45 But he went out, and began to publish *it* much, and to blaze abroad the matter, insomuch that Jesus could no more openly enter into the city, but was without in desert places: and they came to him from every quarter.

Jesus Cures a Leper

And Jesus, moved with compassion, put forth his hand, and touched him, and saith unto him, I will: Be thou clean. (Mark 1:41)

This apparently completely natural composition - another beautiful example of Rembrandt's late, extremely simple style of drawing - was actually carefully considered and is arranged diagonally from top right to bottom left with the more powerfully sketched figure of Jesus in the middle.

Two disciples, by no means at ease, watch their master lovingly bending forward over the leper without going any closer than necessary, carefully touching the man's forehead with the tips of his fingers. Originally the diseased man took hold of the hand Jesus held out. Rembrandt covered over this gesture and then drew Jesus' hand again, this time touching the forehead of the leper.

This drawing is the only surviving version of this subject in Rembrandt's work.

Pen and ink drawing; 14.7 × 17.2 cm.
Ca. 1655-60.
Amsterdam, Rijksprentenkabinet.

Literature: Benesch V, no. 1026 (*ca.* 1656-57); Slive II, no. 330 (*ca.* 1657-60)/Hofstede de Groot, *Rembrandt Bijbel*, N.T.d.II; Rotermund 1963, no. 170; 'Bijbelse Inspiratie', no. 99.

Why are ye so fearful?

Mark 4 AND he began again to teach by the sea side: and there was gathered unto him a great multitude, so that he entered into a ship, and sat in the sea; and the whole multitude was by the sea on the land.

2 And he taught them many things by parables, and said unto them in his doctrine, [...]

34 But without a parable spake he not unto them: and when they were alone, he expounded all things to his disciples.

35 And the same day, when the even was come, he saith unto them, Let us pass over unto the other side.

36 And when they had sent away the multitude, they took him even as he was in the ship. And there were also with him other little ships.

37 And there arose a great storm of wind, and the waves beat into the ship, so that it was now full.

38 And he was in the hinder part of the ship, asleep on a pillow: and they awake him, and say unto him, Master, carest thou not that we perish?

39 And he arose, and rebuked the wind, and said unto the sea, Peace, be still. And the wind ceased, and there was a great calm.

40 And he said unto them, Why are ye so fearful? how is it that ye have no faith?

41 And they feared exceedingly, and said one to another, What manner of man is this, that even the wind and the sea obey him?

The Storm on the Lake of Galilee

And there arose a great storm of wind, and the waves beat into the ship, so that it was now full. And he was in the hinder part of the ship, asleep on a pillow: and they awake him, and say unto him, Master, carest thou not that we perish? (Mark 4:37-38)

It would hardly have been possible to express more realistically and more compellingly than Rembrandt did in this work the wild waves, the scudding wrack, the men desperately fighting the storm on the forward deck, and the terror and misery of the crew in the stern - one of them has become seasick, while others, almost out of their minds, wake up Jesus, shouting to him.

This painting is the first of a series of large-scale dramatic compositions of Biblical and mythological scenes with which Rembrandt attempted to secure his reputation as a historical painter during his first years in Amsterdam, when he was inundated with commissions for portraits. In a drawing dating from the middle of the 1650s (Benesch V, no. 954), he again depicted this rarely used theme.

The little boat on the lake of Galilee, battered by the storm, was seen as a symbol for the Church, 'Peter's ship', which was threatened by a thousand dangers with the Lord on board sailing for the shore of God's peace. In fact the original title of this painting by Rembrandt was *St Pieters scheepje* (St Peter's Ship), and it appeared under this title in the first part of Arnold Houbraken's *De Groote Schouburgh der Nederlantsche Konstschilders en Schilderessen* (The Great Review of Dutch Painters), which was published in 1718. The work was praised for its powerful expression, and was compared with Rembrandt's late work as an example which showed, according to Houbraken, 'that he had more patience in his early years to work on his paintings in detail than he did later'.

Canvas; 159.5 × 127.5 cm.
Signed and dated: *Rembrandt f. 1633.*
Boston, Isabella Stewart Gardner Museum.

Literature: Bredius, no. 547; Bauch, no. 58; Gerson, no. 60; Bredius-Gerson, no. 547/Hofstede de Groot, *Rembrandt Bijbel*, N.T.p.12.

Damsel, I say unto thee, arise

Mark 5   21 And when Jesus was passed over again by ship unto the other side, much people gathered unto him: and he was nigh unto the sea.

22 And, behold, there cometh one of the rulers of the synagogue, Jairus by name; and when he saw him, he fell at his feet,

23 And besought him greatly, saying, My little daughter lieth at the point of death: *I pray thee*, come and lay thy hands on her, that she may be healed; and she shall live.

24 And *Jesus* went with him; and much people followed him, and thronged him.

25 And a certain woman, which had an issue of blood twelve years,

26 And had suffered many things of many physicians, and had spent all that she had, and was nothing bettered, but rather grew worse,

27 When she had heard of Jesus, came in the press behing, and touched his garment.

28 For she said, If I may touch but his clothes, I shall be whole.

29 And straightway the fountain of her blood was dried up; and she felt in *her* body that she was healed of that plague.

30 And Jesus, immediately knowing in himself that virtue had gone out of him, turned him about in the press, and said, Who touched my clothes?

31 And his disciples said unto him, Thou seest the multitude thronging thee, and sayest thou, Who touched me?

32 And he looked round about to see her that had done this thing.

33 But the woman fearing and trembling, knowing what was done in her, came and fell down before him, and told him all the truth.

34 And he said unto her, Daughter, thy faith hath made thee whole; go in peace, and be whole of thy plague.

35 While he yet spake, there came from the ruler of the synagogue's *house certain* which said, Thy daughter is dead: why troublest thou the Master any further?

36 As soon as Jesus heard the word that was spoken, he saith unto the ruler of the synagogue, Be not afraid, only believe.

37 And he suffered no man to follow him, save Peter, and James, and John the brother of James.

38 And he cometh to the house of the ruler of the synagogue, and seeth the tumult, and them that wept and wailed greatly.

39 And when he was come in, he saith unto them, Why make ye this ado, and weep? the damsel is not dead, but sleepeth.

40 And they laughed him to scorn. But when he had put them all out, he taketh the father and the mother of the damsel, and them that were with him, and entereth in where the damsel was lying.

41 And he took the damsel by the hand, and said unto her, Talitha cumi; which is, being interpreted, Damsel, I say unto thee, arise.

42 And straightway the damsel arose, and walked; for she was *of the age* of twelve years. And they were astonished with a great astonishment.

43 And he charged them straitly that no man should know it; and commanded that something should be given her to eat.

The Waking of Jairus' Daughter

... But when he had put them all out, he taketh the father and the mother of the damsel, and them that were with him, and entereth in where the damsel was lying. And he took the damsel by the hand, and said unto her, Talitha cumi; which is, being interpreted, Damsel, I say unto thee, arise.
(Mark 5:40-41)

This thoughtful composition, which is in broad lines a mirror-image repetition of the etching dating from 1642, *The Raising of Lazarus* (see p. 353), again reveals all the characteristics of Rembrandt's late style of drawing. Using surprisingly few techniques, the position and facial expression of each character is assigned exactly the right weight. The boyish figure of John, one of the three privileged disciples Jesus allowed to enter the chamber of death with the girl's parents, is particularly striking among the sympathetic onlookers behind Jesus. As the youngest of the twelve disciples, he is virtually always depicted in Western Christian art as a beardless young man.

Even among Rembrandt's drawings dating from the early 1630s there are several versions (Benesch I, nos. 61, 62 and 95a) depicting the raising of Jairus' daughter. In early Christian art this event was often combined with the immediately preceding healing of a woman suffering from loss of blood, but in later Western art the subject was only rarely used.

Pen and brush drawing; 19.8 × 19.8 cm.
Ca. 1655-60.
Berlin, Kupferstichkabinett der Staatlichen Museen.

Literature: Benesch V, no. 1064 (*ca.* 1660-62); Slive I, no.
151 (*ca.* 1655-60)/Hofstede de Groot, *Rembrandt Bijbel*,
N.T.d.12; Tümpel 1970, no. 75.

John Baptist's head

Matthew 14 AT that time Herod the tetrarch heard of the fame of Jesus,

2 And said unto his servants, This is John the Baptist; he is risen from the dead; and therefore mighty works do shew forth themselves in him.

3 For Herod had laid hold on John, and bound him, and put *him* in prison for Herodias' sake, his brother Philip's wife.

4 For John said unto him, It is not lawful for thee to have her.

5 And when he would have put him to death, he feared the multitude, because they counted him as a prophet.

6 But when Herod's birthday was kept, the daughter of Herodias danced before them, and pleased Herod.

7 Whereupon he promised with an oath to give her whatsoever she would ask.

8 And she, being before instructed of her mother, said, Give me here John Baptist's head in a charger.

9 And the king was sorry: nevertheless for the oath's sake, and them which sat with him at meat, he commanded *it* to be given *her*.

10 And he sent, and beheaded John in the prison.

11 And his head was brought in a charger, and given to the damsel: and she brought *it* to her mother.

12 And his disciples came, and took up the body, and buried it, and went and told Jesus.

The Beheading of St John the Baptist

When artists depicted the beheading of Jesus' intrepid forerunner, who ultimately did not hesitate to tell King Herod the truth to his face, they usually chose the moment just after the execution. Normally the executioner, with the decapitated body at his feet, is seen placing the head of St John the Baptist on a plate in the hands of Salome (Herod's daughter, according to Flavius Josephus) (cf. the drawing on p. 319). To show the way in which the first martyr in the New Testament met his death, Rembrandt chose the moment just before the beheading, a moment that is much less frequently depicted, for this etching dating from 1640. The attention is focused entirely on the figure of St John in the middle in the foreground, kneeling in devout resignation. The camel-hair cloak of the prophet and preacher of penitence is around his waist, and next to him stands his traditional symbol: the staff with a cross and pennant. St John and the executioner, who is on the point of delivering the blow, are the two main figures, brightly illuminated, and the crowds of observers pressing together in the shadows in the background are completely subordinate to them. Although the presence of Salome at the beheading of St John the Baptist is not mentioned in the Bible, Rembrandt has adopted the tradition of including her in the scene, and the girl can be seen in the front row in the background, exactly in the middle. Next to her stands the potentate Herod, wearing a feathered hat. Diagonally behind Salome, we also see Herodias, who is actually responsible for the murder of St John. Rembrandt corrected one tradition in so far as it is not Salome, but a negro boy in the foreground on the right, who holds the plate on which the head of St John the Baptist will be placed after the execution.

Etching; 12.9 × 10.5 cm. First state of two.
Signed and dated: *Rembrandt f. 1640.*
Amsterdam, Rijksprentenkabinet.

Literature: Bartsch, no. 92; Hind, no. 171; Münz, no. 209; Boon, no. 155; Filedt Kok, no. B 92/Hofstede de Groot, *Rembrandt Bijbel*, N.T.e.15; Rotermund 1963, no. 178; Sumowski 1963, no. 31; Tümpel 1970, no. 72.

The Beheading of St John the Baptist

This suggestive, broadly composed sketch, dating from the second half of the 1650s, depicts the same moment as the print dating from 1640 shown on the previous page.

The execution takes place in front of a massive architectural edifice above the dungeon indicated by a barred window, from which the victim has just been taken. As the executioner grabs his sword, John is pushed down on to his knees from the back by one of the executioner's helpers. (Initially he had been drawn slightly further to the left.) Among the observers it is again the figure of Salome who attracts most attention, and, as in the etching dating from 1640, a boy in the foreground on the right holds a plate in readiness for taking the head into the banquet.

Pen and ink drawing; 20.2 × 27.2 cm.
Ca. 1655-60.
Rotterdam, Museum Boymans-van Beuningen.

Literature: Benesch V, no. 1035 (*ca.* 1657-58)/Rotermund 1963, no. 179.

The moment at which the executioner hands the head to Salome is the episode from the story of the death of St John the Baptist which is depicted most often, apart from the scene in which Salome offers the head to her mother.

It is not certain whether this drawing is Rembrandt's own work or that of a talented pupil. The arrangement of the design is virtually the same as that in the etching dating from 1640 (p. 317). St John's head, which is drawn with remarkable détail in comparison with the other heads, forms the focal point of the composition, and all eyes are drawn to it. The figure of the executioner has been damaged by a patch of damp.

Pen and brush drawing; 19.6 × 17.5 cm. At the bottom in later handwriting: *Rembrant.*
Ca. 1640.
Worcester (Mass.), Worcester Art Museum.

Literature: Benesch III, no. 480a (*ca.* 1640).

The Beheading of
St John the Baptist

Lord, save me

13 When Jesus heard *of it*, he departed thence by ship into a desert place apart: and when the people had heard *thereof*, they followed him on foot out of the cities.

14 And Jesus went forth, and saw a great multitude, and was moved with compassion toward them, and he healed their sick.

15 And when it was evening, his disciples came to him, saying, This is a desert place, and the time is now past; send the multitude away, that they may go into the villages, and buy themselves victuals.

16 But Jesus said unto them, They need not depart; give ye them to eat.

17 And they say unto him, We have here but five loaves, and two fishes.

18 He said, Bring them hither to me.

19 And he commanded the multitude to sit down on the grass, and took the five loaves, and the two fishes, and looking up to heaven, he blessed, and brake, and gave the loaves to *his* disciples, and the disciples to the multitude.

20 And they did all eat, and were filled: and they took up of the fragments that remained twelve baskets full.

21 And they that had eaten were about five thousand men, beside women and children.

22 And straightway Jesus constrained his disciples to get into a ship, and to go before him unto the other side, while he sent the multitudes away.

23 And when he had sent the multitudes away, he went up into a mountain apart to pray: and when the evening was come, he was there alone.

24 But the ship was now in the midst of the sea, tossed with waves: for the wind was contrary.

25 And in the fourth watch of the night Jesus went unto them, walking on the sea.

26 And when the disciples saw him walking on the sea, they were troubled, saying, It is a spirit; and they cried out for fear.

27 But straightway Jesus spake unto them, saying, Be of good cheer; it is I; be not afraid.

28 And Peter answered him and said, Lord, if it be thou, bid me come unto thee on the water.

29 And he said, Come. And when Peter was come down out of the ship he walked on the water, to go to Jesus.

30 But when he saw the wind boisterous, he was afraid; and beginning to sink, he cried, saying, Lord, save me.

31 And immediately Jesus stretched forth *his* hand, and caught him, and said unto him, O thou of little faith, wherefore didst thou doubt?

32 And when they were come into the ship, the wind ceased.

33 Then they that were in the ship came and worshipped him, saying, Of a truth thou art the Son of God.

Jesus Saves the Drowning Peter

And when Peter was come down out of the ship, he walked on the water to go to Jesus. But when he saw the wind boisterous, he was afraid; and, beginning to sink, he cried, saying, Lord, save me! And immediately Jesus stretched forth his hand, and caught him, and said unto him, O thou of little faith, wherefore didst thou doubt? (Matthew 14:29-31)

The story of Jesus walking on the water of the lake of Galilee can also be found in the Gospel according to St Mark (6:45-52) and the Gospel according to St John (6:16-21), but the episode about Peter illustrated here is mentioned only in the Gospel according to St Matthew.

It is by no means unlikely that the creation of this baroque composition, drawn with verve and flair and dating from the beginning of the 1630s, is related to the thematically similar painting of the storm on the lake of Galilee, dating from 1633 (see p. 313). Initially this scene of Peter drowning against the background of the disciples' ship being battered by waves was also interpreted as an image of the threatened Church being saved from its downfall by Christ. The detailed precision with which the main characters of Jesus and Peter are elaborated contrasts with the strong lines and general style of drawing in the rest of the picture.

In the British Museum in London, where this drawing is now kept, there is another drawing by Rembrandt of this subject (Benesch V, no. 1043), done about twenty-five years later. That drawing shows how one of the disciples in the boat makes an attempt to help his companion in need.

Pen and ink drawing; 16.8 × 26.5 cm.
Ca. 1632-33.
London, British Museum.

Literature: Benesch I, no. 70 (*ca*. 1632-33); Slive II, no.
531 (*ca*. 1633); Haak, no. 8 (*ca*. 1632-33).

O woman, great *is* thy faith

Matthew 15   21 Then Jesus went thence, and departed into the coasts of Tyre and Sidon.

22 And, behold, a woman of Canaan came out of the same coasts, and cried unto him, saying, Have mercy on me, O Lord, *thou* son of David; my daughter is grievously vexed with a devil.

23 But he answered her not a word. And his disciples came and besought him, saying, Send her away; for she crieth after us.

24 But he answered and said, I am not sent but unto the lost sheep of the house of Israel.

25 Then came she and worshipped him, saying, Lord, help me.

26 But he answered and said, It is not meet to take the children's bread, and to cast *it* to dogs.

27 And she said, Truth, Lord: yet the dogs eat of the crumbs which fall from their masters'table.

28 Then Jesus answered and said unto her, O woman, great *is* thy faith: be it unto thee even as thou wilt. And her daughter was made whole from that very hour.

Jesus and the Woman of Canaan   *Then came she and worshipped him, saying, Lord, help me! But he answered and said, It is not meet to take the children's bread, and to cast it to dogs. And she said, Truth, Lord: yet the dogs eat of the crumbs which fall from their master's table.*
(Matthew 15:25-27)

In this drawing Rembrandt effectively shows how Jesus, while still warding her off, is on the point of succumbing to the belief of the entreating woman.

Benesch and Sumowski state that the scene depicts the curing of the woman who is losing blood, which took place when Jesus was on his way to the house of Jairus, whose daughter was dying (see the Biblical text on p. 314). However, in versions of that scene, the woman kneeling at Jesus' feet usually touches the hem of his cloak. In order to show clearly which story was being portrayed, artists depicting Jesus and the woman of Canaan usually show a dog in the foreground as a reference to the dialogue between Jesus and the woman. In the painting of this subject dating from 1617 by Rembrandt's teacher Pieter Lastman (Amsterdam, Rijksmuseum), there are a couple of dogs playing, as well as two children eating bread in the foreground, by way of clarification. In this late drawing by Rembrandt, there is no such indication. However, according to Rotermund (p. 180) the woman herself is almost like the dog who is satisfied by the breadcrumbs given to it by its lord.

Pen and ink drawing; 15.2 × 22.6 cm.
Ca. 1660.
Vienna, Albertina.

Literature: Benesch V, no. 1052 (*ca.* 1660)/Rotermund 1963, no. 173; Sumowski 1963, no. 55.

322

Go, and do thou likewise

25 And, behold, a certain lawyer stood up, and tempted him, saying, Master, what shall I do to inherit eternal life?

26 He said unto him, What is written in the law? how readest thou?

27 And he answering said, Thou shalt love the Lord thy God with all thy heart, and with all thy soul, and with all thy strength, and with all thy mind; and thy neighbour as thyself.

28 And he said unto him, Thou hast answered right: this do, and thou shalt live.

29 But he, willing to justify himself, said unto Jesus, And who is my neighbour?

30 And Jesus answering said, A certain *man* went down from Jerusalem to Jericho, and fell among thieves, which stripped him of his raiment, and wounded *him*, and departed, leaving *him* half dead.

31 And by chance there came down a certain priest that way: and when he saw him, he passed by on the other side.

32 And likewise a Levite, when he was at the place, came and looked *on him*, and passed by on the other side.

33 But a certain Samaritan, as he journeyed, came where he was: and when he saw him, he had compassion *on him*,

34 And went to *him*, and bound up his wounds, pouring in oil and wine, and set him on his own beast, and brought him to an inn, and took care of him.

35 And on the morrow when he departed, he took out two pence, and gave *them* to the host, and said unto him, Take care of him; and whatsoever thou spendest more, when I come again, I will repay thee.

36 Which now of these three, thinkest thou, was neighbour unto him that fell among the thieves?

37 And he said, He that shewed mercy on him. Then said Jesus unto him, Go, and do thou likewise.

The Good Samaritan Looks After the Wounded Man

But a certain Samaritan, as he journeyed, came where he was: and when he saw him, he had compassion on him, and went to him, and bound up his wounds, pouring in oil and wine ...
(Luke 10:33-34)

The parable of the Good Samaritan, which Rembrandt depicted many times, particularly in drawings, is one of Jesus' most poignant teachings, together with the parable of the Prodigal Son (see pp. 334-39). These two parables can only be found in the Gospel according to St Luke.

In the footsteps of the Church Fathers - who considered the Good Samaritan as an image of Jesus helping man when he has fallen and has been robbed of his innocence, to take him into the inn, his Church - medieval artists sometimes showed the Samaritan in the character of Christ with a halo. It was only in the 16th century that the parable developed as an independent theme in works of art. It became very popular, particularly in prints, not as an allegory with the interpretation given by the early Church, but as a depiction of the example given by Jesus himself of loving your neighbours.

Rembrandt had two favourite episodes in this story: looking after the wounded man in the place where he was attacked, and the arrival at the inn. When they depicted the first scene, shown in this drawing, most artists showed the priest and the Levite in the background. They had also seen the robbed traveller but had walked on, leaving him lying there. It is strange that Rembrandt always left out these figures, though he liked to include motifs in his narrative compositions which referred to events preceding or following the moment depicted.

The drawing reproduced here has the date '1644' in the top right-hand corner, and is therefore of great significance in determining the chronological order of Rembrandt's drawings, which are seldom dated.

Pen and brush drawing; 15.8 × 22.1 cm.
Dated (top right-hand corner): *1644.*
Bottom left in later handwriting: *Rembrand f.*
Berlin, Kupferstichkabinett der Staatlichen Museen.

Literature: Benesch III, no. 556/Rotermund 1963, no.
188; Tümpel 1970, no. 79.

Study for the Good Samaritan with the Wounded Man

But a certain Samaritan, as he journeyed, came where he was: and when he saw him, he had compassion on him, and went to him, and bound up his wounds, pouring in oil and wine ...
(Luke 10:33-34)

Pen and brush drawing; 12.6 × 12.3 cm.
Ca. 1648-50.
Rotterdam, Museum Boymans-van Beuningen.

Literature: Benesch III, no. 621 (*ca.* 1648-49)/Rotermund 1963, no. 189.

The Good Samaritan at the Inn

[And he] brought him to an inn, and took care of him.
(Luke 10:34)

The scene of the arrival at the inn particularly fascinated Rembrandt. His versions of this subject vary a great deal.

In this carefully executed etching dating from 1633, Rembrandt returns to a painting which he did in 1630, showing exactly the same scene in mirror image (London, Wallace Collection; Bredius, no. 545). In that work the realistic motif of the dog, often considered rather disgusting in the last century, was not included.

It has been shown that Rembrandt's composition was based on a copper engraving of the same subject by his slightly older contemporary, Jan van der Velde (*ca.* 1593-1641). Van der Velde's print is in line with the usual style of representation in the 16th century, when it was customary to depict several moments from a story in a single work. Rembrandt copies his example by making the arrival at the inn coincide with the final scene in the parable. While the victim who has just arrived is being lifted off the horse by a stable boy, the Good

Samaritan is talking to the innkeeper, who puts the money paid in advance in his money bag. According to the Bible text, the Samaritan left the money for looking after the wounded man the following morning, when he departed (Luke 10:35).

This large etching by Rembrandt was extremely popular in the 17th and 18th centuries. Filedt Kok disagrees with the view which is often expressed that Rembrandt was helped by his pupils when he made this etching.

Etching; 25.4 × 20.3 cm. Fourth state of four.
Signed and dated: *Rembrandt inventor et feecit, 1633.*
Amsterdam, Rijksprentenkabinet.

Literature: Bartsch, no. 90; Hind, no. 101; Münz, no. 196; Boon, no. 90; Filedt Kok no. B 90/Hofstede de Groot, *Rembrandt Bijbel*, N.T.e.17; J. Bruyn, *Rembrandt's keuze van Bijbelse onderwerpen*, Utrecht 1959, p. 15; Tümpel 1970, no. 81; K. Clark, 'Rembrandt's "Good Samaritan" in the Wallace Collection' in *The Burlington Magazine*, vol. CXVIII, December 1976, pp. 805-09.

· Rembrandt· inventor· et· feecit· 1633·

The Good Samaritan at the Inn

[And he] brought him to an inn, and took care of him.
(Luke 10:34)

In the engraving by Jan van der Velde, which was mentioned above, the scene is shown by night by the light of a torch and a candle. Evidently the print continued to intrigue Rembrandt, for when he returned to the theme again, about ten years after the etching done in 1633, he again showed the arrival at the inn taking place at night with striking contrasts between light and dark, lending a dramatic character to the scene. The Good Samaritan, who is in the centre of the composition, looks on in concern as the wounded man is carried into the inn by helping hands, as carefully as possible. At the top of the stairs the innkeeper stands ready, with a candle in his hand to give more light. Keeping to the Bible text, Rembrandt did not show the Samaritan paying the innkeeper in advance, as he did in the 1633 etching.

Pen and brush drawing; 18.4 × 28.7 cm.
Ca. 1641-43.
London, British Museum.

Literature: Benesch III, no. 518a (*ca.* 1641-43); Slive I, no. 206 (*ca.* 1641-43); Haak, no. 40 (*ca.* 1641-43)/J. Bruyn, *Rembrandts keuze van Bijbelse onderwerpen*, Utrecht 1959, p. 15.

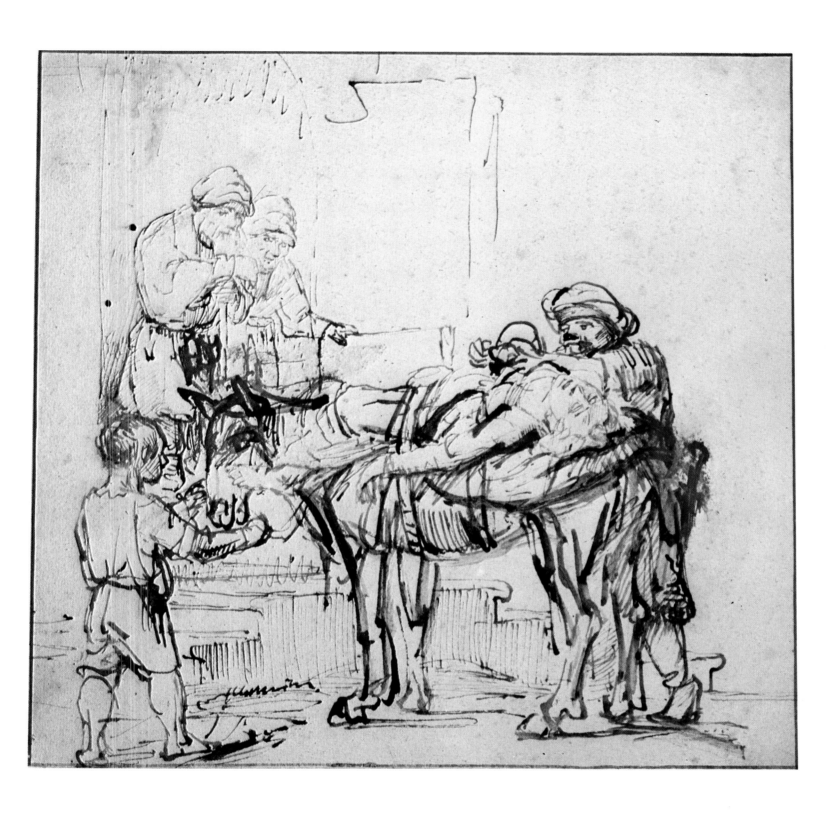

[And he] brought him to an inn, and took care of him.
(Luke 10:34)

The expressive force of Rembrandt's last depiction of
the arrival at the inn transcends all the earlier versions.
The heavily emphasized main group is placed in the
foreground as much as possible, so that the observer is
drawn into the event more than he was before.
Watched by the innkeeper and his wife, the Samaritan
is engaged in untying the bonds with which he secured
the man wounded by the robbers to his beast of
burden. As in the 1633 etching, a boy is holding the reins.

Pen and ink drawing; 19.7 × 20.5 cm.
Ca. 1648-50.
Weimar, Staatliche Kunstsammlungen, Schlossmuseum.

*The Good
Samaritan at the
Inn*

Literature: Benesch III, no. 615 (*ca.* 1648-49)/Rotermund
1963, no. 190; Sumowski 1963, no. 39.

Mary hath chosen that good part

Luke 10 38 Now it came to pass, as they went, that he entered into a certain village: and a certain woman named Martha received him into her house.

39 And she had a sister called Mary, which also sat at Jesus' feet, and heard his word.

40 But Martha was cumbered about much serving, and came to him, and said, Lord, dost thou not care that my sister hath left me to serve alone? bid her therefore that she help me.

41 And Jesus answered and said unto her, Martha, Martha, thou art careful and troubled about many things:

42 But one thing is needful: and Mary hath chosen that good part, which shall not be taken away from her.

Jesus in the House of Martha and Mary

... and came to him, and said, Lord, dost thou not care that my sister hath left me to serve alone? Bid her therefore that she help me. And Jesus answered and said unto her, Martha, Martha, thou art careful and troubled about many things: But one thing is needful: and Mary hath chosen that good part ... ·
(Luke 10:40-42)

In the 16th century, artists often used this subject as an excuse to paint an extravagant still life of a kitchen scene. The combination of material abundance in the foreground with the Biblical subject in the background served to remind the observer that man is not concerned in this life with earthly matters, but with spiritual considerations. In the historical paintings of the 17th century, the emphasis is again on the Biblical story.

All the components of the story - Mary's role, Martha's complaints and Jesus' answer - are clearly expressed in the characters' gestures and facial expressions in this hastily drawn sketch by Rembrandt, a typical example of his lively style at the beginning of the 1630s. It is a popular theme in Dutch art, and in the second half of the 1640s, Rembrandt used it again in drawings several times. The point of the story was in accordance with the teaching of the Reformation that man does not achieve salvation by doing good works, but is saved by his belief, which follows listening to God's word.

Pen and ink drawing; 16 × 19 cm.
Ca. 1632-33.
Haarlem, Teylers Museum.

Literature: Benesch I, no. 79 (*ca.* 1632-33); Slive I, no. 180 (*ca.* 1643)/'Bijbelse Inspiratie', no. 100.

Take heed, and beware of covetousness

Luke 12 13 And one of the company said unto him, Master, speak to my brother, that he divide the inheritance with me.

14 And he said unto him, Man, who made me a judge or a divider over you?

15 And he said unto them, Take heed, and beware of covetousness: for a man's life consisteth not in the abundance of the things which he possesseth.

16 And he spake a parable unto them, saying, The ground of a certain rich man brought forth plentifully:

17 And he thought within himself, saying, What shall I do, because I have no room where to bestow my fruits?

18 And he said, This will I do: I will pull down my barns, and build greater; and there will I bestow all my fruits and my goods.

19 And I will say to my soul, Soul, thou hast much goods laid up for many years; take thine ease, eat, drink, *and* be merry.

20 But God said unto him, *Thou* fool, this night thy soul shall be required of thee: then whose shall those things be, which thou hast provided?

21 So *is* he that layeth up treasure for himself, and he is not rich toward God.

The Rich Fool *Thou fool, this night thy soul shall be required of thee: then whose shall those things be which thou hast provided?* (Luke 12:20)

Until recently, this small painting from Rembrandt's Leyden period was viewed as belonging to a particular genre, and was usually entitled *The Moneychanger*. Tümpel showed that the work actually depicted the rich fool, a theme that had up to then only been dealt with in prints, and then very rarely.

Like the existing depictions of this subject, Rembrandt's version shows the rich man in his treasury. The way in which he examines one of his gold coins by the light of a candle reveals his attachment to earthly possessions. The candlelight clearly shows that the scene takes place at night: 'Thou fool, this night thy soul shall be required of thee' (Luke 12:20).

In older versions, death was usually represented in the allegorical form of a skeleton with an hour-glass. However, this sort of motif, which was not based on visible reality, was considered old-fashioned by 17th-century artists. Therefore Rembrandt shows the presence of death in a completely different way, by surrounding the rich man with piles of books and papers: these refer not only to his financial affairs, but also serve as a sign of the transience of earthly existence. Still lifes of books were a favourite *vanitas* symbol during that period, particularly in the works of artists from Leyden. The Hebrew letters on the bonds serve to identify the scene as a Biblical subject, while its contemporary significance is expressed by the modern presentation.

Panel; 32 × 42 cm.
Signed and dated: *RH(L) 1627*.
Berlin, Gemäldegalerie der Staatlichen Museen.

Literature: Bredius, no. 420; Bauch, no. 110; Gerson, no. 19; Bredius-Gerson, no. 420/Tümpel 1971, pp. 27 *et seq.*

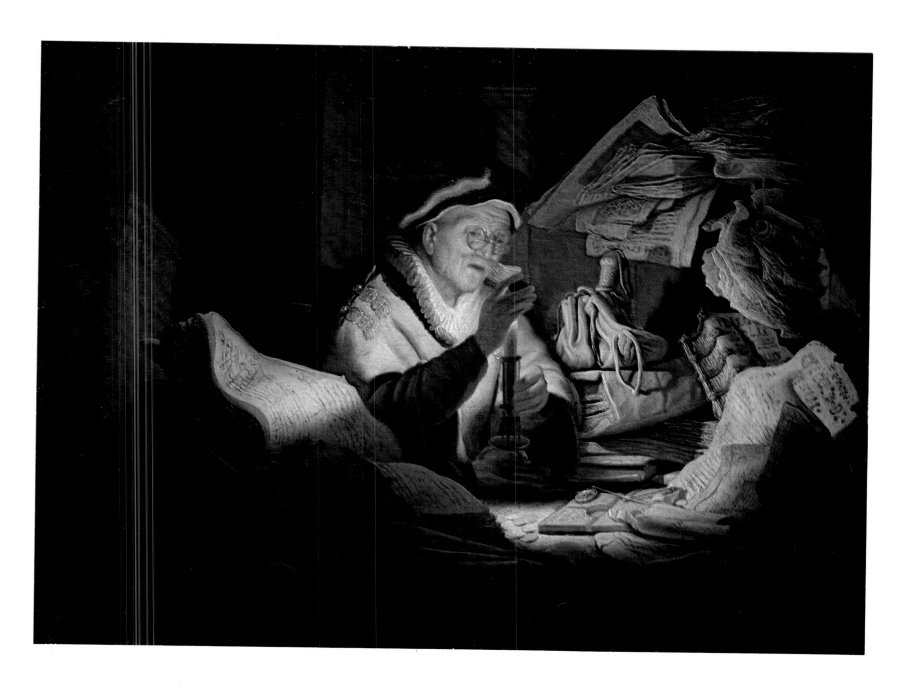

Father, I have sinned against heaven, and before thee

Luke 15 THEN drew near unto him all the publicans and sinners for to hear him.

2 And the Pharisees and scribes murmured, saying, This man received sinners, and eateth with them. [...]

11 And he said, A certain man had two sons:

12 And the younger of them said to *his* father, Father, give me the portion of goods that falleth *to me*. And he divided unto them *his* living.

13 And not many days after the younger son gathered all together, and took his journey into a far country, and there wasted his substance with riotous living.

14 And when he had spent all, there arose a mighty famine in that land; and he began to be in want.

15 And he went and joined himself to a citizen of that country; and he sent him into his fields to feed swine.

16 And he would fain have filled his belly with the husks that the swine did eat: and no man gave unto him.

17 And when he came to himself, he said, How many hired servants of my father's have bread enough and to spare, and I perish with hunger!

18 I will arise and go to my father, and will say unto him, Father, I have sinned against heaven, and before thee,

19 And am no more worthy to be called thy son: make me as one of thy hired servants.

20 And he arose, and came to his father. But when he was yet a great way off, his father saw him, and had compassion, and ran, and fell on his neck, and kissed him.

21 And the son said unto him, Father, I have sinned against heaven, and in thy sight, and am no more worthy to be called thy son.

22 But the father said to his servants, Bring forth the best robe, and put *it* on him; and put a ring on his hand, and shoes on *his* feet:

23 And bring hither the fatted calf, and kill *it*; and let us eat, and be merry:

24 For this my son was dead, and is alive again; he was lost, and is found, And they began to be merry.

25 Now his elder son was in the field: and as he came and drew nigh to the house, he heard musick and dancing.

26 And he called one of the servants, and asked what these things meant.

27 And he said unto him, Thy brother is come; and thy father hath killed the fatted calf, because he hath received him safe and sound.

28 And he was angry, and would not go in: therefore came his father out, and intreated him.

29 And he answering said to *his* father, Lo, these many years do I serve thee, neither transgressed I at any time thy commandment: and yet thou never gavest me a kid, that I might make merry with my friends:

30 But as soon as this thy son was come, which hath devoured thy living with harlots, thou hast killed for him the fatted calf.

31 And he said unto him, Son, thou art ever with me, and all that I have is thine.

32 It was meet that we should make merry, and be glad: for this thy brother was dead, and is alive again; and was lost, and is found.

And he arose, and came to his father. But when he was yet a great way off, his father saw him, and had compassion, and ran, and fell on his neck, and kissed him. And the son said unto him, Father, I have sinned against heaven, and in thy sight, and am no more worthy to be called thy son.
(Luke 15:20-21)

No artist has ever depicted the most moving episode from the parable of the Prodigal Son as often or as effectively as Rembrandt. His first version of this subject is this etching dating from 1636, for which he made use of a woodcut based on a 16th-century master from Haarlem, Maerten van Heemskerck. Following this example, Rembrandt showed the reunion of the father and son on the steps of the parental home, and not at some distance from it, as described in the Bible. The destitute boy has dropped his stick and throws himself into his father's arms, full of repentance. The father's movement reveals his urgency to meet his son with a heartfelt embrace and, above all, his unconditional forgiveness. 'In this way, he expresses the essence of the story, and it is curious to note how stubbornly he held onto this first depiction which

seemed to live on in his mind as an autonomous subject which he can study from various sides, but which has a constant size, always composed of roughly the same motifs' (Bruyn, p. 16). Like Van Heemskerck, Rembrandt anticipates the rest of the story by showing several servants in the doorway. They are coming outside with footwear and new clothes to dress the Prodigal Son most beautifully, make him wear the shoes and offer him a feast of celebration, at the father's command: 'For this my son was dead, and is alive again; he was lost, and is found' (Luke 15:24).

Etching; 15.6 × 13.6 cm. Only state.
Signed and dated: *Rembrandt f. 1636.*
Amsterdam, Rijksprentenkabinet.

Literature: Bartsch, no. 91; Hind, no. 147; Münz, no. 207; Boon, no. 129; Filedt Kok, no. B 91/Hofstede de Groot, *Rembrandt Bijbel*, N.T.e.18; J. Bruyn, *Rembrandts keuze van Bijbelse onderwerpen*, Utrecht 1959, pp. 15 *et seq.*; Rotermund 1963, no. 203; Sumowski 1963, no. 42; 'Bijbelse Inspiratie', no. 40; Tümpel 1970, no. 85.

The Return of the Prodigal Son

The Prodigal Son   Canvas; 161 × 131 cm.

Squanders his   Signed: *Rembrant f. Ca.* 1636.

Inheritance   Dresden, Staatliche Kunstsammlungen Gemäldegalerie.

Literature: Bredius, no. 30; Bauch, no. 535; Gerson, no. 79; Bredius-Gerson, no. 30/Rotermund 1963, p. 185; Tümpel 1968, pp. 116-26; Tümpel 1970, under no. 84.

336

And not many days after, the younger son gathered all together, and took his journey into a far country, and there wasted his substance with riotous living.
(Luke 15:13)

In Dutch 16th- and 17th-century art, the most popular episode in this famous parable was when the Prodigal Son squandered his inheritance on loose women in foreign countries. This aspect is the theme of the painting reproduced here, for which Rembrandt used himself and Saskia as models. In accordance with the traditional representation of the main character, he is wearing a nobleman's clothes with a feathered hat and sword, and the *bon viveur* is sitting at a laden table with a girl on his lap, raising his glass in triumph. The peacock pie on the table symbolizes his arrogance. A board hanging on the wall on the left, with chalk marks showing the bill of fare, indicates that the scene is set in an inn. An X-ray photograph revealed that originally there was a nude figure of a woman playing a mandolin in the background.

Influenced by the prevailing view that everyone should identify with the Prodigal Son, it was not unusual during that period for an artist to depict himself in this negative role.

And when he came to himself, he said, How many hired servants of my father's have bread enough, and to spare, and I perish with hunger! I will arise and go to my father, and will say unto him, Father, I have sinned against heaven and before thee, And am no more worthy to be called thy son: make me as one of thy hired servants.
(Luke 15:17-19)

Undoubtedly Rembrandt was familiar with the celebrated engraving which Albrecht Dürer had devoted to this subject in about 1496, which showed the same moment of repentance by the pig trough. Unlike Dürer, who surrounded the scene with all sorts of buildings, Rembrandt shows only the essential element of the story: the lonely boy, who comes to his senses among the pigs. His emaciated appearance reminds us of the great famine which had swept through the land where he had sought his fortune so lightheartedly. This moving drawing is Rembrandt's only version of this part of the story.

Pen and ink drawing; 15.9 × 23.5 cm.
Ca. 1645-48.
London, British Museum.

Literature: Benesch III, no. 601 (*ca.* 1647-48)/Hofstede de Groot, *Rembrandt Bijbel*, N.T.d.19; Rotermund 1963, no. 200; Sumowski 1963, no. 41.

The Prodigal Son as a Swineherd

The Return of the Prodigal Son

Father, I have sinned against heaven, and in thy sight, and am no more worthy to be called thy son.
(Luke 15:21)

In this drawing Rembrandt restricted himself to the two main characters. In the background there is only a little boy looking on in surprise, leaning against a wall by the entrance to the father's house. This time, the stick which has fallen on the ground belongs to the father, who has come running to his son. The print by J.J. de Claussin (1795-1844), based on this drawing, gives 1642 as the year in which the drawing was done, apparently with good reason.

Pen and brush drawing; 19 × 22.7 cm.
Ca. 1642.
Haarlem, Teylers Museum.

Literature: Benesch III, no. 519 (*ca.* 1642); Slive I, no. 177 (*ca.* 1642)/Rotermund 1963, no. 202; 'Bijbelse Inspiratie', no. 102.

Father, I have sinned against heaven, and in thy sight, and am no more worthy to be called thy son.
(Luke 15:20-21)

In this famous painting from the last years of Rembrandt's life, the emphasis is on the father's total forgiveness, even more strongly than in any of his previous depictions of this subject (including another drawing dating from *ca.* 1644-45, and two drawings done in the 1650s). The old man presses his refound child against him with both hands. The father and son have become one, and the world they inhabit is inaccessible to the other people present, who remain at a distance, in silence.

Canvas; 262 × 206 cm.
Signed (possibly not by Rembrandt himself): *R V Rijn f.*
Ca. 1668-69.
Leningrad, The Hermitage.

Literature: Bredius, no. 598; Bauch, no. 94; Gerson, no. 355; Bredius-Gerson, no. 598/Hofstede de Groot, *Rembrandt Bijbel* N.T.p.17; Sumowski 1963, nos. 43-45.

338

For of such is the kingdom of heaven

Matthew 19

AND it came to pass, *that* when Jesus had finished these sayings, he departed from Galilee, and came into the coasts of Judæa beyond Jordan;

2 And great multitudes followed him; and he healed them there.

3 The Pharisees also came unto him, tempting him, and saying unto him, Is it lawful for a man to put away his wife for every cause?

4 And he answered and said unto them, Have ye not read, that he which made *them* at the beginning made them male and female,

5 And said, For this cause shall a man leave father and mother, and shall cleave to his wife: and they twain shall be one flesh?

6 Wherefore they are no more twain, but one flesh. What therefore God hath joined together, let not man put asunder.

7 They say unto him, Why did Moses then command to give a writing of divorcement, and to put her away?

8 He saith unto them, Moses because of the hardness of your hearts suffered you to put away your wives: but from the beginning it was not so.

9 And I say unto you, Whosoever shall put away his wife, except *it be* for fornication, and shall marry another, committeth adultery: and whoso marrieth her which is put away doth commit adultery. [...]

13 Then were there brought unto him little children, that he should put *his* hands on them, and pray: and the disciples rebuked them.

14 But Jesus said, Suffer little children, and forbid them not, to come unto me: for of such is the kingdom of heaven.

15 And he laid *his* hands on them, and departed thence.

16 And, behold, one came and said unto him, Good Master, what good thing shall I do, that I may have eternal life?

17 And he said unto him, Why callest thou me good? *there is* none good but one, *that is*, God: but if thou wilt enter into life, keep the commandments.

18 He saith unto him, Which? Jesus said, Thou shalt do no murder, Thou shalt not commit adultery, Thou shalt not steal, Thou shalt not bear false witness,

19 Honour thy father and *thy* mother: and, Thou shalt love thy neighbour as thyself.

20 The young man saith unto him, All these things have I kept from my youth up: what lack I yet?

21 Jesus said unto him, If thou wilt be perfect, go *and* sell that thou hast, and give to the poor, and thou shalt have treasure in heaven: and come *and* follow me.

22 But when the young man heard that saying, he went away sorrowful: for he had great possessions.

23 Then said Jesus unto his disciples, Verily I say unto you, That a rich man shall hardly enter into the kingdom of heaven.

24 And again I say unto you, It is easier for a camel to go through the eye of a needle, than for a rich man to enter into the kingdom of God.

25 When his disciples heard *it*, they were exceedingly amazed, saying, Who then can be saved?

26 But Jesus beheld *them*, and said unto them, With men this is impossible; but with God all things are possible.

The Hundred Guilder Print

For the correct interpretation of this famous etching, there is an 'explanation' by Rembrandt's contemporary and friend, Hendrick Waterloos, who wrote a four-verse poem on one of the first prints made from the etching. The second verse in particular shows that Rembrandt has summarized the contents of the Gospel according to St Matthew, chapter 19:

Here Jesus helps the sick. And he blesses the Children (that is God's work): and punishes them who prevent him, But (ah) the young man laments. The scribes mock at The belief of the saints, and Christ's divine grace is radiant.

The procession of the sick and crippled people in the right half of the print serves as a reference to the healing of the sick, referred to in verse 2: 'The Pharisees came to him', the text continued, 'tempting him ...'. The group on the left in the background, which is engaged in discussion, refers to these Pharisees and their argument with Jesus (verses 3-9). The most important scene in the left half of the print refers to the passage about blessing the children (verses 13-14). We see two mothers walking towards Jesus, holding their babies in their arms. One of them hesitates, but is urged on by a small boy who

runs up to follow the woman in front. Rembrandt characterized the disciple who wishes to hold back the first mother as Peter, according to tradition. Jesus stops him with his right hand, and at the same time invites the woman to come closer. Without taking any notice of the fact that after he blessed the children, Jesus left the place (verse 15), Rembrandt shows the rich young man mentioned in the next passage in the same context. With his hand in front of his mouth, he stares disconsolately into space because the size of his wealth prevents him from following Jesus (verses 16-22). Then the Lord says to his disciples: 'Verily I say unto you, That a rich man shall hardly enter into the kingdom of heaven. And again I say unto you, It is easier for a camel to go through the eye of a needle, than for a rich man to enter into the kingdom of God' (verses 23-24). Finally, the camel, walking in through a gate in the background on the right, serves as a reference to these words.

As a rule, Biblical illustrations in the 16th and 17th centuries comprised the successive incidents in an entire chapter, so that they were shown as different scenes taking place at the same time in a single work. However, such simultaneous representations were no longer in accordance with the narrative style which Rembrandt used, which demanded a unity of time, place and action. This is why, when he chose to depict the children being blessed as the main scene, he anticipated the episode of the rich young man, and

when he referred to the preceding scenes - he was forced to abandon the order contained in the story: the sick are still waiting to be cured, and the Pharisees are still discussing what trick questions they can ask Jesus to catch him out. It was only in this way that Rembrandt could bring together all the themes from a whole chapter in a single impressive image with Jesus as the dominant benevolent figure, blessing, healing, teaching and calling upon people to follow him.

Undoubtedly the impossibility of summarizing the subjects in this etching in a single title contributed to the fact that it is generally known by the rather meaningless title of *The Hundred Guilder Print*. This title dates from the beginning of the 18th century, and is based on the story that Rembrandt once had to pay a hundred guilders to buy back a copy of his most popular print.

Etching; 28.3 × 39.5 cm. Second state of two.
Ca. 1648-50.
Amsterdam, Rijksprentenkabinet.

Literature: Bartsch, no. 74; Hind, no. 236; Münz, no. 217; Boon, no. 216; Filedt Kok, no. B 74/Hofstede de Groot, *Rembrandt Bijbel*, N.T.e.19; J. Bruyn, *Rembrandts keuze van Bijbelse onderwerpen*, Utrecht 1959, pp. 21 *et seq*.; Rotermund 1963, no. 186; Sumowski 1963, no. 50; 'Bijbelse Inspiratie', no. 37; Tümpel 1969, pp. 149 *et seq*.; Tümpel 1970, no. 86.

Is thine eye evil, because I am good?

Matthew 20 FOR the kingdom of heaven is like unto a man *that is* an householder, which went out early in the morning to hire labourers into his vineyard.

2 And when he had agreed with the labourers for a penny a day, he sent them into his vineyard.

3 And he went out about the third hour, and saw others standing idle in the marketplace,

4 And said unto them; Go ye also into the vineyard, and whatsoever is right I will give you. And they went their way.

5 Again he went out about the sixth and ninth hour, and did likewise.

6 And about the eleventh hour he went out, and found others standing idle, and saith unto them, Why stand ye here all the day idle?

7 They say unto him, Because no man hath hired us. He saith unto them, Go ye also into the vineyard; and whatsoever is right, *that* shall ye receive.

8 So when even was come, the lord of the vineyard saith unto his steward, Call the labourers, and give them *their* hire, beginning from the last unto the first.

9 And when they came that *were hired* about the eleventh hour, they received every man a penny.

10 But when the first came, they supposed that they should have received more; and they likewise received every man a penny.

11 And when they had received *it*, they murmured against the goodman of the house,

12 Saying, These last have wrought *but* one hour, and thou hast made them equal unto us, which have borne the burden and heat of the day.

13 But he answered one of them, and said, Friend, I do thee no wrong: didst not thou agree with me for a penny?

14 Take *that* thine *is*, and go thy way: I will give unto this last, even as unto thee.

15 Is it not lawful for me to do what I will with mine own? Is thine eye evil, because I am good?

16 So the last shall be first, and the first last: for many be called, but few chosen.

The Labourers in the Vineyard

These last have wrought but one hour, and thou hast made them equal unto us, which have borne the burden and heat of the day. But he answered one of them, and said, Friend, I do thee no wrong: Didst not thou agree with me for a penny? Take that thine is, and go thy way: I will give unto this last even as unto thee.
(Matthew 20:12-14)

It is understandable that depictions of this parable, which tries to show that God is not swayed by human considerations in his sovereign freedom, but bestows his gifts where he wishes, are usually devoted to the episode of the payment of wages. This small painting dating from 1637 is dominated by shades of brown, and Rembrandt has depicted the scene in an unusually fascinating and realistic way, as though it were taking place in the offices of a rich Amsterdam merchant. In the foreground on the left, a number of commodities are standing and lying around, with all sorts of paperwork, and in the background on the right, barrels and chests are being hauled away to a neighbouring warehouse. A group of labourers is engaged in a heated discussion about the wages they have received. The employer is sitting at the table by the windows where there is most light, together with his bookkeeper. The two men making the complaint are clearly told that he does not wish to rescind his decision to pay everybody the same wages.

This little panel must have made a great impression on Rembrandt's contemporaries. Not only some of his pupils, but also some Dutch masters outside Rembrandt's circle, were inspired by it in their own treatments of this subject.

In about 1650, Rembrandt depicted the same scene more concisely in a number of drawings.

Panel; 31 × 42 cm.
Signed and dated: *Rembrandt f. 1637*.
Leningrad, The Hermitage.

Literature: Bredius, no. 558; Bauch, no. 65; Gerson, no.
83; Bredius-Gerson, no. 558/Hofstede de Groot,
Rembrandt Bijbel, N.T.p.18.

Jesus, Master, have mercy on us

Luke 17 11 And it came to pass, as he went to Jerusalem, that he passed through the midst of Samaria and Galilee.

12 And as he entered into a certain village, there met him ten men that were lepers, which stood afar off:

13 And they lifted up *their* voices, and said, Jesus, Master, have mercy on us.

14 And when he saw *them*, he said unto them, Go shew yourselves unto the priests. And it came to pass, that, as they went, they were cleansed.

15 And one of them, when he saw that he was healed, turned back, and with a loud voice glorified God,

16 And fell down on *his* face at his feet, giving him thanks: and he was a Samaritan.

17 And Jesus answering said, Were there not ten cleansed? but where *are* the nine?

18 There are not found that returned to give glory to God, save this stranger.

19 And he said unto him, Arise, go thy way: thy faith hath made thee whole.

Lepers Begging Jesus to Heal them

It is not quite clear which scene from the Gospels Rembrandt is depicting in this drawing. It probably concerns a group of lepers who beg Jesus to take notice of their fate, without coming too close to him. The two figures in the background, standing at a safe distance, reinforce this impression.

Werner Sumowski first related this drawing to the healing of the ten lepers (which is mentioned only in the Gospel according to St Luke), and Christian Tümpel supported this view, 'for there is no doubt that Rembrandt was inspired by other versions of this theme'.

The group of Jesus and his disciples forms a rectangular block opposite the triangular composition of the group of beggars.

Pen and brush drawing; 18 × 24.7 cm.
Ca. 1652.
Berlin, Kupferstichkabinett der Staatlichen Museen.

Literature: Benesch V, no. 900 (*ca.* 1652); Slive II, no. 484 (*ca.* 1655)/Rotermund 1963, no. 171; Sumowski 1963, no. 62; Tümpel 1970, no. 76.

The light of the world

John 9 AND as *Jesus* passed by, he saw a man which was blind from *his* birth.

2 And his disciples asked him, saying, Masters, who did sin, this man, or his parents, that he was born blind?

3 Jesus answered, Neither hath this man sinned, nor his parents: but that the works of God should be made manifest in him. I must work the works of him that sent me, while it is day: the night cometh, when no man can work. As long as I am in the world, I am the light of the world.

6 When he had thus spoken, he spat on the ground, and made clay of the spittle, and he anointed the eyes of the blind man with the clay,

7 And said unto him, Go, wash in the pool of Siloam, (which is by interpretation, Sent.) He went his way therefore, and washed, and came seeing.

8 The neighbours therefore, and they which before had seen him that he was blind, said, Is not this he that sat and begged?

9 Some said, This is he: others *said*, He is like him: *but* he said, I am *he*.

10 Therefore said they unto him, How were thine eyes opened?

11 He answered and said, A man that is called Jesus made clay, and anointed mine eyes, and said unto me, Go to the pool of Siloam, and wash: and I went and washed, and I received sight.

12 Then said they unto him, Where is he? He said, I know not.

13 They brought to the Pharisees him that aforetime was blind.

14 And it was the sabbath day when Jesus made the clay, and opened his eyes.

15 Then again the Pharisees also asked him how he had received his sight. He said unto them, He put clay upon mine eyes , and I washed, and do see.

16 Therefore said some of the Pharisees, This man is not of God, because he keepeth not the sabbath day. Others said, How can a man that is a sinner do such miracles? And there was a division among them. [...]

24 Then again called they the man that was blind, and said unto him, Give God the praise: we know that this man is a sinner.

25 He answered and said, Whether he be a sinner *or no*, I know not: one thing I know, that, whereas I was blind, now I see.

26 Then said they to him again, What did he to thee? how opened he thine eyes?

27 He answered them, I have told you already, and ye did not hear: wherefore would ye hear *it* again? will ye also be his disciples?

28 Then they reviled him, and said, Thou art his disciple; but we are Moses' disciples.

29 We know that God spake unto Moses: *as for* this *fellow*, we know not from whence he is.

30 The man answered and said unto them, Why herein is a marvellous thing, that ye know not from whence he is, and *yet* he hath opened mine eyes.

31 Now we know that God heareth not sinners: but if any man be a worshipper of God, and doeth his will, him he heareth.

32 Since the world began was it not heard that any man opened the eyes of one that was born blind.

33 If this man were not of God, he could do nothing.

34 They answered and said unto him, Thou wast altogether born in sins, and dost thou teach us ? And they cast him out.

35 Jesus heard that they had cast him out; and when he had found him, he said unto him, Dost thou believe on the Son of God?

36 He answered and said, Who is he, Lord, that I might believe on him?

37 And Jesus said unto him, Thou hast both seen him, and it is he that talketh with thee.

38 And he said, Lord, I believe. And he worshipped him.

39 And Jesus said, For judgment I am come into this world, that they which see not might see; and that they which see might be made blind.

40 And *some* of the Pharisees which were with him heard these words, and said unto him, Are we blind also?

41 Jesus said unto them, If ye were blind, ye should have no sin: but now ye say, We see; therefore your sin remaineth.

As long as I am in the world, I am the light of the world.
When he had thus spoken, he spat on the ground, and made
clay of the spittle, and he anointed the eyes of the blind man
with the clay, and said unto him, Go, wash in the pool of
Siloam, (which is, by interpretation, Sent).
(John 9:5-7)

The Gospel according to St John (9:8) describes the
blind man as a beggar, seated at the entrance to the
temple, with his indispensable stick half underneath
him. As he raises his head to Jesus, full of trust, Jesus
bends down over him and touches his eyes with his
fingers. The disciples on the left attentively follow
their master's movements. In the suspicious group of
observers at the top of the steps on the right, there is
already an indication of the Pharisees' opposition and
their refusal to see the healing of the blind man as a
sign of Jesus' Messianic mission.

The composition, with an arch in the background
and a view beyond, resembles the etching *The Sermon of*
Jesus, dating from *ca.* 1652 (see p. 307). The grey wash
areas were added later by someone else.

In ancient Christian times, the healing of the blind
man was one of the miracles which was depicted
particularly frequently. The blind man, who washed
away the clay from his eyes in the pool of Siloam at
Jesus' command, so that the light returned to his eyes,
was the symbol of all those who came to believe
through the Gospels and were consequently purified
and 'enlightened' with the water of baptism. With
reference to the pool of Siloam, the first Christians
called the church where they were baptised 'the house
of enlightenment'.

Pen and brush drawing; 18 × 22.6 cm.
Ca. 1655-60.
Rotterdam, Museum Boymans-van Beuningen.

Literature: Benesch VI, no. C 92 (copy after an
unknown original, dating from *ca.* 1655-57)/Hofstede de
Groot, *Rembrandt Bijbel*, N.T.d.14; Rotermund 1963, no.
213; Sumowski 1963, no. 63.

Jesus Heals the
Blind Man

I am the resurrection and the life

John 11 NOW a certain *man* was sick, *named* Lazarus, of Bethany, the town of Mary and her sister Martha.

2 (It was *that* Mary which anointed the Lord with ointment, and wiped his feet with her hair, whose brother Lazarus was sick.)

3 Therefore his sisters sent unto him, saying, Lord, behold, he whom thou lovest is sick.

4 When Jesus heard *that*, he said, This sickness is not unto death, but for the glory of God, that the Son of God might be glorified thereby.

5 Now Jesus loved Martha, and het sister, and Lazarus.

6 When he had heard therefore that he was sick, he abode two days still in the same place where he was.

7 Then after that saith he to *his* disciples, Let us go into Judæa again.

8 *His* disciples say unto him, Master, the Jews of late sought to stone thee; and goest thou thither again?

9 Jesus answered, Are there not twelve hours in the day? If any man walk in the day, he stumbleth not, because he seeth the light of this world.

10 But if a man walk in the night, he stumbleth, because there is no light in him.

11 These things said he: and after that he saith unto them, Our friend Lazarus sleepeth; but I go, that I may awake him out of sleep.

12 Then said his disciples, Lord, if he sleep, he shall do well.

13 Howbeit Jesus spake of his death: but they thought that he had spoken of taking of rest in sleep..

14 Then said Jesus unto them plainly, Lazarus is dead.

15 And I am glad for your sakes that I was not there, to the intent ye may believe; nevertheless let us go unto him.

16 Then said Thomas, which is called Didymus, unto his fellowdisciples, Les us also go, that we may die with him.

17 Then when Jesus came, he found that he had *lain* in the grave four days already.

18 Now Bethany was nigh unto Jerusalem, about fifteen furlongs off:

19 And many of the Jews came to Martha and Mary, to comfort them concerning their brother.

20 Then Martha, as soon as she heard that Jesus was coming, went and met him: but Mary sat *still* in the house.

21 Then said Martha unto Jesus, Lord, if thou hadst been here, my brother had not died.

22 But I know, that even now, whatsoever thou wilt ask of God, God will give *it* thee.

23 Jesus saith unto her, Thy brother shall rise again.

24 Martha saith unto him, I know that he shall rise again in the resurrection at the last day.

25 Jesus said unto her, I am the resurrection, and the life: he that believeth in me, though he were dead, yet shall he live:

26 And whosoever liveth and believeth in me shall never die. Believest thou this?

27 She saith unto him, Yea, Lord: I believe that thou art the Christ, the Son of God, which should come into the world.

28 And when she had so said, she went her way, and called Mary her sister secretly, saying, The Master is come, and calleth for thee.

29 As soon as she heard *that*, she arose quickly, and came unto him.

30 Now Jesus was not yet come into the town, but was in that place where Martha met him.

31 The Jews then which were with her in the house, and comforted her, when they saw Mary, that she rose up hastily and went out, followed her, saying, She goeth unto the grave to weep there.

32 Then when mary was come where Jesus was, and saw him, she fell down at his feet, saying unto him, Lord, if thou hadst been here, my brother had not died.

33 When Jesus therefore saw her weeping, and the Jews also weeping which came with her, he groaned in the spirit, and was troubled,

34 And said, where have ye laid him? They said unto him, Lord, come and see.

35 Jesus wept.

36 Then said the Jews, Behold how he loved him!

37 And some of them said, Could not this man, which opened the eyes of the blind, have caused that even this man should not have died?

38 Jesus therefore again groaning in himself

Then when Mary was come where Jesus was, and saw him, she fell down at his feet, saying unto him, Lord, if thou hadst been here, my brother had not died.
(John 11:32)

This drawing, first published in 1963, is one of the very rare drawings from the last period of Rembrandt's life, when his drawings were characterized by broad, transparent strokes of the pen.

In the foreground, Mary lies at the feet of Jesus. Her sister Martha is kneeling beside her. Rembrandt repeatedly changed and improved this figure, particularly the position of the head and hands. The figure of a man standing over Martha was covered over and erased. Behind Jesus, there are two disciples, their heads bowed in sorrow. On the right, the composition ends with the group of Jews who had come with Mary.

The story of Martha and Mary at the feet of Jesus by the grave of Lazarus is very old, but it was rarely depicted as a subject in its own right, as Rembrandt did in this case. In the Christian art of the West up to the 12th century, the two sisters kneeling before Jesus were virtually always included in the many versions of the Raising of Lazarus. In later works depicting this miracle they became less prominent, and were usually included among the observers.

Pen and ink drawing; 17.4 × 20.8 cm.
Ca. 1662-65.
Cleveland, The Cleveland Museum of Art.

Literature: O. Benesch, 'A drawing by Rembrandt from his last years', in *The Bulletin of the Cleveland Museum of Art*, March 1963, pp. 42-45; Benesch V, no. 1068A (*ca.* 1662-65).

Martha and Mary at the Feet of Jesus

cometh to the grave. It was a cave, and a
stone lay the grave. It was a cave, and a stone
lay upon it.

39 Jesus said, Take ye away the stone. Martha,
the sister of him that was dead, saith unto
him, Lord, by this time he stinketh: for he
hath been *dead* for days.

40 Jesus saith unto her, Said I not unto thee,
that, if thou wouldest believe, thou shouldest
see the glory of God?

41 Then they took away the stone *from the
place* where the dead was laid. And Jesus lifted
up *his* eyes, and said, Father, I thank thee that
thou hast heard me.

42 And I knew that thou hearest me always:
but because of the people which stand by I
said *it*, that they may believe that thou hast
sent me.

43 And when he thus had spoken, he cried
with a loud voice, Lazarus, come forth.

44 And he that was dead came forth, bound
hand and foot with graveclothes: and his face
was bound about with a napkin. Jesus saith
unto them, Loose him, and let him go.

45 Then many of the Jews which came to
Mary, and had seen the things which Jesus
did, believed on him.

46 But some of them went their ways to the
Pharisees, and told them what things Jesus had
done.

47 Then gathered the chief priests and the
Pharisees a council, and said, What do we? for
this man doeth many miracles.

48 If we let him thus alone, all *men* will

believe in him: and the Romans shall come
and take away both our place and nation.

49 And one of them, *named* Caiaphas, being
the high priest that same year, said unto them,
Ye know nothing at all,

50 Nor consider that it is expedient for us,
that one man should die for the people, and
that the whole nation perish not.

51 And this spake he not of himself: but being
high priest that year, he prophesied that Jesus
should die for that nation;

52 And not for that nation only, but also he
should gather together in one the children of
God that were scattered abroad.

53 Then from that day forth they took
counsel together for to put him to death.

54 Jesus therefore walked no more openly
among the Jews; but went thence unto a
country near to the wilderness, into a city
called Ephraim, and there continued with his
disciples.

55 And the Jews' passover was nigh at hand:
and many went out of the country up to
Jerusalem before the passover, to purify
themselves.

56 Then sought they for Jesus, and spake
among themselves, as they stood in the
temple, What think ye, that he will not come
to the feast?

57 Now both the chief priests and the
Pharisees had given a commandment, that, if
any man knew where he were, he should shew
it, that they might take him.

---

*The Raising of
Lazarus*

*And when he thus had spoken, he cried out with a loud
voice, Lazarus, come forth. And he that was dead came
forth, bound hand and foot with grave clothes; and his face
was bound about with a napkin.*
(John 11:43-44)

This highly significant miracle of Jesus, which is
mentioned only in the Gospel according to St John,
was one of the favourite subjects of artists, both in
early Christian times and in the following centuries.
For believers, the raising of Lazarus from death was
the symbol of their own resurrection on the Last Day.
Jesus had said to Martha: 'I am the resurrection, and
the life: he that believeth in me, though he were dead,
yet shall he live' (John 11:25). Just as Jesus had raised
Lazarus, he would resurrect every believer to a new
life at the Last Judgment.

In this painting dating from *ca.* 1630, the young

Rembrandt attempted to portray the miracle as
dramatically and with as much penetrating detail as
possible. The figure of Jesus facing us stands on the
stone that has been pulled back. He raises his right
hand authoritatively and commands Lazarus to rise
from his grave 'with a loud voice'. It is as though the
dead man in his white grave clothes is waking up from
a deep sleep when he hears this voice.

The scene takes place in a sepulchre. The light
coming in from the left accentuates Jesus' raised arm,
Lazarus as he rises from the grave, and the group of
observers next to Jesus - including the sisters of
Lazarus, who look on in amazement and can hardly
believe their eyes. The light also touches on some
weapons hanging on the wall: the weapons of Lazarus,
who served in the army as a soldier, according to the
Legenda Aurea.

Panel; 93.5 × 81 cm.
Ca. 1630.
Los Angeles, Los Angeles County Museum of Art.

Literature: Bredius, no. 538; Bauch, no. 51; Gerson, no. 16; Bredius-Gerson, no. 538.

And when he thus had spoken, he cried out with a loud voice, Lazarus, come forth. And he that was dead came forth, bound hand and foot with grave clothes; and his face was bound about with a napkin.
(John 11:43-44)

This large etching dating from *ca.* 1632 is a variation on the painting reproduced on the previous page, and contains broadly the same elements. The dramatic figure of Jesus, this time viewed from the back and placed further in the foreground, dominates the work even more than in the painting, and the feelings of amazement and shock among the observers are translated into extremely pathetic gestures and facial expressions. The large number of states of this print reveal Rembrandt's constant concern to ensure that every figure is as expressive as possible.

Etching; 36.6 × 25.8 cm. Fifth state of ten.
Signed: *RHL van Rijn f.*
Ca. 1632.
Amsterdam, Rijksprentenkabinet.

Literature: Bartsch, no. 73; Hind, no. 96; Münz, no. 192; Boon, no. 85; Filedt Kok, no. B 73/Hofstede de Groot, *Rembrandt Bijbel*, N.T.e.16; Sumowski 1963, no. 64; Tümpel 1970, no. 73.

And when he thus had spoken, he cried out with a loud voice, Lazarus, come forth. And he that was dead came forth, bound hand and foot with grave clothes; and his face was bound about with a napkin.
(John 11:43-44)

For this small print dating from 1642, Rembrandt also returned to his composition on this subject dating from *ca.* 1630, but the character of the scene has completely changed. As in the earlier painting, the figure of Jesus is facing us, but he is no longer the giant performing a shocking miracle with a theatrical gesture; his figure is once again shown in human proportions, and the calm gesture with which he brings Lazarus back to life is barely perceptible. Obviously the onlookers are astonished by the miracle, but they no longer recoil in shock, as in the etching done ten years earlier. The baroque movements are replaced by an atmosphere of quiet attention.

Etching; 15 × 11.5 cm. First state of two.
Signed and dated: *Rembrandt f. 1642.*
Amsterdam, Rijksprentenkabinet.

Literature: Bartsch, no. 72; Hind, no. 198; Münz, no. 214; Boon, no. 177; Filedt Kok, no. B 72/Rotermund 1963, no. 112; Sumowski 1963, no. 65; 'Bijbelse Inspiratie', no. 39; Tümpel 1970, no. 74.

The Raising of Lazarus

The zeal of thine house hath eaten me up

John 2 13 And the Jews' passover was at hand, and Jesus went up to Jerusalem,

14 And found in the temple those that sold oxen and sheep and doves, and the changers of money sitting:

15 And when he had made a scourge of small cords, he drove them all out of the temple, and the sheep, and the oxen; and poured out the changers' money, and overthrew the tables;

16 And said unto them that sold doves, Take these things hence; maken not my Father's house an house of merchandise.

17 And his disciples remembered that it was written, The zeal of thine house hath eaten me up.

18 Then answered the Jews and said unto him, What sign shewest thou unto us, seeing that thou doest these things?

19 Jesus answered and said unto them, Destroy this temple, and in three days I will raise it up.

20 Then said the Jews, Forty and six years was this temple in building, and wilt thou rear it up in three days?

21 But spake of the temple of his body.

22 When therefore he was risen from the dead, his disciples remembered that he had said this unto them; and they believed the scripture, and the word which Jesus had said.

23 Now when he was in Jerusalem at the passover, in the feast *day*, many believed in his name, when they saw the miracles which he did.

24 But Jesus did not commit himself unto them, because he knew all *men*,

25 And needed not that any should testify of man: for he knew what was in man.

Jesus Drives the Moneychangers from the Temple

And when he had made a scourge of small cords, he drove them all out of the temple, and the sheep, and the oxen; and poured out the changers' money, and overthrew the tables; And said unto them that sold doves, Take these things hence; make not my father's house an house of merchandise.
(John 2:15-16)

In 1626, the young Rembrandt had already chosen this story as the subject of one of his very first paintings (Leningrad, The Hermitage; Bredius, no. 532), and it is not surprising that in the 1630s he returned to this forceful theme, which asks for movement, in order to depict it in his characteristic dramatic style. The scene, which moves from right to left, is an exact illustration of the description of Jesus clearing the temple given in the Gospel according to St John. The other Gospels do not mention the sheep and the oxen, and do not refer to the scourge which Jesus made to drive everyone and everything from the temple. In order to emphasize the fact that Jesus is acting in holy wrath, the halo which normally surrounds his head is now shining around Jesus' punishing hand in the centre of the composition. The priests and scribes angrily looking on in the background serve to remind us of the Jewish authorities who were hostile to Jesus and did not understand him. At the end they demand that he give them a sign to legitimize himself as a defender of God's honour.

In contrast with St John, who deliberately included this story at the beginning of his Gospel because he wished to start his account of Jesus' actions as the Messiah with a dramatic deed, the other Gospel writers, Matthew (21:12-13), Mark (11:15-18) and Luke (19:45-48), only mention the clearing of the temple after the entry into Jerusalem at the beginning of the week of the Passion. For them, the event plays an important role in the conflict which ends with the death of Jesus. This is why some series depicting different episodes from the Passion also include the scene of the clearing of the temple - as does, for example, *The Small Passion*, by Albrecht Dürer, which comprises no fewer than thirty-six small woodcuts. Rembrandt based the figure of Jesus in this etching on that print by Dürer.

During the Reformation the clearing of the temple was often seen as an image of Luther's actions in the countries of north-west Europe.

Etching; 13.6 × 16.9 cm. First state of two.
Signed and dated: *Rembrandt f. 1635.*
Amsterdam, Rijksprentenkabinet.

Literature: Bartsch, no. 69; Hind, no. 126; Münz, no. 206;
Boon, no. 114; Filedt Kok, no. B 69/Hofstede de Groot,
Rembrandt Bijbel, N.T.e.21; Rotermund 1963, no. 214;
Sumowski 1963, no. 67; Tümpel 1970, no. 89.

When they had heard *these words*, they marvelled

Matthew 22 15 Then went the Pharisees, and took counsel how they might entangle him in *his* talk.

16 And they sent out unto him their disciples with the Herodians, saying, Master, we know that thou art true, and teachest the way of God in truth, neither carest thou for any *man*: for thou regardest not the person of men.

17 Tell us therefore, What thinkest thou? Is it lawful to give tribute unto Cæsar, or not?

18 But Jesus perceived their wickedness, and said, Why tempt ye me, *ye* hypocrites?

19 Shew me the tribute money. And they brought unto him a penny.

20 And he saith unto them, Whose *is* this image and superscription?

21 They say unto him, Cæsar's. Then saith he unto them, Render therefore unto Cæsar the things which are Cæsar's: and unto God the things that are God's.

22 When they had heard *these words*, they marvelled, and left him, and went their way.

The Tribute Money

And they brought unto him a penny. And he saith unto them, Whose is this image and superscription? They say unto him, Caesar's. Then saith he unto them, Render therefore unto Caesar the things which are Caesar's, and unto God the things that are God's. When they had heard these words, they marvelled ...
(Matthew 22:19-22)

Jesus' answer to the trick question posed by the Herodians has always provoked admiration. If he had denied the taxation obligation, he would have come into conflict with the Roman authorities. If he had simply declared that man was obliged to pay taxes to the Emperor, he would have lost his reputation as the Messiah among the people because he was recognizing a temporal authority - and in fact, an authority exercised by a foreign tyrant.

According to the story in the Gospel, the scene takes place as a series of arguments between Jesus and the members of the Jewish High Council. These discussions are held in the temple, where Jesus gives instruction to the people every day after his entry into Jerusalem (cf. Matthew 21:23 and Luke 20:1). Therefore Rembrandt was justified in showing this scene, which had only been regularly depicted since the 16th century, inside the temple rather than in the open air, as several of his predecessors had done. The beautiful composition of the etching, dating from the middle of the 1630s, bears a close resemblance to Rembrandt's small painting dating from 1629 (Ottawa, National Gallery of Canada; Bredius, no. 536) which treats the subject in the same spirit, but in a vertical composition. Jesus' raised right hand indicates his answer: 'Render therefore unto Caesar the things that are Caesar's; and unto God the things that are God's'. Rembrandt expressed the astonishment provoked by these words among his interlocutors in a masterful way. He makes a brief reference to the Pharisees mentioned at the beginning of the story, on whose behalf the trick question was put to Jesus, by showing a group of observers expectantly awaiting the answer in the archway in the background on the left.

Etching; 7.3 × 10.3 cm. First state of two.
Ca. 1635.
Amsterdam, Rijksprentenkabinet.

Literature: Bartsch, no. 68; Hind, no. 124; Münz, no. 200;
Boon, no. 110; Filedt Kok, no. B 68/Rotermund 1963,
no. 183; Sumowski 1963, no. 68; Tümpel 1970, no. 90.

Ye shall be hated of all nations for my name's sake

Matthew 24 AND Jesus went out, and departed from the temple: and his disciples came to *him* for to shew him the buildings of the temple.

2 And Jesus said unto them, See ye not all these things? verily I say unto you, There shall not be left here one stone upon another, that shall not be thrown down.

3 And as he sat upon the mount of Olives, the disciples came unto him privately, saying, Tell us, when shall these things be? and what *shall be* the sign of thy coming, and of the end of the world?

4 And Jesus answered and said unto them, Take heed that no man deceive you.

5 For many shall come in my name, saying, I am Christ; and shall deceive many.

6 And ye shall hear of wars and rumours of wars: see that ye be not troubled: for all *these things* must come to pass, but the end is not yet.

7 For nation shall rise against nation, and kingdom against kingdom: and there shall be famines, and pestilences, and earthquakes, in divers places.

8 All these *are* the beginning of sorrows.

9 Then shall they deliver you up to be afflicted, and shall kill you: and ye shall be hated of all nations for my name's sake.

10 And then shall many be offended, and shall betray one another, and shall hate one another.

11 And many false prophets shall rise, and shall deceive many.

12 And because iniquity shall abound, the love of many shall wax cold.

13 But he that shall endure unto the end, the same shall be saved.

14 And this gospel of the kingdom shall be preached in all the world for a witness unto all nations; and then shall the end come.

15 When ye therefore shall see the abomination of desolation, spoken of by Daniel the prophet, stand in the holy place, (whoso readeth, let him understand:)

16 Then let them which be in Judæa flee into the mountains:

17 Let him which is on the housetop not come down to take any thing out of his house:

18 Neither let him which is in the field return back to take his clothes.

19 And woe unto them that are with child, and to them that give suck in those days!

20 But pray ye that your flight be not in the winter, neither on the sabbath day:

21 For then shall be great tribulation, such as was not since the beginning of the world to this time, no, nor ever shall be.

22 And except those days should be shortened, there should no flesh be saved: but for the elect's sake those days shall be shortened.

23 Then if any man shall say unto you, Lo, here *is* Christ, or there; believe *it* not.

24 For there shall arise false Christs, and false prophets, and shall shew great signs and wonders; insomuch that, if *it were* possible, they shall deceive the very elect.

25 Behold, I have told you before.

26 Wherefore if they shall say unto you, Behold, he is in the desert; go not forth: behold, *he is* in the secret chambers; believe *it* not.

27 For as the lightning cometh out of the east, and shineth even unto the west; so shall also the coming of the Son of man be.

28 For wheresoever the carcase is, there will the eagles be gathered together.

29 Immediately after the tribulation of those days shall the sun be darkened, and the moon shall not give her light, and the stars shall fall from heaven, and the powers of the heavens shall be shaken:

30 And then shall appear the sign of the Son of man in heaven: and then shall all the tribes of the earth mourn, and they shall see the Son of man coming in the clouds of heaven with power and great glory.

31 And he shall send his angels with a great sound of a trumpet, and they shall gather together his elect from the winds, from one end of heaven to the other.

32 Now learn a parable of the fig tree; When his branch is yet tender, and putteth forth leaves, ye know that summer *is* nigh:

33 So likewise ye, when ye shall see all these things, know that it is near, *even* at the doors.

34 Verily I say unto you, This generation shall not pass, till all these things be fulfilled.

35 Heaven and earth shall pass away, but my words shall not pass away.

36 But of that day and hour knoweth no *man*, no, not the angels of heaven, but my Father only.

It is difficult to be sure which story in the Gospels is illustrated by this large drawing, one of Rembrandt's most elaborate known drawings. Because of the young man with closed eyes in the centre of the circle, some critics interpreted the scene as the Raising of Lazarus and others as the healing of the boy possessed by a spirit (Mark 9:14-29). However, there is no doubt that this figure is actually the Apostle John, the youngest of the twelve, in a characteristic pose in line with Christian tradition as an introverted and spiritual young man and the most profound Gospel writer. St Augustine wrote that his eyes had seen the inner and eternal light. In the catalogue of the exhibition 'Bijbelse Inspiratie', the drawing was first related to the passage from the Gospel according to St Matthew, which begins with the words: 'And as he sat upon the Mount of Olives, the disciples came unto him privately, saying, Tell us, when shall these things be? And what shall be the sign of thy coming and of the end of the world?' (Matthew 24:3). The sharp contrasts between light and dark give the drawing a mysterious and

Jesus Surrounded by his Disciples

dramatic character, which accords perfectly with the threatening content of this speech, and the serious nature of the warnings given by Jesus is reflected in the faces of his disciples. The trunk and branches of the olive trees are visible in the dark background on the left.

The drawing is signed and dated 1634, and it seems to have been done as a work in its own right, but it is also quite possible that it was intended as a preliminary study for a painting or an etching (which was never executed), a night-time scene with strong light and dark effects in the style of the angel appearing to the shepherds, which dates from the same year (see p. 229).

Black and red chalk drawing with pen and brush, elaborated in various colours; 35.5 × 47.6 cm.
Signed and dated: *Rembrandt f. 1634.*
Haarlem, Teylers Museum.

Literature: Benesch I, no. 89; Slive I, no. 175; Haak, p. 17/ Rotermund 1963, no. 184; 'Bijbelse Inspiratie', no. 108.

He which had received the one talent

Matthew 25 14 For *the kingdom of heaven is* as a man travelling into a far country, *who* called his own servants, and delivered unto them his goods.

15 And unto one he gave five talents, to another two, and to another one; to every man according to his several ability; and straightway took his journey.

16 Then he that had received the five talents went and traded with the same, and made *them* other five talents.

17 And likewise he that *had received* two, he also gained other two.

18 But he that had received one went and digged in the earth, and hid his lord's money.

19 After a long time the lord of those servants cometh, and reckoneth with them.

20 And so he that had received five talents come and brought other five talents, saying, Lord, thou deliveredst unto my five talents: behold, I have gained beside them five talents more.

21 His lord said unto him, Well done, *thou* good and faithful servant: thou hast been faithful over a few things, I will make thee ruler over many things: enter thou into the joy of thy lord.

22 He also that had received two talents came and said, Lord, thou deliveredst unto me two talents: behold, I have gained two other talents beside them.

23 His lord said unto him, Well done, good and faithful servant; thou hast been faithful over a few things, I will make thee ruler over many things: enter thou into the joy of thy lord.

24 Then he which had received the one talent came and said, Lord, I knew thee that thou art an hard man, reaping where thou hast not sown, and gathering where thou hast not strawed:

25 And I was afraid, and went and hid thy talent in the earth: lo, *there* thou hast *that is* thine.

26 His lord answered and said unto him, *Thou* wicked and slothful servant, thou knewest that I reap where I sowed not, and gather where I have not strawed:

27 Thou oughtest therefore to have put my money to the exchangers, and *then* at my coming I should have received mine own with usury.

28 Take therefore the talent from him, and give *it* unto him which hath ten talents.

29 For unto every one that hath shall be given, and he shall have abundance: but from him that hath not shall be taken away even that which he hath.

30 And cast ye the unprofitable servant into outer darkness: there shall be weeping and gnashing of teeth.

The Lazy Servant Before his Master

Then he which had received the one talent came and said, Lord, I knew thee that thou art an hard man, reaping where thou has not sown, and gathering where thou hast not strawed: And I was afraid, and went and hid thy talent in the earth: lo, there thou hast that is thine.
(Matthew 25:24-25)

Relying on his exceptional skill in imagining people's attitudes in a given situation, Rembrandt shows the moment at which the lazy and fearful servant, who realizes he has failed his master, takes out the talent entrusted to him to give it back to his master, unused. He explains his conduct by appealing to his master's hardness and uncommon greed. His dissatisfied master's dark look bodes ill. Meanwhile, the bookkeeper, peering at a voluminous cash book, pretends not to listen. The contemporary furnishings, with a Dutch fireplace on the right, are so simple and basic that they do not detract in any way from the timeless significance of this scene.

The drawing, which dates from the beginning of the 1650s, is the only version of this parable, which can also be found in the Gospel according to St Luke in a slightly different form as the parable of the ten pounds (19:11-27).

Pen and ink drawing; 17.3 × 21.8 cm.
Ca. 1652.
Paris, The Louvre.

Literature: Benesch V, no. 910 (*ca.* 1652); Slive I, no. 152
(*ca.* 1652)/Hofstede de Groot, *Rembrandt Bijbel*,
N.T.d.20; Rotermund 1963, no. 193.

This woman was taken in adultery

John 8 2 And early in the morning he came again into the temple, and all the people came unto him; and he sat down, and taught them.

3 And the scribes and Pharisees brought unto him a woman taken in adultery; and when they had set her in the midst,

4 They say unto him, Master, this woman was taken in adultery, in the very act.

5 Now Moses in the law commanded us, that such should be stoned: but what sayest thou?

6 This they said, tempting him, that they might have to accuse him. But Jesus stooped down, and with *his* finger wrote on the ground, *as though he heard them not.*

7 So when they continued asking him, he lifted up himself, and said unto them, He that is without sin among you, let him first cast a stone at her.

8 And again he stooped down, and wrote on the ground.

9 And they which heard *it,* being convicted by *their own* conscience, went out one by one, beginning at the eldest, *even* unto the last: and Jesus was left alone, and the woman standing in the midst.

10 When Jesus had lifted up himself, and saw none but the woman, he said unto her, Woman, where are those thine accusers? hath no man condemned thee?

11 She said, No man, Lord. And Jesus said unto her, Neither do I condemn thee: go, and sin no more.

Jesus and the Adulterous Woman

And the scribes and Pharisees brought unto him a woman taken in adultery; and when they set her in the midst, they say unto him, Master, this woman was taken in adultery, in the very act. Now Moses in the law commanded us, that such should be stoned: but what sayest thou?
(John 8:3-5)

In his first and most famous version of this story, which had been a favourite subject with artists since the late Middle Ages, Rembrandt painted in detail the introduction to the clever argument that Jesus puts to his opponents. At the top of the wide stairs which lead into the temple, the observer sees a Pharisee dressed in dark clothes, who turns to Jesus, accusingly pointing at the woman who has been brought into the temple, and on whom the attention is focused as she kneels in the light. Apart from that one Pharisee, no one in the beautifully dressed group makes any movement. Aware of his mildness towards sinners, the opponents are counting on Jesus to let the woman go, so that they can discredit him with the law of Moses. There is great tension as they await his answer, for the rabbi from Nazareth will have to show his hand.

Meanwhile, a religious ritual is taking place in the background of the soaring architecture of the temple, in the presence of the High Priest who is sitting on a richly decorated throne.

It is quite likely that Rembrandt deliberately did this painting, dating from 1644, in the same finely detailed style as *The Song of Simeon*, dating from 1631 (see p. 267). In fact, there are many similarities with this work, including its structure and the use of light. Nevertheless, the development in the artist's work in the intervening years is evident. The composition as a whole is much calmer, the colours are richer, and the arrangement of the figures is more comprehensible.

Panel; 83.8 × 65.4 cm.
Signed and dated: *Rembrandt f. 1644.*
London, National Gallery.

Literature: Bredius, no. 566; Bauch, no. 72; Gerson, no. 208; Bredius-Gerson, no. 566/Hofstede de Groot, *Rembrandt Bijbel*, N.T.p.14; Sumowski 1963, no. 47.

Jesus and the Adulterous Woman

But Jesus stooped down, and with his finger wrote on the ground.
(John 8:6)

A number of drawings show that during the second half of the 1650s Rembrandt was again intensely concerned with this subject. In the sketch reproduced above, he shows the moment when Jesus allows the Pharisees and scribes to believe that he has been tempted to answer their question by writing on the ground with his finger. Most of them are too curious to wait patiently until he has finished writing.

It is striking how Rembrandt managed to depict this simple yet lively scene, using predominantly straight lines. The composition was probably inspired by an engraving after Pieter Bruegel, which depicts the same moment in a comparable manner. It must be assumed that Rembrandt was familiar with this engraving, as his inventory of 1656 mentions a book full of prints by Bruegel the Elder (Hofstede de Groot, *Urkunden* 169, no. 204).

Pen and ink drawing; 18.9 × 24.8 cm.
Ca. 1658-59.
Stockholm, Nationalmuseum.

Literature: Benesch V, no. 1038 (*ca.* 1658-59); Slive I, no. 229 (*ca.* 1655)/Rotermund 1963, no. 211.

So when they continued asking him, he lifted up himself, and said unto them, He that is without sin amongst you, let him first cast the stone at her.
(John 8:7)

This drawing, in which the contours are even more rigid and the forms even starker than in the last sketch, is on the back of an invitation for a funeral on 14 May 1659, and was probably done shortly after that date. On a strip of paper attached to the bottom of the drawing, Rembrandt wrote: 'The scribe was in such a hurry to trick Christ in his answer that he could not wait for the answer'.

This caption - one of the rare occasions on which Rembrandt wrote anything about his work - shows that the drawing is related to the verse quoted above, the turning point in the story: while the impatient scribes and Pharisees urge him to give an answer, Jesus has drawn himself up to silence his questioners once and for all. The fact that the moment shown here is not the same as that depicted in the painting dating from

1644, but follows the moment in the drawing now in Stockholm reproduced on the previous page, is also clear from the scene itself: on Jesus' left, one of the disciples is trying to decipher what his master has just written on the ground.

The composition is reminiscent of the main group in the painting in London, but it also bears a strong resemblance to the etching *The Sermon of Jesus* (p. 307), dating from *ca.* 1652.

Pen and brush drawing; 17 × 20.2 cm.
Red and grey wash added later by someone else.
Ca. 1659-60.
Munich, Staatliche Graphische Sammlung.

Literature: Benesch V, no. 1047 (*ca.* 1659-60); Slive II, no. 442; Haak, no. 89 (*ca.* 1659-60).

*Jesus and the
Adulterous Woman*

I have given you an example

John 13   NOW before the feast of the passover, when Jesus knew that his hour was come that he should depart out of this world unto the Father, having loved his own which were in the world, he loved them unto the end.

2 And supper being ended, the devil having now put into the heart of Judas Iscariot, Simon's *son,* to betray him;

3 Jesus knowing that the Father had given all things into his hands, and that he was come from God, and went to God;

4 He riseth from supper, and laid aside his garments; and took a towel, and girded himself.

5 After that he poureth water into a bason, and began to wash the disciples' feet, and to wipe *them* with the towel wherewith he was girded.

6 Then cometh he to Simon Peter: and Peter saith unto him, Lord, dost thou wash my feet?

7 Jesus answered and said unto him, What I do thou knowest not now; but thou shalt know hereafter.

8 Peter said unto him, Thou shalt never wash my feet. Jesus answered him, If I wash thee not, thou hast no part with me.

9 Simon Peter saith unto him, Lord, not my feet only, but also *my* hands and *my* head.

10 Jesus saith to him, He that is washed needeth not save to wash *his* feet, but is clean every whit: and ye are clean, but not all.

11 For he knew who should betray him; therefore said he, Ye are not all clean.

12 So after he had washed their feet, and had taken his garments, and was set down again, he said unto them, Know ye what I have done to you?

13 Ye call me Master and Lord: and ye say well; for *so* I am.

14 If I then, *your* Lord and Master, have washed your feet; ye also ought to wash one another's feet.

15 For I have given you an example, that ye should do as I have done to you.

The Washing of the Feet

Peter saith unto him, Thou shalt never wash my feet. Jesus answered him, If I wash thee not, thou hast no part with me. Simon Peter saith unto him, Lord, not my feet only, but also my hands and my head.
(John 13:8-9)

The story of Jesus washing his disciples' feet is found only in the Gospel according to St John, where Jesus' example of loving service is directly seen in the dark context of Judas' plan to betray his master, thus indicating that the events leading up to his death on the Cross have already commenced.

Like virtually all the depictions of this story, Rembrandt's concise drawing, dating from the middle of the 1650s, is basically concerned with the washing of Peter's feet. The tense attitude of the perfectly characterized apostle as he submits to being served by his master shows that he initially protested against it. The composition forms a right-angled triangle, combining the firmly but simply sketched figures in a single group in which the figure of Jesus sitting on his haunches is the focal point.

Rembrandt apparently also did a painting of Jesus washing his disciples' feet. Two 17th-century inventories reveal that in 1660 Abraham Jacobsz Greeven owned a small painting by Rembrandt of Christ washing his disciples' feet, and in 1678 it was owned by Harmen Becker - both of these were in Amsterdam.

Pen and ink drawing; 15.6 × 22 cm.
Ca. 1655.
Amsterdam, Rijksprentenkabinet.

Literature: Benesch V, no. 931 (*ca.* 1653); Slive I, no. 238 (*ca.* 1655); Haak, no. 77 (*ca.* 1653-55)/Rotermund 1963, no. 215; Sumowski 1963, no. 71; 'Bijbelse Inspiratie', no. 107.

Verily I say unto you, that one of you shall betray me

20 Now when the even was come, he sat down with the twelve.

21 And as they did eat, he said, Verily I say unto you, that one of you shall betray me.

22 And they were exceeding sorrowful, and began every one of them to say unto him, Lord, it is I?

23 And he answered and said, He that dippeth *his* hand with me in the dish, the same shall betray me.

24 The Son of man goeth as it is written of him: but woe unto that man by whom the Son of man is betrayed! it had been good for that man if he had not been born.

25 Then Judas, which betrayed him, answered and said, Master, is it I? He said unto him, Thou hast said.

26 And as they were eating, Jesus took bread, and blessed *it*, and brake *it* and gave *it* to the disciples, and said, Take, eat; this is my body.

27 And he took the cup, and gave thanks, and gave *it* to them, saying, Drink ye all of it;

28 For this is my blood of the new testament, which is shed for many for the remission of sins.

29 But I say unto you, I will not drink henceforth of this fruit of the vine, until that day when I drink it new with you in my Father's kingdom.

30 And when they had sung an hymn, they went out into the mount of Olives.

The Last Supper

And as they did eat, he said, Verily I say unto you, That one of you shall betray me. And they were exceeding sorrowful, and began every one of them to say unto him, Lord, is it I? (Matthew 26:21-22)

From the Middle Ages the theme of most depictions of the Last Supper was not so much the institution of the Holy Supper, but rather Jesus' announcement of Judas' betrayal. The reaction of the disciples to their master's shocking declaration gave artists an opportunity of portraying a greater variation in the positions and gestures of the thirteen figures at the table. When the depiction of the Last Supper was part of a Passion series, the tragedy of that moment was in harmony with the content of the following scenes from the story of the Passion. The art of the Counter-Reformation once again emphasized the sacrament of the Eucharist.

Rembrandt did not produce his own version of the Last Supper. His only known works are a number of studies after Leonardo da Vinci's *The Last Supper*, which were based on an early 16th-century engraving inspired by the famous fresco in the Santa Maria delle Grazie in Milan. The studies date from *ca.* 1635, and subsequently the influence of this dialogue with Leonardo regularly recurred in Rembrandt's work.

In the studies in red chalk shown here, the twelve apostles are rhythmically grouped in twice two interrelated groups of three, on either side of Jesus, just as in Leonardo da Vinci's work. The real subject is the consternation which has arisen among the disciples when Jesus predicts that one among them will betray him. Judas is the figure withdrawing with a moneybag, and together with Peter and John he forms the group of three on Jesus' right hand.

In this drawing there are actually two superimposed drawings. The first, a fairly faithful copy of the above-mentioned engraving, carefully executed in thin lines, can still be clearly identified in the figure of Jesus and the group of three apostles on his left. Later, Rembrandt drastically altered the drawing. He simplified most of the figures and added a canopy above Jesus and the group of apostles on his left. He also changed Jesus' position. The drawing is now dominated by the high canopy which is raised against the back wall, just to the right of centre, so that the initially classical symmetry of the picture changes into an asymmetrical baroque composition. The effects of this change can also be seen in Rembrandt's etching dating from 1654, showing the related theme of the meal in Emmaus (see p. 428). The risen Lord, clearly inspired by the Christ figure in Leonardo da Vinci's *The Last Supper*, is again seated at a table under a similar canopy, though this time in the centre of a composition which is symmetrical.

Drawing in red chalk; 36.5 × 47.5 cm.
Signed (bottom right): *Rembrant f.*
Ca. 1635.
New York, The Metropolitan Museum of Art (Robert Lehman Collection).

Literature: Benesch II, no. 443 (*ca.* 1635); Slive I, no. 100 (*ca.* 1635); Haak, no. 16 (*ca.* 1635)/Rotermund 1963, no. 216; Sumowski 1963, no. 70; Joseph Ganter, *Rembrandt und die Verwandlung klassischer Formen*, Berne 1964, pp. 36 *et seq.*

My soul is exceeding sorrowful, even unto death

Matthew 26 31 Then saith Jesus unto them, All ye shall be offended because of me this night: for it is written, I will smite the shepherd, and the sheep of the flock shall be scattered abroad.

32 But after I am risen again, I will go before you into Galilee.

33 Peter answered and said unto him, Though all *men* shall be offended because of thee, *yet* will I never be offended.

34 Jesus said unto him, Verily I say unto thee, That this night, before the cock crow, thou shalt deny me thrice.

35 Peter said unto him, Though I should die with thee, yet will I not deny thee. Likewise also said all the disciples.

36 Then cometh Jesus with them unto a place called Gethsemane, and saith unto the disciples, Sit ye here, while I go and pray yonder.

37 And he took with him Peter and the two sons of Zebedee, and began to be sorrowful and very heavy.

38 Then saith he unto them, My soul is exceeding sorrowful, even unto death: tarry ye here, and watch with me.

39 And he went a little farther, and fell on his face, and prayed, saying, O my Father, if it be possible, let this cup pass from me: nevertheless not as I will, but as thou *wilt*.

40 And he cometh unto the disciples, and findeth them asleep, and saith unto Peter, What, could ye not watch with me one hour?

41 Watch and pray, that ye enter not into temptation: the spirit indeed *is* willing, but the flesh *is* weak.

42 He went away again the second time, and prayed, saying, O my Father, if this cup may not pass away from me, except I drink it, thy will be done.

43 And he came and found them asleep again: for their eyes were heavy.

44 And he left them, and went away again, and prayed the third time, saying the same words.

45 Then cometh he to his disciples, and saith unto them, Sleep on now, and take *your* rest: behold, the hour is at hand, and the Son of man is betrayed into the hands of sinners.

46 Rise, let us be going: behold, he is at hand that doth betray me.

Jesus in Gethsemane *And he went a little farther, and fell on his face, and prayed, saying, O my Father, if it be possible, let this cup pass from me: nevertheless not as I will, but as thou wilt. (Matthew 26:39)*

The way in which Rembrandt expressed Jesus' mortal despair in this scene makes this small print, dating from the second half of the 1650s, a high point in his etchings. The scene is set on the Mount of Olives in the Garden of Gethsemane, just outside Jerusalem. In the background, by the light of the full moon, which is partially concealed behind a veil of dark clouds, the sinister silhouette of a circular tower of a fortress rises up above the city walls. While Jesus wrestles with his fear, supported by an angel, Peter and the two sons of Zebedee quietly sleep at the foot of the rock on which he is kneeling. Meanwhile, the crowd which is to capture Jesus is already approaching through the gate in the distance on the left. Thus the scene is not a separate episode, but is part of the series of events which will end with the Crucifixion on Golgotha.

In the traditional method of depicting this scene, Rembrandt did not base this etching only on the similar details given in the Gospels according to St Matthew and St Mark, but to a significant extent also relied on the more concise version in the Gospel according to St Luke. Unlike Matthew and Mark, Luke does not mention that Jesus took only the three

privileged disciples, Peter, James and John, to the place where he went to pray, nor that he sought their support in vain and prayed three times. On the other hand, the angel which supports Jesus is mentioned only in the Gospel according to St Luke. After relating Jesus' words in prayer to his Father, the Gospel continues: 'And there appeared an angel unto him from heaven, strengthening him. And being in agony he prayed more earnestly: and his sweat was as it were great drops of blood falling down to the ground' (Luke 22:43-44). It is clear that this passage from the Gospel according to St Luke is central in this etching.

The preliminary study which is now in Hamburg (Benesch V, no. 899) shows that initially Rembrandt intended to depict a traditional cup of sorrows next to the angel. The origin of this motif, which had been popular since the 14th century, lies in Jesus' prayer, which was quoted above, in which he describes his suffering as a cup from which he must drink. Normally this cup is held out to Jesus by an angel descending from heaven, who sometimes also carries the Cross and the other symbols of the Passion. Rembrandt's much more natural interpretation of the Gospel story is based on a style of representation introduced in the 16th century, which does not incorporate the symbolically intended cup of sorrows. Jesus has turned his gaze inward and fights a hopeless struggle against himself, while the angel supports and consoles him.

Etching; 11.1 × 8.4 cm. Only state.
Signed and dated: *Rembrandt f. 165-.*
Ca. 1657.
Amsterdam, Rijksprentenkabinet.

Literature: Bartsch, no. 75; Hind, no. 293; Münz, no. 225
(*ca.* 1653); Boon, no. 275; Filedt Kok, no. B 75/Hofstede
de Groot, *Rembrandt Bijbel*, N.T.e.22; Rotermund 1963,
no. 217; Sumowski 1963, no. 72; 'Bijbelse Inspiratie', no.
41; Tümpel 1968, pp. 96-102; Tümpel 1970, no. 92.

Jesus Finds the Apostles Asleep

And he cometh unto the disciples, and findeth them asleep, and saith unto Peter, What! could ye not watch with me one hour?
(Matthew 26:40)

As he is facing death, Jesus seeks the support of his disciples three times, and each time finds that they are asleep. Rembrandt used this part of the story of Gethsemane several times in his drawings, though it was rarely depicted by other artists. In this drawing dating from *ca.* 1655, we see Jesus returning to Peter and the two sons of Zebedee for the first time, broken and overcome by fear. When his master speaks to him, Peter seems to recoil in shock at his appearance. The sword, which is invariably shown in this context, and which he will use to attack the servant of the High Priest, can also be seen in the etching on the previous page, with the hilt protruding just above his right arm.

Pen and brush drawing; 17.8 × 24.3 cm.
Ca. 1655.
Berlin, Kupferstichkabinett der Staatlichen Museen.

Literature: Benesch V, no. 940 (*ca.* 1654-55); Slive I, no. 33 (*ca.* 1655)/Hofstede de Groot, *Rembrandt Bijbel*, N.T.d.24; Rotermund 1963, no. 219; Tümpel 1970, no. 93.

And he came and found them asleep again: for their eyes were heavy. And he left them, and went away again, and prayed the third time, saying the same words. (Matthew 26:43-44)

Everything indicates that in this drawing, which was not done much earlier or later than the previous one, Rembrandt wished to depict the moment at which Jesus returned to the three sleeping disciples for the second time. His gesture expresses both disappointment and resignation, and he does not attempt to awaken any of his disciples. In the skilfully composed landscape where the scene is set, the Mount of Olives is shown on the right, while the city of Jerusalem can be seen in the background.

Pen and brush drawing; 18.3 × 28 cm.
Ca. 1655.
Williamstown (Mass.), Sterling and Francine Clark Art Institute.

Literature: Benesch V, no. 941 (*ca.* 1654); Slive I, no. 258 (*ca.* 1655).

Jesus Finds the Apostles Asleep

Are ye come out as against a thief

Matthew 26

47 And while he yet spake, lo, Judas, one of the twelve, came, and with him a great multitude with swords and staves, from the chief priests and elders of the people.

48 Now he that betrayed him gave them a sign, saying, Whomsoever I shall kiss, that same is he: hold him fast.

49 And forthwith he came to Jesus, and said, Hail, master; and kissed him.

50 And Jesus said unto him, Friend, wherefore art thou come? then came they, and laid hands on Jesus, and took him.

51 And, behold, one of them which were with Jesus stretched out *his* hand, and drew his sword, and struck a servant of the high priest's, and smote off his ear.

52 Then said Jesus unto him, Put up again thy sword into his place: for all they that take the sword shall perish with the sword.

53 Thinkest thou that I cannot now pray to my Father, and he shall presently give me more than twelve legions of angels?

54 But how then shall the scriptures be fulfilled, that thus it must be?

55 In that same hour said Jesus to the multitudes, Are ye come out as against a thief with swords and staves for to take me? I sat daily with you teaching in the temple, and ye laid no hold on me.

56 But all this was done, that the scriptures of the prophets might be fulfilled. Then all the disciples forsook him, and fled.

Jesus is Arrested

Then came they, and laid hands on Jesus, and took him. And, behold, one of them which were with Jesus stretched out his hand, and drew his sword, and struck a servant of the High Priest, and smote off his ear.
(Matthew 26:50-51)

The Gospel according to St John reveals that it was Peter who used his sword, and that the High Priest's servant who was struck was called Malchus (John 18:10). The incident is described in all four Gospels, and therefore Peter's deed is seldom left out in depictions of Jesus' arrest. In Rembrandt's drawing the skirmish takes place in the foreground on the right. This drawing, one of the best examples of Rembrandt's strong style - which is devoid of any superfluous decoration - in the second half of the 1650s, shows the moment just after the kiss of Judas. Threatened and surrounded by the crowd sent to capture him, Jesus commands Peter to cease resisting and refers to the power of the Father who would immediately send him 'more than twelve legions of angels' if he asked for them, 'But how then shall the Scriptures be fulfilled, that thus it must be?'

The stories in the Gospels clearly indicate that by the time of his arrest Jesus had regained his former self-control and decisiveness. To express this, Rembrandt strongly emphasized the majestic quality of Jesus' personality, both in this drawing and in one on the same subject done slightly earlier (Benesch V, no. 1022). Jesus, and not the armed men, dominates the scene of confusion. 'But this is your hour, and the power of darkness' are the last words of Jesus' speech to the crowd in the Gospel according to St Luke. In the background on the right Rembrandt has indicated the disciples fleeing from the scene.

Pen and brush drawing; 20.5 × 29.8 cm.
Ca. 1655-60.
Stockholm, Nationalmuseum.

Literature: Benesch V, no. 1044 (*ca.* 1659-60); Slive I, no. 230 (*ca.* 1655-60)/Hofstede de Groot, *Rembrandt Bijbel*, N.T.d.25.

Woman, I know him not

Luke 22 54 Then took they him, and led *him*, and brought him into the high priest's house. And Peter followed afar off.

55 And when they had kindled a fire in the midst of the hall, and were set down together, Peter sat down among them.

56 But a certain maid beheld him as he sat by the fire, and earnestly looked upon him, and said, This man was also with him.

57 And he denied him, saying, Woman, I know him not.

58 And after a little while another saw him, and said, Thou art also of them. And Peter said, Man, I am not.

59 And about the space of one hour after another confidently affirmed, saying, Of a truth this *fellow* also was with him: for he is a Galiæan.

60 And Peter said, Man, I know not what thou sayest. And immediately, while he yet spake, the cock crew.

61 And the lord turned, and looked upon Peter. And Peter remembered the word of the Lord, how he had said unto him, Before the cock crow, thou shalt deny me thrice.

62 And Peter went out, and wept bitterly.

Peter Denies Christ In this monumental night scene painted in 1660, with its mysterious chiaroscuro, Rembrandt combined the three denials of Peter in a single scene, based on the description in the Gospel according to St Luke. In order to concentrate the successive episodes of the story in a single moment, he was forced to show the three individuals who recognized Peter as one of Jesus' disciples together with the apostle at the same time, although they appear separately in the account in the Bible.

Dressed in a voluminous cloak, Peter, who had followed his master to the High Priest's house after he had been captured, is unexpectedly stopped by a young woman who carefully observes his face by the light of a candle, and then says, 'This man was also with him' (verse 56). The helmeted soldier corroborates this and says, 'Thou art also of them' (verse 58). Then another soldier also starts to interfere. Waiting to take a drink from his wine flask, he takes a careful look at the impressive figure opposite him and declares: 'Of a truth, this fellow also was with him; for he is a Galilean' (verse 59). Unexpectedly faced with three pairs of questioning eyes, Peter denies them and then tries to avoid the threatening danger with an evasive answer, 'Man, I know not what thou sayest' (verse 60). In the background the Lord, standing before Caiaphas with his hands bound together, turns round to his disciple (verse 61), realizing that his prediction has come true. This scene, where the diagonal line of the composition comes to an end, does not merely intensify the dramatic tension. It also serves as a narrative element which, referring back to the previous capture of Jesus and anticipating his sentence by the high court, places the tragic note of Peter's denial in the context of the larger tragedy of the Passion.

During the first half of the 17th century, the theme was particularly popular with followers of the Italian painter, Caravaggio, because of the opportunity provided in the story for the use of exciting light effects. A number of details in Rembrandt's painting suggest that he was familiar with an engraving after one of the many depictions of this subject by the Antwerp follower of Caravaggio, Gerard Seghers, dating from between 1620 and 1628.

Canvas; 154 × 169 cm.
Signed and dated: *Rembrandt 1660*.
Amsterdam, Rijksmuseum.

Literature: Bredius, no. 594; Bauch, no. 92; Gerson, no. 353; Bredius-Gerson, no. 594/Hofstede de Groot, *Rembrandt Bijbel*, N.T.p.20; H.E. van Gelder, *Rembrandt, Saul en David, Petrus verloochent Christus* (Rembrandt, Saul and David, Peter Denies Christ), Leiden 1948; Rotermund 1963, p. 262; Sumowski 1963, no. 77.

He hath spoken blasphemy

Matthew 26 59 Now the chief priests, and elders, and all the council, sought false witness against Jesus, to put him to death;

60 But found none: yea, though many false witnesses came, *yet* found they none. At the last came two false witnesses,

61 And said, This *fellow* said, I am able to destroy the temple of God, and to build it in three days.

62 And the high priest arose, and said unto him, Answerest thou nothing? what *is it which* these witness against thee?

63 But Jesus held his peace. And the high priest answered and said unto him, I adjure thee by the living God, that thou tell us whether thou be the Christ, the Son of God.

64 Jesus saith unto him, Thou hast said: nevertheless I say unto you, Hereafter shall ye see the Son of man sitting on the right hand of power, and coming in the clouds of heaven.

65 Then the high priest rent his clothes, saying, He hath spoken blasphemy; what further need have we of witnesses? behold, now ye have heard his blasphemy.

66 What think ye? They answered and said, He is guilty of death.

67 Then did they spit in his face, and buffeted him; and others smote *him* with the palms of their hands.

68 Saying, Prophesy unto us, thou Christ, Who is he that smote thee?

Jesus Before Caiaphas

Then did they spit in his face, and buffeted him; and others smote him with the palms of their hands, saying, Prophecy unto us, thou Christ, Who is he that smote thee?
(Matthew 26:67-68)

When artists depicted the trial in their series of the Passion, they usually chose the moment at which the High Priest is sitting in his chair or jumping up, and rents his clothes in indignation at Jesus' blasphemous answer that he is actually the Christ, the Son of God. Anticipating the final scene, it is also customary to show a soldier striking the bound Jesus in the face.

In this drawing Rembrandt deals with the last scene from the story. Caiaphas has pronounced his judgment and the sentence is passed: 'He is guilty of death.' A hand is raised, ready to strike, in front of Jesus' face. One of the guards takes hold of him: 'Prophecy unto us, thou Christ, who is he that smote thee?' The man who points at Jesus and speaks to the High Priest serves as another reference to the trial that took place, in which there were many false witnesses, according to the Gospel.

Pen and brush drawing; 15.1 × 19.7 cm.
Ca. 1650.
Berlin, Kupferstichkabinett der Staatlichen Museen.

Literature: Benesch III, no. 645 (*ca.* 1649-50)/Rotermund, 1963, no. 224; Sumowski 1963, no. 76; Tümpel 1970, no. 95.

I have sinned in that I have betrayed the innocent blood

Matthew 27 WHEN the mornig was come, all the chief priests and elders of the people took counsel against Jesus to put him to death:

2 And when they had bound him, they led *him* away, and delivered him to Pontius Pilate the governor.

3 Then Judas, which had betrayed him, when he saw that he was condemned, repented himself, and brought again the thirty pieces of silver to the chief priests and elders,

4 Saying, I have sinned in that I have betrayed the innocent blood. And they said, what *is that* to us? see thou *to that.*

5 And he cast down the pieces of silver in the temple, and departed, and went and hanged himself.

6 And the chief priests took the silver pieces, and said, It is not lawful for to put them into the treasury, because it is the price of blood.

7 And they took counsel, and bought with them the potter's field, to bury strangers in.

8 Wherefore that field was called, The field of blood, unto this day.

9 Then was fulfilled that which was spoken by Jeremy the prophet, saying, And they took the thirty pieces of silver, the price of him that was valued, whom they of the children of Israel did value;

10 and gave them for the potter's field, as the Lord appointed me.

Judas Returns the Thirty Pieces of Silver

Then Judas, which had betrayed him, when he saw that he was condemned, repented himself, and brought again the thirty pieces of silver to the chief priests and elders, Saying, I have sinned in that I have betrayed the innocent blood. And they said, What is that to us? see thou to that.
(Matthew 27:3-4)

Judas' desperate end is described only in the Gospel according to St Matthew. Like Peter, the traitor apparently wished to know what would happen, and stayed in the neighbourhood of Caiaphas's palace. When he realized that Jesus' death was inevitable, he lost his mind, seeing no solution.

Rembrandt's painting, one of his first large-scale works, dating from 1629, shows the moment at which Judas describes his horror of his own betrayal to his accomplices. However, he has done the chief priests and elders the service and they are no longer interested in him and leave him to his own despair.

The autobiographical notes of Constantijn Huygens, written in about 1630 - which include a long passage about Rembrandt and Jan Lievens, who were working together in Leyden at that time - show that this gifted art lover was deeply impressed by this painting. In view of the date on the work, it must just have been completed when Huygens saw it. He refers to it as an example of all Rembrandt's work, and in an elaborate Latin sentence he praises above all the way in which the young artist expressed Judas' despair: 'The figure of Judas tortured by his remorse - not to speak of all the other admirable figures in this one work - I repeat: just the figure of Judas alone, raging, lamenting, begging forgiveness, but no longer even hoping for it, judging by the expression on his face, his haggard features, his unkempt hair, his torn clothes, distorted arms and hands clasped so hard they are almost bleeding as he impulsively throws himself onto his knees, while his whole body shrivels up with remorse and sorrow in the most piteous way, this figure is comparable to anything produced in the arts in centuries gone by ...' In Huygens's eyes the young Rembrandt had achieved in this painting the ideal of a historical painting: the convincing portrayal of human emotions and passions in a dramatic situation. The fact that there are a number of 17th-century copies of this painting reveals that he was not alone in his admiration of this work. It is also significant that in 1634 the figure of Judas was used in a print by Jan Joris van Vliet to serve as an example of a successful portrayal of remorse.

Panel; 79.5 × 102 cm.
Signed and dated: *RHL 1629.*
England, private collection.

Literature: Bauch, no. 47; Gerson, no. 12; Bredius-Gerson, no. 539a/Hofstede de Groot, *Rembrandt Bijbel*, N.T.p.21 (an old copy which was still considered as the original and which came to light only in 1939); Sumowski 1963, no. 90; B. Haak, 'Nieuw licht op Judas en de Zilverlingen van Rembrandt' in *Album Amicorum J.G. van Gelder*, The Hague 1973, p. 155 *et seq.*

Why, what evil hath he done?

Matthew 27

11 And Jesus stood before the governor: and the governor asked him, saying, Art thou the King of the Jews? And Jesus said into him, Thou sayest.

12 And when he was accused of the chief priests and elders, he answered nothing.

13 Then said Pilate unto him, Hearest thou not how many things they witness against thee?

14 And he answered him to never a word; insomuch that the governor marvelled greatly.

15 Now at *that* feast the governor was wont to release unto the people a prisoner, whom they would.

16 And they had then a notable prisoner, called Barabbas.

17 Therefore when they were gathered together, Pilate said unto them, Whom will ye that I release unto you? Barabbas, or Jesus which is called Christ?

18 For he knew that for envy they had delivered him.

19 When he was set down on the judgment seat, his wife sent unto him, saying, Have thou nothing to do with that just man: for I have suffered many things this day in a dram because of him.

20 But the chief priests and elders persuaded the multitude that they should ask Barabbas, and destroy Jesus.

21 The governor answered and said unto them, Whether of the twain will ye that I release unto your? They said, Barabbas.

22 Pilate saith unto them, What shall I do then with Jesus which is called Christ? *They* all say unto him, Let him be crucified.

23 And the governor said, Why, what evil hath he done? But they cried out the more, saying, Let him be crucified.

24 When Pilate saw that he could prevail nothing, but *that* rather a tumult was made, he took water, and washed *his* hands before the multitude, saying, I am innocent of the blood of this just person: see ye *to it*.

25 Then answered all the people, and said, His blood *be* on us, and on our children.

26 Then released he Barabbas unto them: and when he had scourged Jesus, he delivered *him* to be crucified.

Pilate Gives the People the Choice Between Barabbas and Jesus

Now at that feast the governor was wont to release unto the people a prisoner, whom they would. And they had then a notable prisoner, called Barabbas. Therefore, when they were gathered together, Pilate said unto them, Whom will ye that I release unto you? Barabbas, or Jesus which is called Christ?
(Matthew 27:15-17)

As the council was able to pronounce the death sentence, but the approval and execution was left to the Roman governor, Jesus was taken before Pontius Pilate. The accusation that he had blasphemed against God would have made little impression on the Roman, and therefore the chief priests and elders now emphasized that his crime was of a political nature. In the Gospels according to St Matthew and St Mark, the nature of his crime must be derived from Pilate's question to Jesus: 'Art thou the king of the Jews?'; while the Gospel according to St Luke describes the accusations which were made in detail: 'We found this fellow perverting the nation, and forbidding to give tribute to Caesar, saying that he himself is Christ a King' (Luke 23:2). With regard to the governor, who is only interested in the last and most important accusation, Jesus confirms that he is the king of the Jews, but the Gospel according to St John states that Jesus explains to Pilate that his kingdom is 'not of this world' (John 18:36-37), so that the Roman comes to the conclusion that the affair is of a purely religious nature, and the man is no threat to Roman authority.

As the members of the council stubbornly continue to insist that Jesus is condemned, Pilate seeks a solution and appeals to the people, suggesting that they make a choice between Jesus and the notorious Barabbas, convinced that they will elect to free Jesus.

The large print in which Rembrandt reveals this decisive moment dates from 1655, and is often considered a counterpart to his other large print of the Passion, *The Three Crosses*, dating from 1653 (see p. 400). The scene is full of figures and is set in the courtyard of a monumental court of law in which the facade is decorated with the statues of Justitia and Fortitudo, symbolizing justice and power. The two main characters stand at the front of the platform, framed by the darkness of the main entrance: Pilate, and Jesus, who has been handed over to him. Between Jesus and the tired governor, holding a long staff in his hand as a sign of his judicial authority, we see the cruel head of Barabbas. Pointing at Jesus, Pilate asks the question, 'Whom will ye that I release unto you? Barabbas, or Jesus which is called Christ?' In the thronging mass below a few voices loudly choose Barabbas. The scribe, sitting behind the raised stone pedestal to the left of the governor, attentively notes everything down. In a little while he will have to make note of a small incident mentioned only in the Gospel according to St Matthew, involving Pilate's wife. We can see her sitting in the window in the top left-hand corner. The messenger, who is to inform her husband of her dream, is just leaving. On the far left of the platform

Rembrandt shows a boy with a bowl and a jug of water in his hands, which serves as a reference to Pilate washing his hands, the symbolic act with which the governor finally pushes aside all responsibility for the course of events.

As this scene from the Passion described in the Gospel according to St Matthew is often confused with the scene described in the Gospel according to St John - where Pilate has Jesus taken outside again after he has been scourged and crowned with thorns, and utters the well-known words 'Ecce homo' (Behold the man) (see p. 389), the print is also often, though incorrectly, called *Ecce homo*. However, there is no question that other versions of the subject in which Jesus always wears a crown of thorns served Rembrandt as examples. His main source of inspiration was the large *Ecce homo* print by Lucas van Leyden, dating from 1510, but Rembrandt's composition also bears a great similarity to many other depictions of this subject.

Etching; 38.3 × 45.5 cm. Third state of eight.
Signed and dated from the seventh state: *Rembrandt f. 1655.*
Amsterdam, Rijksprentenkabinet.

Literature: Bartsch, no. 76; Hind, no. 271; Münz, no. 235; Boon, no. 261; Filedt Kok, no. B 76a/Hofstede de Groot, *Rembrandt Bijbel*, N.T.e.23; Rotermund 1963, no. 226; Sumowski 1963, no. 80; E. Winternitz, 'Rembrandt's "Christ presented to the people" - 1655', in *Oud Holland* 84 (1969), pp. 177 *et seq.*; Tümpel 1970, no. 97.

Pilate Gives the
People the Choice
Between Barabbas
and Jesus

Therefore, when they were gathered together, Pilate said
unto them, Whom will ye that I release unto you? Barabbas,
or Jesus which is called Christ?
(Matthew 27:17)

Compared with the third state reproduced on the
preceding page, the eighth and last state of this print
reveals a number of striking differences. After the
third state, Rembrandt cut a strip off the plate at the
top and elaborated the architecture on the right.
However, a much more far-reaching change was the
removal of the people in the foreground in front of
the platform after the fifth state. Rembrandt replaced
them with two dark arches at the front of the scene.
The bearded figure, looking rather like a river god,
between these two arches was largely removed again in
the last state. The figures on the platform, and
particularly the figure of Jesus, were given more detail
and contrast. Rembrandt also elaborated the wall
between the two statues above the central group. He
added a few figures in the left doorway and placed his
signature and the date '1655' over the right doorway to

indicate that he considered the print was completed.

As the foreground is now empty, the observer is
directly confronted with the scene taking place on the
platform. Initially he could still hide behind the Jews,
but now it is he, and not the inflamed mob, who calls
for Barabbas to be freed, and then answers Pilate's
question, 'What shall I do then with Jesus who is called
Christ?' screaming, 'Let him be crucified.' It is as
though Rembrandt wished to show what had already
been expressed by the theologian and poet, Jacob
Revius:

It is not the Jews, Lord Jesus, who crucified you,
It was I, O Lord, it was I who did it.

Etching; 35.8 × 45.5 cm. Eighth state of eight.
Signed and dated: *Rembrandt f. 1655.*
Amsterdam, Rijksprentenkabinet.

Literature: Bartsch, no. 76; Hind, no. 271; Münz, no. 235;
Boon, no. 262; Filedt Kok, no. B 76b.

When Pilate saw that he could prevail nothing, but that rather a tumult was made, he took water, and washed his hands before the multitude, saying, I am innocent of the blood of this just person: see ye to it.
(Matthew 27:24)

Only the Gospel according to St Matthew describes the ceremony in which Pilate publicly washes his hands to show his innocence and absolve himself of the consequences of murdering an innocent man. The arrangement in Rembrandt's drawing of this frequently depicted scene is strongly reminiscent of that in the etching dating from 1655 reproduced on the preceding page, particularly because of the platform with steps leading up on which Pilate is standing. Another drawing dating from the first half of the 1650s (Benesch V, no. 927), indicates that when Rembrandt had the idea of making a print of a scene with Pontius Pilate, he initially thought of depicting this view from the side, and only later decided on a front view, like that in the large print by Lucas van Leyden which was mentioned earlier.

In this concise and rapidly drawn composition there is a greater emphasis on Pilate as the central figure.

As a quiet slave meekly pours water over his hands, he turns deliberately to the inflamed crowd which insists on taking on the responsibility for Jesus' death. The victim of Pilate's scheming has just been taken away. On the right of the stage we still see one of the soldiers leading the prisoner away.

Pen and ink drawing; 20.1 × 26.5 cm.
Ca. 1652-54.
Cambridge (Mass.), Fogg Art Museum, Harvard University.

Literature: Benesch V, no. 937 (*ca.* 1653-54).

Pilate Washes his Hands

Hail, King of the Jews!

Matthew 27   27 Then the soldiers of the governor took Jesus into the common hall, and gathered unto him the whole band *of soldiers*.
28 And they stripped him, and put on him a scarlet robe.

29 And when they had platted a crown of thorns, they put *it* upon his head, and a reed in his right hand: and they bowed the knee before him, and mocked him, saying, Hail, King of the Jews!
30 And they spit upon him, and took the reed, and smote him on the head.

Jesus is Mocked   *And when they had platted a crown of thorns, they put it upon his head, and a reed in his right hand, and they bowed the knee before him, and mocked him, saying, Hail, King of the Jews!*
(Matthew 27:29)

Rembrandt followed the description given in the Gospel according to St Matthew very literally. Only the red robe in which the soldiers dressed the target of their mockery is lacking. The torture pillar rising up behind Jesus has a hook on the top to draw a rope through so that the victim can be tied up, and this is a reminder of the torture he has already suffered. Jesus' cloak is hanging over the pillar.

The catalogue of the exhibition *Rembrandt After Three Hundred Years* (Chicago-Minneapolis-Detroit 1969, no. 129) states that for the depiction of the seated main character the artist was undoubtedly influenced by depictions of the theme dating from the late Middle Ages; 'Christ on the cold stone' was a subject that was particularly popular in the religious art of Northern Europe. The conscious representations of a profoundly sad Saviour, crowned with thorns, and dressed only in a loincloth, do not depict a historical moment in the Passion but are a sort of summary of the whole Passion and were intended to stimulate the observer to contemplate the Lord's suffering. Jesus' loneliness is all the more prominent in Rembrandt's composition because the mocking soldiers and those observing events from a distance are grouped in couples.

In a drawing dated slightly later (Benesch V, no. 1024), Rembrandt dealt with this subject again in the same spirit, but this time against an empty background.

Pen and ink drawing; 15.5 × 21.5 cm.
Ca. 1652-55.
New York, The Pierpont Morgan Library.

Literature: Benesch V, no. 920 (*ca.* 1652-53)/Rotermund 1963, no. 227; Sumowski 1963, no. 82.

Behold the man!

John 19

4 Pilate therefore went forth again, and saith unto them, Behold, I bring him forth to you, that ye may know that I find no fault in him.

5 Then came Jesus forth, wearing the crown of thorns, and the purple robe. And *Pilate* saith unto them, Behold the man!

6 When the chief priests therefore and officers saw him, they cried out, saying, Crucify *him*, crucify *him*. Pilate saith unto them, Take ye him, and crucify *him*: for I find no fault in him.

7 The Jews answered him, We have a law, and by our law he ought to die, because he made himself the Son of God.

8 When Pilate therfore heard that saying, he was the more afraid;

9 And went again into the judgment hall, and saith unto Jesus, Whence art thou? But jesus gave him no answer.

10 Then saith Pilate unto him, Speakest thou not unto me? knowest thou not that I have power to crucify thee, and have power to release thee?

11 Jesus answered, Thou couldest have no power *at all* against me, except it were given thee from above: therfore he that delivered me unto thee hath the greater sin.

12 And from thenceforth Pilate sought to release him: but the Jews cried out, saying, If thou let this man go, thou art not Cæsar's friend: whosoever maketh himself a king speaketh against Cæsar.

13 When Pilate therefore heard that saying, he brought Jesus forth, and sat down in the judgment seat in a place that is called the Pavement, but in the Hebrew, Gabbatha

14 And it was the preparation of the passover, and about the sixth hour: and he saith unto the Jews, Behold your King!

15 But they cried out, Away with *him*, away with *him*, crucify him. Pilate saith unto them, Shall I crucify your King? The chief priests answered, We have no king but Cæsar.

16 Then delivered he him therefore unto them to be crucified. And they took Jesus, and led *him* away.

Jesus is Shown to the People (Ecce homo)

Then came Jesus forth, wearing the crown of thorns, and the purple robe. And Pilate saith unto them, Behold the man! When the chief priests therefore and officers saw him, they cried out, saying, Crucify him, crucify him. Pilate saith unto them, Take ye him, and crucify him: for I find no fault in him. (John 19:5-6)

The Gospel according to St John, which describes the conflict between Pilate and the Jewish leaders for Jesus' life in by far the most detail, relates that the Roman governor has the prisoner brought out again after he has been tortured and mocked, and makes another attempt to save Jesus from crucifixion. It was only when he realized that his opponents were implacable that he pronounced the death sentence.

In this grisaille painted on paper in 1634, which served as a preliminary study for an etching completed in 1636 (Bartsch, no. 77), Rembrandt depicts the final stage of the trial before Pilate, which is described only in the Gospel according to St John. Although Jesus, exhibited as a mocked king, has a dominant place in the painting of this busy scene, Rembrandt was above all concerned with showing the conflict between the governor and the chief priests, who have crowded right up to the seat of justice, their faces distorted. As Pilate rises and explains to his opponents that he does not wish to meet their demands, one of the priests grabs hold of his staff, the symbol of his judicial authority. In Tümpel's opinion, Rembrandt used this motif, which he made up himself, to show that the Jewish leaders took the law into their own hands, appealing to their own law when Pilate persisted in his refusal to pronounce the death sentence on Jesus. 'We have a law, and by our law he ought to die, because he made himself the Son of God' (verse 7). A bust of the Roman Emperor placed on a tall pillar, which rises up above the large multitude in the square like an exclamation mark, serves as a reference to their rejection of the Messiah-King at the end of the story (verse 15) in the words: 'We have no king but Caesar.' In the background the hand of the clock with Roman numbers shows the hour at which, according to John, Jesus was condemned to death, at the sixth hour, i.e., at about noon.

This painting is very probably the same as the *Ecce homo* grisaille which was mentioned in Rembrandt's inventory in 1656: 'An excehomo in greys by Rembrant' (Hofstede de Groot, *Urkenden* 169, no. 121).

Paper on canvas; 54.5 × 44.5 cm.
Signed and dated: *Rembrandt f. 1634.*
London, National Gallery.

Literature: Bredius, no. 546; Bauch, no. 62; Gerson, no. 72; Bredius-Gerson, no. 546/Hofstede de Groot, *Rembrandt Bijbel*, N.T.p.22; Tümpel 1970, under no. 96.

For if they do these things in a green tree

Luke 23 26 And as they led him away, they laid hold upon one Simon, a Cyrenian, coming out of the country, and on him they laid the cross, that he might bear *it* after Jesus.

27 And there followed him a great company of people, and of women, which also bewailed and lamented him.

28 But Jesus turning unto them said, Daughters of Jerusalem, weep not for me, but weep for yourselves, and for your children.

29 For, behold, the days are coming, in the which they shall say, Blessed *are* the barren, and the wombs that never bare, and the paps which never gave suck.

30 Then shall they begin to say to the mountains, Fall on us; and to the hills, Cover us.

31 For if they do these things in a green tree, what shall be done in the dry?

32 And there were also two other, malefactors, led with him to be put to death.

33 And when they were come to the place, which is called Calvary, there they crucified him, and the malefactors, one on the right hand, and the other on the left.

34 Then said Jesus, Father, forgive them; for they know not what they do. And they parted his raiment, and cast lots.

35 And the people stood beholding. And the rulers also with them derided *him*, saying, He saved others; let him save himself, if he be Christ, the chosen of God.

36 And the soldiers also mocked him, coming to him, and offering him vinegar.

37 And saying, If thou be the king of the Jews, save thyself.

38 And a superscription also was written over him in letters of Greek, and Latin, and Hebrew, THIS IS THE KING OF THE JEWS.

39 And one of the malefactors which were hanged railed on him, saying, If thou be Christ, save thyself and us.

40 But the other answering rebuked him, saying, Dost not thou fear God, seeing thou art in the same condemnation?

41 And we indeed justly; for we receive the due reward of our deeds: but this man hath done nothing amiss.

42 And he said unto Jesus, Lord, remember me when thou comest into thy kingdom.

43 And Jesus said unto him, Verily I say unto thee, To day shalt thou be with me in paradise.

Carrying the Cross *And as they led him away, they laid hold upon one Simon, a Cyrenian, coming out of the temple, and on him they laid the cross, that he might bear it after Jesus. And there followed him a great company of people, and of women, which also bewailed and lamented him.*
(Luke 23:26-27)

In Roman times it was customary for a condemned man to carry his own instrument of punishment. Only the Gospel according to St John mentions that Jesus had to carry his cross himself: 'and he bearing his cross went forth into a place called the place of a skull, which is called in the Hebrew, Golgotha' (John 19:17). Matthew, Mark and Luke indicate that when the procession was outside the city, the soldiers forced a man returning to the city, Simon, a Cyrenian, to carry the Cross.

In early Christian art Jesus carries the Cross on his shoulder, walking upright, as though it is not an oppressive burden but a symbol of his victory. Simon the Cyrenian is also shown bearing the Cross, and in a number of early medieval works it is Simon who goes

ahead carrying the Cross, followed by Jesus, who has his hands bound. However, from the 13th century onwards, when there was an increasing emphasis in religious experience on Christ's suffering, Jesus usually carried the Cross himself, either alone or helped by Simon the Cyrenian.

There are no known paintings or etchings by Rembrandt of the road to Calvary, on the way to Golgotha. The theme only appears in two of his drawings: a baroque sketch full of movement, dating from the middle of the 1630s (Benesch I, no. 97), and this forcefully drawn composition from the second half of the 1650s drawn in a comparable style to *Jesus is Arrested*, now in Stockholm (p. 375). The way in which the scene is depicted is largely based on existing artistic tradition, rather than on the Biblical text. The Gospels do not mention Jesus collapsing under the burden of the Cross, although it may be assumed that the soldiers pressed a passer-by to take over the Cross because the victim was too exhausted to be able to carry it any further himself. It is this scene with Simon the Cyrenian that is depicted in the drawing on the right.

The Gospels do not mention Veronica's act in relation to Jesus' collapse, as shown by Rembrandt. This is derived from an old legend, according to which this devout lady from Jerusalem washed Jesus' face with a cloth as he was bearing the Cross, and as a result Jesus' features remained printed on the cloth. Behind Veronica there is one of the lamenting women, part of the multitude following Jesus, as described in the Gospel according to St Luke.

Jesus' collapse under the Cross, the involvement of Simon the Cyrenian and Veronica's act are all separate episodes on the road to Calvary, a series of illustrations ('stations') - initially seven, and later fourteen - which, since the 15th century, had shown the path of Jesus from Pilate's courthouse to Golgotha. Just as Rembrandt had condensed successive incidents in an entire chapter in a single moment in *The Hundred Guilder Print*, he did the same again in three emotional 'stations' from the traditional road to Calvary.

Pen and brush drawing; 17.4 × 27.3 cm.
Ca. 1655-60.
Haarlem, Teylers Museum.

Literature: Benesch V, no. 923 (*ca.* 1653)/Rotermund 1963, no. 228; Sumowski 1963, no. 84; 'Bijbelse Inspiratie', no. 110; Tümpel 1970, under no. 98.

The Erection of
the Cross

*And when they were come to the place which is called
Calvary, there they crucified him, and the malefactors, one
on the right hand, and the other on the left.*
(Luke 23:33)

The Gospels are extremely succinct with regard to the
way in which Jesus' crucifixion was carried out. Up to
the end of the 14th century there are works in
Byzantine and Italian art depicting the theme of Jesus
ascending the Cross. They show how he gets onto the
Cross as it stands upright in the ground, sometimes
with and sometimes without a ladder, while the
executioners are ready to nail him onto the Cross,
standing on two ladders leaning against the horizontal
crosspiece. After the 14th century, Western European
art usually showed Jesus being nailed to the Cross as it
is lying on the ground. In the gradually expanding
series of scenes of his suffering, the erection of the
Cross fills the gap between Jesus being nailed onto the
Cross and the age-old representation of the
Crucifixion. It was particularly during the baroque
period, when there was a preference for dynamic
compositions with a diagonal structure, that this theme
was frequently adopted.

In Rembrandt's realistic work, it is striking that
virtually all the light is focused on the body of the
crucified Christ. Golgotha is already shrouded in the
darkness which has swallowed up the whole land in the
middle of the day (Matthew 27:45, Mark 15:33, Luke
23:44). In the Gospels this phenomenon characterizes
the death of Jesus as the beginning of the end of the
'day of the Lord', of which the prophet Amos had said:
'And it shall come to pass in that day, saith the Lord
God, that I will cause the sun to go down at noon, and
I will darken the earth in a clear day' (Amos 8:9). With
an awareness that Jesus is crucified again and again
through the sins of man, Rembrandt shows himself as
one of the executioners' helpers who are pulling and
pushing to draw the Cross upright, supervised by a
mounted centurion. The spade shown in the ground
indicates the hole which has been dug for planting the
Cross. On the left of the painting we see the Jewish
authorities. Mocking the signs of Jesus' Messianic
mission, they jeer at him and call out: 'He saved
others; let him save himself, if he be Christ, the chosen
of God' (Luke 23:35). In the background on the right,
preparations are made for crucifying one of the
criminals.

Together with *The Descent from the Cross* (p. 403), *The*
Entombment (p. 410), *The Resurrection* (p. 415) and *The
Ascension* (p. 435), this painting is one of Rembrandt's
five scenes of the Passion commissioned by Prince
Frederik Hendrik during the 1630s. Constantijn
Huygens, the Prince's secretary and adviser on his
purchases of works of art, acted as an intermediary in
this commission. Huygens was one of the first to
recognize the talent of the young artist (see p. 380),
and it may be assumed that Rembrandt received the
commission on his recommendation. Seven surviving
letters from Rembrandt to Huygens - Rembrandt's
only known letters - reveal that the delivery of the
paintings which had been ordered did not take place
without difficulties. The first works to be done were
The Erection of the Cross and *The Descent from the Cross*,
and these vied with the large altarpieces devoted to
these subjects by Rubens, who was much admired at
the court in The Hague. The two paintings are not
dated, but it is probable that they were delivered in
ca. 1633-34. Rembrandt refers to them in the first letter,
written at the beginning of 1636. In this letter he
informs Huygens that he is still busy working on the
other scenes commissioned by His Excellence from the
Passion, i.e., an Entombment, a Resurrection and the
Ascension of Christ. He states that these works are 'in
accord' with *The Erection of the Cross* and *The Descent
from the Cross*, which have already been delivered, and
that one of the three, in which Christ ascends to
heaven, has been completed, while the other two are
more than half done. *The Ascension of Jesus* was sent to
the Prince shortly afterwards, but the last two
paintings were not delivered for another three years,
even though they had been more than half finished. It
was not until January 1639 that Rembrandt wrote to
Huygens that he had also completed *The Entombment*
and *The Resurrection of Christ*.

All five paintings are now in the Alte Pinakothek in
Munich, as well as *The Shepherds Worshipping the Infant
Jesus*, one of the two works which supplemented the
series in 1646 (see pp. 232-33).

Canvas, rounded at the top; 96 × 72 cm.
Ca. 1632-33.
Munich, Alte Pinakothek.

Literature: Bredius, no. 548; Bauch, no. 57; Gerson, no.
64; Bredius-Gerson, no. 548/Hofstede de Groot,
Rembrandt Bijbel, N.T.p.25; Tümpel 1970, under no. 99.

Jesus is Crucified Between the Two Criminals

And one of the malefactors which were hanged railed on him, saying, If thou be Christ, save thyself and us. But the other answering rebuked him, saying, Dost not thou fear God, seeing thou art in the same condemnation? And we indeed justly; for we receive the due reward of our deeds: but this man hath done nothing amiss. And he said unto Jesus, Lord, remember me when thou comest into thy kingdom. And Jesus said unto him, Verily I say unto thee, Today shalt thou be with me in paradise.
(Luke 23:39-43)

All four Gospels mention that two criminals were crucified at the same time as Jesus, one on his right and one on his left. Therefore the words in Isaiah 53:12 about the servant of God were applicable to the Lord, who died according to the Scriptures: 'And he was numbered with the transgressors' (Mark 15:28). It is only in the Gospel according to St Luke that a distinction is made between the two, and 'the good murderer' admits that he deserves his punishment and recognizes Jesus as the Messiah. In this oval etching of the three crosses, Rembrandt depicts the moment at which Jesus promises the criminal looking at him that he will be in paradise today, because of his belief.

The atmosphere in Rembrandt's representations of the scene on Golgotha is always determined by sorrow and despair. Christian Tümpel pointed out that

Rembrandt deliberately omitted narrative details, such as the casting of lots for Jesus' clothes (Luke 23:34), which artists had formerly frequently used as an excuse for a quarrel, because this would detract from the intended mood of the scene. Rembrandt's main concern was to show the reactions of those who were affected by Jesus' death. In this print, in which the shades vary from light grey to deep black, the mood of despondency appears in particular in the sorrowing women at the foot of the Cross. 'The sadness hangs like a leaden weight around the figures shrouded in darkness. Only Christ himself is radiant with a heavenly light, which just touches upon the good murderer' ('Bijbelse Inspiratie', no. 44). The reed with the sponge soaked in vinegar which the soldiers give to the condemned men stands to the back of the Cross on the left (Luke 23:36).

Etching; 13.6 × 10 cm. Second state of two.
Ca. 1641.
Amsterdam, Rijksprentenkabinet.

Literature: Bartsch, no. 79; Hind, no. 173; Münz, no. 215 (*ca.* 1643-44); Boon, no. 172; Filedt Kok, no. B 79/'Bijbelse Inspiratie', no. 44; Tümpel 1968, pp. 101-02; Tümpel 1970, no. 102.

According to the story of the Passion in the Gospel according to St John, the friends and relations of Jesus who witnessed the Crucifixion included his mother and the apostle John, the disciple 'whom he loved'. 'When Jesus therefore saw his mother, and the disciple standing by whom he loved, he saith unto his mother, Woman, behold thy son! Then saith he to the disciple, Behold thy mother! And from that hour that disciple took her unto his own home' (John 19:26-27).

This moving print, dating from *ca.* 1635, reminds us of these words of Jesus. From the very beginning, Mary and John were the main figures, and often the only figures depicted under the Cross in Christian art. Rembrandt's print shows how Mary has collapsed, overwhelmed by grief. Supported by one of the other women, she raises her eyes to Jesus, who looks at his mother from the Cross. Mary Magdalene kneels at the foot of the Cross, as is customary. The figures lamenting the death of Jesus are divided into two groups opposite each other, connected by the unmoved Jewish priest in the foreground in the centre.

The motif of Mary, helplessly collapsing under the Cross, is not derived from the Biblical text but is based on the artistic tradition of the late Middle Ages, when Mary was made more prominent than ever as a 'co-Saviour'. This resulted in religious art emphasizing the suffering of the mother of sorrows and her son, for our sake. In his own words, Rembrandt aimed in his historical works to express as much natural movement as possible (see p. 414), and he considered this effective motif from pre-Reformation tradition eminently suitable for moving the observer so that he could experience the drama on Golgotha as intensely as possible. In fact, the motif recurs regularly in his scenes of the Passion (see pp. 399, 400, 403 and 404).

Jesus on the Cross

Etching; 9.5 × 6.8 cm. Only state.
Signed: *Rembrandt f.*
Ca. 1635.
Amsterdam, Rijksprentenkabinet.

Literature: Bartsch, no. 80; Hind, no. 123; Münz, no. 202; Boon, no. 111; Filedt Kok, no. B 80/J. Bruyn, *Rembrandt's keuze van Bijbelse onderwerpen*, Utrecht 1959, p. 8; Tümpel 1970, nos. 100 and 101.

My God, my God, why hast thou forsaken me?

Matthew 27

45 Now from the sixth hour there was darkness over all the land unto the ninth hour.

46 And about the ninth hour Jesus cried with a loud voice, saying , Eli, Eli, lama sabachthani? that is to say, My God, my God, why hast thou forsaken me?

47 Some of them that stood there, when they heard *that*, said, This *man* calleth for Elias.

48 And straightway one of them ran, and took a spunge, and filled *it* with vinegar, and put *it* on a reed, and gave him to drink.

49 The rest said, Let be, let us see whether Elias will come to save him.

50 Jesus, when he had cried again with a loud voice, yielded up the ghost.

51 And, behold, the veil of the temple was rent in twain from the top to the bottom; and the earth did quake, and the rocks rent;

52 And the graves were opened; and many bodies of the saints which slept arose,

53 And came out of the graves after his resurrection, and went into the holy city, and appeared unto many.

54 Now when the centurion, and they that were with him, watching Jesus, saw the earthquake, and those things that were done, they feared greatly, saying, Truly this was the Son of God.

55 And many woman were there beholding afar off, which followed Jesus from Galilee, ministering unto him:

56 Among which was Mary Magdalene, and Mary the mother of James and Joses, and the mother of Zebedee's children.

Jesus on the Cross

Now from the sixth hour there was darkness over all the land until the ninth hour. And about the ninth hour Jesus cried with a loud voice, saying, Eli! Eli! lama sabachthani? that is to say, My God! My God! why hast thou forsaken me?
(Matthew 27:45-46)

Works such as this painting, in which Jesus is shown hanging on the Cross in complete loneliness against an empty dark background, only became popular in the 17th century as an expression of the terrible desolation of the death of the Son of God. Rembrandt's interpretation of this subject has a very personal stamp because of the powerful chiaroscuro and daring realism particularly evident in the crucified Christ's face, which is distorted with suffering. The notice nailed to the top of the Cross states the reason for the Crucifixion as given by Pilate, in Hebrew, Greek and Latin: 'Jesus of Nazareth, the King of the Jews'. It is not surprising that the Jewish chief priests asked Pilate to change the text, as related in the Gospel according to St John: 'Write not, the King of the Jews; but that he said, I am King of the Jews. Pilate answered, What I have written I have written' (John 19:21-22).

In 1959 Rembrandt's signature and the date 1631 were discovered when this painting, which had been rescued from oblivion, was carefully examined. This date, the subject, the execution and the dimensions of the work mean that it is very probable that it is related to the scenes from the Passion mentioned on p. 392, which Rembrandt was commissioned to paint in the 1630s for Prince Frederik Hendrik through the mediation of Constantijn Huygens. Gerson suggested that Rembrandt designed it as the centrepiece for three works, and that it should have been hung between *The Erection of the Cross* (p. 393) and *The Descent from the Cross* (p. 403). He thought that Huygens must have seen the paintings when they were made, and bought them for the Prince. Then Rembrandt was supposedly commissioned to paint another three scenes from the Passion in the same style. However, Rembrandt's first letter to Huygens, dating from 1636, does not mention a Crucifixion, and refers only to a completed erection of the Cross and descent from the Cross (see p. 392). Therefore it is by no means certain that this work belongs in the Passion series that is now in Munich. Certainly even if the Prince did buy the painting, it did not remain in his collection. In 1805, Xavier Duffour, who had bought the painting at an auction in Dunkirk, donated it to the parish church of his birthplace, Le Mas d'Agenais. Thus this painting is the only religious work by Rembrandt which now hangs in a church.

Canvas on panel, rounded at the top; 100 × 73 cm.
Signed and dated: *RHL 1631*.
Le Mas d'Agenais, parish church.

Literature: Bauch, no. 54; Gerson, no. 56; Bredius Gerson, no. 543A/K. Bauch, 'Rembrandts Christus am Kreuz' in *Pantheon* 20 (1962), pp. 137 *et seq.*; Sumowski 1963, no. 86.

Jesus is Given Vinegar to Drink on the Cross

And about the ninth hour Jesus cried with a loud voice, saying, Eli! Eli! lama sabachthani? That is to say, My God! My God! why hast thou forsaken me? Some of them that stood there, when they heard that, said, This man calleth for Elias. And straightway one of them ran, and took a sponge, and filled it with vinegar, and put it on a reed, and gave him to drink.
(Matthew 27:46-48)

The Gospel according to St John describes how Jesus was passed the sponge when, just before his spirit departed from him, he said: 'That the Scripture might be fulfilled, saith, I thirst' (John 19:28). The Gospel refers to the words of Psalm 69, verse 21: 'They gave me also gall for my meat; and in my thirst they gave me vinegar to drink.'

This drawing, which dates from the first half of the 1650s, shows the three crosses viewed from the side in the same arrangement as in the oval etching, dating from *ca.* 1641 (see p. 394). The rapidly and broadly sketched scene shows the very last act before Jesus' death. The temple of Jerusalem can be seen in the background, where in a few moments, the veil between the Holy and the Holy of Holies will be rent in twain (Matthew 27:51). On the right the composition ends with a centurion keeping guard. Shortly, when he sees what happens when Jesus dies, he will say: 'Truly this was the Son of God' (Matthew 27:54).

Pen and brush drawing; 20.5 × 28.5 cm.
Ca. 1650-55.
Paris, The Louvre.

Literature: Benesch III, no. 652 (*ca.* 1649-50); Slive I, no. 164 (*ca.* 1650-55)/Hofstede de Groot, *Rembrandt Bijbel*, N.T.d.28; 'Bijbelse Inspiratie', under no. 112.

Jesus, when he had cried again with a loud voice, yielded up the ghost.
(Matthew 27:50)

Matthew and Mark do not say what Jesus called out just before he died. In the Gospel according to St Luke, his last words are: 'Father, into thy hands I commend my spirit' (Luke 23:46). The Gospel according to St John gives as his last words: 'It is finished' (John 19:30).

Rembrandt's drawing devoted to this moment, which dates from the second half of the 1640s, is dominated by the one Cross, which draws the attention all the more because it is slightly off centre. The reed with the sponge soaked in vinegar which has just been given to Jesus lies at the foot of the Cross. The crucified Christ, staring ahead into the distance, bears a great resemblance to the dying Redeemer in the famous

etching, *The Three Crosses* (p. 400), which was done about five years later. To the right of the Cross, Mary has collapsed in sorrow and is supported and consoled by the sympathetic women around her. On the other side of the Cross, mocking words can still be heard, but the tension in the centurion who stands guard opposite Jesus reveals a trace of the astonishment mixed with fear which will result in his conversion. The oppressive atmosphere of sorrow and despair is expressed most strongly in the figure of John, who is bent over a rock in the foreground on the left, alone in his sorrow.

Golgotha

Pen and brush drawing; 16.5 × 23.8 cm.
Signed on the back: *Rembrandt.*
Ca. 1645-50.
Frankfurt am Main, Städelsches Kunstinstitut.
Literature: Benesch III, no. 586 (*ca.* 1647).

The Three Crosses

Now when the centurion, and they that were with him watching Jesus, saw the earthquake, and those things that were done, they feared greatly, saying, Truly this was the Son of God.
(Matthew 27:54)

This monumental print dating from 1653 is reproduced here at barely half of its actual size. Rembrandt has recreated the drama of Golgotha in a breathtaking scene in which the death of Jesus is revealed as the victory of light over dark. Now that the Lord has fulfilled his mission, the darkened sky over Golgotha breaks open and a sea of light floods over the raised Cross. Unbelievers flee from the light in consternation. However, the Roman centurion has dismounted from his horse and with the characteristic gesture used by Rembrandt to indicate a sudden overwhelming awareness of the presence of God, he kneels down before the Cross in prayer. The friends and relations of Jesus have assembled in the glow to the right of the Cross.

John stretches out his hands to heaven in desperation; the women take care of Mary, who has swooned in her sorrow. Above them the 'good murderer' also shares the light. The face of the obdurate criminal remains shrouded in darkness.

There are very few differences between the first three states of this etching. Rembrandt signed the third state and dated it 1653. He made drastic changes to the print in the fourth state, so that it looks quite different.

Etching; 38.5 × 45 cm. First state of five.
The third state is signed and dated: *Rembrandt f. 1653*. Amsterdam, Rijksprentenkabinet.

Literature: Bartsch, no. 78; Hind, no. 270; Münz, no. 223; Boon, no. 244; Filedt Kok, no. B 78/Hofstede de Groot, *Rembrandt Bijbel*, N.T.e.24; Rotermund 1963, no. 232; Sumowski 1963, no. 87; 'Bijbelse Inspiratie', no. 45; Tümpel 1970, no. 103.

With his powerful imagination, Rembrandt conjured up and depicted many different moments in the tragedy on Golgotha. In this drawing, which again dates from the first half of the 1650s when he did so many scenes from the Passion, the Roman soldiers have already started to leave the place of judgment. Jesus has died. He hangs on the Cross, having fought the fight. But the scribes and Pharisees, blinded with hatred, are still not satisfied and their shouts drown the lament of Jesus' followers. In this way they confirm the lashing words which Jesus had addressed to his opponents a few days earlier: 'Woe unto you, scribes and Pharisees, hypocrites! because ye build the tombs of the prophets, and garnish the sepulchres of the righteous. And say, If we had been in the days of our fathers, we would not have been partakers with them in the blood of the prophets. Wherefore ye be witnesses unto yourselves, that ye are the children of them which killed the prophets. Fill ye up then the measure of your fathers' (Matthew 23:29-32).

Pen and brush drawing; 24.7 × 21.1 cm.
Ca. 1650-53.
Stockholm, Nationalmuseum.

Literature: Benesch V, no. 924 (*ca.* 1653)/Rotermund 1963, no. 230; 'Bijbelse Inspiratie', under no. 112.

Jesus on the Cross

And now when the even was come

Mark 15 42 And now when the even was come, because it was the preparation, that is, the day before the sabbath,

43 Joseph of Arimathæa, an honourable counsellor, which also waited for the kingdom of God, came, and went in boldly unto Pilate, and craved the body of Jesus.

44 And Pilate marvelled if he were already dead: and calling *unto him* the centurion, he asked him whether he had been any while dead.

45 And when he knew *it* of the centurion, he gave the body to Joseph.

46 And he bought fine linen, and took him down, and wrapped him in the linen, and laid him in a sepulchre which was hewn out of a rock, and rolled a stone unto the door of the sepulchre.

47 And Mary Magdalene and Mary *the mother* of Joses beheld where he was laid.

The Descent from the Cross

All four Gospels relate how a certain Joseph of Arimathea, one of Jesus' disciples, 'but secretly for fear of the Jews' (John 19:38) went to Pilate shortly after Jesus' death and asked the governor for permission to take his body down from the Cross and bury it. Only the Gospel according to St John mentions that the important Nicodemus, a Pharisee, who had once had a serious night-time conversation with Jesus (John 3:1-21) also came, bringing a mixture of myrrh and aloes with him (John 19:39).

Rembrandt's painting of the descent from the Cross, one of the two earliest works in the series of scenes from the Passion commissioned by Prince Frederik Hendrik (see p. 392), shows how Joseph of Arimathea, aided by four helpers, carefully takes the lifeless body down from the high Cross in the dark of the approaching evening. Jesus' distorted face testifies to the pain he has suffered. In the chiaroscuro only the essential elements are visible: the blood-covered Cross, the pale greyish body of Jesus, the faces and gestures of the helpers and bystanders who are moved with pity. As in the painting of the erection of the Cross, the artist again included himself. We recognize as the young Rembrandt the young man in blue who is standing on the ladder holding Jesus' right arm. Nicodemus, who came along, stands on the right, calm and dignified. According to legend, Jesus' mother was also present at the foot of the Cross when the body of her son was taken down, and she is virtually always shown in depictions of this subject.

Rembrandt shows her in the shadows in the foreground on the left, where she has collapsed in sorrow and despair, supported by two women. (For this motif, which is based on late medieval tradition, see the explanatory text on p. 395.) It has often been pointed out that Rembrandt's composition was influenced by Rubens's famous painting in Antwerp Cathedral. Rembrandt must have been familiar with this work through the print by Lucas Vorsterman, dating from 1620. Nevertheless, it is clear from his realism and the way in which he emphasizes the mystery of Jesus' suffering by means of the strong contrast between light and dark that his vision of the subject is very different from that of the Flemish master. He did not idealize the body of Jesus as Rubens had done. In Rembrandt's work we see a real corpse, weak and heavy, being taken down from the Cross.

In order to make sure that this composition became well known, Rembrandt reproduced this painting in the form of a large etching dated 1633 (Bartsch, no. 81). The precise date of the painting itself is not certain, but it was undoubtedly painted at the same time as *The Erection of the Cross* (p. 393), during Rembrandt's first years in Amsterdam. In 1634 he did a second painting on the same theme (Bredius, no. 551; Leningrad, The Hermitage) in which the Cross is viewed from the front, as in Rubens's work. As the number of bystanders is considerably larger and the attention is focused on much more than the central event, that composition lacks the serenity and calm which emanates from this painting in Munich.

Panel, rounded at the top; 89.5 × 65.2 cm.
Ca. 1632-33.
Munich, Alte Pinakothek.

Literature: Bredius, no. 550; Bauch, no. 56; Gerson, no. 65; Bredius-Gerson, no. 550/J. Bruyn, *Rembrandt's keuze van Bijbelse onderwerpen*, Utrecht 1959, p. 7V; Sumowski 1963, no. 91; Tümpel 1970, under no. 104.

The Descent from the Cross

The descent from the Cross depicted in this print is rather different from versions of the subject which Rembrandt had done earlier. While Mary Magdalene, who can be recognized by her long, loosely hanging hair, stands by the Cross weeping, one of the helpers of Joseph of Arimathea is already taking Jesus' right hand off the crossbar of the Cross, having taken down the left hand. Meanwhile, the lifeless body is held up by a taut sheet. The crown of thorns has been removed and placed on a dish at the bottom right of the picture. In the foreground on the left, the composition is completed with the figure of a kneeling woman who looks up at Jesus while she supports the mother of the Lord, who has collapsed in despair.

The motif of 'Adam's skull', which became popular in the 9th century, can also be seen at the foot of the Cross. According to an ancient legend, the place outside Jerusalem where Jesus was crucified was called Golgotha, which means the place of skulls, because Adam's skull was buried there. By depicting the skull

at the foot of the Cross, the historical significance of Jesus' death was expressed. What Adam had lost by his sin was regained by Jesus, the new Adam, through his death on the Cross. As St Paul wrote to the Romans: 'For as by one man's disobedience many were made sinners; so by the obedience of one shall many be made righteous' (Romans 5:19). When the legend of Adam's skull being buried at Golgotha was no longer believed, the skull was still depicted at the foot of the Cross, usually together with some bones, to show that by his death Jesus was victorious over death. In Rembrandt's scenes of Golgotha, this age-old motif can be found only in this etching of the descent from the Cross.

Etching; 14.9 × 11.6 cm. Only state.
Signed and dated: *Rembrandt f. 1642.*
Amsterdam, Rijksprentenkabinet.

Literature: Bartsch, no. 82; Hind, no. 199; Münz, no. 213; Boon, no. 179; Filedt Kok, no. B 82/Tümpel 1970, no. 105.

404

In Rembrandt's last composition of the descent from the Cross, which is not comparable with any of his other versions, the scene takes place along a diagonal line from top left to bottom right, where Joseph of Arimathea is spreading out the shroud on the bier on which the body of Jesus is to be carried to the sepulchre. The light shining down, which reveals the sad event in the darkness, comes from a torch held between the vertical post of the Cross and the sheet. The way in which the heaviness of the dead, weak body is expressed again bears witness to Rembrandt's realistic vision. It is as though we see the man who is respectfully taking down the body tottering under its weight, an impression that is further strengthened by the hand stretched out that is lit up in the dark. Unlike most depictions of this subject, the work does not show Jesus' mother and Mary Magdalene.

It is possible that this print is part of a group including *The Entombment* (p. 413), *The Meal in Emmaus* (p. 428), and *The Presentation in the Temple* p. 277), which are all virtually the same size.

Etching; 21 × 16.1 cm. Only state.
Signed and dated: *Rembrandt f. 1654.*
Amsterdam, Rijksprentenkabinet.

Literature: Bartsch, no. 83; Hind, no. 280; Münz, no. 232; Boon, no. 257; Filedt Kok, no. B 83/Hofstede de Groot, *Rembrandt Bijbel*, N.T.e.26; Rotermund 1963, no. 233; Sumowski 1963, no. 92; 'Bijbelse Inspiratie', no. 47; Tümpel 1970, no. 108.

The Descent from the Cross

The Pietà None of the Gospels describes the lamentation after Jesus' death. This theme dates from the late Middle Ages, when the lamentation, between the descent from the Cross and the entombment, developed to become one of the most frequently depicted scenes from the Passion, as a result of the emphasis on the suffering of Christ.

Combining this scene with the descent from the Cross, Rembrandt's *pietà* in this expressive sketch is set at the foot of the Cross. Mary's sorrow is the central theme. She passionately enfolds her dead son in her arms, pressing her face against his. Nicodemus, Joseph of Arimathea and the others who helped to take Jesus down from the Cross look on with deep emotion.

According to Otto Benesch, Rembrandt's composition was inspired by a 15th-century work by the Flemish master Rogier van der Weyden.

Drawing in pen; 17.1 × 15.4 cm.
Ca. 1635.
Berlin, Kupferstichkabinett der Staatlichen Museen.

Literature: Benesch I, no. 100 (*ca.* 1635); Slive I, no. 11 (*ca.* 1635)/Sumowski 1963, no. 93; Tümpel 1970, no. 109.

In this sketch in oils, which was probably intended as a study for an etching which was never executed, the event is again closely related to the descent from the Cross. Apart from the empty Cross of Jesus, we also see two crosses to his left and right with the sentenced criminals. The arrangement of the three crosses is the same as that in the oval etching of the three crosses dating from *ca.* 1641 (see p. 394). In the light which focuses attention on the main characters, the inconsolable mother of sorrows sits with her son's body on her lap. The body is rigid in death, and Mary Magdalene embraces Jesus' feet. In the distance, Jerusalem is lit up against a pale grey sky.

A preparatory study (Benesch I, no. 154), which - like this sketch in oils - underwent many changes, shows that originally Rembrandt had intended a horizontal composition for this work.

Paper and canvas on a panel; 32 × 26.5 cm.
Ca. 1640-42.
London, National Gallery.

Literature: Bredius, no. 565; Bauch, no. 69; Gerson, no. 89; Bredius-Gerson, no. 565.

406

Jesus is Carried to the Sepulchre

... and laid him in a sepulchre which was hewn out of a rock ...
(Mark 15:46)

Holding a burning torch in his hand, Joseph of Arimathea accompanies the two men who are carrying Jesus' body to the sepulchre. One of the women walks along with him, weeping and wiping her tears with a cloth.

This study, dating from the early 1630s, was probably done in connection with the scenes from the Passion commissioned by Prince Frederik Hendrik on which Rembrandt was working at the time (see p. 392). Works on the theme of Jesus' burial, either as an independent subject or as part of a series on the Passion, usually depicted the entombment, and not the body being carried to the sepulchre. For the painting on this subject for the Prince, which was completed in 1639, Rembrandt also finally chose the actual entombment (see p. 410).

Drawing in pen; 12.4 × 14.9 cm.
Ca. 1632-33.
Berlin, Kupferstichkabinett der Staatlichen Museen.

Literature: Benesch I, no. 60 (*ca.* 1632-33); Slive I, no. 285 (*ca.* 1633)/Rotermund 1963, no. 235; Sumowski 1963, no. 94; Tümpel 1970, no. 110.

... and laid him in a sepulchre which was hewn out of a rock ...
(Mark 15:46)

The Gospel according to St John gives the most details about the sepulchre where Jesus' body was taken: 'Now in the place where he was crucified there was a garden; and in the garden a new sepulchre, wherein was man never yet laid. There they laid Jesus therefore, because of the Jews' preparation day; for the sepulchre was nigh at hand' (John 19:41-42).

Rembrandt's first work depicting Jesus being carried to the sepulchre was outlined in the sketch dating from *ca.* 1632-33 reproduced on the preceding page. The next version of this subject was this etching dating from *ca.* 1645. Four men carry their dead master on a bier to his final resting place, leading the funeral procession which is approaching the entrance to the sepulchre. The despondency weighing upon the small group of faithful followers is individually expressed in all the characters.

This print is one of the most beautiful examples of Rembrandt's Biblical etchings because of the deeply moving way in which he depicted the quiet procession without any excessive virtuosity.

Etching; 13.1 × 10.8 cm. Only state.
Signed: *Rembrant.*
Ca. 1645.
Amsterdam, Rijksprentenkabinet.

Literature: Bartsch, no. 84; Hind, no. 215; Münz, no. 224 (*ca.* 1653); Boon, no. 194; Filedt Kok, no. B 84/Rotermund 1963, no. 236; Sumowski 1963, no. 95; 'Bijbelse Inspiratie', no. 48; Tümpel 1970, no. 111.

Jesus is Carried to the Sepulchre

... *and laid him in a sepulchre which was hewn out of a rock ...*
(Mark 15:46)

Of the five scenes of the Passion commissioned by Prince Frederik Hendrik (see p. 392), Rembrandt only delivered the last two, including this entombment, in 1634. In the letter to Huygens in which he stated that he had completed the two paintings, he described the work with the dead body of Christ being placed in the sepulchre. The hill of Golgotha with the three crosses can be seen through the strangely illuminated opening in the sepulchral cave.

Canvas, rounded at the top; 92.3 × 69 cm.
Completed in 1639.
Munich, Alte Pinakothek.

Literature: Bredius, no. 560; Bauch, no. 68; Gerson, no. 87; Bredius-Gerson, no. 560/Hofstede de Groot, *Rembrandt Bijbel*, N.T.p.28; Tümpel 1970, under no. 110.

... *and laid him in a sepulchre which was hewn out of a rock ...*
(Mark 15:46)

This beautiful sketch in oils is probably identical with 'A sketch of the entombment of Christ by Rembrant' mentioned in Rembrandt's inventory drawn up on 25 and 26 July 1656 (Hofstede de Groot, *Urkunden* 169, no. 111). The main group broadly corresponds to the painting reproduced on the preceding page, which is now in Munich. The grisaille was previously considered to be a preliminary study for that painting, but nowadays it is considered to be a design done in the 1640s for an etching which was never completed.

Panel; 32.2 × 40.5 cm.
Ca. 1645.
Glasgow, Hunterian Art Gallery.

Literature: Bredius, no. 554; Bauch, no. 74; Gerson, no. 217; Bredius-Gerson, no. 554 (painted in the 1630s).

The Entombment of Jesus

The Entombment of Jesus

... *and laid him in a sepulchre which was hewn out of a rock ...*
(Mark 15:46)

Rembrandt's 1656 inventory clearly reveals that he was very familiar with Italian art. This semicircular composition of the entombment is direct proof of his interest in the work of the Italian masters. The drawing is actually a fairly accurate copy of a composition of the school of Raphael which has survived as three drawings (illus. in Benesch V, pp. 326-27). Rembrandt's copy has most in common with the version now in the Fogg Art Museum in Cambridge (Mass.), which is normally ascribed to Raphael's pupil Perino-del Vaga (1501-47). However, in some of the details it more closely resembles the other two. Therefore it is by no means out of the question that Rembrandt was familiar with another version which has now disappeared, possibly the lost original by Raphael himself on which the three known drawings are based.

Pen and brush drawing; 18 × 28.3 cm.
Bottom right in later handwriting: *Rembrandt.*
Ca. 1655.
Haarlem, Teylers Museum.

Literature: Benesch V, no. 1208 (*ca.* 1657-58); Slive I, no. 179 (*ca.* 1655-60)/'Bijbelse Inspiratie', no. 113; Tümpel 1970, under no. 112.

... *and laid him in a sepulchre which was hewn out of a rock ...*
(Mark 15:46)

The above-mentioned Italian composition must have fascinated Rembrandt. In addition to making a copy of it, he also assimilated and adapted certain elements from it in this etching of the entombment dating from 1654. In accordance with the Biblical text, he changed the Renaissance-style tomb from his example into a hollow sepulchre hewn from the rock. Nevertheless, the background, where two skulls grin at us from the edge of a stone wall in a dark niche, reveals that in creating this vault he was influenced by the Italian drawing. The figure seen from the back which is in the foreground and forms part of the group lowering the body of Jesus into the grave is also derived from that drawing. One of the disciples has already descended into the sepulchre to take the mortal remains of his master. In his arrangement of the figures, Rembrandt abandoned the composition of his example; the witnesses to the entombment are silently mourning, assembled on the left half of the print. He did retain another basic pattern which was used in the Italian composition: the arch of the vault is continued in the semicircle where the tall Nicodemus, Mary and the group with the body of Jesus are arranged. In this way we gain an impression of the way in which Rembrandt deviated from his examples and how he adapted the elements to correspond with his own imagination.

In the later states of the etching, Rembrandt used shading to darken and deepen the shadows shown in this print even further, so that the whole place is in darkness and in the strongly concentrated light only the body of Jesus and the figures and features of those around him can be distinguished.

This print, together with the etching mentioned on p. 405, is often considered to be part of a group which might have been intended to form a series on the life of Jesus.

Etching; 21.1 × 16.1 cm. First state of four.
Ca. 1654.
Amsterdam, Rijksprentenkabinet.

Literature: Bartsch, no. 86; Hind, no. 281; Münz, no. 241 (*ca.* 1658-59); Boon, no. 259; Filedt Kok, no. B 86/Hofstede de Groot, *Rembrandt Bijbel*, N.T.e.27; Sumowski 1963, no. 96; Tümpel 1970, no. 113.

His countenance was like lightning

Matthew 28 IN the end of the sabbath, as it began to dawn toward the first *day* of the week, came Mary Magdalene and the other Mary to see the sepulchre.

2 And, behold, there was a great earthquake: for the angel of the Lord descended from heaven, and came and rolled back the stone from the door, and sat upon it.

3 His countenance was like lightning, and his raiment white as snow:

4 And for fear of him the keepers did shake, and became as dead *men*.

5 And the angel answered and said unto the women, Fear not ye: for I know that ye seek Jesus, which was crucified.

6 He is not here: for he is risen, as he said. Come, see the place where the Lord lay.

7 And go quickly, and tell his disciples that he is risen from the dead; and, behold, he goeth before you into Galilee; there shall ye see him: lo, I have told you.

The Resurrection of Jesus

And, behold, there was a great earthquake: for the angel of the Lord descended from heaven, and came and rolled back the stone from the door, and sat upon it. His countenance was like lightning, and his raiment white as snow: And for fear of him the keepers did shake, and became as dead men. (Matthew 28:2-4)

To connect the story of the Passion with the appearance of the resurrected Lord, the Gospels each in their own way tell the story of the women who visit the grave on Easter morning and are told: 'He is not here; for he is risen.' The mystery of the Resurrection itself is not described. In the art of the Western Church it was not until the 13th century that the event in which Jesus was resurrected from the grave - which is not described in the Gospels - was depicted. Initially the resurrected Lord steps out of the open tomb with a banner of victory in his hand, one leg over the edge. Later on, he was depicted floating in a shroud of light and cloud above the empty grave, while the soldiers on guard collapse in amazement and disbelief, or otherwise sleep on undisturbed in great peace. In this painting of the Resurrection - which is part of the series of the Passion commissioned by Prince Frederik Hendrik - Rembrandt shows Jesus just as he had earlier depicted Lazarus in his works entitled *The Raising of Lazarus*, in the movement of the awakening from the sleep of death, wrapped in a white shroud (cf. pp. 351-52). He is the only artist to show Jesus in this way.

The Entombment (p. 410) and *The Resurrection*, which were both more than half finished in 1636 (see p. 392), were not completed and delivered until 1639. In Rembrandt's third letter to Huygens, dated 12 January 1639, he stated that these two last works were now also finished, and described his painting of the Resurrection: 'Christ rising up from the dead to the great amazement and terror of the guards'. X-rays, as well as copies of an earlier version of this painting, have revealed that initially Rembrandt left out the figure of Jesus rising up from the grave, and merely showed how an angel of lightning suddenly lifted up the cover of the empty tomb to the amazement and horror of the soldiers - as described in the Gospel according to St Matthew. In order to turn the painting into a depiction of the actual Resurrection, as commissioned, he added the figure of Christ later on. As described in the text of the Gospel according to St Matthew, only two women are shown at the bottom right, Mary Magdalene and the other Mary, instead of the three that are customarily present (see Mark 16:1-8). B. Broos pointed out the relationship between Rembrandt's work and the painting by his teacher Pieter Lastman, *The Resurrection of Jesus*, dating from 1610 (Amsterdam, Rijksmuseum); in the latter the Resurrection also includes the appearance of an angel who lifts up the cover of the sepulchre. The theme is not found again in Rembrandt's Biblical works.

In the above-mentioned letter, Rembrandt told Huygens that the Prince would undoubtedly be pleased with the works which had been completed with great diligence and industry because the greatest naturalness and movement was observed. He added that this was the reason that it had taken so long to complete the works. It is known that Huygens thought highly of Rembrandt as a historical painter because he was able to express the moods of the characters in his works realistically and effectively (see p. 380). However, it is not known whether he considered Rembrandt's concern to achieve the greatest possible naturalness and movement as a valid excuse for the artist's delay in completing the two paintings.

Canvas on panel, rounded at the top; 92 × 67 cm.
Signed and dated: *Rembr..t 163(9)*.
Munich, Alte Pinakothek.

Literature: Bredius, no. 561; Bauch, no. 67; Gerson, no. 88; Bredius-Gerson, no. 561/Hofstede de Groot, *Rembrandt Bijbel*, N.T.p.29; Sumowski 1963, no. 97; K. Bauch, 'Ikonographischer Stil' in *Studien zur Kunstgeschichte*, Berlin 1967, pp. 129-31; B.P.J. Broos, 'Rembrandt en zijn eeuwige leermeester Lastman' in *De kroniek van het Rembrandthuis*, 26 (1972), pp. 84-90.

He is risen

Mark 16 AND when the sabbath was past, Mary Magdalene, and Mary the *mother* of James, and Salome, had bought sweet spices, that they might come and anoint him.

2 And very early in the morning the first *day* of the week, they came unto the sepulchre at the rising of the sun.

3 And they said among themselves, Who shall roll us away the stone from the door of the sepulchre?

4 And when they looked, they saw that the stone was rolled away: for it was very great.

5 And entering into the sepulchre, they saw a young man sitting on the right side, clothed in a long white garment; and they were affrighted.

6 And he saith unto them, Be not affrighted: Ye seek Jesus of Nazareth, which was crucified: he is risen; he is not here: behold the place where they laid him.

7 But go your way, tell his disciples and Peter that he goeth before you into Galilee: there shall ye see him, as he said unto you.

8 And they went out quickly, and fled from the sepulchre; for they trembled and were amazed: neither said they any thing to any *man*; for they were afraid.

The Women by the Sepulchre

And they said among themselves, Who shall roll us away the stone from the door of the sepulchre? And when they looked, they saw that the stone was rolled away: for it was very great. (Mark 16:3-4)

Before it became popular to show the Resurrection of Jesus in a direct way in Western Christian art in the 13th century, the Easter scene was usually devoted to the modest story of the women who go to the grave with sweet scented herbs as the sun rises on the first day of the week, and then see that the stone has been rolled away from the entrance.

This fascinating drawing, a high point in Rembrandt's Biblical drawings of the 1650s, portrays the rarely depicted story in a very simple and restrained way. The women unsuspectingly enter the dark cave from the early light of the new day. The three crosses on Golgotha and the walls of Jerusalem can be seen in the distance through the arched opening. The women's eyes immediately turn to the entrance to the grave. Soon they will discover that the heavy cylindrical stone (bottom left) has been rolled away from the low entrance to the crypt, where they, together with Joseph of Arimathea, had placed the body of Jesus on Friday evening. The rays of light coming through the opening indicate the presence of the angel by the grave who will tell the women that Jesus is resurrected.

A comparison of this drawing with the painting of the entombment dating from 1639 (p. 410) or with that of Jesus' appearance to Mary Magdalene dating from 1638 (p. 419), clearly shows that Rembrandt's ideas concerning the construction of Jesus' sepulchre changed significantly in the course of the years.

Pen and brush drawing; 15.9 × 23.1 cm.
Bottom right in later handwriting: *Rembrandt.*
Ca. 1655.
Rotterdam, Museum Boymans-van Beuningen.

Literature: Benesch V, no. 1009 (*ca.* 1656)/Rotermund 1963, no. 237; Sumowski 1963, no. 98.

Woman, why weepest thou?

John 20 11 but Mary stood without at the sepulchre weeping: and as she wept, she stooped down, *and looked* into the sepulchre,

12 And seeth two angels in white sitting, the one at the head, and the other at the feet, where the body of Jesus had lain.

13 And they say unto her, Woman, why weepest thou? She saith unto them, Because they have taken away my Lord, and I know not where they have laid him.

14 And when she had thus said, she turned herself back, and saw Jesus standing, and knew not that it was Jesus.

15 Jesus saith unto her, Woman, why weepest thou? whom seekest thou? She, supposing him to be the gardener, saith unto him, Sir, if thou have borne him hence, tell me where thou hast laid him, and I will take him away.

16 Jesus saith unto her, Mary. She turned herself, and saith unto him, Rabboni; which is to say, Master.

17 Jesus saith unto her, Touch me not; for I am not yet ascended to my Father: but go to my brethren, and say unto them, I ascend unto my Father, and your Father; and *to* my God, and your God.

18 Mary Magdalene came and told the disciples that she had seen the Lord, and *that* he had spoken these things unto her.

The Resurrected Lord Appears to Mary Magdalene

And when she had thus said, she turned herself back, and saw Jesus standing, and knew not that it was Jesus. Jesus saith unto her, Woman, why weepest thou? whom seekest thou? (John 20:14-15)

Jesus' appearance to Mary Magdalene, who had remained behind by the empty sepulchre weeping, is described only in the Gospel according to St John. In this charming painting dating from 1638, Rembrandt depicts the scene in the garden mentioned by John, with the new sepulchre where Jesus had been placed after being taken down from the Cross (see p. 409). In her despair over the disappearance of the body, Mary Magdalene can only think that the grave has been desecrated, and hardly notices the angels talking to her. She is seen at the moment when she turns round and sees Jesus standing there, but she doesn't recognize him. In order to express this, Rembrandt uses the technique which is used in most depictions of this popular theme: he shows the resurrected Lord with a spade in his hand and a broad-brimmed hat, as the gardener Mary mistakes him for. The soft morning light of the first 'day of the Lord' shines over the figures and the landscape, in which the temple of Jerusalem rises up in the background.

The poet Jeremias de Decker (1609-66), a friend of Rembrandt, composed the following poem to go with the painting, with the inscription, 'To the illustration of the resurrected Christ and Mary Magdalene, painted by the excellent Mr Rembrant van Rijn for H.F. Waterloos':

When I read the story described by St John,
And next to it see this artistic scene,
I think, where has a painter ever followed the writer so
closely, Or dead paint brought so much to life?
It seems that Christ is saying: Mary do not tremble.
It is I. Death has not taken your Lord.
She believes this, but not entirely,
And seems to hover between joy and sorrow, fear and hope.
The rock dominating the grave soars high up in the air in
this painting.
That rock and the shadows it casts
Create beauty and majesty in the rest of the work.
Your masterly strokes of the brush,
Friend Rembrandt, I first saw on this panel.
Therefore my pen will write an ode to your gifted brush
And my ink will praise your paint.

The words of this poem, which was first published in 1660, were written on the back of the painting.

Panel; 61.5 × 50 cm.
Signed and dated: *Rembrandt f. 1638.*
London, Buckingham Palace (Royal Collection).

Literature: Bredius, no. 559; Bauch, no. 66; Gerson, no. 82; Bredius-Gerson, no. 559/Hofstede de Groot, *Rembrandt Bijbel*, N.T.p.31; 'Bijbelse Inspiratie', under no. 114.

The Resurrected Lord Appears to Mary Magdalene

Jesus saith unto her, Woman, why weepest thou? whom seekest thou? She, supposing him to be the gardener, saith unto him, Sir, if thou have borne him hence, tell me where thou hast laid him, and I will take him away.
(John 20:15)

The moment depicted in this drawing immediately follows on from the scene depicted on the panel dating from 1638, which is now in London. Mary Magdalene hopelessly turns to the man she believes to be the gardener and, without looking at him, she begs him to tell her where he has placed the body of her dear master. The background shows the hill of Golgotha, with the three crosses, as well as the city of Jerusalem.

In broad lines the composition coincides with that of the panel in Buckingham Palace. It is therefore considered probable that the drawing was done during the time that Rembrandt was working on that painting. In addition to this drawing, there is in the Rijksprentenkabinet in Amsterdam another drawing of this subject which Rembrandt did at the same time (Benesch III, no. 538). However, because of the style of drawing, Otto Benesch believes that the two drawings were done *ca.* 1643, i.e., about five years after the painting.

Pen and ink drawing; 15.2 × 19 cm.
Ca. 1638.
Amsterdam, Rijksprentenkabinet.

Literature: Benesch III, no. 537 (*ca.* 1643); Slive II, no. 331; Haak, no. 24 (*ca.* 1638?)/Rotermund 1963, no. 238; 'Bijbelse Inspiratie', no. 114.

Jesus saith unto her, Mary! She turned herself, and saith unto him, Rabboni! which is to say, Master! Jesus saith unto her, Touch me not; for I am not yet ascended to my Father: but go to my brethren, and say unto them, I ascend unto my Father, and your Father; and to my God, and your God. (John 20:16-17)

Of all the scenes from this popular story, the scene depicted here has always appealed most to the imagination. By restricting the space in the painting to virtually no more than the foreground, Rembrandt brings the scene right up to the observer. Mary Magdalene recognizes the Lord by the familiar tone in which he pronounces her name. Assuming that her master has returned in his former earthly form, she stretches out her hands to him, but Jesus - who is now recognized, and therefore no longer appears as a gardener with a hat and spade - withdraws, and says to her: 'Touch me not.' Their earlier form of contact is over. Jesus' presence among his people will henceforth

be of a different nature. The first light of the new day glimmers over the trees in the background on the left.

The painting dates from 1651. In a drawing which he did later (Benesch V, no. 993), Rembrandt depicted the same scene again. Two further drawings from the same period (Benesch V, nos. 869a and 929) reveal how much this story fascinated him. These drawings concern the moment before recognition, and therefore the resurrected Lord is again portrayed in the guise in which he appeared in the works on the two preceding pages.

Canvas; 65 × 79 cm.
Signed and dated: *Rembrandt f. 1651*.
Brunswick, Herzog-Anton-Ulrich Museum.

Literature: Bredius, no. 583; Bauch, no. 83; Gerson, no. 269; Bredius-Gerson, no. 583/Hofstede de Groot, *Rembrandt Bijbel*, N.T.p.32; Sumowski 1963, no. 99; 'Bijbelse Inspiratie', under no. 115.

The Resurrected Lord Appears to Mary Magdalene

To a village called Emmaus

Luke 24 13 And, behold, two of them went that same day to a village called Emmaus, which was from Jerusalem *about* threescore furlongs.

14 And they talked together of all these things which had happened.

15 And it came to pass, that, while they communed *together* and reasoned, Jesus himself drew near, and went with them.

16 But their eyes were holden that they should not know him.

17 And he said unto them, What manner of communications *are* these that ye have one to another, as ye walk, and are sad?

18 And the one of them, whose name was Cleopas, answering said unto him, Art thou only a stranger in Jerusalem, and hast not known the things which are come to pass there in these days?

19 And he said unto them, What things? And they said unto him, Concerning Jesus of Nazareth, which was a prophet mighty in deed and word before God and all the people:

20 And how the chief priests and our rulers delivered him to be condemned to death, and have crucified him.

21 But we trusted that it had been he which should have redeemed Israel: and beside all this to day is the third day since these things were done.

22 Yea, and certain women also of our company made us astonished, which were early at the sepulchre;

23 And when they found not his body, they came, saying, that they had also seen a vision of angels, which said that he was alive.

24 And certain of them which were with us went to the sepulchre, and found *it* even so as the women had said: but him they saw not.

25 Then he said unto them, O fools, and slow of heart to believe all that the prophets have spoken:

26 Ought not Christ to have suffered these things, and to enter into his glory?

27 And beginning at Moses and all the prophets, he expounded unto them in all the scriptures the things concerning himself.

28 And they drew nigh unto the village, whither they went: and he made as though he would have gone further.

29 But they constrained him, saying, Abide with us: for it is toward evening, and the day is far spent. And he went in to tarry with them.

30 And it came to pass, as he sat at meat with them, he took bread, and blessed *it*, and brake, and gave to them.

31 And their eyes were opened, and they knew him; and he vanished out of their sight.

32 And they said one to another, Did not our heart burn within us, while he talked with us by the way, and while he opened to us the scriptures?

33 And they rose up the same hour, and returned to Jerusalem, and found the eleven gathered together, and them that were with them,

34 Saying, The Lord is risen indeed, and hath appeared to Simon.

35 And they told what things *were done* in the way, and how he was known of them in breaking of bread.

The Meal in Emmaus And it came to pass, as he sat at meat with them, he took bread, and blessed it, and brake, and gave to them, and their eyes were opened, and they knew him ... (Luke 24:30-31)

The series of works in which Rembrandt depicted the climax of the Emmaus story in different ways throughout the years starts with this small painting dated *ca.* 1628, a fascinating night scene which is one of the most beautiful works from his early period. The young artist made use of the possibilities of chiaroscuro, a technique he had just discovered, with great virtuosity. With penetrating effect he shows the moment at which the tension which had slowly been building up is released. As though struck by lightning, the two disciples suddenly recognize the mysterious stranger breaking the bread to be their Lord. In the dark in the foreground one of the men falls down on his knees before Jesus, throwing over his chair. The other, illuminated by a light from an invisible source, recoils in shock and stares at the Lord in amazement. The dominant figure of the resurrected Lord is darkly outlined against the brightly lit wooden wall. The contours of his silhouette are repeated on a smaller scale in the glimpse of the women working in the kitchen at the back, ignorant of what has happened. There is no striking use of colour in this painting; the colour is subordinate to the dramatic lighting.

Paper on panel; 39 × 42 cm.
Signed: *RHL*.
Ca. 1628.
Paris, Musée Jacquemart-André.

Literature: Bredius, no. 539; Bauch, no. 49; Gerson, no.
14; Bredius-Gerson, no. 539/Sumowski 1963, no. 104.

On the Road to Emmaus with Jesus

And it came to pass, that, while they communed together and reasoned, Jesus himself drew near, and went with them. But their eyes were holden that they should not know him. And he said unto them, What manner of communications are these that ye have one to another, as ye walk, and are sad? (Luke 24:15-17)

Throughout his life, Rembrandt was fascinated by this famous Easter story from the Gospel according to St Luke. In his numerous versions of the final episode, the meal in Emmaus, the sudden recognition of Jesus is the central theme, but in this drawing of the walk to Emmaus it is precisely the lack of recognition that is emphasized. This sheet, characteristic of Rembrandt's unique style of drawing in about 1655, depicts the moment at which the resurrected Lord joins the two disciples who are returning home from Jerusalem disconsolately after the disturbing events of the previous two days. Politely the elder of the two takes off his hat to greet the stranger walking by, who is looking for company and unexpectedly joins in their conversation. His young companion, who is carrying their baggage, is not very enthusiastic either, and merely takes the opportunity of closely observing the stranger. The men both look at him, but they do not see who he is, for 'their eyes were holden that they should not know him'. As they go on their way and he explains to them what the Scriptures have to say about the suffering and death of the Messiah, they begin to glow inwardly, and in retrospect they are surprised that they had not recognized their master before.

In two drawings from an earlier date (Benesch I, no. 68A (*ca.* 1632-33) and Benesch III, no. 585 (*ca.* 1647)), Rembrandt also devoted some attention to the much less frequently depicted episode of the arrival in Emmaus, when the two men insistently invite their travelling companion, who pretends that he must go on, to stay with them.

Pen and ink drawing; 16.6 × 22.4 cm.
Ca. 1655.
Paris, The Louvre.

Literature: Benesch V, no. 987 (*ca.* 1655-56)/J.Q. van Regteren Altena, 'Rembrandt's Way to Emmaus' in *Kunstmuseets Arsskrift* 35-36 (1948-49), pp. 1-25.

And it came to pass, as he sat at meat with them, he took bread, and blessed it, and brake, and gave to them, and their eyes were opened, and they knew him ...
(Luke 24:30-31)

This small print dating from 1634 is closely related to the early painting reproduced on the left in its dynamic interpretation of the subject. The three figures at the table fill virtually the whole print. The robust figure of Jesus, illuminated against a dark background, is again viewed from the side, to the right of centre. As the Lord breaks the bread and pronounces the blessing, the man who has started to carve the meat suddenly stays his hand, and looks at him in astonishment. His companion opposite Jesus has already recognized the master and is speechless with amazement. Initially, Rembrandt also included a servant in the background on the left, but later he removed this figure as best he could with shading.

This commonly depicted theme was particularly popular in the 17th century as a symbol of the liturgical meal of the Lord in which the resurrected Lord is still recognized by believers in 'breaking the bread'. This wider interpretation is revealed most strongly in Rembrandt's versions of the subject which appear in the following pages: sacred scenes in which the breaking of the bread is the focal point, and the reactions of the disciples reveal an awe of holiness rather than shock.

Etching; 10.2 × 7.3 cm. Only state.
Signed and dated: *Rembrandt f. 1634.*
Amsterdam, Rijksprentenkabinet.

Literature: Bartsch, no. 88; Hind, no. 121; Münz, no. 203; Boon, no. 109; Filedt Kok, no. B 88/Tümpel 1970, no. 115.

The Meal in Emmaus

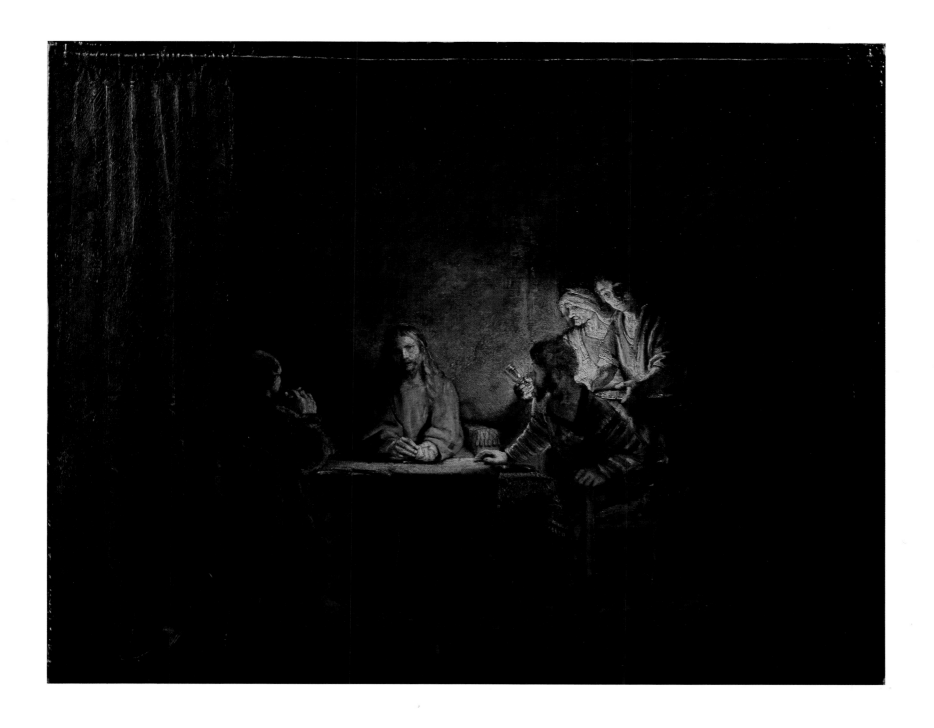

And it came to pass, as he sat at meat with them, he took bread, and blessed it, and brake, and gave to them, and their eyes were opened, and they knew him ...
(Luke 24:30-31)

Rembrandt's most famous version of this theme for the first time shows Jesus as the central figure of the group sitting at the table. The tall monumental niche rising up behind him emphasizes the majesty of his soft and radiant appearance. The startling light effects of twenty years before have been replaced by a much more subtle chiaroscuro which imbues the silent scene with a solemn character. While the disciples suddenly begin to see, the servant bringing the dish does not notice anything special.

Panel; 68 × 65 cm.
Signed and dated: *Rembrandt f. 1648.*
Paris, The Louvre.

Literature: Bredius, no. 578; Bauch, no. 82; Gerson, no. 218; Bredius-Gerson, no. 578/Sumowski 1963, no. 103.

And it came to pass, as he sat at meat with them, he took bread, and blessed it, and brake, and gave to them, and their eyes were opened, and they knew him ...
(Luke 24:30-31)

By simplifying the background and concentrating on the lighting, Rembrandt has created a much more intimate atmosphere in this variation on the previous painting, which also dates from 1648. Nevertheless, it is filled with a mysterious tension. As in the panel, *The Holy Family* (see p. 287), which is now in Kassel, there is a drawn curtain in this painting, as though Rembrandt wishes to say that the sacred scene can barely tolerate the gaze of the outside world.

Canvas; 89.5 × 111.5 cm.
Signed and dated: *Rembrandt f. 1648.*
Copenhagen, Statens Museum for Kunst.

Literature: Bredius, no. 579; Gerson, no. 219; Bredius-Gerson, no. 579/Hofstede de Groot, *Rembrandt Bijbel*, N.T.p.33.

The Meal in Emmaus

The Meal at Emmaus

And it came to pass, as he sat at meat with them, he took bread, and blessed it, and brake, and gave to them, and their eyes were opened, and they knew him ...
(Luke 24:30-31)

What Rembrandt had endeavoured to do in the two paintings shown on the previous pages was only fully achieved in this large-scale print dating from 1654. Up to then he had depicted the breaking of the bread in the customary fashion, but this time he chose to show the moment at which the Lord passes the broken bread to the men. He based the radiant Christ figure with outstretched arms on one of his drawings after *The Last Supper* by Leonardo da Vinci, from which he

also took the all-embracing canopy (see p. 369). The landlord in the foreground, who is going down to the cellar, can see that something strange is happening to his guests, but the meaning is lost on him.

Etching; 21.1 × 16 cm. Second state of three.
Signed and dated: *Rembrandt f. 1654.*
Amsterdam, Rijksprentenkabinet.

Literature: Bartsch, no. 87; Hind, no. 282; Münz, no. 233; Boon, no. 256; Filedt Kok, no. B 87/Hofstede de Groot, *Rembrandt Bijbel*, N.T.e.28; Rotermund 1963, no. 244; Sumowski 1963, no. 105; 'Bijbelse Inspiratie', no. 49; Tümpel 1970, no. 117.

... *And he vanished out of their sight.*
(Luke 24:31)

The two men stare in bewilderment at the empty chair where the Lord had been sitting at supper with them only a moment before. Next to the chair the discerning observer will see the vague outlines of a transparent figure departing with his back to us. Only his left heel is still sharply outlined. Where the head should be, there is light shining on all sides. This moment had never been depicted in such a way before in the history of art, though there are a number of medieval works of art which show Jesus' feet at the edge at the top just before they disappear into the clouds, as in many versions of the Ascension.

In 1718 Arnold Houbraken did an etching to illustrate the biography of Rembrandt in his work, *Groote schouburgh der Nederlantsche Konstschilders en Schilderessen* (Great Review of Dutch Artists), which was based on this drawing (or on a painting by Rembrandt which has now disappeared, and for which this drawing served as a preliminary study). The copy was intended to serve as a 'guide for untrained young artists'.

Pen and brush drawing; 19.8 × 18.3 cm.
Ca. 1648-49.
Cambridge, Fitzwilliam Museum.

Literature: Benesch IV, no. C 47 (probably a copy by a pupil after an original dating from *ca.* 1648-49, which has been lost)/Rotermund 1963, no. 245.

Jesus'
Disappearance in
Emmaus

My Lord and my God

John 20 19 Then the same day at evening, being the first *day* of the week, when the doors were shut where the disciples were assembled for fear of the Jews, came Jesus and stood in the midst, and saith unto them, Peace *be* unto you.

20 And when he had so said, he shewed unto them *his* hands and his side. Then were the disciples glad, when they saw the Lord.

21 Then said Jesus to them again, Peace *be* unto you: as *my* Father hath sent me, even so send I you.

22 And when he had said this, he breathed on *them*, and saith unto them, Receive ye the Holy Ghost:

23 Whose soever sins ye remit, they are remitted unto them; *and* whose soever *sins* ye retain, they are retained.

24 But Thomas, one of the twelve, called Didymus, was not with them when Jesus came.

25 The other disciples therefore said unto him, We have seen the Lord. But he said unto them, Except I shall see in his hands the print of the nails, and put my finger into the print of the nails, and thrust my hand into his side, I will not believe.

26 And after eight days again his disciples were within, and Thomas with them: *then* came Jesus, the doors being shut, and stood in the midst, and said, Peace *be* unto you.

27 Then saith he to Thomas, Reach hither thy finger, and behold my hands; and reach hither thy hand, and thrust *it* into my side: and be not faithless but believing.

28 And Thomas answered and said unto him, My Lord and my God.

29 Jesus saith unto him, Thomas, because thou hast seen me, thou hast believed: blessed *are* they that have not seen, and *yet* have believed.

The Doubting Thomas

Then saith he to Thomas, Reach hither thy finger, and behold my hands; and reach hither thy hand, and thrust it into my side: and be not faithless, but believing. And Thomas answered and said unto him, my Lord and my God.
(John 20:27-28)

Most works depicting this subject show Thomas placing his hand in the wound in Jesus' side. However, the Gospel according to St John does not suggest in any way that the apostle follows Jesus' suggestion. On the contrary, he is immediately convinced, and calls out: 'My Lord and my God'. It is in this spirit that Rembrandt interprets Thomas's reaction in this painting. The risen Lord, radiant in the centre of the composition, invites the doubter to feel his wounds. But it is no longer necessary, and following the shock of recognition, the formerly doubting Thomas makes the most beautiful confession of faith that is given in the Gospels. The other disciples are grouped around Jesus in a circle. The urge to look is no less in most of them than it was for Thomas. Only one of the apostles respectfully folds his hands without looking, and in this way confirms Jesus' words: 'Blessed are they that have not seen, and yet have believed.' Curiously, the greatest visionary of all Jesus' disciples, the apostle John, is shown sleeping, or rather, engaged in inner contemplation. Rembrandt also shows him in this pose in the large drawing *Jesus Surrounded by his Disciples* in Teylers Museum in Haarlem (see p. 359), which dates from 1634, like this painting. In this pose he is characterized in Christian art as the most profound writer of the Gospels and beholder of God's secrets, as described in the Revelation of St John.

Panel; 53 × 51 cm.
Signed and dated: *Rembrandt f. 1634.*
Moscow, Pushkin Museum.

Literature: Bredius, no. 552; Bauch, no. 60; Gerson, no. 67; Bredius-Gerson, no. 552/Tümpel 1970, under no. 118.

The Doubting Thomas

Then saith he to Thomas, Reach hither thy finger, and behold my hands; and reach hither thy hand, and thrust it into my side: and be not faithless, but believing. And Thomas answered and said unto him, my Lord and my God. (John 20:27-28)

It is a peculiar aspect of Rembrandt's interpretation that again he does not show Thomas placing his hand in Jesus' side. As in the painting dating from 1634 discussed above, he emphasizes how, in accordance with the Biblical text, the apostles' provisional belief immediately changes to an unconditional belief when the Lord shows them his wounds. The disciples are depicted in various poses, arranged randomly around a clear focal point. Amongst them the meekly kneeling figure of Thomas is emphasized through the heavier outline. The drawing dates from the middle of the 1650s, and is closely related to the etching dating from 1656 reproduced on the right.

Pen and ink drawing; 15 × 24 cm.
Ca. 1655.
Paris, The Louvre.

Literature: Benesch V, no. 1010 (*ca.* 1656)/'Bijbelse Inspiratie', under no. 50.

432

Then saith he to Thomas, Reach hither thy finger, and behold my hands; and reach hither thy hand, and thrust it into my side: and be not faithless, but believing. And Thomas answered and said unto him, my Lord and my God. (John 20:27-28)

The almost unreal appearance of this print dating from 1656 is in perfect harmony with the extraordinary character of the event being portrayed. A supernatural glow permeates all the figures when the impressive figure of the risen Lord suddenly appears among his disciples, and convinces the shocked Thomas that he is truly resurrected. The varied reactions of the others are expressed both concisely and characteristically. Few artists have succeeded in portraying the glorious vision of the resurrected Lord as convincingly as Rembrandt did in this etching.

Etching; 16.2 × 21 cm. Only state.
Signed and dated: *Rembrandt f. 1656.*
Amsterdam, Rijksprentenkabinet.

The Doubting Thomas

Literature: Bartsch, no. 89; Hind, no. 237; Münz, no. 220; Boon, no. 268; Filedt Kok, no. B 89/Hofstede de Groot, *Rembrandt Bijbel*, N.T.e.29; Rotermund 1963, no. 241; Sumowski 1963, no. 100; 'Bijbelse Inspiratie', no. 50; Tümpel 1970, no. 118.

433

And carried up into heaven

Luke 24 44 And he said unto them, These *are* the words which I spake unto you, while I was yet with you, that all things must be fulfilled, which were written in the law of Moses, and *in* the prophets, and *in* the psalms, concerning me.
45 Then opened he their understanding, that they might understand the scriptures,
46 And said unto them, Thus it is written, and thus it behoved Christ to suffer, and to rise from the dead the third day:
47 And that repentance and remission of sins should be preached in his name among all nations, beginning at Jerusalem.
48 And ye are witnesses of these things.
49 And, behold, I send the promise of my Father upon you: but tarry ye in the city of Jerusalem, until ye be endued with power from on high.
50 and he led them out as far as to Bethany, and he lifted up his hands, and blessed them.
51 And it came to pass, while he blessed them, he was parted from them, and carried up into heaven.
52 And they worshipped him, and returned to Jerusalem with great joy:
53 And were continually in the temple, praising and blessing God. Amen.

The Ascension of Jesus

And he led them out as far as to Bethany; and he lifted up his hands, and blessed them. And it came to pass, while he blessed them, he was parted from them, and carried out into heaven.
(Luke 24:50-51)

As the apostles who remained behind on earth gaze up at him, Jesus rises up to heaven, dressed in white and radiant with the glory of the Lord shining all around him, and accompanied by angels. The wounds of the nails, the signs of his humiliation, without which he could not have been raised up, can still be seen on his raised hands. In the Acts of the Apostles 1:9, there is a description of the cloud coming from the right, which in a moment will pass over the figure of the rising Lord like a veil, so that he will disappear from sight. The Gospel according to St Luke concludes with the Ascension of Jesus, and the Acts of the Apostles starts with it: 'And when he had spoken these things, while they beheld, he was taken up; and a cloud received him out of their sight.' Rembrandt expressed the awe and astonishment with which the apostles observe these events in a range of feeling in their faces and gestures.

The painting is one of the five scenes of the Passion which Rembrandt was commissioned to paint by Prince Frederik Hendrik during the 1630s (see p. 392). The painting is dated 1636. This accords with the presumed date at the beginning of 1636 of Rembrandt's first letter to Constantijn Huygens, in which he wrote that of the three works of the Passion still to be delivered, one of Christ ascending to heaven had now been completed. When he sent the work, he informed Huygens in a short letter (dated February 1636, in another hand), that he would soon go to The Hague to see how the work fitted in with the other paintings.

It is probable that Rembrandt started on it shortly after completing the first two works in about 1634. This explains the similarity of the painting to the etching, *The Angel Appears to the Shepherds*, which was done in the same year. In that work, the heavens open in the same way to the amazement of a number of mortals, though in that case it is to announce the coming of the Lord (see p. 229). However, Rembrandt's most important source of inspiration for this composition is considered to be Titian's painting, *The Ascension of Mary* in the Frari church in Venice, which was painted between 1516 and 1518. Rembrandt must have had a print or a painted copy of this work. X-rays have shown that initially Rembrandt showed the figure of God the Father above Christ's head in the same way as he appears in Titian's painting over Mary, as she ascends. At a later stage he must have thought it was more sensible to take into account the Calvinist prohibition against depicting the Invisible. Therefore he painted an aura over this figure with in the centre a dove, the traditional symbol of the Holy Ghost.

In older works up to the 12th century, the right hand of the Father appears at the top of the picture enclosing the hand stretched out by his Son, and in many works from the late Middle Ages the Lord ascending up to heaven has already largely disappeared from the picture, leaving only his feet at the top of the picture.

Canvas, rounded at the top; 92.7 × 68.3 cm.
Signed and dated: *Rembrandt f. 1636.*
Munich, Alte Pinakothek.

Literature: Bredius, no. 557; Bauch, no. 64; Gerson, no. 80; Bredius-Gerson, no. 557/Hofstede de Groot, *Rembrandt Bijbel*, N.T.p.34; Sumowski 1963, no. 106.

SUMMARY OF REMBRANDT'S LIFE

1606   Rembrandt was born in Leyden on 15 July. His father, the miller Harmen Gerritsz van Rijn, the only member of the family to convert to Calvinism as an adult, had married the well-to-do baker's daughter Neeltje van Suydtbroek in the Pieterskerk in 1589. Since 1572 this church had been used for the Reformed service. On her mother's side, she came from an old family of regents in Leyden, which had remained Catholic. Rembrandt was the eighth of their nine children. The year of his birth was a turning point in the history of the young Republic of the United Netherlands. After 1606, secret discussions were held between trusted agents on the Spanish side and diplomatic representatives of the Republic in order to bring about an end to the war between the two parties which had been dragging on since 1568. In 1609 these discussions were concluded with the Twelve-Year Armistice, which actually implied the Spanish recognition of Dutch independence. The Republic entered a period of great cultural development.

1613   In preparation for his classical education, Rembrandt's parents sent him to the strict Calvinist Latin School in Leyden when he was 7 years old.

1620   On 20 May, Rembrandt was enrolled as a student in the faculty of arts at the University of Leyden. Later that year he left the University and was apprenticed to the Leyden artist, Jacob van Swanenburgh, who had worked in Italy from *ca.* 1600 to 1617 and mainly painted depictions of hell, inspired by Hieronymus Bosch and Pieter Bruegel.

1624   To complete his training, Rembrandt went to Amsterdam for six months to be apprenticed to Pieter Lastman, one of the most highly esteemed historical painters in Holland. Rembrandt apparently had an ambition to become a historical artist also, i.e., to paint historical, and in particular Biblical and mythological, subjects in which the human form and human emotions and passions are the main theme.

1625   The beginning of Rembrandt's career as an independent artist in Leyden, where he shared a studio with Jan Lievens (1607-74), who had also been apprenticed to Lastman. Rembrandt's earliest known painting, *The Stoning of St Stephen*, dates from this year.

1628   The Utrecht lawyer Arnold van Buchell wrote in his diary about the 22-year-old Rembrandt: 'The miller's son from Leyden is praised very highly, but this is premature.' This note is the first written comment on Rembrandt's art.

In November, Constantijn Huygens, the eclectic and gifted secretary of the Stadtholder, Prince Frederik Hendrik, came to Leyden and presumably on that occasion visited the studio of Rembrandt and Lievens. In his autobiographical notes written slightly later, he devotes an enthusiastic passage to the two young artists. Through Huygens's mediation they received several commissions from The Hague.

1630   Rembrandt's father died and was buried in the Pieterskerk in Leyden on 27 April.

1631   In June, Rembrandt lent the Amsterdam art dealer Hendrick van Uylenburgh 1000 guilders. It was probably at the end of that year that he moved to Amsterdam, where he moved in with van Uylenburgh, who lived in the Sint-Anthoniesbreestraat (now the Jodenbreestraat). This could indicate that the latter exerted pressure on Rembrandt to come to Amsterdam, where the opportunities for a young, ambitious painter were greater than in Leyden.

1632   Rembrandt rapidly gained great popularity as a portrait painter. One of his portraits was of Amalia van Solms, the wife of Prince Frederik Hendrik. At roughly the same time, the Stadtholder commissioned Rembrandt to paint a series of scenes from the Passion of Jesus.

1634   On 22 June, Rembrandt married Saskia van Uylenburgh, a niece of Hendrick van Uylenburgh, in the Reformed church of Sint-Anna-Parochie in Friesland. Saskia was born in Leeuwarden on 2 August 1612. Her father, Rombout van Uylenburgh, had been burghermaster of that town and had held many other prominent positions. When both her parents had died - her mother died when she was 6 years old, her father when she was 11 - she went to live with a family in Amsterdam. As well as her cousin Hendrick, at whose home she undoubtedly met Rembrandt, her cousin Aaltje van Uylenburgh also lived in Amsterdam. Aaltje, who was forty years her senior, was married to the pastor Jan Cornelisz Sylvius. She had been Saskia's guardian until she came of age.

1638   On 22 July, a daughter, Cornelia, was christened. The child died within three weeks and was buried on 13 August.

1639   On 5 January, Rembrandt bought a respectable house on the Sint-Antoniesbreestraat, two houses away from that of Hendrick van Uylenburgh. It cost 13,000 guilders. The repayment of that sum became an increasing financial burden for him.

1640   On 29 July, a second daughter, also called Cornelia, was christened, but she died within two weeks and was buried on 12 August. A month later Rembrandt's mother died. She was buried in the Pieterskerk in Leyden on 14 September.

1641   In the second edition of his *Beschrijvinge der Stadt Leyden* (Description of the Town of Leyden), J.J. Orlers published the first biography of Rembrandt.

On 22 September Titus was christened. He was the only one of Rembrandt and Saskia's children to reach maturity.

1642   On 5 June Saskia wrote her will as she lay ill in bed. She died on 14 June and was buried five days later in the Oude Kerk in Amsterdam. Rembrandt was left on his own with Titus, who was 9 months old. He employed Geertge Dircx, a young childless widow from Noord Holland, to look after the child, and she soon became his lover.

1648   The Peace of Munster brought an end to the war between Spain and the Republic of the United Netherlands. Spain recognized the independence of the Republic, which abandoned its claims to the southern Netherlands.

1649   Big problems arose between Rembrandt and Geertge Dircx. Meanwhile, a new servant had come into Rembrandt's house and Geertge realized she would have to make way for her. After leaving Rembrandt's house in June, she instigated legal proceedings against him on 25 September for failing to fulfil his promise of marriage. Rembrandt appeared before the court only after the third summons. He avoided a forced wedding with Geertge, but the three commissars of marital affairs decided that he would have to pay her a single sum of 160 guilders and 200 guilders per year for the rest of his life. Apparently all this affected Rembrandt so much that he was barely able to work. At any rate, there are no known paintings and etchings dating from that year.

1650   By bribing bailiffs and regents, Rembrandt managed to have Geertge committed to a penal institution in Gouda on 4 July. In 1651, he tried to ensure that she would remain imprisoned for another eleven years. Despite Rembrandt's dire threats, Geertge's friends succeeded in freeing her in May 1655. She probably died in 1656 or shortly afterwards.

1653   Rembrandt's financial affairs became increasingly hopeless. Fourteen years after purchasing the expensive house in the Antoniesbreestraat he still owed 7000 guilders of the 13,000 guilders of his debt, as well as the interest on it since 1649, and part of the tax. It was clear that his income was no longer sufficient for the repayments.

1654   In July, his mistress Hendrickje Stoffels, was summoned by the Amsterdam Council of Churches because she was living with Rembrandt. She appeared before them on 23 July after the third summons. She admitted that she had been 'guilty of whoring with Rembrandt the artist, was severely punished, and ordered to pay a fine and excluded from the Lord's table (the evening meal)'.

In October their daughter Cornelia was born.

1656   Rembrandt applied to be allowed to make available his total assets to pay his creditors. This meant that he voluntarily paid all the money raised on his entire property to his creditors. On 25 July, an inventory of his possessions was drawn up for the city auctioneer.

1657   On 4 December, a three-week-long auction was held of Rembrandt's possessions in the inn, The Keyserskroon. In February 1658, his house was auctioned, but he was allowed to continue to live there for another two years. In the autumn of 1658, a special auction was held to sell the prints and drawings in Rembrandt's possession. The total sum that was raised was by no means sufficient to satisfy all the creditors.

1660   Rembrandt moved with his family to a house on the Rozengracht. As a decree of the Artists' Guild had ruled that following the public sale of his work, he was no longer permitted to sell his own work, Titus and Hendrickje established an art dealers' business together on 15 December. If necessary, Rembrandt was to act as their adviser, as no one could be better informed than he, and in exchange for his livelihood he agreed to pass all his work to the business.

1663   Hendrickje had already been physically ill though she was still active on 7 August 1661 when she made her will. She was buried on 24 July in the Westerkerk.

1668   On 10 February, Titus married Magdalena van Loo, the daughter of a silversmith. He died less than seven months later and was buried in the Westerkerk on 7 September.

1669   Titus's daughter Titia van Rijn was born in March, six months after her father's death.

Rembrandt died on 4 October and was buried in the Westerkerk on 8 October. Magdalena van Loo, Titus's widow, died a few days later.

Epilogue

The Old Testament

THE HISTORY OF THE PATRIARCHS

A large proportion of Rembrandt's paintings, etchings and drawings of Old Testament subjects are devoted to subjects taken from the book of Genesis. For example, this applies to ten of the eighteen etchings. This attention to the stories of the patriarchs was a general feature of the religious art of the northern Netherlands in the 17th century. Almost half of the paintings of Old Testament subjects dating from this period are devoted to themes from the stories in the book of Genesis. A great deal of material was also provided by other narrative books of the Old Testament. In contrast with the Middle Ages, when scenes from Jesus' childhood, Mary's life and the Crucifixion were predominant, at this time Old Testament scenes were regularly adopted as independent subjects for prints and paintings. The stories of Noah, Abraham, Isaac and Jacob, which revealed so much spirituality and piety, particularly fascinated the 17th-century artists and were used as examples.

During the Middle Ages the figures and events described in the Old Testament had been explained as precursors of those in the New Testament. For the believers of that time the only significance of the Old Testament lay in its relationship to the New Testament; a story from the Old Testament was only relevant in so far as it referred to an episode in the life of Jesus. In the frescoes and painted ceilings of churches, and the statues and altarpieces that decorated them, Old Testament themes were always of lesser importance. For example, in the medieval view, the story of Abraham, who was prepared to obey God and sacrifice his only son Isaac, was a reference to God the Father, who so loved man that he was prepared to sacrifice his only begotten son. Isaac, tied to the sacrificial woodpile, was viewed as an anticipatory representation of Christ on the Cross. Thus Abraham's sacrifice was only ever depicted in relation to a representation of Christ on the Cross, and it was always explained in these terms. The adventures of Joseph, Jacob's favourite son, were also always explained and represented as a foreshadowing of Jesus' passion and death. Like Jesus, Joseph was betrayed and rejected by his brothers, and through his eventual exaltation he achieved the salvation of a great nation. Jesus' resurrection from the grave was anticipated in the prophet Jonah, who was spewed up on to land after spending three days and three nights inside a fish. As in the Middle Ages the Old Testament served only to explain the New Testament, the interrelated episodes from the Old and New Testaments were often depicted together.

The beginning of the 16th century saw the end of the Middle Ages, and this increasingly contrived explanation of Old Testament events gradually lost its general currency. Under the influence of Biblical humanism and the doctrines of the Reformation, a new interest developed in the Bible, and this led to a different interpretation of the Old Testament. The literal/historical interpretation which henceforth became increasingly predominant had an effect on religious art. There was room for new possibilities. The individual character and religious significance of Old Testament stories were increasingly acknowledged, and it was no longer accepted unquestioningly that when artists depicted Old Testament subjects, their choice and treatment would be determined by the long-held principles. These changes were reflected most clearly in 16th-century prints. Series of saints and prints devoted to the suffering of Jesus had long been among the regular repertoire of every print artist. It was a new development that series of prints now also depicted the events in the lives of Abraham, Isaac and Jacob, the adventures of Joseph and those of other great Old Testament figures - as subjects in their own right, as they related to each other and in chronological order, because they had their own significance and were important figures. In this way the printmakers of the time created works using many different themes from the Old Testament which had never, or hardly ever, been used before in art. It is clear that the historical painters of the 17th century found models in the graphic work of the 16th century for the Old Testament scenes they painted.

In the footsteps of his teacher Pieter Lastman and of his other precursors (including the brothers Jan and Jacob Pynas), Rembrandt was often inspired by this wealth of illustrative material. Research into his large collection of prints - which largely consisted of 16th- and 17th-century Dutch, German and Italian masters, according to his inventory dated 1656 - shows that he had one or more examples of virtually all the Biblical subjects which he used in his own work, and in many cases they served as a source for his own compositions. The fact that in the choice and treatment of his Biblical themes Rembrandt did not simply use the stories of the Bible itself, but based his work primarily on existing prints, is most evident from his frequent use of themes which he could not have taken from the text in the Bible, but must have borrowed from the traditional representation of the scenes by earlier artists in examples known to him. The traditional image was generally accorded greater weight than the written word, particularly when it increased the graphic quality of an event, as in the case of the angel intervening at the scene of Abraham's sacrifice. Rembrandt's exceptional talent as an interpreter of the Bible therefore does not lie in the independent relationship to tradition often ascribed to him, but in the unique way in which he made use of it. Concentrating on the emotions of the main characters at a critical moment in a story - which he clearly knew thoroughly, as revealed by the way in which he chose to refer to the context - he was able as no other to affect the observer and involve him in the event.

FROM MOSES TO THE DAYS OF THE KINGS AND PROPHETS

In choosing his Biblical themes, Rembrandt repeatedly revealed a preference for stories about the experiences of a particular figure. He seldom chose a subject in which the masses play a leading role. Therefore with regard to the Old Testament, we should not be surprised that Rembrandt often worked on the stories of Samson, Ruth, Saul and David, but paid hardly any attention to the experiences of Israel during the Exodus from Egypt, the journey through the desert or the conquest of the Promised Land. Unlike Rubens, for example, Rembrandt was never attracted to painting scenes of crowds with many different figures. From the very beginning, he preferred to restrict himself to a few figures. He attempted to express the emotions and passions of these characters as realistically and clearly as possible by means of their posture, gestures and facial expressions.

In 1629, the young Rembrandt and Jan Lievens, who had shared a studio for some years in Leyden, were visited by Constantijn Huygens, the influential secretary of the Stadtholder-Prince Frederik Hendrik, who was not only a poet and musician, but had a penetrating understanding of art. Huygens described this visit in detail in his autobiographical notes, written in Latin, in about 1630. Comparing the two young painters, he said that Lievens liked to paint his figures life-size or even larger, endeavouring to express all that is elevated and wonderful, while Rembrandt, whose 'taste and lively sensitivity' surpassed that of Lievens, in his opinion, preferred to 'achieve an effect which others might attempt to produce in vain on colossal canvases' in very small and compact works. As an example of Rembrandt's talent, he mentioned the illustration of the despairing Judas, when he returns his thirty pieces of silver to the High Priests. The works in this volume include five of these expressive panels, which are usually small, dating from Rembrandt's period in Leyden and highly valued by Huygens. The rate at which the young artist developed during these early years can be seen from a comparison of the rather crudely painted *Balaam and the Ass*, dating from 1626, with the painting of Samson and Delilah, dating from 1628, which could almost be called a masterpiece.

In the autumn of 1631 Rembrandt moved from Leyden to Amsterdam, where he was better able to undertake an increasing number of attractive commissions for portraits. In Amsterdam he soon became one of the most sought-after portrait painters. However, his real ambition was still to paint historical works of Biblical and mythological scenes, for these won an artist the most acclaim in those days. According to the official theory of art at the time, the stories from the Bible and from classical antiquity provided the noblest subjects for paintings and, furthermore, the invention with which an artist managed to re-create and bring to life a particular story with his own vision was the best indication of his skill and imagination.

In comparison with the work of a historical painter, paintings of portraits, landscapes and still lifes were considered second-rate art, and no more than an imitation of reality. Carel van Mander, the author of the *Schilder-boeck*, which was published in 1604, regretted the fact that in his time painters in the Netherlands had little opportunity to excel by painting historical works because of the lack of sufficient commissions. 'For what they are mainly given to do is to paint portraits from life, so that most artists often take this side road of art, attracted by the financial rewards or in order simply to make a living ..., so that a great deal of pure and noble talent has been fruitlessly and permanently extinguished and art has suffered.'

Certainly Rembrandt also painted portraits, 'attracted by financial rewards or in order simply to make a living', but his consistent production of paintings, etchings and drawings of themes taken from the Bible and classical mythology clearly shows that he continued to endeavour to be primarily a historical painter. In 17th-century Holland, there were no artists who could afford to do only historical works, as his teacher Pieter Lastman had done. Searching for a new style, and undoubtedly also aiming to enhance his reputation as a historical painter, he designed a number of dramatic large-scale compositions during his first years in Amsterdam, as well as small works like those he had done before. No fewer than three of these are devoted to an episode in the story of Samson. Just as his representation of Judas had aroused the admiration of Constantijn Huygens, now his large painting of Samson's marriage feast, dating from 1638, elicited the praise of the Leyden painter Philips Angel in 1641. Angel praised it as an example worthy of being copied, because it showed that the painter had first read the story concerned very carefully, as was proper, and then did everything to depict the story as faithfully as possible.

During the 1640s there was a remarkable change in the style of Rembrandt's Biblical representations. In general the scenes were again fairly small, and they were calmer, with a sensitivity which was absent in the turbulent baroque scenes from the 1630s. This change can be seen in his painting, *The Departure of the Shunamite Woman*, dating from 1640, and also in *David's Parting from Jonathan*, dating from 1642, in which the emotions of the two figures embracing each other is expressed in a very controlled way.

It was not until about the 1650s that Rembrandt again started to paint large-scale Biblical compositions with life-size figures, such as his *Bathsheba*, dating from 1654, and the impressive *Moses*, dating from 1659. However, no matter how much the style of his historical works and the way in which he approached his subjects changed over the course of the years, his preference was always for the moment in a story when a figure was taken over by strong emotions.

THE STORIES OF ESTHER, DANIEL, TOBIT AND JUDITH

The events in the book of Judith principally take place on Israelite soil, but we find ourselves in the books of Esther, Daniel and Tobit far from the ancient fatherland, amongst the Jews in exile. We are told of the pious Jew Tobit that he was exiled by the Assyrians to Nineveh when his tribe, the Naphtali, were deported. Daniel is one of the aristocratic young Jewish boys brought by King Nebuchadnezzar to his court in Babylon to be educated. And the story of Esther, adopted daughter of the Jew Mordechai, who is reputed to be one of the first exiles taken from Jerusalem by Nebuchadnezzar, takes place at the royal court in the Persian capital of Shushan.

The following text from the Psalms could be placed as a motto at the beginning of the story of Esther:

Behold, he travaileth with iniquity, and hath conceived mischief, and brought forth falsehood.
He made a pit, and digged it, and is fallen into the ditch which he made.
His mischief shall return upon his own head, and his violent dealing shall come down upon his own pate.
(Psalm 7:14-16)

The compelling story of the Jew-hating Haman, whose scheme for the total annihilation of the Jews in the Persian kingdom is thwarted by Mordecai and Esther, and who then suffers the fate he had planned for his enemy, is rich in sharp contrasts, thanks to the personalities of the chief characters, and laden with great emotions. It is no wonder that it is one of the Biblical stories for which Rembrandt and his pupils had a preference. The Esther story, with its theme of intimidation and salvation, was also particularly popular in the young republic of the Netherlands. The Calvinistic section of the population, who identified with the chosen people of the Bible, could read into an account such as this the story of their own successful struggle against coercion and repression.

Rembrandt's most important works with a theme from the book of Esther date from the last period of his life. The painting *Haman and Ahasuerus at Banquet with Esther* bears the date 1660, and it is generally accepted that the imposing canvas *Haman Sets Forth to Honour Mordecai* was produced around 1665 or even a little later. These are the last paintings with an Old Testament subject by Rembrandt of which we know. At this point he scarcely makes any effort to indicate the setting in which the scene takes place. His only concern now is to portray the emotions which are affecting the figures in the painting.

In 1636 Rembrandt made an etched portrait of Menasseh ben Israel, the renowned and at that time 32-year-old Amsterdam rabbi who was closely associated with several of Rembrandt's depictions of themes from the book of Daniel. Born in Lisbon, Menasseh ben Israel emigrated with his parents to Amsterdam in 1605 when he was barely a year old. In Amsterdam he became involved with the teaching of the Hebrew language at the early age of 18. With the establishment of a Hebrew printing shop in 1627, he

laid the foundations for Hebrew typography in Amsterdam. It is thanks to his initiative as the first Jewish printer-publisher that Amsterdam developed over the course of the 17th century into a world centre for Jewish book production, and was long to remain so.

It may be presumed that Rembrandt was a friend of Menasseh ben Israel. He lived in the Breestraat, which Rembrandt had left shortly before 1636 but where the painter once again came to live in 1639. It is, at any rate, almost a certainty that Rembrandt, who did not know any Hebrew himself, consulted this expert when around the middle of the 1630s he wished to make an extra impression in a large painting of the feast of King Belshazzar (Daniel, chapter 5) by depicting in Hebrew script the *mene tekel* which appears in the painting. Twenty years later, in 1655, it was Menasseh ben Israel who approached Rembrandt for four illustrations for his Messianic tract, written in Spanish, concerning the mysterious stone which destroyed the image Nebuchadnezzar had seen in his dreams (Daniel, chapter 2). At that time Menasseh was just about to leave for England, where he intended to persuade Oliver Cromwell to reopen the country to the Jews, who had been banned from England since 1290. He believed that the Messiah would come soon, but thought that the coming could only take place once the Jews had spread themselves throughout the world.

The story of Susanna, one of the later additions to the book of Daniel, and the books of Tobit and Judith, belong to a group of late Jewish writings which in the Catholic Church are deemed part of the Bible, but are considered apocryphal by the churches of the Reformation. Luther, however, did include the Apocrypha in his German translation of the Bible, as an appendix to the Old Testament. In his opinion, the apocryphal books may not have been in line with the canonical books but it was good for men to read them nevertheless. We also find them in the first editions of the Dutch Authorized Version, although at the very end, without marginalia and prefaced by a 'Warning to the Readers'. Later they gradually disappeared from the common editions of the Protestant Bible.

With regard to the book of Tobit, it is certainly the case that it was still much read in the 17th century, and was no less popular than the stories of the patriarchs and the book of Esther. Rembrandt in particular shows in his work a remarkable predilection for this book. Fascinated by the poignant depiction of human nature in this edifying family story, whose pious, sorely tested hero is nevertheless ultimately permitted to discover that 'the ways of God bear witness to his mercy and truth' (Tobit 3:2), he repeatedly turned to this book as no one else in his age did. In his surviving work we find no fewer than twenty drawings, five paintings and three etchings connected with it, and almost every episode from the story is represented in these. The book of Tobit can be justifiably described as Rembrandt's favourite book.

The New Testament

THE BIRTH AND CHILDHOOD OF JESUS

Throughout the centuries, artists have created countless works of art depicting the great moments in the story of Jesus' birth and childhood. The Annunciation by the Angel Gabriel, the Nativity in the stable in Bethlehem, the Circumcision, the Presentation in the temple - the Church calendar commemorates all these events with particular holy days, providing a rich source for Christian art, and, together with the story of the Passion, they provide some of the main themes.

Only two of the Gospel writers, St Matthew and St Luke, have given us details about Jesus' birth and childhood. However, painters, sculptors and engravers did not find inspiration only in the stories of the Bible. From the 2nd century AD there were apocryphal scriptures (not recognized by the Church) about Jesus' childhood and the lives of Mary and Joseph, the carpenter. These filled the gaps in the sparse Bible text with abundant imaginative detail which was further elaborated in medieval legends based on them. They provided the simple people with something the Gospels did not: anecdotal stories, sentiment and romanticism. These stories - which often contained miracles - in the *Legenda Aurea* (Golden Legends), written in a popular style and read throughout Western Europe following the invention of the printing press, had a great influence on the religious art of the late Middle Ages. In the course of the 16th century, humanism - which had a particularly Biblical character in the Netherlands - and the Reformation sought to establish a purer form of Christianity in north-west Europe, directly inspired by the holy book. The apocryphal stories became less significant, another factor being the Roman Catholic Church's strong opposition to all kinds of naïve medieval beliefs and ideas in its fight against the Reformation. However, although many of the old traditions were doomed to disappear, some of the deeply rooted ideas, particularly in the field of art, persisted for a long time.

As Rembrandt was inspired to a significant extent by examples of 15th- and 16th-century prints in his choice and interpretation of Biblical subjects, it is not really surprising that among his representations of the stories of the Nativity and childhood of Jesus there are many themes and motifs which are not based on the Bible, but which find their origin in the apocryphal scriptures or religious imagination of the late Middle Ages. He depicted a number of scenes entitled *The Rest on the Flight in to Egypt*, which had for a long time been a popular subject in Dutch art: Mary feeding the infant with the meal prepared by Joseph on a wood fire; the parents resting in silence under the open sky; their attempts to make the arduous journey. In his many representations of the Holy Family in Nazareth, which are not based on episodes which appear in the Bible, he did not merely portray the figures of Jesus, Mary and Joseph, but also showed St Anne a number of times. She was the devout lady who was the mother of Mary, according to the Apocrypha, although she is not mentioned anywhere in the canon of the Gospels. In

general, Rembrandt adopted the customary ways of representing the traditional themes from the Nativity, even when these were not supported by a Biblical text, and even when particular ideas conflicted with the literal text. For example, in accordance with tradition, he represented the wise men from the East as three kings with a large retinue. Departing from the Gospel story of Mary's visit to Elizabeth, which describes how Mary enters Zachariah's house and greets Elizabeth (Luke 1:40), he painted this scene as a meeting outside the house, rather than inside. It had been depicted in this way for centuries - for example, by Albrecht Dürer in his large woodcut of this subject, with which Rembrandt was familiar. On the other hand, there is no sign of an ox and an ass in Rembrandt's works of the shepherds worshipping the infant Jesus; these animals had virtually always been shown by the manger since the 5th century, even though there is not a word about them in St Luke's story of the Nativity.

The event in the childhood of Jesus which interested Rembrandt most throughout his life - his many works on the subject clearly differing from the traditional depiction - is the story of Simeon's meeting with Jesus as a child when he is presented at the temple. Misled by a tradition based on one of the apocryphal scriptures, artists had for a long time been inclined to combine the stories of the meeting with the old man, Simeon (which, according to the Gospel of St Luke, had taken place before) and the actual Presentation in the temple. Thus the old man was identified with the High Priest serving in the temple, who stands by the altar to take the infant Jesus from Mary's hands. From the very beginning Rembrandt avoided this erroneous interpretation and placed Simeon, singing praises and prophesying with the child in his arms, not by the altar but in the middle of the temple. Therefore it has justifiably been noted that these works by Rembrandt should not be entitled *The Presentation at the Temple*.

Despite his respect for the traditions of the past, Rembrandt interpreted them in his own way. Endeavouring to depict the Biblical stories as clearly and movingly as possible, he was able to find new ways of doing this when he thought it was necessary, and was helped in this by his knowledge of the Scriptures.

THE LIFE OF JESUS OF NAZARETH

The events during the life of Jesus are not all emphasized as strongly in the liturgical Church calendar as the story of his birth, the Passion and his death. Therefore, the religious art of the Middle Ages, which was based on the liturgy of the Church, devoted considerably less attention to the stories in the Gospels about Jesus' life as a prophet than to the stories of his birth and the drama of Golgotha. This changed only in the 16th century, when there was an increasing demand in the countries of the Reformation for greater access to the whole message of the Bible, and when the choice of subjects in religious art became determined to a lesser extent by liturgy and devotion than before. The parables of Jesus, which had previously rarely been depicted, became particularly popular, especially in prints. Engravers of that time produced series of prints illustrating the whole story of the best-loved parables, such as those of the Good Samaritan (Luke 10:30-37) and the Prodigal Son (Luke 15:11-32). In many cases, these formed the starting point for the interpretations of later artists. Rembrandt, who was very familiar with new themes in 16th-century art through his large and diverse collection of prints, was also stimulated and influenced by them throughout his life. It goes without saying that the two parables mentioned above, which are among Jesus' most moving teachings, have a special place amongst Rembrandt's depictions of Jesus' illustrative stories. Adapting the examples dating from the 16th century or later versions of these into his own idiom, he shows us again and again how the Good Samaritan takes pity on the traveller attacked by robbers; and no other artist has expressed so often and so movingly the wonderful goodness of the father in the parable of the Prodigal Son, when he takes his 'reborn' child into his arms. There was a lack of interest among medieval artists in the miracles performed by Jesus, though the early Christians had enjoyed depicting these as signs of a new reality. With the arrival of humanism and the Reformation, interest in them waned even further. Those who were aiming at a purer form of Christianity inspired by the Bible concentrated on Jesus' preaching and not on his miracles. According to Erasmus (1528), Christianity is not based on miracles. The Raising of Lazarus (John 11:1-44), in which Jesus described himself as the source of the resurrection and the life, is one of the few miracles which rarely failed to attract attention throughout the centuries. The many works depicting this event in early Christian art were restricted to the essence of the miracle: Jesus, with a staff in his hand, commanding Lazarus to rise up from the grave. Later, in baroque art in particular, the narrative element was predominant, and the spectacular element of the story was emphasized. In these works Jesus performed the miracle among crowds of onlookers, and their amazement gave the artist the opportunity to express a large range of gestures and facial expressions. The young Rembrandt also portrayed this age-old subject in a theatrical and dramatic style, first in a painting, and shortly afterwards in a large etching. Both compositions contain the apocryphal motif of the weapons which, according to legend, Lazarus bore as a soldier in the army. Ten years later, in 1642, Rembrandt gave a completely different interpretation of this miracle in another etching, which is much more profound in its subdued feeling. The Raising of Lazarus is the only one of Jesus' miracles portrayed by Rembrandt in works which were intended for public view: his etchings and paintings. It was only in his drawings, which were in the first instance intended for his own use, that he devoted attention to other miracles. The drawings concerned mainly date from the 1650s, and Rembrandt's plain renderings of these Gospel stories exude the quiet dignity which is characteristic of the scenes of miracles in early Christian art.

Although Rembrandt never really deviated from the traditional Christ figure dating from the Middle Ages - a serene figure with long wavy hair, parted in the centre, and a not too long beard, divided in two - there is a clear development in the character portrayed by him as Jesus of Nazareth. Initially, his portrayal of the figure of Jesus was not without an idealized heroic aspect, influenced by the artistic views of the baroque period. However, by the beginning of the 1640s, this impressive figure made way for a much more human character, a quiet, simple man, who is hardly different from the people around him. Jesus was first portrayed in this way in the etching mentioned above dating from 1642, of the Raising of Lazarus, though his figure seems to be slightly larger than the other figures in the work. This is how we see him in the so-called *The Hundred Guilders Print*, Rembrandt's most admired etching, as the incarnation of God's love for mankind, and as the man who said of himself, 'I am the light of the world: he that followeth me shall not walk in darkness, but shall have the light of life' (John 8:12). In this work the story of a whole chapter (Matthew 19) is condensed in a totally new way in a single image. The figure of Jesus preaching in an etching dating from *ca.* 1652 is even more effective because of its simplicity. This must be Rembrandt's most beautiful portrayal of the man from Nazareth who travelled round the whole of Galilee, preaching the word of God.

THE PASSION, DEATH AND RESURRECTION OF JESUS

As long as death by crucifixion, the most cruel and dreadful degradation which existed in ancient times, was still used as a punishment, it was not possible for the earliest Christian communities to imagine or accept the image of the crucified Christ which is so familiar to us. In fact, the early Church was less interested in the tragedy of the Cross than in the overwhelming concept of the Resurrection. It was more concerned with Christ's victory over death than with his degradation on the Cross. It was only many centuries later that the Church became accustomed to the image of the terrible death to which Pontius Pilate had sentenced Jesus.

When the first pictures of the Cross appeared in Western Europe in about AD 1000, the insult and physical suffering were still concealed behind the figure of a crucified but victorious Christ, as seen in the Byzantine culture of the Eastern Church. With head raised and open eyes, robed in a long garment and crowned with gold, the Lord hangs on the Cross like a living God-king, inseparable from the sign of his victory. However, a completely different picture emerged in the course of the 13th century, when Christianity started to realize how great a price had been paid for man's redemption through God's incarnation, and attempted to understand with increasing self-deprecation the suffering inflicted upon the Redeemer. The time came when Christ was portrayed on the Cross dead or dying, his weak body collapsed and clearly showing the traces of the torture he had suffered. This was followed by moving works of Christ being taken down from the Cross, *pietàs* and entombments. Believers turned towards the man of suffering, a pitiable figure, wounded and bloody, with a crown of thorns on his head. The mystic Jan van Ruusbroec (1293-1381), who lived in the monastery of Groenendael near Brussels, expressed the poignancy evoked in believers by the contemplation of Jesus's suffering in the following way: 'When man thinks of the torture and the suffering of the precious body of Christ, this gives rise to such a feeling of loving devotion and so much pity that he wishes to be nailed to the Cross with Christ and spill his blood to honour Christ, and he presses into the wounds and the open heart of Christ, his Saviour.' In the 15th century, Stations of the Cross appeared along the roads to well-known places of pilgrimage, and later also in churches. These were depictions which helped believers to follow Jesus step by step on his path of suffering from the courthouse of Pontius Pilate to Golgotha. Soon there was hardly a print maker who had not made several series of woodcuts or copper engravings to portray the various episodes in this story of suffering. These series of the Passion, which comprised varying numbers of depictions, usually started with the Last Supper or with Jesus in the Garden of Gethsemane. Normally the series concluded with a depiction of the Resurrection.

Rembrandt owned one or more examples of all these themes of the Passion which became common in the late Middle Ages, for he had an extensive collection of prints. Translated into his own 'idiom' they can virtually all be found among the many drawings, etchings and paintings which he devoted to the Passion in the course of his life. These include themes which are not based on a particular passage in the Gospels, but whose origin lies in the devout reflections on the Passion in previous centuries, such as *The Erection of the Cross* and *The Pietà*.

Rembrandt's work, *The Erection of the Cross*, completed *ca*. 1632-33, is the first of five paintings of the Passion commissioned by Prince Frederik Hendrik in the 1630s. Rembrandt did not deliver the last two paintings, *The Entombment* and *The Resurrection* until January 1639, although he had written to tell Constantijn Huygens, the Prince's secretary, who was acting as an intermediary, that they were already more than half finished in February 1636. He stated that the reason for the delay was that he had tried to include as much natural movement as possible. His goal in depicting the Passion was to express the deepest human emotions as realistically and convincingly as possible through every gesture and movement. For Rembrandt the Passion, with its many tragic moments, was primarily a psychological drama. Even in his works depicting the cruel event on Golgotha, there is less emphasis on the physical suffering of Jesus than on the actions and feelings of those who are observing it, whether they are profoundly sad or mocking and rejoicing in the humiliation inflicted on the man from Nazareth.

Rembrandt attracted the admiration of his contemporaries early on in his career through the expressive power with which he had portrayed the despair of Judas in his painting, *Judas Returns the Thirty Pieces of Silver*, which dates from 1629. His first depiction of *The Meal in Emmaus* also dates from this period. This theme was to interest him throughout his life, and every time he focused on the astonishment of the two disciples when they suddenly recognized this stranger sitting at the table as the risen Lord.

The means which he used through the years changed, but his aim always remained the same.

Of Rembrandt's surviving drawings showing scenes from the Passion, by far the majority date from the years 1650-55. His most important etchings of scenes from the Passion also date from this period, including his two masterpieces on this theme: *The Three Crosses*, dating from 1653, and *Pilate Gives the People the Choice Between Barabbas and Jesus*, dating from 1655.

Rembrandt's last great work on a theme from the Passion is the painting *Peter Denies Jesus*, dating from 1660. This monumental canvas shows all the episodes from the story related in the Gospel according to St Luke around the figure of the cornered apostle, combined in a single moment of the greatest psychological tension. One could not imagine a more perfect historical work.

BIBLIOGRAPHY

LIST OF THE WORKS MENTIONED IN ABBREVIATED FORM

BARTSCH: A. Bartsch, *Catalogue raisonné de toutes les estampes qui forment l'oeuvre de Rembrandt, et ceux de ses principaux imitateurs,* 2 vol., Vienna 1797.'

BAUCH: K. Bauch, *Rembrandt. Gemälde,* Berlin 1966.

BENESCH: O. Benesch, *The Drawings of Rembrandt.* Enlarged and edited by Eva Benesch, 6 vol., London 1973.

'BIJBELSE INSPIRATIE': Catalogus van de tentoonstelling *Bijbelse Inspiratie. Tekeningen en prenten van Lucas van Leyden en Rembrandt,* Rijksmuseum Amsterdam 1964/65.

BOON: K.G. Boon, *Rembrandt de etser. Het volledige werk,* Amsterdam 1963.

BREDIUS: A. Bredius, *Rembrandt: schilderijen,* Utrecht 1935.

BREDIUS-GERSON: A. Bredius, *Rembrandt. The complete edition of the paintings.* Revised by H. Gerson, London 1969.

FILEDT KOK: J.P. Filedt Kok, *Rembrandt etchings & drawings in the Rembrandt House. A catalogue,* Maarssen 1972.

GERSAINT: E.F. Gersaint, *Catalogue raisonné de toutes les pièces qui forment l'oeuvre de Rembrandt,* Paris 1751.

GERSON: H. Gerson, *De schilderijen van Rembrandt,* Amsterdam 1969.

HAAK: B. Haak, *Rembrandt tekeningen,* Amsterdam 1976.

HIND: A.M. Hind, *A catalogue of Rembrandt's etchings,* 2 vol., London 1923².

HOFSTEDE DE GROOT, *Rembrandt Bijbel:* C. Hofstede de Groot, *Rembrandt Bijbel. Bevattende de verhalen des Ouden en Nieuwen Verbonds, welke door Rembrandt met penseel, etsnaald en teekenstift zijn in beeld gebracht* 2 vol., Amsterdam s.a. (1906-1910).

HOFSTEDE DE GROOT, *Urkunden:* C. Hofstede de Groot, *Die Urkunden über Rembrandt* (1575-1721), The Hague 1906.

MÜNZ: L. Münz, *Rembrandt's etchings,* 2 vol., London 1952.

ROTERMUND 1963: H.-M. Rotermund, *Rembrandts Handzeichnungen und Radierungen zur Bibel,* Lahr/ Schwarzwald and Stuttgart 1963.

SLIVE: S. Slive, *Drawings of Rembrandt. With a selection of drawings by his pupils and followers,* 2 vol., New York 1965.

SUMOWSKI 1963: W. Sumowski, *Das Leben Jesu in Bildern, Handzeichnungen, Radierungen von Rembrandt,* Witten/Berlin 1963.

TÜMPEL 1968: Chr. Tümpel, 'Ikonographische Beiträge zu Rembrandt', in: *Jahrbuch der Hamburger Kunstsammlungen* 13 (1968), pp. 95-126.

TÜMPEL 1969: Chr. Tümpel, 'Studien zur Ikonographie der Historien Rembrandts', in: *Nederlands Kunsthistorisch Jaarboek* 20 (1969), pp. 107-198.

TÜMPEL 1970: Chr. Tümpel, *Rembrandt legt die Bibel aus. Zeichnungen und Radierungen aus dem Kupferstichkabinett der Staatlichen Museen Preussischer Kulturbesitz* exhibition catalogue), Berlin 1970.

TÜMPEL 1971: Chr. Tümpel, 'Ikonographische Beiträge zu Rembrandt', in: *Jahrbuch der Hamburger Kunstsammlungen* 16 (1971), pp. 20-38.

MONOGRAPHS AND STUDIES

O. Benesch, *Rembrandt as a draughtsman,* London 1960.

O. Benesch, *Collected Writings. Volume I: Rembrandt,* edited by Eva Benesch, London 1970.

I. Bergström, 'Rembrandts double-portrait of himself and Saskia at the Dresden Gallery. A tradition transformed', in: *Nederlands Kunsthistorisch Jaarboek* 17 (1966), pp. 143-169.

J. Bolten/H. Bolten-Rempt, *Rembrandt,* Wiesbaden 1977.

D. Bomford, Chr. Brown, Ashok Roy, *Art in the Making: Rembrandt,* Oxford 1988.

B.P.J. Broos, *Index to the formal sources of Rembrandt's art,* Maarssen 1977.

J. Bruyn, *Rembrandt's keuze van Bijbelse onderwerpen,* Utrecht 1959.

K. Clark, *Rembrandt and the Italian Renaissance,* London 1966.

J.A. Emmens, *Rembrandt en de regels van de kunst,* Utrecht 1968.

R.H. Fuchs, *Rembrandt en Amsterdam,* Rotterdam 1968.

J. Gantner, *Rembrandt und die Verwandlung klassischer Formen,* Berne and Munich 1964.

H.E. van Gelder, *Rembrandt en de Heilige Schrift,* Palet-serie, Amsterdam s.a. (1964).

L. Goldscheider, *Rembrandt. Paintings, drawings and etchings,* London 1960.

J. and M. Guillaud, *Rembrandt, the Human Form and Spirit,* Paris 1986.

H. Guratzsch, *Rembrandts Darstellungen der Lazaruserweckung,* in: Die Auferweckung des Lazarus in der niederländischen Kunst von 1400-1700, 2 vol., Kortrijk 1978.

B. Haak, *Rembrandt, zijn leven, zijn werk, zijn tijd,* Amsterdam s.a. (1968).

R. Haussherr, *Rembrandts Jacobssegen,* Opladen 1976

J. Held, *Rembrandt-Studien,* Leipzig 1983

E.S. Levitin, *Rembrandt Etchings,* Leningrad 1985.

C.W. Mönnich/Michel van der Plas, *Het Woord in beeld. Vijf eeuwen bijbel in het dagelijks leven,* Baarn 1977.

L. Münz, *Rembrandt,* Cologne 1967.

J. Rosenberg, *Rembrandt. Life and work,* London 1964.

H.-M. Rotermund, 'Rembrandts Bibel', in: *Nederlands Kunsthistorisch Jaarboek* 8 (1957), pp. 123-150.

H.-M. Rotermund 'Unidentifizierte bzw. missverstandene Zeichnungen Rembrandts zu biblischen Szenen', in: *Wallraf-Richartz-Jahrbuch* 21 (1959), pp. 173-209.

J.L.A.A.M. van Rijkevorsel, *Rembrandt en de traditie,* Rotterdam 1932.

G. Schwartz, *Rembrandt: All the etchings reproduced in true sizes,* Maarssen 1977.

G. Schwartz, *Rembrandt, his life, his paintings,* Maarssen 1984.

J. Seibert, *Lexikon christlicher Kunst. Themen, Gestalten, Symbole,* Freiburg-Basle-Vienna 1980.

S. Slive, *Rembrandt: Bible Paintings,* London 1959.

W. Sumowski, *Bemerkungen zu O. Beneschs Corpus der Rembrandt-Zeichnungen I und II,* Berlin 1956-1957 and 1961.

Chr. Tümpel, *Rembrandt, in Selbstzeugnissen und Bilddokumenten,* Reinbek bei Hamburg 1977.

Chr. Tümpel, *Rembrandt - Mythos und Methode,* Königstein 1986.

J. Veth, *Rembrandts leven en kunst,* Amsterdam 1906, second edition, with an introduction and commentary by J.Q. van Regteren Altena, Amsterdam 1941.

W.A. Visser 't Hooft, *Rembrandts weg tot het Evangelie,* Amsterdam 1956.

A.B. de Vries, *Rembrandt,* Baarn s.a. (1956).

Chr. White, *Rembrandt and his world,* London 1963.

Chr. White, *Rembrandt as an etcher,* 2 vol., London 1969.

446

EXHIBITION CATALOGUES

AMSTERDAM-ROTTERDAM 1956: *Rembrandt. Tentoonstelling ter herdenking van de geboorte van Rembrandt op 15 juli 1606*, 3 vol., Schilderijen, Tekeningen, Etsen. Rijksmuseum, Amsterdam; Museum Boymans-van Beuningen, Rotterdam.

AMSTERDAM 1969: *Rembrandt 1669/1969, tentoonstelling ter herdenking van Rembrandts sterfdag op 4 oktober 1669*, Rijksmuseum, Amsterdam.

AMSTERDAM 1985: *Rembrandt en zijn voorbeelden*, Museum het Rembrandthuis.

CHICAGO-MINNEAPOLIS-DETROIT 1969-1970: *Rembrandt after Three Hundred Years*, The Art Institute of Chicago; The Minneapolis Institute of Arts; The Detroit Institute of Arts.

HAMBURG 1987: *Rembrandt, Hundert Radierungen*, Kunsthalle.

PARIS 1969-1970: *Les plus belles eaux-fortes de Rembrandt, choisies dans les quatre principales collections de Paris*, Musée du Louvre.

PARIS 1970: *Rembrandt et son temps. Dessins des collections publiques et privées conservées en France*, Musée du Louvre.

PARIS 1986: *Rembrandt, eaux-fortes*, Musée du Petit Palais.

ROTTERDAM 1988: *Rembrandt and his School, Paintings and Drawings*, Museum Boymans-van Beuningen.

SOURCES OF ILLUSTRATIONS

Allschwill-Bâle, Colorphoto Hans Hinz
Amsterdam, Gemeentemusea
Amsterdam, Rijksmuseum
Bayonne, Photo Etienne
Berlin, Bildarchiv Preussischer Kulturbesitz (Jörg P. Anders)
Besançon, Studio R. Schwartz
Birmingham, The Barber Institute of Fine Arts, The University of Birmingham
Boston, Isabella Stewart Gardner Museum
Braunschweig, Herzog-Anton-Ulrich-Museum (Bernd-Peter Keiser)
Cambridge (G.B.), Fitzwilliam Museum
Cambridge (Mass.U.S.A.), Fogg Art Museum
Chicago, The Art Institute of Chicago
Cleveland, The Cleveland Museum of Art
Constance, Bildarchiv der Stadt Konstanz
Detroit, The Detroit Institute of Arts
Dublin, The National Gallery of Ireland
Ecublens (Switzerland), André Held
Edinburgh, The National Gallery of Scotland
Frankfurt a/Main, Kurt Haase
Gauting (Munich), Kunst-Dias Blauel
Glasgow, Hunterian Art Gallery
Groningen, Groninger Museum
Haarlem, Teylers Museum
The Hague, Gemeentemuseum 's Gravenhage
The Hague, Koninklijk Kabinet van Schilderijen, Mauritshuis
Hamburg, Fotografisches Atelier Ralph Kleinhempel
Hornbaek (Denmark), Hans Petersen
Kassel, Staatliche Kunstsammlungen Kassel
Leipzig-Mölkau, Farbenfotografie Gerhard Reinhold
London, John Freeman Group
London, The National Gallery
London, Photographic Service British Museum
London, Victoria and Albert Museum
Los Angeles, Los Angeles County Museum of Art
Moscow, v/o Vneshtorgizdat (Litho: Toppan, Tokio)
Naples, Museo di Capodimonte
New York, The Metropolitan Museum of Art
New York, The Pierpont Morgan Library
Oxford, Ashmolean Museum
Paris, Ecole Nationale Supérieure des Beaux-Arts
Paris, Photo Bulloz
Paris, Photographie Giraudon
Paris, Service de Documentation Photographiques de la Réunion des Musées Nationaux
Philadelphia, Philadelphia Museum of Art
Rotterdam, Museum Boymans-Van Beuningen
Stockholm, Nationalmuseum
Stuttgart, Staatsgalerie
Vienna, Lichtbildwerkstätte Alpenland
Voorburg, Frequin-Photos
Washington, National Gallery of Art
Weimar, Klaus G.Beyer
Weimar, Nationale Forschungs- und Gedenkstätte der klassischen Deutschen Literatur
Williamstown (Mass.), Sterling and Francine Clark Art Institute
Worcester (Mass.), Worcester Art Museum
Private collections